TIBET: TODAY AND YESTERDAY

76
80
84
USSR
Shufu
Soche
SINKIA
Hotien
Chok
36
Srinagar
Leh
Indus
T
32
Simla
Gartok
I
B
ARI
Tangra Tso
Delhi
28
NEPAL
Shigatse
Gyangtse
Katmandu
Sikkim
Puna
BHUT
Darjeeling
INDIA
24
N
Brah
Calcutta
20
VIRGINIA M. EDWARDS
84
88
92

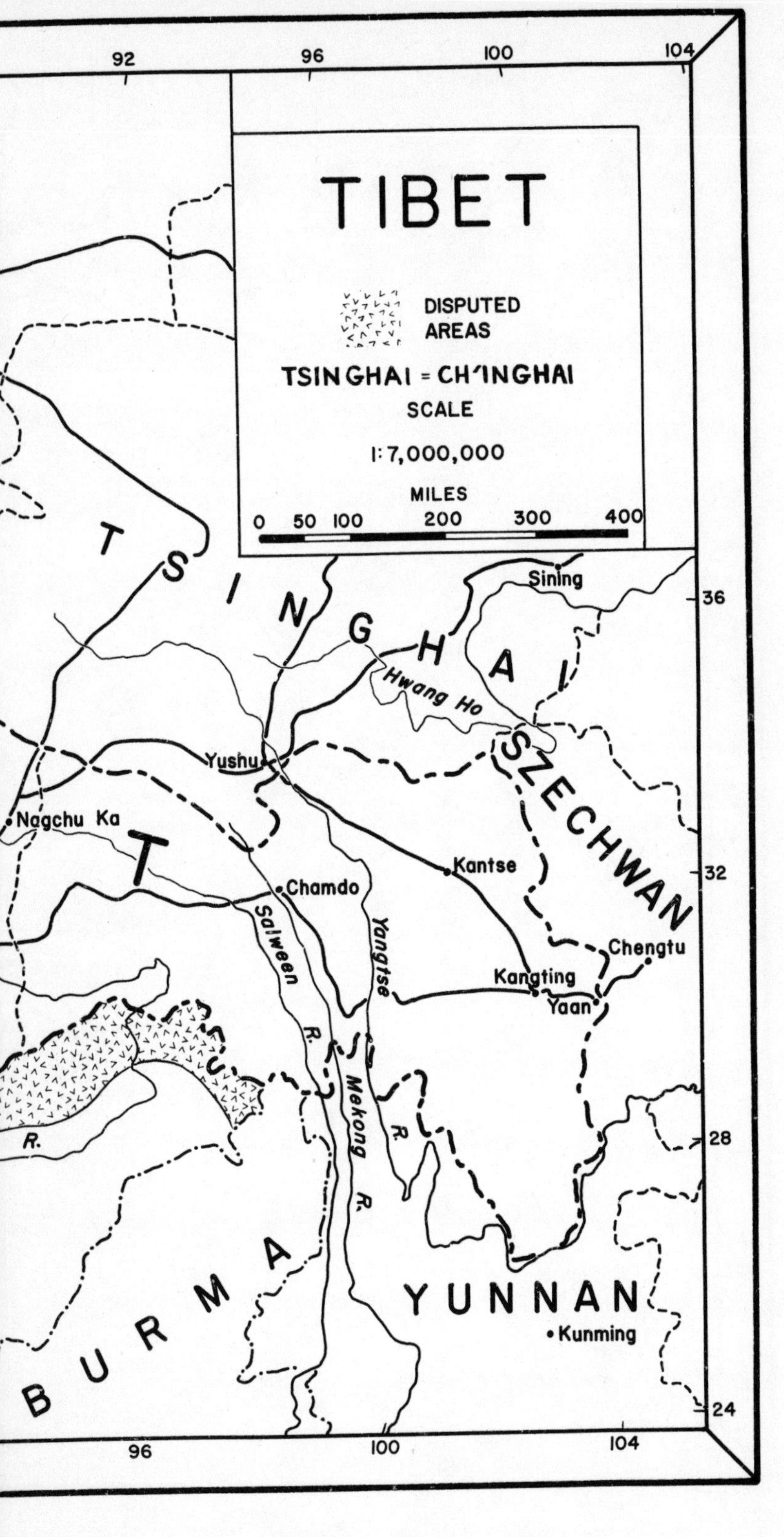

TIBET
DISPUTED AREAS
TSINGHAI = CH'INGHAI
SCALE
1:7,000,000
MILES
0 50 100 200 300 400
92
96
100
104
36
32
28
24
TSINGHAI
Sining
Hwang Ho
SZECHWAN
Yushu
Nagchu Ka
Chamdo
Kantse
Chengtu
Kangting
Yaan
Salween R.
Yangtse R.
Mekong R.
R.
BURMA
YUNNAN
Kunming

TIBET

Today and Yesterday

By TIEH-TSENG LI

BOOKMAN ASSOCIATES
NEW YORK

Library of Congress Catalog Card Number: 60-8548

MANUFACTURED IN THE UNITED STATES OF AMERICA

CONTENTS

INTRODUCTION

Since the March revolt in Lhasa, Tibet has become a household word in the United States. In a way, Tibet is now better known; but I am afraid it is still misunderstood in many of its aspects. The deep mystery enshrouding Tibet must be attributed not only to its remoteness and comparative inaccessibility, but also, and in a greater degree, to a lack of information, even to positive misinformation concerning this so-called hidden land in the snow mountains.

Even Tibet's boundaries cause confusion. In referring to popular sources of information such as *Information Please* (469,413 sq. mi.) and the *World Almanac* (475,000 sq. mi.) one would find a discrepancy of 5,587 square miles, while Chinese sources usually give Tibet's area, including the Chamdo District as 1,221,600 square kilometers. An accurate figure would be possible only after the frontier between India and Tibet has been entirely demarcated and the disputed territory settled. India's claim of the McMahon frontier, based on the alleged Simla Convention, is disputable and has been, in fact, repudiated by the Chinese National Government.[1]

First of all a distinction has to be made between the Tibet of history and the area we call Tibet on our maps, which, unfortunately do not always demarcate the actual domain over which the Lhasa authority is exercised. Among the 2,775,622 Tibetans according to the census of 1953, only 1,273,969, that is, less than one half live in Tibet, while the rest form minority groups in neighboring provinces: Sikang, Szechwan, Ch'ing-hai, Kansu and Yünnan. The present Dalai Lama and the present Panch'en Lama both were born in Tibetan families in Ch'inghai beyond the jurisdiction of the Lhasa government. The Khamba tribesmen, who are very much in the news nowadays because of their resistance to the Communist rule, belong to Sikang, not Tibet.[2]

For a time Tibet extended its control eastward over a part of Ch'inghai and Kansu, and most of Sikang, as well as some districts of Yünnan; and ruled the western frontier states of Nepal, Sikkim, Bhutan, and Kashmir's Ladakh, where even today Tibetans constitute an important part of the population and exercise a considerable cultural and religious influence. An ethnologist would draw the ethnic boundary of Tibet further east to the Chengtu plain in the heart of the province of Szechwan, and further west to the Zo-Gi-La pass, only a little more than thirty-five miles east of Srinagar, the capital of Kashmir.[3]

The boundary problem however appears simple by comparison with the complexities of the status of Tibet. In the first place, the status of a nation is not a matter of how that nation regards itself, or even how another nation regards it: status is to be found somewhere in the relations which obtain between the nation in question and all the other nations which may affect it and which it may affect. In the second place, the status of a nation is something which changes through a process of time in relation to each of the nations concerned with it, and the nations themselves are changing too. In the present study whenever the writer presents as a historical fact that Tibet has long been an integral part of China, it does not mean that he is of the opinion that it is only fair and just that Tibet continues in this status. By the same token, anyone who advocates independence for Tibet need not deny such a historical fact.

It is much to be regretted that throughout the manifesto attached to a letter addressed to the Indian Prime Minister and signed by Gyalo Thondup, a brother of the Dalai Lama living at Kalimpong, a copy of which the writer obtained while taking a study trip to the Far East last fall, there is denial of any existence of friendship between China and Tibet even in ancient times. The manifesto went so far as to say that King Sron-tsan Gampo obtained his Chinese bride, Princess Wên-ch'êng, "by force." Granted the non-existence of the record of the marriage in the *Documents de Touen-Houang* and the *T'ang shu,* and of the text of the Treaty of Amity inscribed on the 821 stone pillar which is still standing in the Tibetan capital today, who would believe that at a time when the great T'ang Dynasty was at the zenith of its power, the Chinese Emperor could have been forced to give the Princess in marriage to the Tibetan king? The manifesto characterized Chao Erh-feng as "the butcher." But in Chapter III we find that his work was praised and favorably commented upon by such British authorities on Tibetan affairs as Sir Francis Younghusband, Sir Eric Teichman, and Brigadier-General M. E. Willoughby. On the question whether there ever existed any degree of friendship between China and Tibet and how the rule of Tibet by Peking Court was regarded by the Tibetan people, the readers are requested to refer to the conclusions of the American and the British authorities on Tibet, W. W. Rockhill and Sir Charles Bell, quoted in the following chapters, and to draw conclusions of their own.

As to Tibet's actual status, there is a prevailing misunderstanding. In some dispatches Tibet is even referred to as a republic. However, nothing is farther from the truth than assertions to the effect that Tibet has always been or was until recently an independent country with sovereign power. A factual answer to these assertions will be found in this book which deals, among other things, with such matters as how Tibetans regard themselves, whether there is evidence to show that they are able and willing to assume and fulfill international obligations—an essential criterion of statehood—and how Tibet is regarded by all powers concerned as shown in international treaties and in discussions in the United Nations.

As the scope of this book is confined to Tibet yesterday and today, no attempt should be made to hazard a conjecture concerning its tomorrow. But the abortive revolt and the flight of the Dalai Lama have definitely created an aftermath on the international scene. One can not help wondering if history is repeating itself and how far the parallel will go. The present Dalai Lama is living in exile in India as his immediate predecessor did forty-nine years ago, and the Panch'en Lama is being backed by Peking as was his immediate predecessor, with the only difference that this time it is a Communist Party that is in power on the Chinese mainland and India is no longer under the British rule.

As is related in some detail in Chapter V, India for a time attempted to assume the role in Tibet previously played by the British. Indian Prime Minister Mr. Nehru once said that geography is a compelling factor. He made it plain that his country's security is the primary consideration of the Indian Government in dealing with the Tibetan issue. On the other hand, the Chinese Communists who fought their way through the Tibetan borderland in their "Long March," and whose former capital, Yenan, is situated in China's "Wild West," where they have been putting a big effort into the development of oilfields, industrial construction, and the building of roads, railways, and airfields, must certainly realize, if only for defense considerations, how vital it is to keep the Tibetan plateau from being taken over by a foreign power.

Now, New Delhi and Peking have lately exchanged accusations. They have used stronger words than in their diplomatic duel in 1950 as cited in Chapter V. But there is still restraint shown on both sides. However, the situation is very delicate and fraught with danger. It remains to be seen if these two populous Asiatic Powers, who demonstrated a remarkable degree of solidarity and collaboration at the Bandung Conference, will again reach a harmonious understanding or this time come to an irreparable rupture in their relations. It is worth mentioning that Mr. Nehru, who had talked with King Mahendra of Negal about the situation in Tibet at the border town of Bhimnagar on April 30th, paid a visit to the Napalese capital during the second week of June to confer with the King again and with Premier B. P. Koirala, the head of Nepal's first popularly elected Government, on international affairs including Tibet. He said at a news conference before leaving Katmandu that Communist China's suppression of the Tibetan revolt last March posed no threat to the Indian and Napalese frontiers.[4]

After all, Tibet's status will continue to be a factor in Indo-Chinese relations which may in turn greatly affect world politics. With a view to helping the reader appraise the present-day Tibetan situation in general and Tibetan status in particular—status as it is and as it should be—the writer ventures to present several aspects of the problem and, whenever necessary, to offer his personal opinion.

First, besides being a defense issue for China, as mentioned above, the Tibetan problem is also a Chinese minority issue. Aside from Han nationality, which constitutes 93.94% of the Chinese population, there are scores of national minorities with a combined population of more than 35 million. Those national minorities with a population of one million or above each are as follows: Chuang, Uighur, Hui, Yi, Tibetan, Miao, Manchu, Mongol, Puyi and Korean. In other words, Tibetans rank fifth in numerical order among national minorities.

China for a century has lived under threat of being cut into slices like a melon. Russia from the north and Japan from the east, in addition to outright seizure of territories, set up so-called independent states in the name of the Mongols and the Manchus, while colonial powers from the West established concessions and settlements along the coast and created a buffer state in Tibet, all aiming at undermining the authority of the Chinese government. Outer Mongolia became legally ceded as a result of the secret agreements reached at the Yalta Conference without China's participation. The U.S.S.R. has played with the minority issue and backed the Uighurs to claim a so-called independent region of Ili in Sinkiang, which is no longer heard of since the establishment of the Communist regime on the entire Chinese mainland.

The Chinese, whether of Han nationality or of any minority group, have had enough bitter experience to learn that in unity there is strength. China should be dealt with as a whole. Any attempt to weaken China's position by backing one or more of her national minorities will prove futile in the long run.

Secondly, the Tibetan problem is not so much religious as social. Generally speaking, China has been tolerant toward the different religions professed by her people and throughout Chinese history we do not find such conflicts between state and church as are recorded in Europe. But under the theocratic form of government any event taking place in Tibet must have something to do with its religion. However, the Dalai Lama can not claim either that he is the state or that he is the church. The development of his office and authority is narrated in the chapters to follow. As pointed out by Professor George E. Taylor in a Foreword written for Messrs. Tsung-lien Shen and Shen-chi Liu's book on *Tibet and the Tibetans,* "though the church controls the state the two are separate entities."

The present fourteenth Dalai Lama, age 24, is not a "Strong Man," but an influential symbol which any contestant for power in Tibet would like to have on his side. That is why the Communist China's People's Congress still retains his name as one of its Vice-Chairmen even after its election in April, when he had already been given asylum in India. He could have easily crossed the Indian frontier in 1950 when he fled Lhasa and stayed at the border town of Yatung, though this time his emergence safe and sound after a perilous fifteen-day trek over some of the world's most treacherous mountain area with Chinese Communist searching planes overhead has brought more joy to his well-wishers. In 1950 he chose to send a delegation to Peking, who signed a seventeen-article Agreement with the Chinese Communists the following year. This year he told the Indian Prime Minister at Mussoorie on April 24 that he had had "no definite idea" of leaving Lhasa before the fighting broke out in the capital on March 17. He admitted that the letter written to Communist China's chief political commissar in Tibet informing the latter of the threats of "reactionary evil elements," delivered on the eve of his departure, published later in Peking and questioned by many observers, was written by his hand. He also told Mr. Nehru that he had never opposed progressive reforms in Tibet and repeated his belief that Tibet was "very backward" socially and economically.[5]

While almost all media of communication here in America have been praising the Dalai Lama as a god-king leading his people heroically in anti-communist activities, the Panch'en Lama is often described as a puppet or stooge put up by the Peking reigme. In fact, both the present Dalai Lama and the present Panch'en Lama were installed in solemn ceremonies officiated by the Chairman of the Commission for Mongolian and Tibetan Affairs of the Chinese National Government before the Chinese Communists founded their government in Peking.

The Dalai Lama and the Panch'en Lama are believed to be the reincarnations of two outstanding disciples of the great reformer Tsong K'a-pa, called the Luther of Tibet, who established the Yellow Sect of Lamaism. The present Dalai Lama is the fourteenth generation, while the present Panch-en Lama is the tenth. Their predecessors throughout all these generations had at times been rivals for power, but for the most time they were on good terms serving as tutor and disciple to each other by turns.

More about the Panch'en Lama as an institution is given in Chapters III-V. Here are the words of Sir Charles Bell, a close friend of the thirteenth Dalai Lama, on the standing of the Panch'en Lama as compared with that of the Dalai Lama from a religious point of view: "It is, however, argued that as the Panch'en is the Incarnation of Ö-pa-me and the Dalai of Chen-re-zi, and as the former is the spiritual father of the latter, therefore the Panch'en must be the higher. . . . His worldly preoccupations, though not absent, are far less than those of the Dalai Lama, and his time for spiritual work is proportionately greater."[6]

In this connection, the words of Mr. Shen Tsung-lien, former director of the Office of the Mongolian and Tibetan Affairs Commission in Tibet, are worth noting: "The Communist government issued several proclamations to safeguard religious freedom, to protect lama monasteries, and to respect the existing customs of Tibet. The prestige of the Dalai Lama as the pillar of Lamaist Buddhism was counteracted greatly by that of the Panch'en Lama, the other pillar."[7]

Though their introduction of modern medical services to Tibet —where rampant malaria, smallpox and venereal disease took a heavy toll of lives annually, and where the people used to rely on prayers for their cure—and though their introduction of a modern Communist style educational system for Tibetan children and youth—who hitherto could only acquire some learning from monasteries—must have affected the position of the Lamas, the Chinese communists have left the church alone and no serious complaints have been reported from ecclesiastical circles except about the reduction of their income. What actually precipitated the March revolt, so far as the writer's knowledge goes, is social rather than religious.

We must bear in mind that the Tibetan social order is somewhat like the manorial system and chattel slavery of medieval Europe. The landed aristocrats and feudal lords used to monopolize trade making exorbitant profits which they have now been deprived of by the Communist state-owned trade organs. In an article written in May, 1958 on the seventh anniversary of the signing of the seventeen-article Agreement, the Dalai Lama declared that "good progress has been made in agriculture, live-stock breeding, forestry, the medical services, transportations and communications in Tibet," and that "power stations have been built and schools set up in many localities to promote Tibetan culture." Whether or not there has been good progress, we can gauge from the Dalai Lama's statement on the extent of the Communists' activities in Tibet and the effect of subverting the old society.

As indicated elsewhere in the book, to adjust a feudal society and a theocratic and aristocratic government to the Peking pattern would unavoidably cause serious friction. Chinese Communists hoped to avoid major trouble in Tibet by pronouncing at the end of 1956 a moratorium on changes in Tibet's political, economic and social structure, for the next six years. But Chang Kuo-hua, Vice-Chairman and Commander of the People's Liberation Army in Tibet made it clear at the twentieth meeting of the Standing Committee of the Preparatory Committee for the Tibet Autonomous Region presided over by the Dalai Lama as chairman that, "This does not, however, imply that reforms will not be carried out in Tibet at all. It is definite that Tibet must take to the road of reforms but only when the conditions are mature for such reforms."

Accordingly, no revolutionary social or political changes have been openly decreed since the end of 1956. But the reforms have continuously been carried out as scheduled in the Tibetan districts in Szechwan and in Yünnan Provinces. To the landed aristocrats and feudal lords the handwriting on the wall must have been clear, for even if no further reforms were to be introduced in the distant future, two accomplished facts have already upset their social order: (1) the peaceful penetration of highways and (2) the continuous indoctrination of the Tibetan youth. No moratorium on changes could have made them rest assured.

By January 1957, more than six thousand kilometers of motor

roads had been opened to traffic there since the Chinese Communists took over the control of Tibet. The highways to eight Chichiao areas (i.e. administrative districts: Lhasa, Shigatse, Chamdo, Nagchuka, Takung, Shannan, Gyantse and Ari) had all been linked. With Lhasa as the hub of the highway network, there were five trunk highway lines, namely, Kanting-Tibet, Ch'inghai-Tibet, Nagchuka-Ari, Lhasa-Yatung, and Lhasa-Chitang. Another two highways from Nagchuka to Chamdo with a total length of 720 kilometers and from Bamda to Ningtsin covering 280 kilometers were then under construction, and surveying of three other highways about 900 kilometers (1, from Shigatse to Nilam; 2, from a point on Kangting-Tibet highway to Chayu on the southeastern part of the Tibetan Plateau; 3, to connect Chushul with Gyantse which will shorten the distance between Lhasa and Gyantse by over 170 kilometers) was expected to be completed before the end of 1957.

As to their indoctrination program, Chinese Communists showed no less intensity. By April, 1957, Tibet had more than seventy primary schools with six thousand pupils, while a year before it had only twenty. The first secondary school was founded in Lhasa in the fall of the same year with the capacity of admitting two hundred students. It was reported in June, 1956, that five hundred youths left Tibet to take up studies in the Central Institute for Minorities in Peking and the Southwestern Institute for Minorities in Chengtu. There is a school in Hsien-yang, Shensi, for the exclusive training of Tibetan youth, which is said to have an enrollment of three thousand. The Chinese Communist Party Work Committee in Tibet and the Preparatory Committee for Tibet Autonomous Region have been training local Tibetan cadres in large numbers. Chamdo District was expected to recruit more than 3,300 before the end of 1956, while Lhasa was assigned to absorb no less than 5,100 during the same period. Thupten Tenthar, Secretary-General of the Lhasa Local Government, declared in May, 1958 that "in the past seven years, the Central Government trained about 5,000 Tibetans in the fields of administration, finance and economy, posts and telecommunications, public health, animal husbandry and veterinary, and other work."

The preceding information may be exaggerated.[8] But whatever discount the reader likes to give, the fact remains that the Tibetan problem is more social than religious. From now on, as Tiliman Durdin commented in a special article to the *New York Times* (April 5), "the Tibetan rising may indeed force more direct Chinese intervention and hasten the overturn of the old society through communization."

Thirdly, the Tibetan problem has been accorded so much attention not because of Tibet's trade, nor even because of its natural resources, but rather because of its strategic position. The Earl of Rosebury who described Tibet as "a huge monastery inhabited by a nation of monks, with a subject population inhabiting the most inhospitable region in the world, in the worst climate which is habitable by human beings," told the House of Lords that "There is little or no commerce to be got out of Tibet."[9] The American Consul at Bombay, Mr. Henry D. Baker, in reporting 1913 Indo-Tibetan trade figures to his government, added: "The statistics of land trade of British India with foreign countries published by the Commercial Intelligence Department of the Government of India, show that the trade between India and Tibet is extremely small, considering the vast area of Tibet, and is not even as large as such comparatively smaller states in the Himalaya Mountains as Nepal, Sikkim, and Bhutan."[10]

Alan Winnington, the first English journalist to have been allowed freedom of travel throughout Tibet since Chinese Communists took control of the land, in commenting on the Tibetan trade mission brought to Great Britain and the United States in 1947-48, wrote that the total volume of Tibetan trade at that time was less than 500,000 pounds yearly.[11]

The earliest Chinese record of the mineral products of Tibet is the *Hsin T'ang shu* which mentions "gold, silver, copper and tin produced in Sifan." *Wei-tsang T'u shih* gives a list of products including minerals, found in different parts of ethnological Tibet west of Tach'ienlu. A Japanese writer by the name of Hatsuo Yamagata, gathered information on minerals and other products of Tibet, and devoted a chapter to them in his book giving a general review of Tibet.[12] According to W. W. Rockhill, besides gold,—silver, copper, and iron are all found and to some extent worked in south-eastern Tibet.[13] Sir Charles Bell says that "it is possible that Tibet is rich, perhaps very rich, in minerals," but adds: "Nothing definite can be said, until the ground has been prospected scientifically and with some approach to thoroughness."[14] This he suggested accordingly in his seven-item proposal for formulating a new policy toward Tibet, presented to the Indian Government in 1921. Sir Henry Hayden, at one time Director General of the Geological Survey of India, was then chosen by the Foreign Secretary of the Indian Government to examine Tibet's mineral resources. He was generally recognized as a noted geologist, competent in his work. "His report was not favorable as regards commercial possibilities."[15]

One might argue that since motor traffic is now available between major cities and towns of Tibet where there was not a single highway up to 1951, consequently shortening the time in traversing tremendous distances (For example, it took two years to make a return trip from the east end of Tibet to its west end because snow-capped mountains and turbulent rivers blocked traffic; now it can be done in two months.), such improved communications and transport, not to count the air traffic which has already been inaugurated, should bring expanded trade, and should make possible the working at a profit of the natural resources. But up to now, it is neither its trade nor its natural resources that has earned the world-wide attention paid to Tibet.

It seems that it is its strategic position that counts. Yet heretofore, Tibet was always considered as a military backwater, for its road led nowhere.[16] It was no less due to its lack of strategic value than to respect for its religious influence that it was often left alone in its secluded position. Even the Manchu expeditions and Dzungar and Gurkha invasions into Tibet were motivated not so much by strategic, as by religio-political considerations. Emperor Kao-tsung, known as Chien-lung the Great on account of his ten successful military campaigns, told his court ministers that to take military steps in Tibet was to "use the useful in a non-beneficial place" and therefore unnecessary.[17] These words show clearly the absence of strategic value of Tibet itself in the eyes of the Emperor who was forced by the march of events to resort to force twice in Tibet during his long reign. But today the operation of air power has made warfare truly three-dimensional.

In a shrinking world divided into two hostile camps such an extended area as Tibet, situated on the roof of the world, has certainly new strategic importance. Amaury de Reincourt, speaking of the 1942 American expedition to Tibet headed by Lt. Col. Ilia Tolstoy, told us that the latter was "convinced . . . that its strategic importance was very great in an age of increasing air power."[18] These quoted words were said before the A-bomb was made known. We can well imagine how much greater is its strategic importance in a nuclear age with H-bombs and guided missiles as main weapons.

Finally, the Tibetan problem presents the issue of Tibetan autonomy. Tibetans have enjoyed autonomy ever since the Mongolian Emperor of China, Kublai Khan, made Phagspa the first Priest-King of Tibet in the 1270's. Their autonomy is clearly provided in the seventeen-article Agreement mentioned above. The Constitution of the People's Republic of China contains provisions defining regional autonomy for the national minorities, while the Constitution of the Republic of China (Art. 120) specifically stipulates that "Tibet's autonomy shall be duly guaranteed."

The question is how to interpret the autonomy of Tibet. What the British wanted was that (to quote the words of the British Secretary of State for India) Tibet should remain in that state of isolation," but on condition that "British influence should be recognized at Lhasa in such a manner as to exclude that of any other power."[19] The position of the British Government of India was made clear in its message of advice and farewell to the thirteenth Dalai Lama when he ended his exile in India and was about to return to Tibet: "The desire of the Government is to see the internal autonomy of Tibet under Chinese suzerainty maintained without Chinese interference so long as Treaty obligations are duly performed and cordial positions preserved between Tibet and India."[20]

The position of the Government of China, on the other hand, has always been, since her first contact with the West, and still is, to claim sovereignty over Tibet and to regard what happens in Tibet as within her domestic jurisdiction.

Independent India in her communications with Peking stressed the fact of Tibetan autonomy. But in view of the radical changes in the power position and in time and tide, and of the fact that India signed a pact with Communist China in May, 1954 accepting the principle that Tibet constitutes an integral part of China and pledging mutual non-interference in each other's internal affairs, the British version of Tibetan autonomy cannot be revived without upsetting the present world order. Mr. Nehru, a devoted socialist, who spent thirteen years in prison in his fight for India's independence and who has steered his country on a course of non-alignment, is in a unique position to influence Communist China's policy. His statesmanship is being put to test on this issue of preserving autonomy in the neighboring Tibet.

Sir Charles Bell told us what the thirteenth Dalai Lama wanted was to have Tibet manage its own internal affairs.[21] The present Dalai Lama has not yet made his position clear. Among his retinue at Mussoorie, India, some are urging a proclamation of independence. Former American Ambassador to U.S.S.R. W. Averell Harriman and former American Ambassador to India Chester Bowles told the House Foreign Affairs Committee that the United States should not be the first to "rush" toward recognition of a Tibetan government-in-exile, should the Dalai Lama set one up. They both cautioned against efforts to give "a cold war twist" to the situation.[22]

The writer has faith in Asian nationalism, but detests those who make all sorts of pretenses in the name of nationalism, while engaging in activities contrary to the national interest of their own country. Indeed, nationalism has broken and is still breaking colonial empires; but this does not mean that all multi-nationality countries should be divided into independent national states. The elevation of Alaska and Hawaii to the status of states in the United States shows another trend toward unity instead of division.

The writer believes in the words of President Wilson that "Self-determination . . . is an imperative principle of action." Tibet's independence should be, therefore, the Tibetan people's choice. But I do not think that those landed aristocrats and feudal lords of Tibet who took refuge in India can speak for the Tibetan people. Their number and rank are no doubt very impressive; but we must not lose sight of the fact that some noted landed aristocrats, like bka'blon Ngabou Ngawang Jigme, who headed the Tibetan delegation and signed the seventeen-articles Agreement, remain in Lhasa and are still collaborating with the Chinese Communists. Of course, whether or not the local Lhasa government before the March revolt could speak for the Tibetan people is an open question.

Studies have been made on criteria of a nation's capacity for independence. And, as yet, there is no agreed-upon yardstick to measure a nation's maturity toward its attainment. However, should Tibet be made today a "sovereign" state out of strategic considerations, it would, like Jordan, in view of its very limited resources and other handicaps, not be able to remain economically independent, and might most likely become a liability or even an Achilles' heel to its distant patronal power.

The reader might question why, in making the present study, reliance has to be placed on sources other than Tibetan. Besides acknowledging the fact that he does not read Tibetan, the writer offers the following explanation:

The Tibetans lack a sense of history as understood by other peoples. The number of their historical works known to the outside world is by no means small—as early as 1838 the great Hungarian traveler and scholar, Alexander Csoma de Körös, enumerated a long list of them.[23] They are, however, histories of a religion rather than chronicles of a people. The reason is that as the authors were lamas, they considered the greatest events in the reign of a king to be his gifts to monasteries and his building of chortens. Other events such as military campaigns, for instance, are either ignored or only referred to briefly. As Sir Charles Bell remarked: "History, unless it centers on religion, does not appeal to the Tibetan mind."[24] In other words, Tibetan annals are to the history of Tibet what Bede's *Ecclesiastical History* is to the history of England.

Not only are the Tibetan annals devoid of critical perspective; they conflict with one another. For example, W. W. Rockhill pointed out at one place, "Csoma, Sanang Setsen and Sarat Chandra Das, our chief authorities, do not agree on any one date."[25] S. W. Bushell, also commented in his article in the *Journal of the Royal Asiatic Society, "In Georgii Alphabetum Tibetanum,*

Schmidt's translation of Sanang Setsen, Csoma de Körös' *Tibetan Grammar* and Emil Schlagintweit's *Könige von Tibet,* the genealogical lists differ very widely both from each other and from the dates of the Chinese T'ang Histories."[26]

For foreign sources of information we naturally turn to countries neighboring on Tibet. *The Cambridge History of India,* commenting on Indian literature of the early days, makes the remark: "As records of political progress they are deficient. By their aid alone it would be impossible to sketch the outline of the political history of any one of the nations of India before the Muhammadan Conquest."[27] We cannot, therefore, gather any substantial information from Indian sources that will throw light on the earlier status of Tibet.

Another neighboring country, with which Tibet has been brought into closer contact than with India, is Nepal, and here again we find ourselves on equaly barren ground. "Nepal possesses numerous local chronicles, which are, however, of little historical value for the early period, and their chronology, when it can be checked, is unreliable."[28]

Chinese records thus become, for the early period at least, the only foreign sources from which one can draw information having a bearing on the status of Tibet. Western writers on Tibet have, as a rule, preferred Chinese records, the accuracy and authenticity of which are generally recognized. Nontheless no one would deny that there are valuable historical data in Tibetan records, and it is not to be supposed that the Chinese records are entirely without error.

PREFACE

This book was published under the title: *The Historical Status of Tibet* by the King's Crown Press, Columbia University in 1956. Its first edition was sold out in April, 1958. Though it was favorably reviewed by leading periodicals and received highly encouraging commendations from such noted authorities as Professors Schuyler V. R. Cammann, Taraknath Das, and Franz Michael, which would indicate its further usefulness, it did not seem practicable at the time to consider a second edition.

Since the I hasa uprising three months ago, the Tibetan issue has become a matter of first interest to the public and there is therefore a demand for books on Tibet. My present publisher suggested for this edition a more fitting title. I am glad to have been afforded an opportunity to improve my book through revision, to correct some errors in the early edition, and by re-writing the Introduction to present a more comprehensive picture with a view to helping create a better understanding of the Tibetan issue. I have also added an appendix which, I believe, will be helpful to those readers who are not familiar with the Far Eastern politics and central Asiatic affairs.

However, I find that my original conclusions have stood the test of the current developments and would prefer to leave them untouched. Even if I had time, a revision of my main theme would not be called for either. I realize that being Chinese it might be assumed that I am biased and predisposed to maintain the Chinese point of view in those instances where a possible doubt exists. I stated in the original introduction that I would like to put on record the fact that while engaged on this work, I have endeavored to be as impartial as possible. I further stated that no man can rid himself of every source of error in judgment, though

Descartes thought that he had. But if the writer puts the desire for truth above other desires, he has, if accused of partiality, provided grounds for extenuation if not for acquittal. It is gratifying to find these words in the review of my book by Professor Alex Wayman of the University of California in the *Journal of the American Oriental Society* Vol. 76, No. 3, 1956: "I feel that he has been fair within the limits of his data," and in the review by Professor Schuyler V. R. Cammann of the University of Pennsylvania in the *Journal of Asian Studies* Vol. XVI, No. 3, May, 1957: "Very commendably, in spite of his loyalty to his mother country, which is always apparent, he has generally managed to avoid writing an obvious *apologia pro patria sua,* but for the most part has maintained a high level of objectivity throughout this study." Nevertheless, I am sorry to find one reviewer who did not grant me a bit of extenuation. Professor William M. McGovern of Northwestern University in the *American Political Science Review* Vol. L, No. 4, though he said some kind words of my book, called me a vigorous propagandist. Professor McGovern, who went to Lhasa in disguise thirty-seven years ago, raised a serious objection to the statement on p. 211 that Tibet absorbed civilization mainly from China and only in a lesser degree from India. In fact, it is not a claim of my own, but a statement made by the British authority on Tibetan affairs and one of the distinguished civil servants of British India, Sir Charles Bell, in his book *Tibet: Past and Present,* which I quoted with a footnote indicating its source on p. 12.

In chapter V, a reference was made to the activities of Mr. H. E. Richardson, the former British Trade Agent in Tibet, in connection with the Tibetan civil strife in 1947. I based my information on an article written by Professor Lo Chia-lun, a historian and former Chinese ambassador to India up to the eve of the latter's recognition of the Peking government. The Columbia University Press notified me of its receipt of a letter from Mr. Richardson to say that the statement was not true. As I have no way of checking what actually took place and Mr. Richardson certainly deserves every benefit of the doubt, I have therefore deleted the passage from the present edition.

I wish to register again my deep gratitude to Professors L. Carrington Goodrich, Leland M. Goodrich, Philip C. Jessup, Nathaniel Peffer, and C. Martin Wilbur of Columbia University for their encouragement and guidance. Whenever I take up my pen to write on a topic in the field of international relations, I am reminded of my indebtedness to Professors S. R. Chow and C. A. W. Manning, without whose inspiring instruction I would have strayed into another walk of life.

In addition to those mentioned in the acknowledgment written in May 1955, my thanks are also due to my friend Professor Chiang Yee who was studying Tibetan at the School of Oriental Studies of the London University at the time when I was a research student at the London School of Economics and Political Science, for his trouble in going through my book and writing a detailed comment on it. I would have quoted his comment here, were it not for the reason that I should not cite a friend's words as if I were using them for advertising purpose. I owe Mr. Beverly H. Brown of the Division of Orientalia of the Library of Congress an apology. When I was collecting data in preparation of this work at the Library, Mr. Brown kindly showed me a manuscript prepared by a friend and told me that I could make use of it but, for political reasons, I could not mention it nor its author. Through an oversight, I did not thank him in the acknowledgments included in the first edition for having let me use this manuscript.

TIEH-TSENG LI

University of Hartford
June 20, 1959

CHAPTER I

FOREIGN RELATIONS UP TO THE THIRTEENTH CENTURY

The Earliest Contact

ACCORDING to Chinese writers, contact was established between China and Tibet as early as 2220 B.C., when the Emperor Shun drove the San-meaou tribesmen into a region called San-wei, the location of which was not indicated at the time.[1] In a decree of 1720 A.D., the learned Emperor Shêng-tsu told the scholars of his court that after many years of intensive study he came to the conclusion that San-wei constituted three parts of Tibet.[2] There is, however, still much doubt among Chinese scholars as well as Western Sinologists as to the accuracy of the Emperor's conclusion. Western Sinologists nowadays dismiss data and dates from Chinese literature about the third millennium B.C. as of almost no value. Unless written materials like bronzes and oracle bones, of an earlier period than those now available, come to light, they will not, of course, accept such assertions at all.

In the histories of the Chinese dynasties Shang (ca. 1523-1028 B.C.; Chinese traditional chronology assigns to the Shang dynasty the dates 1765-1123 B.C.), Chou (ca. 1027-256 B.C.), Han (202 B.C.-220 A.D.), Tsin (265-420), and Sui (589-618), there are stray references to tribes named Jung or Ch'iang,[3] who are identified by Chinese historians as peoples of Tibet. But whether they were ancestors of present Tibetans is an open question.

Tibetan records of the corresponding periods contain references to China or the Chinese. *Dub-thah-leg-shad sel-kyi mélon* [4] mentioned a Chinese sage, Leg-tan-man, in the early years of the Bon religion.[5] During the reign of Namri-sron-tsan, or Gnam-ri slon mchan,[6] who ascended the throne of Tibet in the latter part of the sixth century, the Tibetans obtained their first knowledge of arithmetic and medicine from the Chinese.[7]

Definite Relations First Established

Definite relations, however, were not established until the T'ang dynasty (618-907). It was during the period of this dynasty [8] that no fewer than one hundred missions went from one country to the other.[9] Some were sent to announce the death of a sovereign or to tender congratulations on auspicious occasions. Others were either missions of tribute from Tibet to the Emperor of China, or missions bearing presents to the Tsanpu of Tibet from the Emperor. Most of them, however, were sent to sue for peace, renew friendly relations, and settle boundaries, or to conclude sworn treaties or matrimonial alliances. The close contact may be seen from the fact that in the second and eleventh months of the year 805 two missions were sent from China to Tibet and in the seventh and tenth months of the same year two missions were sent from Tibet to China. The Tibetan manuscripts found at Tunhuang, which give a very succinct year-by-year account of the great events from A.D. 650-747, record the receiving of Chinese envoys by the Tibetan King in every year from 729-37 and 742-44, besides the earlier references to Chinese missions.[10]

The two countries were often at war—one side being victorious at one time and the other at another—and frontier conflicts were common. Once the Tibetans led by a traitor general named Kao Hui entered the Chinese imperial capital, Ch'ang-an, and occupied it for fifteen days (763 A.D.). One (?) Tibetan record reports (and this may be a later interpolation) that the Chinese captured the Tibetan capital, Lhasa, after the death of Sron-tsan Gampo.[11] It is significant that neither the Chinese historical annals nor the highly important Tibetan manuscripts found at Tunhuang mention a Chinese capture of Lhasa.

In spite of the frequent armed conflicts, diplomatic relations were, more often than not, maintained between the two countries. On the deaths of the Tsanpus Ch'i-tsung-lung-tsan in 650, Chilipapu in 679, Ch'inuhsilung in 705, Ch'ilisulungliehtsan in 755, Mukhri-bcan-po in 804, name omitted in 817,[12] and Tamo, also known as Glang Dhama or Landarma, in 842, the Chinese Emperor was informed.[13] He sent special envoys to convey his condolences, or to offer sacrifices, or to participate in the ceremonies at funerals. Sometimes he went into mourning and closed the court for one to three days.

The Tibetans were likewise informed of the deaths of the Chinese emperors and of the accessions of their successors in 805 and 820. Missions to offer condolences on the deaths of the emperors and to make sacrifices at the funerals were sent from Tibet. The 805 mission, moreover, brought gold, silver, robes, oxen, and horses as offerings for the mausoleum of Te-tsung who reigned from 780-805.[14]

Eight treaties were solemnly and ceremoniously signed during this period. The first was concluded during the reign of Chung-tsung (705-10),[15] the second, known as the treaty of Ch'ih-ling, in 730, the third in 756, the fourth in 765, the fifth in 766, the sixth, known as the treaty of Ch'ing-shui, in 783,[16] the seventh in 784, and the eighth in 821.

In addition to these, a ceremony of swearing a treaty was treacherously broken up by the Tibetans at Ping-liang in 787. The treaty of 783 and the treaty signed in Ch'ang-an in 821 and confirmed at Lhasa by religious ceremonies in the following year were inscribed on stone pillars in front of the large temple, called by the Chinese Ta-chao-ssu, in the city of Lhasa. Bushell made a facsimile of part of the 821 pillar. A translation from the Tibetan text was appended to Sir Charles Bell's *Tibet*.[17] *Shên chou kuo kuang chi* (Shanghai, 1909), No. 7, reproduced the four sides of the pillar in two plates accompanied by Lo Chên-yü's (1866-1940) article in which the author added in print a transcript of the entire Chinese portion of the monument, inclusive of the thirty-four names so far as decipherable.[18]

These relations were strengthened by military assistance from Tibet. In 648 Tibet sent an army in collaboration with 7,000 cavalry from Nepal to support the Chinese envoy, Wang Hsüan-ts'e, in subduing the usurper of Magadha. The latter was taken prisoner and brought to Ch'ang-an.[19] In 784 Tibet offered its troops to help settle the difficulties of the State of China. A Chinese envoy was therefore sent to Tibet to devise a plan of campaign, and the joint army recovered the capital, Ch'ang-an, and relieved Feng-tien, in which the Emperor was besieged.

Matrimonial Alliances and Their Effect on the Religions of Tibet

To strengthen the bond of neighborly friendship, two matrimonial alliances were made. In 641 Emperor T'ai-tsung gave the Princess Wên-ch'êng of the Imperial House in marriage to the celebrated Tsanpu Ch'i-tsung-lung-tsan. In 703 the ruling Empress Wu-tsê-t'ien granted the request of Tsanpu Ch'inuhsilung for a matrimonial alliance, but the latter died during the war with Nepal and P'o-lo-mên (Brāhmana), and the marriage did not take place. In 710 the Emperor Chung-tsung gave his adopted daughter with the title of Princess Chin-ch'eng in marriage to Tsanpu Ch'ilisutsan. Thus, the two courts had been united by marriages which, according to the treaty of 783, had, by the time of its signing, established a nephew-uncle relationship for nearly two hundred years[20]—an exaggeration of at least fifty years.

The Tibetan record[21] registered the marriage of Ch'i-tsung-lung-tsan and Princess Wên-ch'êng, but gave the name of the Tsanpu as Sron-tsan Gampo. Ch'i-tsung-lung-tsan was probably a transcription of his name prior to his accession (that is Khri-ldan-srong-btsan).[22] The name of the princess was given as Hun-shin. The record also registered the marriage of the Tsanpu Khri-lde gtsug btsan mes Ag-ts'oms and Princess Kyim-shan, daughter of the Chinese Emperor Wai-jun. This must have been the marriage between Ch'ilisutsan and Princess Chin-ch'eng, as the Chinese name gives a quite correct pronunciation of the first four syllables of this Tibetan name, and Kyim-shan is only a different rendering of Chin-ch'eng.[23] But the story of the engagement and marriage is very different from the account in *T'ang shu.* The *Documents de Touen-Houang,* which began its record from 650, mentioned the earlier (641) arrival of the Princess Wên-ch'êng (the name was rendered as Mun-čhan) and revealed the fact that she did not live together with the King until six years of their marriage had elapsed. The *Documents* records the arrival of the Princess Kim-san in 710, which agrees with *T'ang shu.* Other Mongolian and Tibetan accounts, as those of Sanang Setsen, *Bodhimur,*[24] and the *Mani Bkah-hbum,*[25] although they distort many of the related facts, agree substantially with the Chinese record as far as the marriage itself is concerned.[26]

These two weddings had a remarkable effect upon the religions of Tibet. The two Chinese princesses and, in the case of Wên-ch'êng, jointly with a Nepalese princess whom her husband married, exerted great influence in the propagation of Buddhism in that country.[27] In his book on Buddhism, M. V. Vassilief quotes the Tibetan historian, Buston, as saying that "at the beginning the Chinese Kachanna were the guides of the Tibetans in Buddhism."[28] The Princess Wên-ch'êng is regarded by the Tibetans as the incarnation of the Divine Mother (Tara) and her image in the famous Ta-chao-ssu is still an object of worship.[29]

The Extent of Chinese Influence

The facts related in the present and following paragraphs show the extent of the Chinese influence in Tibet. "As the Princess disliked their custom of painting their faces red, Lung-tsan [Ch'i-tsung-lung-tsan] ordered his people to put a stop to the practice, and it was no longer done. He also discarded his felt and skins, put on brocade and silk, and gradually copied Chinese civilization. He also sent the children of his chiefs and of rich men to request admittance into the national schools to be taught the classics, and invited learned scholars from China to compose his official reports to the Emperor."[30] He later asked for silkworms' eggs, mortars and presses for making wine, and for workmen to manufacture paper and ink and to construct water mills. All these requests were granted, and in addition a calendar was sent.[31] The *T'ang hui yao*[32] records that he asked the Emperor for workmen to manufacture writing-brushes. In this connection it is interesting to note that the Tibetans actually employ for writing a wooden or bamboo stylus in the same manner as the ancient Chinese did prior to the invention of the brush.

In giving away the Princess Chin-ch'eng, the Emperor Chung-tsung sent as a dowry several tens of thousands of pieces of brocaded and plain silk, various kinds of apparatus with skilled workmen, and Chin-ts'ŭ musical instruments. The Princess asked for a copy of the classical works *Mao-shih, Li-chi, Tso-chuan,* and

Hsiao T'ung's compilation known as *Wên-hsüan;* and, in spite of the memorial of remonstrance presented by the scholar and high official, Yü Hsiu-lieh, a decree ordered the officers in charge to make a copy of the classics and the literature and issue them to the Princess.[33]

The Mongolian and Tibetan works also record that Sron-tsan introduced from China silkworms and mulberry trees,[34] that his Chinese Princess introduced "Nas-chang, or whiskey, barley beer, and cheese," and that the people were taught how to make pottery works and water mills.[35] The Chinese method of divination by means of the tortoise, in which the system of the "pa kua" was employed, is believed to have been imported by the Chinese Princess Wên-ch'êng. According to Laufer, the Tibetan transcriptions of "pa kua" have partially preserved the ancient initial sonants and the ancient finals of Chinese: they are thus well attested as coming down from the T'ang period.[36] The great Tsanpu, Sron-tsan Gampo, though the stories about his literary and linguistic prowess are not substantiated in early literature, is said to have acquired a fair knowledge of Chinese, which helped him to converse with the Chinese ambassadors.[37]

Princess Wên-ch'êng brought with her the great image of Buddha and several volumes of Buddhist scripture, besides a few treatises on medicine and astrology. At the age of twenty-five Sron-tsan sent his ministers to North China to erect 108 chapels at Re-ro-tse-ña, the chosen residence of Manjuśri towards the north of Peking. He invited Hoshang Mahá-tshe from China and others from Nepal and India for the great work of the translation of the Buddhist scriptures from the Sanskrit and Chinese originals into the newly formed written language of Tibet.[38]

According to K. S. Chen, the earliest work translated from Chinese into Tibetan was the *Pai-pai ch'an-hui ching,* which is not found in the present Chinese or Tibetan canon.[39] Lü Chêng in his book on Tibetan Buddhism[40] says that the canon then translated was the *Pao yün ching* (Ratnamegha-sûtra) and the *Pao ch'ieh ching.*[41] Liu Li-ch'ien's compilation[42] also mentions the translation of *Pao yün, Pao ch'ieh,* and nineteen others, but relates the legend that the *Pai-pai ch'an-hui ching* and the *Pao ch'ieh ching* had been dropped from heaven during the reign of the 27th Tsanpu, five generations before the Sron-tsan Gampo. He gives the Chinese name of Hoshang Mahá-tshe as Han-ta-shou-t'ien without any explanation.

During the reign of Dgung-srong (Khri-'dus-sron, or Ch'inuhsi-lung as he is called in *T'ang shu*), tea, which afterwards became the national beverage, was first brought from China.[43] The Tsanpu Khri-lde gtsug btsan mes Ag-ts'oms (Chinese Ch'ilisutsan) obtained the volumes of Buddhist scriptures, called Ser-hod-tampa, from the province of Kuń-shi[44] in China, besides a few treatises on medicine, all of which he ordered to be translated into Tibetan.[45] Another source recorded that he had these volumes (*Suvarna prabhasa sûtra* in Sanskrit) translated into Tibetan. He also had several Chinese works on medicine, astrology, and works concerning religious ceremonies translated.[46]

While his son Thi-sron-de-tsan[47] reigned, a Chinese sage named Hoshang-Maháyána arrived in Tibet and converted the ignorant classes to his tenets.[48] Later, when the great teacher of India, Kamalasila, came to Lhasa upon the heels of the celebrated Padma Sambhava in response to the Tsanpu's invitation, he met with a great deal of opposition from Maháyána and perhaps also from Hoshang Zab-mo, author of two works in the Bstan-hgyur (Mdo. XXX, XXXIII).[49] *Le Concile de Lhasa,* a translation of the Chinese Touen-Houang manuscript by Paul Demieville (Paris, 1952), registered the debates engaged in by these Hoshangs. It is no wonder that we should have found some Chinese monks in Tibet at a time when diplomatic relations and other contacts were being maintained. For one thing, the Chinese monks Fa-hsien,[50] Hui-sheng,[51] Hsüan-tsang,[52] and Wu-k'ung[53] went as far as India, though not through Tibet.[54] Also, the *Ta T'ang hsi yü chiu fa kao sêng chuan* by I-tsing (635-713) and the *Fa yüan chu lin* by Tao-shih (completed in 668) recorded the passages of sramanas Hsüan-chao, Tao-hsi, and Hsüan-t'ai and five others through Tibet in the T'ang dynasty; and the interview of Hsüan-chao with Princess Wên-ch'êng while in Lhasa.

The Tsanpu Ralpachan, or Khri-ral (Kolikotsu in *T'ang shu*), not being satisfied with the translations of Sanskrit works already in his possession, obtained fresh manuscripts from China and other neighboring countries.[55] He had all the events of his reign recorded according to the Chinese system of chronology, and introduced standard weights and measures similar to those used in China.[56]

From the above we have seen the widespread influence of Chinese culture on the early life of Tibet. As conceded by Sir Charles Bell, "we may in fact say that the present civilization of Tibet was taken mainly from China, and only in a lesser degree from India.[57] There was indeed very early religious contact between India and Tibet—not to mention the legend told by those lama-authors who always liked to link time immemorial with the land of the birth of Buddhism. But the Tibetans, as shown by a study of the loan-words in their language, appear to have received names and objects from the Chinese prior to their contact with India.[58]

There is very scanty information about commercial relations. It seems that Sron-tsan Gampo first established such relations with China.[59] *T'ang shu* recorded in 730 the request of the Tibetans for the privilege of bartering horses at Ch'ih-ling and setting up an exchange mart at Kansungling. The latter was not granted for strategic considerations. Later they requested the establishment of an exchange mart at the Lungchou barrier, which was allowed by decree in the early years of the ninth century.[60]

Status at This Time Difficult to Define in Modern Terms

We have considered the close and changing relations between Tibet and China during the period of the T'ang dynasty, but it is impossible to describe the political status of Tibet in relation to China in modern terms. The French scholar Grenard[61] wrote that Sron-tsan Gampo recognized the suzerainty of the Emperor of China. There is evidence to support this view, but from the following interesting incident, recorded in Chinese annals, one may form some idea of the actual position:

> When Ch'ang Lü, with the envoy Ts'ui Han-hêng, first arrived at their hotel (781), the Tsanpu (Ch'i-li-tsan) ordered them to stop, and made them first produce the official despatch. That having been done, he sent this message to Han-hêng, "The imperial despatch you bring says, 'The things offered as tribute have all been accepted and now we bestow upon our son-in-law a few presents for him to take when they arrive.' Our great Fan and Tang nations are allied by marriages, and how is it that we are treated with the rites due to a subject? . . .

Let, then, Han-hêng send a messenger to report to the Emperor that he may act."

Lü was sent back and the imperial despatch was accordingly altered, the words "offered as tribute" changed to "presented," "bestowed" to "given" and "for him to take" to "for his acceptance." The following words were added, "The former minister, Yang Yen, departed from the old practice and is responsible for these errors. . . ."[62]

With Landarma (Tamo in Chinese), the famous "Julian the Apostate of Buddhism," ended the long line of Tibetan sovereigns, and his descendants henceforth ceased to exercise authority over the whole of the country.[63] Both Chinese and Tibetan records agree on this. According to the history of the Sung dynasty (960-1279),[64] Tibet became weak and declined in power during the later years of the T'ang dynasty.[65] The tribes formed clans of various sizes, and the country was no longer united. In Das's article we find the partition of the kingdom between Landarma's two sons, Hodsrun and Yumten, and the later subdivisions. The accompanying diagram is designed to show how their possessions were subsequently divided.

Tibetan History after Landarma, written by Nag-dbaṅ-dge-legs in 1643 and translated from Tibetan into Chinese by Liu Li-chien in 1945, supplements Das's account and gives a more detailed chronology showing further subdivisions. For example, while Das's account based upon *Deb-ther-sṅon-po, Chho-jur,* and others gives only a table of the genealogical succession from Yumten, here a more detailed subdivision is given showing where his descendants subsequently established themselves. It also informs us of the retreat of Tasi-tségpal's descendants to La-stod and Thi Kyi-de Ṅimagon's descendants to Mṅah-ric, both under the pressure of Yumten's branch.

It further records that Tsede's fifth descendant, Btsan-phyug, went to Ya-tser and became king and founder of the Ya-tser House which lasted another six generations. Its more detailed account of the subdivisions into different tribes of Tasi-tségpal's branch, especially the spread of Thichhun's heirs, gives a clear picture of how Tibet was further weakened politically, while its religion revived. In describing the genealogical development of this branch, it mentions the visit of the younger son of Sakya-bkraśis

- **LANDARMA**
  - **HODSRUN** (took possession of western Tibet)
    - **PALKHOR-TSAN**
      - **THI TASI-TSÉGPAL**
        - **PALDE** — His descendants made themselves masters of Guñthañ, Lugyalwa, Chyipa, Lhatse, Lan-lun, and Tsakor, where they severally ruled as petty chiefs.
        - **HODDÉ**
          - **PHAB-DE-SE** became master of Tsañ-roñ.
          - **THI-DE** took possession of Amdo and Tsonkha.
          - **THICHHUN** became king of U and removed capital to Yar-lung; his seventh descendant, SAKYA-GON, a great patron of Sakya Pandita; his ninth descendant, TAGPA RIMPCHHE, accompanied the Illustrious Phagspa on his visit to the Emperor of China and obtained Imperial Patents.
          - **NAGPA** also succeeded as master of Tsañ-roñ.
        - **KYIDE** — His descendants spread over Mu, Jan, Tanag, Ya-rul-lag, and Gyal-tse districts where they ruled as petty princes over their respective possessions.
  - **THI-DE YUMTEN** (took possession of eastern province)
      - **THI-KYI-DE NIMAGON** (went to Nahri, founded capital at Purañ)
        - **DERIGPA-GON** (Declared himself king of Mañ-yul)
        - **TASIDE-GON** (Seized Purañ)
        - **DETASUG-GON** (Became king of Shañ-shuñ [modern Gugé])
          - **KHOR-RÉ** (became monk, known as YESE-HOD)
            - **LHADE**
              - **HODDÉ**
                - **TSEDE**
              - **SHI-VA-HOD**
              - **CHYAN CHHUB-HOD** (invited Atisá from India, 1042)
          - **SRON-NE**

in Phagspa's company to the Emperor Kublai, the founder of Chinese Yüan dynasty, and the receipt of the Imperial Patents from the latter. The same is related in Das's account.

In the Reverend Francke's *History of Western Tibet* is found a rather different version of the story. Both Kyi-de Ñimagon and Tasi-tségpal were robbed of their possessions in central Tibet by Yumten and fled to western Tibet. The latter became king of the most eastern portion of western Tibet, called Yar-lung. The former conquered western Tibet completely and divided his kingdom among his three sons. All records agree that the country was mainly divided into two parts with their respective subdivisions.

The history of the Sung dynasty dealt only with the bordering tribes of eastern and northeastern Tibet, presumably the descendants of Yumten, of whom scarcely a trace of any systematic record can be found except some genealogical tables as mentioned above. As Tibet was then divided and not strong enough to endanger the security of China in any way, the Chinese who had originally neither the desire nor the necessity to exploit a region so economically poor, and who themselves were under attack from the north during much of the Sung period, had only its frontier closely guarded. They adopted a laissez-faire policy toward what was going on in that neighboring land, whose people had once been a source of so much trouble.

Throughout the Sung dynasty (960-1279), therefore, the writer has been able to find nothing more than the acceptance of the submission of the native tribes, their presentation of tribute and occasional expeditions against rebellious tribes or invaders of the protected tribes. For instance, there was one expedition against Li Chi-chien and another against Yuanha. On the whole, the Chinese Emperor then maintained a peaceful policy towards the Tibetan tribes.[67] He even bestowed favors upon them.

In 961 Shang-po-kan, chief of the Chinchow tribes, killed the Chinese soldiers who came over to his region to gather some wood. The Chinese Governor arrested forty-seven of his men and submitted a report to the Court. The Emperor replaced the Governor and sent Shang-po-kan a message to announce his pardon. That led the chief to make his submission. Thirty-four years later the Governor, Wên Chung-shu, reported his success in driving the native tribes beyond Wei-pei. The Emperor, Tai-tsung, this time transferred the Governor to another post to avoid further conflict. Generous gifts and high honors were used to pacify the Tibetan tribes. Whenever the chieftains submitted tribute, mostly horses but sometimes sheep and camels, the Emperor gave them either tea, brocade, silk, robes, or apparatus in return, or richly rewarded them with money. Several chieftains were appointed governors with seals and tablets and some were made generals. Among the latter the most outstanding figure was Che-pu-lung-po, who came to the Imperial Court in 998 and was promoted to the rank of general-in-chief. In 1032 the same honor was conferred upon Kuo-szu-lo, a descendant of Tsanpu.

We may assume that most of these chieftains presented tribute as a commercial proposition rather than as a mark of allegiance. There are records of the giving of seventy-six kinds of Chinese medicine to the Tibetan tribes during the prevalence of a plague, and presents of bows, arrows, and other weapons—a departure from the old practice—to the faithful tribes. Moreover, the royal surname was conferred on loyal and deserving chieftains, and hostages—usually sons and brothers of the chiefs who had submitted—were returned as friendly gestures and proofs of confidence. All these benefactions were highly appreciated, and throughout the Sung dynasty the Chinese western frontier was generally quiet.

The religious tie, so close during the T'ang dynasty and maintained during this period between western Tibet and its western neighbor,[68] does not seem to have been altogether severed between China and eastern Tibet. In 966, Chi-pu-kuo-chih, the Tibetan chief of Hsi-liang, reported to the Chinese Imperial Court the arrival of a group of more than sixty Chinese monks, who declared that they were on their way to India, but had been robbed by the natives. As Chinese history does not pay much attention to religious matters, it is highly probable that many more religious events in connection with China and Tibet in this period were not recorded.

The weakened and divided Tibet was, however, not entirely free from the encroachment of her western nighbor. According to the *Cambridge History of India,* in 1205 Ikhtiyār-ud-dīn of

Bengal, dreaming of carrying his arms beyond the Himalayas, set out with an army of ten thousand horse on his perilous adventure. When he penetrated deep into the Tibetan borderland and found it impossible to take a garrisoned city, he began to retreat. Then he found the natives had destroyed or obstructed the road and burnt all vegetation so that neither fodder nor fuel was procurable. Those who managed to get back to the river found the bridge already destroyed, and no boats were at hand. He finally succeeded in reaching the opposite bank with about one hundred horsemen with which sorry remnant of his army he returned to Lakhnāwatī.[69]

Historians could ascribe Tibet's immunity from Chinese encroachment at that period to the fact that since the death of Landarma[70] the T'ang dynasty was on the decline and China was later facing foreign aggression and civil strife, and that during the Sung dynasty, "although its troops fought heroically often, they never succeeded in breaking the iron ring forged around the imperial boundaries by the Khitan (until 1125), the Jurchen Tungus (until 1234), and the Mongols in the north; by the Tangut . . . (ca. 990-1227) and the Mongols in the northwest; and by Annam and Nan Chao in the southwest and south,"[71] and were, therefore, too hard pressed to be in a position to acquire new additions to China's domain at the expense of Tibet. Historians could also explain the noninterference of the Sung emperors in the affairs of a weak and divided Tibet in terms other than those of power politics. Anyhow, it was partly due to the laissez-faire, or as someone put it, isolationist, policy of the Sung dynasty and partly due to the natural barrier against India that Tibet was left alone in its secluded position until the Mongolian Khan brought a fundamental change to its status.

CHAPTER II

TIBET AS A VASSAL STATE

Conquest by the Mongols

SINO-TIBETAN RELATIONS between the seventh and ninth centuries were, as shown in the preceding chapter, close indeed, but the status of Tibet even then was rather vague. During that period Tibet as a military power was by no means inferior to China; but when later it was divided and weakened, and its foreign relations were reduced almost to naught, its status naturally became even less clear. In any case, owing partly to differences in setting—an environment of a thousand years ago compared with the world of today—and partly to differences between Chinese and Western, and between ancient and modern, conceptions of the term, we prefer to leave the political status of Tibet in this early period undefined. We can, however, be sure of one thing, that is, the strong influence of Chinese culture in Tibet, especially during the T'ang dynasty.

It is beyond the scope of this study to analyze the characteristics of Chinese culture and its effect on China's policy toward neighboring nations. Suffice it to say that, thanks more to the fact that "the history of China is the record of an expanding culture, not that of a conquering empire," [1] than to any other factor, Tibet's status, however we may conceive it, was maintained even at a time it was split and impotent after the reign of Landarma (died 842). But this status was bound to be affected as a result of what now occurred—Jenghis Khan's [2] conquest and the rise of the Mongolian Empire.

According to Das, as soon as the great and mighty warrior came in the beginning of the thirteenth century, the whole of Tibet, without much resistance, succumbed to his power. The different chieftains and petty princes became his abject vassals. The Chinese records, however, show that his conquest extended only as far as Hsi Hsia (Tangut), known to the Chinese as Ho-hsi.[3]

It was his grandson, Möngä,[4] who established, soon after the submission of the Tibetan tribes in 1253, an administrative center at Hochow, in the present province of Kansu, and the pacification bureaus at Tiao-men, Yü-t'ung, Li, Ya, Ch'ang-ho-hsi, and Ning-yüan, all along the western border of present Szechwan.

When Kublai, who had commanded the forces that overran eastern Tibet on his way in 1253 to conquer Ta-li (in Yünnan),[5] succeeded Möngä as Khan in 1260, he enforced the pacification policy of the latter with even greater energy. In 1269 he established a pacification bureau in Wussutsang, which was farther in the interior of Tibet and dominated the two principal provinces, Dbus (U) and Gtsang (Tsang). Later he divided Tibet into districts (Chün and Hsien) as in China Proper, and established various offices and a system of local government.[6]

The history of the Yüan dynasty records the assimilation of the Tibetan army under the command of a Mongolian prince Auluchi (whose title in Chinese was Ping-hsi-wang) and the employment of it in subduing the Chien-tu tribe in 1272, and also the further use of force in bringing the Tibetans into submission.[7]

Apparently Kublai Khan found the warlike Tibetans a difficult people to rule, and resolved to reduce them to a condition of docility through the influence of religion. Buddhism was reaffirmed[8] as the religion best calculated to tame the wild tribesmen of Tibet, and as it had already secured a firm foothold there,[9] the project was by no means an impractical one. The policy was effectively enforced, and the cooperation of Sakya Pandita of the large monastery at Sakya was secured by his being invited to the Mongolian court.[10]

Tibet as a Theocracy

According to the Chinese records, Sakya Pandita's nephew Phagspa went to see Kublai in 1253. This young visitor[11] pleased him so much that as soon as he was made Khan he asked Phagspa to be his spiritual guide, or national mentor. As a reward for his adaptation of Tibetan and Brahmic script to the existing spoken Mongolian language,[12] Phagspa was raised to the rank of priest-king (Ta-pao-fa-wang or prince of the holy law) and constituted the ruler of (1) Tibet proper, comprising the thirteen districts of U and Tsang, (2) Kham, and (3) Amdo. From that time Tibet was ruled by the Sakyapa lamas as a theocracy.

In 1275 Phagspa, who had remained at the Mongolian court except for a short visit to his home in 1264 and a brief journey a few months before, asked for a long leave to return to Tibet. Permission was only reluctantly granted. He left his half-brother, Ling-ching (rim-rgyal in Tibetan), to take his place at the court. He died five years later.[13] Phagspa had been granted the right to make the succession to the throne hereditary in his family and had received all the highest honors that could be conferred on a lama. He had a seat in Ulterior Tibet called Sakya-Jong.[14]

In order to understand better how this theocratic rule worked and the new status that resulted from such a change, it seems not out of place here to devote a few lines to the situation in which Tibet found herself. In the preceding chapter mention was made of the revival of Buddhism after the death of Landarma[15] and the subsequent religious contact between India and Tibet.[16] At the end of the twelfth century the Pala and Sena dynasties in India were swept away by a Mohammedan invasion led by Muhammad Bakhtyar. The rich and Buddhist country of Bengal succumbed without much resistance. "The town of Bihar was taken by surprise by only two hundred horsemen. The monks were put to the sword, and the slaughter was so great that, when the victor wanted someone to explain to him the books in the library, not a soul could be found to do so! Those monks who escaped took refuge in Tibet, taking with them Sanskrit manuscripts which were translated into Tibetan. Copies of these may be seen in the libraries at Lhasa and other Tibetan Monasteries today."[17] The tragic stories of the massacre by invaders of an alien faith told by these refugees, and the news of the above-mentioned Ikhtiyār's encroachment on Tibet, though abortive, must have frightened the Tibetans and made them more dependent on the powerful Mongolian court which had shown repeated favors to Buddhism. And as a result of the stoppage of the route to Bengal which never escaped from the rule of Mohammedans for any considerable time until they were superseded in the eighteenth century by the

British, and the decline of Buddhism in India, increasing influences on Tibetan culture in general and religion in particular tended to come from China.

The institution of a national mentor was maintained throughout the period of the Yüan dynasty.[18] Unusual respect was paid to the holder of the office, who enjoyed important privileges. Some of the privileges were extended even to his relatives. The national mentor and high lamas did not, however, always live up to the requirements of their offices, and some of them grossly abused the indulgence of the emperors. They misappropriated money, accepted bribes, desecrated graves, and were guilty of seduction, oppression, and even murder. Moreover, they used their influence to help their friends to avoid the payment of taxes and obstructed the course of justice.

There is a wealth of evidence concerning the highhandedness of the highly placed lamas. Yang-lien-chen-chia, the Pontiff of Buddhists in southeastern China appointed by Kublai, rifled the imperial cemeteries of the Sung dynasty and made a very large fortune by unlawful means. In 1308 some Tibetan lamas stole a stock of fuel from a civilian. When the case was brought up in court they nearly lynched the plaintiff, and yet the culprits were pardoned. In 1309 a group of eighteen lamas assaulted a princess, while she was traveling. They were arrested but released. In later years even the national mentor became corrupt. It was recorded that the last occupant of this office during the Yüan dynasty supplied the emperor with aphrodisiacs and encouraged him in vice in order to win his favor.[19]

The extraordinary tolerance that the court extended to the lamas had the effect of enabling the latter to sap the resistance of the bellicose Tibetans. Eventually Tibetan bloodthirstiness was converted into a passion for spiritual satisfaction. Thus, through the religious link between China and Tibet, China was able to exercise a dominant influence over her vassal state or, in terms of Buddhist statecraft, her "patronized state," without using force or establishing colonies in the country.

In Tibet the Sakya lamas were no better, if not worse, than the Sakya lamas in China. The regents[20] who held the real power under the puppet Sakya hierarchy waged war against each other.

The country became a hotbed of conspiracies and assassinations. The emperors at Peking do not seem to have made any attempt to alter this state of affairs. So long as their own authority was not threatened they left the rise and fall of Tibetan rival monasteries to take their own course.

From the Tibetan records we find that one Mongol emperor preferred one sect, while his successor showed special favors to a different sect, usually by means of giving land together with thousands of families for the maintenance of the monasteries under its charge, and numerous feudal chiefs were thus created.[21] The regents received patents and seals directly from the court of Peking.[22] One regent, or Dpon-chen as the office was called in Tibetan, abused his power to such an extent that the disciples of Phagspa petitioned to the Emperor who then sent troops to Bya-rog-rdoñ and put him to death.[23] During a later feud (about 1290) between Sakya and Hbri-gun sects, the regent named A-ña-lan suppressed the latter sect with the aid of Mongolian military forces.[24]

The figurehead Sakya priest-kings always maintained close relations with the emperors at Peking by sending their brothers or sons to be national mentors and reside near the court. Carla, who succeeded his brother Phagspa and whose son Dharma-palarak-sita, a former national mentor, succeeded him as priest-king, married a Mongolian princess. The dispute on the succession of Carla was brought to the Emperor, who upheld his son and banished a claimant; at the death of Dharma-palarak-sita, the installation of priest-king was held up for years because of the Emperor's disapproval of the choice.[25] Apparently it was by the emperor's authority that the Sakyapa hierarchs were maintained till the middle of the fourteenth century.[26]

During the latter part of the Yüan dynasty the emperors were weak and waning in power, but it does not seem to have been their weakness that prevented them from interfering in the affairs of such a chaotic state as Tibet. Besides the effective ideological control by means of religion, they must have taken the international situation of that part of the world into consideration. An event related below must have deeply affected the thinking of the Tibetans, bringing closer their tie with China and therefore making the Mongol emperors feel assured that no interference was necessary.

An Indian Attack

In the early part of the fourteenth century Muhammad Tughluq of India believed that his forces could traverse the mountains and take Tibet and China by surprise. He had no idea of the nature of the country and the inhabitants, the narrow passes, the perilous mountain paths, and the sheer precipices. Nor did he realize the bitter cold that would have to be endured by troops bred in the scorching plains of India. In 1337-38 he embarked upon this hazardous undertaking by sending an army of 100,000 horse and a large number of foot soldiers under the command of Malik Nīkpāī by way of Nāgarkot or Kāngra. This was by far a greater expedition than that led 132 years earlier by Ikhtiyār-ud-dīn of Bengal,[27] and it met an even greater disaster.

While climbing on a narrow road along the precipitous mountain side the army was overtaken by the heavy and drenching rains of the mountains, which spread disease among men and horses and destroyed large numbers of both. Mountaineers had assembled to harass their retreat and occupied the gorges and defiles, and so thoroughly did they perform their task that they destroyed the army almost to a man. Nīkpāī, two other officers, and about ten horsemen were all who returned to Delhi.[28]

The authors of *An Advanced History of India* are of the opinion that

> Muhammad-bin-Tughluq never entertained the fantastic idea of conquering Tibet and China. But Barni, a contemporary officer, and Ibn Batutah clearly refer to his design of "capturing the mountain of Kara-jal—which lies between the territories of Hind (India) and those of China." [29]

No matter what may have motivated the Moslem ruler, his military campaign on such a large scale could not possibly escape the notice of the Tibetans and fail to produce some psychological effect on them despite their lack of the sense of solidarity, a lack common in those days. With the western frontier freed from the threat of force as a result of this calamitous military adventure, the emperors at Peking could comfortably afford to leave the Tibetans alone and not meddle in their affairs.

Even in the establishment of the Sitya regime the Emperor did not lend a hand but contented himself with giving it the sanction of his authority, although the circumstances of the country were repeatedly brought to his notice.

Chyañ-chhub as Undisputed Master

The founder of the new regime, Chyañ-chhub Gyal-tshan, better known by his name of Phagmo-du, was a member of the famous Bkah-brgyud-pa sect,[30] although he visited the Sakya monastery at the age of fourteen and stayed there for some time. His ancestors had received patents from the Peking court,[31] and he himself was appointed at the age of eighteen to the command of 10,000 families by patent from the Emperor and entrusted with a seal for his own use.[32]

During a dispute with the chiefs, nobles, and lamas of U and Tsang, the Emperor decided in his favor, furnished him with renewed patents and seals, and bestowed on him, to be enjoyed as hereditary possessions, the province of U, leaving Tsang to the Sakyapas. Five years later,[33] after having defeated the Sakyapas and other rivals on the battlefield, Chyañ-chhub presented to the court of Peking charges of imbecility and dissensions of the Sakyapa authorities and the local chiefs to justify this action, and the Emperor permitted him to annex the remaining parts of Tibet and Kham to his possessions.[34] He assumed the title of King of Situ and became the undisputed master of the whole of Tibet.

There was hardly any change in the relations between China and Tibet; nor was there any change in Tibet's status, as a result of the change of regime. The close relation between the court of Peking and the Sitya regime may be gathered from Das's account.[35] He states that Sákya Rin-chheñ, the fourth in descent from Phagmo-du, became a favorite minister of Togon-Timur (reigned 1333-68), the last emperor of the Yüan dynasty. At first entrusted with guarding the palace, Sákya Rin-chheñ was later given the office of collector of the revenue from one of the great provinces of China.

The Founding of the Ming Dynasty and Its Relation to Tibet

When Chu Yüan-Chang (titled Ming T'ai-tsu) overthrew the Mongolian regime and founded the Ming dynasty in 1368,[36] he was greatly impressed by the extent of the religious influence in Tibet so successfully exploited by his predecessors. Having himself once been a Buddhist monk in Huang-chüeh monastery, he was only too glad to further the Buddhist cause.

In the second year of his reign the Chinese Emperor issued a decree inviting the leading Tibetan lamas to come to him for the renewal of their appointments and the change of their tablets of authority. There was apparently little response to the decree. He then sent a high official, Hsu Yün-tê, to Tibet on a mission to explain the continued pro-Buddhist policy of the new regime.[37] As a result, the acting national mentor of the previous dynasty, Nan-chia-pal-tsang-po, sent an envoy to the Emperor and three years later himself came to the Chinese court. He was warmly received and generously rewarded. His sixty subordinate officials, whose reappointment he recommended, were confirmed in their posts, and he himself received a jade seal and a new title. After that precedent, many of the leading lamas,[38] including the descendants of Phagspa, sent their representatives to ask for the reappointment of their subordinates, and the requests were always granted.[39]

As a precautionary measure against the failure of his peaceful overtures, the Emperor appointed in 1372 General Têng Yü as commander-in-chief to make preparations for a military campaign in Tibet, and five years later, the latter did score a decisive victory over those Tibetan tribes who blocked the passage of tributes from Wussutsang.[40] Afterwards, when the missions were found to be successful, the Emperor set up command posts at Wussutsang and To-kan-sze[41] for the supervision of a number of pacification bureaus and offices. Most of the offices were hereditary under the Yüan dynasty. Their occupants, in command of one thousand or ten thousand families, were reappointed with new patents.

In the reign of Ch'êng-tsu (son of T'ai-tsu), who usurped the throne from the legitimate successor, Yün-wên, generally known as Hui-ti (son of the crown prince), Buddhism gained even greater importance. The Emperor invited the famous Halima [42] to come from Tibet to China. He arrived in the winter of 1406 and is reported to have performed many miracles in the presence of the Emperor. He was made a prince of the holy law, Ta-pao-fa-wang in Chinese—a title previously held by Phagspa—and his three disciples received titles of honor and tablets. Titles of different grades were also conferred on a large number of lamas of various monasteries.

As the Emperor Ch'êng-tsu made an extensive search for learned lamas, he could not have missed the great reformer Tsong-k'a-pa who founded the Yellow Sect during his reign. Yü Tao-ch'üan discovered from Tibetan sources the record of the missions sent by the Emperor to invite him to his court and the letter sent in reply by the latter, in which Tsong-k'a-pa gave illness as the reason for declining the Emperor's invitation.[43] In 1413 the Emperor again sent an envoy with a letter asking the great reformer to dispatch a disciple on his behalf, if he himself could not come in person. With this Tsong-k'a-pa complied and he sent one of his outstanding disciples, Çakya Yeçes, whom Yü Tao-ch'üan, using a Mongolian source, identified as the Ta-tz'u-fa-wang mentioned in the *Ming shih*.[44]

As a result of the high favors repeatedly shown by the emperors toward Buddhism, the highways were filled with lamas coming and going. The *Ming shih* comments that their missions or envoys caused congestion and inconvenience on the official postal route and their reception and reward was a great drain on the treasury and a source of resentment among the people.[45]

At first they were sent back as soon as their mission was accomplished. During the reign of Hsüan-tsung (1426-35) they began the practice of staying in the capital for long periods, and the expenses of their entertainment became a great burden to the treasury. To combat this evil the Court was compelled to issue stringent regulations.

There was always feeling against the lamas at Court, and the position of the lamas in China fluctuated with the moods of the emperors. For example, Ying-tsung, after his restoration in 1457, changed his attitude towards the Tibetan lamas, and many regents and pontiffs were degraded. It was not a change in the traditional policy towards the Buddhist priesthood of Tibet. His action was only motivated by a desire to enforce measures which would show contrast to the acts of his half-brother, Ching-tsung, who had occupied the throne during his absence as a prisoner of war in the hands of the Wala (Oirat) Mongols.[46]

Ying-tsung's son and heir, Hsien-tsung, who reigned from 1465 to 1486, was in favor of the lamas and showered titles and honors upon them. In contrast, his son, Hsiao-tsung, who reigned from 1488 to 1505, treated the Tibetan lamas with severity. In his later years, however, he went to the other extreme and indulged them. Wu-tsung (reigned 1506-22), son of Hsiao-tsung, was originally uninterested in lamaism. Three pontiffs were degraded when he ascended the throne, but he soon became very indulgent towards lamas. He studied the Tibetan language and the Buddhist canons, and it is said that he gave himself a title equivalent to that of Dharma Raja, and conferred new titles upon his favorite high lamas. It was he who sent a very costly but fruitless mission to Tibet to invite to the court a man who, he was told, was a living Buddha: the mission with a large retinue and many extravagant presents was raided and robbed by Tibetans en route and never arrived at its destination.

His cousin, Shih-tsung (reigned 1522-66), was the first real enemy the lamas encountered among the emperors. He degraded and sent back to Tibet many of the lamas. He embraced Taoism and strove to suppress Buddhism. From his day till the end of the Ming dynasty in 1644 lamas seldom went to China. Nevertheless, Buddhism continued to serve this dynasty like the preceding one by preserving peace between China and Tibet.

It must not be supposed that force was not employed by the Chinese in maintaining their hold upon Tibet. Military expeditions supported pacification through religion in the early years of this period. Several expeditions were sent against turbulent tribes. In 1425 a Chinese army pursued tribesmen far beyond the Kuenlun Mountains. Since 1509 Mongolian tribesmen had been moving down to Kokonor and soon occupied this vast fertile region.[47] The state of affairs in Tibet resembled the dark days which had followed the succession of the apostate Landarma to the throne,[48] and as such Tibet was not in a position to lend a helping hand to its people in the north. The native Tibetans, deprived of their possessions and livelihood, were obliged to knock on the doors of Sining and Kansu and try to enter them even by force. Thus peace was no longer maintained along the northwestern borderland and fighting between the Chinese garrison forces and Tartar hordes or native Tibetans was common. These operations were, however, of a local character. There was no general war and force was never employed on a large scale.

Nor must it be supposed that Buddhism was the only factor responsible for the preservation of peace between China and Tibet. Economic factors were also operating. One was the benefit derived from missions sent to the Chinese Court, as they were lavishly rewarded by the Emperor. It is recorded that native monks of Tao and Ming districts in present-day Kansu made handsome profits by sending fraudulent and spurious tributes in the name of missions.[49] The bartering of horses, Tibet's staple product, for tea, which was what its people wanted most from abroad, was highly profitable, and it was often the imposition of restrictions upon this traffic that led to uprisings of the Tibetan tribes.[50] Finally hereditary titles tended to consolidate Chinese power by their psychological effect upon the Tibetan mind.

The Yellow Sect and the Ming Dynasty

It now remains to define, as far as it is possible, the relationship which existed between the newly established Yellow Sect and the Ming dynasty. As mentioned above, the Emperor Ch'êng-tsu did get in touch with its founder Tsong-k'a-pa. But throughout the *Ming shih* and the *Ming shih lu* no mention was made of the latter.[51] Just when this Luther of Tibet lived is a matter of dispute among writers. According to Csoma, he lived from 1355 to 1417; according to Liu Li-chien, Eugène Obermiller, and Huc from 1357 to 1419; according to Rockhill from 1360 to 1422 (?); and according to Grünwedel and Pander's *Pantheon* from 1378 to 1441. Sir Charles Bell placed his birth at 1358. Hackin placed his death at 1417; while Pelliot seems to be quite certain that he died in 1419. Georgi gives his life period as 1232-1312, which is *prima facie* incorrect because of its apparent anachronism.[52] Chinese sources, which did not record anything about Tsong-k'a-pa until the Ch'ing dynasty, give the life period of this great religious reformer of Tibet as 1417-78. The year 1478 as the year of his death was mentioned by the Emperor Kao-tsung in an imperial edict issued in 1792.[53] Parker, basing his information on a Chinese source, gives the life period of Tsong-k'a-pa as 1417-69.[54] But judging by the year in which he built the famous monastery of Gah-Dan[55] and also by the life period of his disciple and successor, Ganden-Truppa, known as the first Dalai Lama (1391-1474), this source is obviously unreliable.

This error in Chinese sources as well as the wrong identification of Ta-tz'u-fu-wang as a lama of Red Sect[56] were probably the result of the suppression of information in connection with Tsong-k'a-pa and the Yellow Sect by the historians of the Ming dynasty. In China not only the Emperor could do no wrong, but also his prestige and dignity had to be upheld at any cost. Had the fact been made known to the public that Ch'êng-tsu's repeated invitations extended to Tsong-k'a-pa were declined, the Emperor's prestige and dignity would have been considered as lowered to a contemptible degree, especially at a time when his policy to show high favors toward lamas was by no means popular and had already caused resentment among the people.[57] This explains why no mention of Tsong-k'a-pa and the Yellow Sect was made in the *Ming shih* and *Ming shih lu*.[58]

Some Chinese writers prior to Yü Tao-ch'üan's discovery advanced a thesis that knowledge of the Tibetan religious reform did not reach the Chinese until the time of the Ch'ing dynasty, as during the lifetime of Tsong-k'a-pa and the early years of the new sect its influence was then confined to part of central and western Tibet.[59] But Western writers had long maintained that there was early contact between the Yellow Sect and the Ming Court and Grenard even says that the Yellow Sect triumphed with the Ming dynasty.[60]

The historians of the Ming dynasty could not, however, suppress altogether an outstanding historical fact for very long. Instead of disclosing the name of the Yellow Sect, which would make the public inquisitive of its origin and its early contact with the Emperor, they later mentioned only the existence of a living Buddha or a lama prophet. The abortive mission sent by the Emperor Wu-tsung to invite a living Buddha[61] was presumably intended for Ganden Gyatso, the second Dalai Lama. In the reign of Shen-tsung (1573-1619) the Chinese heard of a lama prophet named Sonam Gyatso. At the suggestion of the Altan Khan, the chieftain of a Mongolian tribe, now known as Tumed, a great patron of the Yellow Sect,[62] the lama prophet sent a letter together with presents to the minister, Chang Chu-cheng, who accepted them with the Imperial assent. The lama's request to make presents in the future was granted.[63] Later the Emperor sent to the lama an invitation delivered by a special envoy who arrived only to witness the lama's passing into silence.[64] Sonam Gyatso can be unhesitatingly identified with the name of the third Dalai Lama.

The introduction of the Yellow Sect of lamaism into Mongolia through the efforts of the third Dalai Lama has a bearing not only upon the status of Tibet but also upon the whole picture of that part of the world. The occupation of Kokonor as mentioned above[65] had its natural consequences. It had always been the high policy of the Chinese Government to prevent the Hiung-Nu and the Ch'iang (the Tibetans) from joining hands. The policy had been inaugurated by Han-wu-ti (reigned 140-88 B.C.) when he set up command posts and garrison forts in Kansu to drive a wedge between these two warlike neighbors. With their presence at Kokonor, the Mongols soon became involved in the political affairs in Tibet.

During the civil strife the Yellow Sect at first met with reverses in their struggle for power on account of the powerful help which the Chief of Tsang had given to the Red Sect. The reformers then invited the help of the Mongolian hordes, who succeeded in restoring to them their lost territorial endowments and their beloved monasteries. The Chief of Tsang and the Karma-pa hierarch of the Red Sect, failing in their military enterprise, also sought help from Mongolian chiefs.[66] Such a situation, occurring as it did at a time when China was facing serious rebellions in Manchuria and in China Proper and the weakened Ming government was itself in a helpless condition,[67] could lead only to making Tibet the occupied territory of the Khoshote Mongols.

As a result of further bloodshed, the new dynasty founded by Karma-pa of Tsang Province to replace the Sitya[68] was overthrown by the Mongolian army under Gushi Khan, who, at the earnest entreaties of the representatives of the Yellow Sect, marched into Tibet to punish their enemies. Having crushed the army of 40,000 Tartars of the Chog-thu Khan of Kokonor, who espoused the cause of the Red Sect, and having further led his army to defeat the King Beri of Kham, who followed the Bon religion and who, like Landarma, had destroyed all the Buddhist institutions of Kham belonging to the Red and the Yellow Sects, Gushi Khan had little difficulty in overcoming the resistance of Tsang, and he put the fallen monarch to death. He then proclaimed his authority over the whole country and made the fifth Dalai Lama the undisputed spiritual ruler of Tibet.[69]

It was only natural that the Yellow Sect should have appealed to Mongolians for help. In 1580 the third Dalai Lama, Sonam Gyatso, at the invitation of Altan Khan, went to Mongolia where he died after eight years' residence.[70] As a result of his effort, Buddhism as interpreted by the Yellow Sect spread there far and wide.

Tibet's connection with Mongolia was further cemented by the birth of the fourth Dalai Lama in the princely Mongol family—being reincarnated in the person of no other than Altan Khan's great-grandson. During the lifetime of the fourth Dalai Lama the teachings of the Yellow Sect had already taken such a firm root in Mongolia that the Khalka Mongols asked for the establishment of a special and permanent patriarch in Khalka to take charge of the ecclesiastical affairs of their vast land. It was the fourth Dalai Lama who gave sanction to their request and chose the reincarnated Hutukhtu of the third disciple[71] of Tsong-k'a-pa as the occupant of this new and responsible post. From that time onward Tibet and Mongolia not only joined hands because of geographical propinquity but also had a meeting of minds by means of religion. The Mongols were asked to come as defenders of a common faith.

The Status of Tibet

From the above account we have seen that Tibet became a vassal state of China from the time of Kublai Khan and remained in such a status throughout the Yüan and Ming dynasties. At one time the Emperor at Peking exercised his authority over local administration in Tibet; for example, in effecting the change of a governor or in issuing patents to local officers in command of one thousand or ten thousand families. At other times he left the Tibetans alone to manage their affairs so long as his own authority was not challenged or as long as both parties of a civil strife paid allegiance or even lip-service to him. The writer wonders why Rockhill states so dogmatically that there is not a single reference in the histories of the Yüan and Ming dynasties to political relations having been established at any time with the temporal rulers of Tibet.[72] As mentioned above, the history of the Yüan dynasty records the assimilation of the Tibetan army under the command of a Mongolian prince and the employment of it in a military campaign. At least, Kublai's relation with Phagspa, as recorded in *Yüan shih,* cannot be dismissed as non-political, even if we do not agree with Das[73] that "a change of official seals [as recorded in the history of the Ming dynasty] generally signifies a change of Vassalage," and even if we dismiss all tribute-missions sent from Tibet to the Yüan and Ming emperors as nothing but profit-making business. The Tibetan sources alone as quoted in this chapter bear sufficient evidence to show that during the Yüan and Ming dynasties, Tibet was in a status resembling or suggesting that of a vassal in the full sense of the word.

CHAPTER III

THE ESTABLISHMENT OF CHINESE SOVEREIGNTY IN TIBET

From Occupation by the Khoshote-Mongols to the Recognition of the Suzerainty of the Manchu Court

TIBET became the occupied territory of the Khoshote-Mongols in 1642[1] and two years later China Proper was lost to the Manchus. For some time there had been a struggle for supremacy between the Mongols and the Manchus. According to Parker, "in 1624 the Manchus defeated the Genghizide Mongols, half of whom went over to the Chahars, . . . by 1632 the Manchus had practically conquered the Chahars, and had even succeeded in wringing from China official recognition of Manchu superiority over the Mongols in rank; subject, however, to the suzerainty of China."[2] In 1633 the Manchus started a continuous southward movement. All the Mongol tribes, nomads in the eastern regions of China, one after another yielded to the terrible conquerors or fled before them. Hu-tun-t'u (Lindan Khan) with his Chahar people made a last effort to resist. He suffered defeat and died in 1634.[3]

When therefore Shih-tsu under the regency of his uncle ascended the throne of China in Peking, he had only the Outer Mongols north of the desert and the Oelot, or Eleuths, west of it to deal with. Yet this remaining task was still so formidable and he was so occupied with it that he was not in a position to use force against Tibet. He was, however, not prevented from employing diplomatic means to come to an understanding with the Tibetan authorities.

Contact had already been established with the Lamaist hierarchy in Tibet. In 1639, following a suggestion made two years before by the three Khans of the Khalka Mongols, the Manchurian Emperor T'ai-tsung (Shih-tsu's father) sent an envoy with a message to the Khan of Tibet, the temporal ruler at Shigatse, inviting the Holy Priest to come to his court.[4] Another invitation was addressed to the Dalai Lama direct. In response to the invitations, the Dalai Lama, the Panch'en (or Tashi) Lama, Tsangpa Khan, and Gushi Khan sent representatives to Mukden to offer presents in 1642.[5]

When Shih-tsu at the invitation of Wu San-kuei entered Peking in 1644 and replaced the Ming dynasty which he was supposed to be coming to rescue, he promptly sent an envoy to invite the Dalai Lama, who dispatched return missions in 1646[6] and 1647. Desiring to establish personal contact when he took over the reins of government, Shih-tsu sent another envoy to the Dalai Lama in 1651, urging him to come.[7] The invitation was accepted, and in the following year the Dalai Lama came to Peking, bringing tribute. He was warmly received, and the Emperor treated him with great respect and courtesy. In fact, the Emperor would have met him at the frontier had he not been dissuaded by his ministers.[8] The Dalai Lama remained in Peking until the next spring. When he left he took away with him a golden tablet, a golden seal, and a new title.[9]

The friendly relations between the emperors and the Dalai Lamas established an unwritten *concordat*. The Dalai Lama gave powerful aid to the Chinese Government by lending the weight of his great name and authority to its administration in Mongolia, where, as we have seen in the preceding chapter, the Yellow Sect had secured a firm footing since the days of the third Dalai Lama.[10] The Dalai Lama had equally good reasons for cultivating the friendship of the emperors. The recognition of the Dalai Lama as the head of the Buddhist world naturally added enormously to the strength of his position and enhanced its prestige. That was important, in view of the fact that the leading lama of the Red Sect, whose waning authority had still to be reckoned with, had sent envoys to the Manchu court to submit declarations of loyalty and respect and had received patents from the Emperor.[11]

This unwritten *concordat* worked to the great advantage of the

Emperor. It bore fruit especially during the reign of his son, Shêng-tsu, when the Khalka-Mongols deliberated whether to seek Russian or Chinese protection. It was only through the influence of the Grand Lama Cheptsundampa, hierarch of the Yellow Sect in Mongolia, that they decided for China.[12]

Sir Charles Bell in his latest work gives full endorsement to Rockhill's cônclusion (*sic*) about the fifth Dalai Lama's visit to Peking in 1652, although elsewhere in the book he speaks of his observation as seriously in error. Here are his words: "W. W. Rockhill . . . dealt with the question of Tibetan independence of China, and obtained his information for the most part from Chinese sources. As a result of his enquiries, he came to the conclusion that the fifth Dalai Lama, when visiting Peking in A.D. 1652, came there as an independent monarch, being at that time neither under China nor under any other nation." [13]

But from the contents of the messages sent from T'ai-tsung to the Khan of Tibet and to the Dalai Lama, which were confined to religious matters and were devoid of any political references,[14] and also from the facts (1) that the invitation was first sent through the Khan, and (2) that the first Tibetan mission to Mukden was originally suggested by Gushi Khan and sent in collaboration with Tsangpa Khan, we can safely draw the inference that the Dalai Lama at the time had only very limited, if any, temporal power.

At first, the Dalai Lama's temporal power, if any, must have been confined to U, while Tsang was dominated by the Red Sect and ruled by Tsangpa Khan (Khan or Chief of Tsang).[15] In 1641 Diba Sang-kieh (Desi Sanggye-gyatso),[16] who acted as a regent for the Dalai Lama to relieve him of much of the responsibility for mundane affairs, called on Gushi Khan for help to crush the Red Sect. The latter, as mentioned in the preceding chapter, responded to the appeal and marched his army against Tsangpa Khan, whom he killed in the following year.[17] Gushi Khan donated the conquered territories to the Dalai Lama, who, in turn, constituted his old preceptor, the fourth Panch'en, the Grand Lama of Tashi-lhunpo with theoretical control over Tsang, otherwise known as Ulterior Tibet.[18] It was only then that the Dalai Lama was made the spiritual ruler of the whole of Tibet.

Gushi Khan withdrew after the victory, leaving one of his sons as commander of the garrison and another as the assistant commander.[19] We can well imagine what military commanders with foreign garrison forces could do in those days. They were in absolute control of the armed forces and everything connected with them. Petech says they were nominal heads of the civil government and quotes Tucci to the effect that the regent to whom the executive power was at first delegated was a nominee of the Khan.[20] It is no wonder that Das, who made a profound study of Tibetan history from Tibetan sources, should call Tibet from 1643 on a dependency of Mongolia. The writer of this study fails to find any evidence to support Sir Charles's words referred to above, and wonders if Rockhill ever came to such a dogmatic conclusion as Sir Charles asserts.

Rockhill was correct in saying that the Dalai Lama had been treated with all the ceremony which could have been accorded to any independent sovereign. Indeed, the Emperor treated him well, and took every precaution not to offend him. Though he did not meet the Lama at the frontier, he sent a royal prince as his representative with a letter to notify his guest of his pretext for not having met him at Tai-ka as previously arranged.[21] He did not ask him about the state of affairs nor for his advisory opinion, lest the Lama feel hurt if his opinion were not adopted.

But as Cammann points out, the manner of the Dalai Lama's reception alone is not sufficient evidence that he was considered an independent sovereign.[22] Beyond any doubt, the ceremony was full of pomp. But nothing can be found in Chinese works to indicate that the Lama was looked upon as "an independent monarch, being at that time neither under China nor under any other nation." From the wording of the letter sent from T'ai-tsung to the Dalai Lama and especially the citation issued by Shih-tsu in conferring on the Lama a new title, we find rather some implications to the contrary. A lack of respect for the Lama's opinion underlies the discussion between Shih-tsu and his court ministers on the question whether the Lama should be asked for any advisory opinion, as does the ruling of the Emperor that there was "no need to ask," in spite of the memorial of remonstrance of those who held that the Lama might be equally offended if not asked at all.[23]

Even the ceremony itself does not bear full evidence that he was regarded as an independent monarch. During the audience with the Emperor, the Lama had knelt before he was given a seat.[24] Even so he was considered as having been shown a special courtesy, since he was exempted from touching the ground with his forehead, a formality known as "kowtow." But, after all, no independent monarch would be required to touch the ground with his right knee on meeting the chief of another state, especially when the latter does not return the courtesy in the same way.

The Emperor's treatment of the Lama was necessarily tactful. As Rockhill correctly says, "at this period of China's relations with Tibet, the temporal power of the Lama, backed by the arms of Gushi Khan and the devotion of all Mongolia, was not a thing for the emperor of China to question."[25] As explained above, the Emperor was too occupied with the problems of Mongolia and, in the meantime, his position in China Proper was not yet consolidated. He and his immediate successor, Shêng-tsu, could only adopt towards Tibet a policy of marking time, even while the Tibetan authorities were giving Shêng-tsu repeated provocation by intriguing with Wu San-kuei and later with Wu's grandson Wu Shih-p'an and still later with Galdan, the usurping Khan of the Dzungar-Mongols.[26]

As Lord Grey of Fallodon wrote, "In great affairs there is much more in the mind of the events than in the mind of the chief actors." It is the march of events rather than the designs of some individuals that brings Sino-Tibetan relations into a new phase. Because of the reasons explained above, the court of Peking could so far exercise only a general suzerainty over Tibet or fill the role of patron of Tibetan Lamaism. Several successful military expeditions, however, enabled the Ch'ing dynasty to strengthen its hold on Tibet, and eventually it went so far as to depose the Dalai Lama. For a time the Imperial Government not only exercised sovereignty over the territory but also ruled it through the Lhasa Government which had been brought under Chinese control.

Events Leading to the First Campaign

In 1682 the fifth Dalai Lama died. The regent Sang-kieh suppressed the news of his death and ruled in his name. He instigated his protégé, the above-mentioned Galden, whom he had made Dzungdan Khan by usurpation, to go to war with the Khalka. When Galden defeated the Khalka and then invaded Inner Mongolia, the Chinese Emperor led an army against him and inflicted a severe defeat upon him in 1696. The Emperor, who had long suspected[27] that the Dalai Lama was dead, had his suspicions confirmed by prisoners he had taken,[28] who informed him the Dalai Lama had died fourteen years before.[29]

The Emperor called upon Sang-kieh for an immediate declaration of the facts. The latter confessed in the following year that the Dalai was dead and that his reembodiment was now fifteen years of age.[30] In a humble apology for his conduct the Regent begged the Emperor to keep the revelation a secret until the enthronement of the new Dalai Lama so as to avert the danger of an outbreak among the rank and file of his own followers. The Emperor granted his request,[31] but soon discovered that Sang-kieh was engaged in fresh intrigues.

On the question of the enthronement of the new Dalai Lama, Sang-kieh and Latsang Khan, the great-grandson[32] of Gushi Khan and commander of the Lhasa garrison, were divided, and the dispute made them bitter enemies. Sang-kieh failed in an atempt to poison Latsang Khan and was killed by him in 1705.[33] Latsang reported the facts to the Imperial Court and was given a title equivalent to that of a king.[34]

In compliance with the repeated orders of the Emperor, but in defiance of the request of Galdan's successor Chewanlaputan (Tsewang Araptan)[35]—a no less deadly enemy of the Emperor—Latsang sent Tsang-yang Gyatso, the romantic sixth Dalai Lama installed by Sang-kieh, to Peking. The latter died on the way in Kokonor in 1707.[36]

The question of the enthronement had still not been settled. Latsang then collaborated with the Panch'en Lama[37] and apparently with the consent of the priesthood in Lhasa produced a lama named Yeshes as the true incarnation of the fifth Dalai Lama and enthroned him in the Potala. The election was confirmed by the Emperor,[38] but the Mongols and the Kokonor tribes refused to recognize the new occupant of the pontifical chair[39] and brought forward a child, who had been born at Li-t'ang, as the incarnation of the sixth Dalai Lama.[40] The Emperor, fearing the situation might lead to war, sent in 1709 a special envoy[41] to effect a compromise and as the attempt failed, he finally ordered the new claimant to be moved to Sining.[42] Meanwhile, the dissension gave rise to an invasion.

Chewanlaputan was not forgetful of Latsang's refusal to send Tsang-yang, the deposed lama, to him. At first he lulled Latsang into a false sense of security by offering him a matrimonial alliance. In 1716, two years after the marriage of his daughter to Latsang's eldest son, Chewanlaputan took advantage of the internal strife to send his crack army of 6,000 men to invade Tibet under the pretext that he was replacing on the throne of the Potala the true incarnation of the Dalai Lama. His army crossed the desert and arrived at the frontier the next autumn. The aged Latsang, relying on his relationship by marriage to the invader rather than on the national forces, and against the warnings of the Emperor, left the strategic points unguarded. He was taken by surprise and killed in action. The Tibetan capital was then pillaged.[43] The Dalai Lama, Yeshes, who was the subject of the dispute, was imprisoned in a temple. The regime set up by Gushi Khan in 1642 now came to an end.

The First Campaign and Its Consequences on Tibetan Status

The sudden and complete success of the Dzungar expedition to Tibet created a situation fraught with great danger for the Emperor. It might have been the prelude to the successful founding of a Mongol Empire including Tibet under a common religion—a fear that had long haunted him. He could not look on with folded arms.

At the critical moment, Latsang appealed to the Emperor for help.[44] On receiving his message, the Emperor dispatched an army of several thousand men to the aid of Tibet. The army was attacked by the Dzungars when it crossed the Kalawusu river in the autumn of the year (1718) and annihilated after a resistance of over one month.[45]

In 1720 the Emperor, against the remonstrance of his court ministers,[46] sent two armies, one from Kokonor and the other from Tach'ienlu under the command of his fourteenth son. A third army was dispatched to raid Urumchi and Turfan with the object of attacking the enemy in the rear.[47] After a series of victories on all fronts, the Chinese troops by way of Tach'ienlu entered Lhasa first, the Dzungars withdrawing to Ili after sustaining heavy losses.

The new claimant, who had been proclaimed (officially the sixth, but actually the seventh) Dalai Lama at the beginning of this campaign and who had accompanied the army all the way through Kokonor,[48] was now installed at the Potala[49] and given a new title. Yeshes was deposed and brought a prisoner to Peking.[50] Two ministers of Latsang known as Sonamyapo of Khang-ch'en (K'an-c'en-nas) and Sonam-stob-gyal of Polhare (P'o-lha-nas), who rendered valuable assistance in the campaign, were entrusted with the administration of temporal affairs of anterior and ulterior Tibet respectively.[51] The head of the puppet government, sTag-rtse-pa, and his two ministers were found by a Chinese military court guilty of cooperation with the Dzungars and put to death in spite of the entreaty of the Dalai Lama to spare sTag-rtse-pa's life.[52] A garrison force of 3,000,[53] composed of Mongol, Szechwan, and Yünnan soldiers, was left behind and the road between Tach'ienlu and Lhasa was kept open by patrols of troops. A large inscribed stone in commemoration of the victory was erected below the Potala Castle.[54]

The victory in this campaign, as remarked by the eyewitness Father Desidiri, "insured Chinese suzerainty over the whole of Tibet including Bhutan."[55] In making preparations for the campaign, the Imperial Army in 1719 occupied Ba-t'ang and Li-t'ang, two strategic areas connecting Tach'ienlu with Tibet proper,[56] and recovered in the next year Chungtien[57] which Wu Shih-p'an in rebellion had ceded to the Kokonor Mongols as the price of their promised aid.[58] After the victory Lhasa and the other strategic points were garrisoned by imperial forces. The temporal rulers of both anterior and ulterior Tibet together with three councillors of state[59] who formed a bKa'-blon, or cabinet with Sonamyapo of Khang-ch'en as their head, were all selected and appointed by the Emperor. Above all, it is especially significant that in a nation like Tibet, the spiritual ruler,[60] the Dalai Lama, was installed on the throne at the Potala by the Imperial Army which brought him all the way from Sining.

The Emperor was, however, not exercising direct control of political affairs in Tibet. His primary concern was the Mongolian problem, making every endeavor to prevent the Khoshotes from joining the Dzungars.[61] For the dual purpose of showing favors to the Khoshotes, whose power in Tibet had been destroyed by the Dzungar invasion, but whose strength in Kokonor was still considerable, and of giving the Tibetans to understand that his armies were sent as defenders of their faith, not for his own self-aggrandizement, he chose to leave the administration in the hands of some Tibetans, who were officials of the last regime and who had rendered appreciable service to the campaign, rather than to set up a residency in this remote region and in the midst of this unruly people.[62]

Events Prior to the Second Expedition

In 1723 when Emperor Shih-tsung succeeded to the throne of China he ordered the evacuation of the imperial troops from Tibet, and they left immediately in spite of the request made by the Tibetan authorities for them to stay.[63] A garrison was then set up at Chamdo to secure communications.[64] As the Dzungar menace was by no means over, and the condition of Tibet was still turbulent, the Emperor found it necessary to make some sort of provision for the continuance of imperial supervision and sent O-lai (Orai) there to "supervise its affairs." [65]

Two years later when the rebellion of some Kokonor chiefs headed by Cing-wang Blo-bzan-bstan-adsin was completely crushed, the Emperor proceeded to reorganize the imperial administration in the frontier districts of Tibet. As a new favor shown to the Dalai Lama he gave back to the government of Lhasa all the country between Ba-t'ang Li-t'ang and U, mainly the region of Lho-roṅ-rdsoṅ. K'an-c'en-nas and Ṅa-p'od-pa were formally appointed as prime minister (tsung-li) and deputy prime minister (hsieh-li), respectively, under imperial letters patent.[66]

For a brief period after the first expedition, Tibet appears to have enjoyed peace, but it was not long before serious dissensions arose between the newly created Tibetan ministers. The prime minister and his three colleagues were at loggerheads, forming two hostile camps with the father of the Dalai Lama behind the scene who, bound to Lum-pa-nas by marriage, was in favor of K'an-c'en-nas's opposition. This may be said to have been a clash of personalities. But actually the very composition of the cabinet carried in itself the seeds of strife. As the ministers were at the same time governors of provinces, the cabinet gradually became a desultory meeting of powerful regional rulers, rather than an administrative body.

The Emperor sent through one of his envoys (either O-ch'i or Panti) a message of stern warning which had some effect, but which did not produce any lasting consequence.[67] O-ch'i, on his return to Peking, presented a report on the situation.[68] Seng-ko and Mala were then sent to Tibet with a rescript ordering the cabinet to cooperate with them but without clear instructions as to what definite measures were to be taken.[69]

The news of the appointment of these officials set the opposition in action. They were afraid that the Emperor was backing K'an-c'en-nas to the full and that the arrival of the imperial mission would discourage their partisans and proportionally increase the following of the prime minister. At a cabinet meeting on August 5, 1727,[70] they murdered K'an-c'en-nas.

The Emperor, on receiving P'o-lha-nas's report of the outbreak and his request for armed help,[71] was afraid that the Dzungars might have been involved. He mobilized an expeditionary force consisting of 400 Manchu soldiers from Sian-fu and 15,000 Chinese troops from Shensi, Szechwan, and Yünnan. But he soon found the outbreak was only a quarrel between the Tibetan ministers—a matter of little importance. He immediately ordered the mobilization to halt.[72] After some hesitation, however, the expeditionary forces were dispatched under the command of Jalangga.[73]

In the meantime civil war was being waged between Na-p'od-pa, Lum-pa-nas, and sByar-ra-ba on the one hand, who formed a triumvirate after their successful coup, and P'o-lha-nas on the other, who, known by the name of Mi-dbaṅ, i.e., ruler of men, skillfully organized a resistance movement against them in mNa'-ris and Tsang.

For our study of the status of Tibet, it is interesting to note that notwithstanding the outbreak of civil war, the imperial mission succeeded in reaching Lhasa without being opposed by the new rulers; they were received by the Dalai Lama and remained undisturbed in Lhasa during the whole war. Some officials of the mission could even cross the theater of war and reach Tashi-lhunpo where they laid before the Panch'en Lama the complimentary presents of the Emperor.[74] According to Fr. Gioachino,[75] both sides had sent envoys to the Emperor. The defeated triumvirate entertained the hope that if they could hold the palace for two or three months, the imperial troops would arrive and rescue them. When they submitted to P'o-lha-nas through the good office of the Dalai Lama, they were told by the victor that the final judgment belonged to the envoys of the Emperor.[76]

But in fact the Emperor had long since decided in favor of P'o-lha-nas. He passed orders to send word, secretly and by trusted men, to Seng-ko and Mala, who were then in Lhasa, not to do anything that might jeopardize P'o-lha-nas's action.[77] He did this at a time when P'o-lha-nas's situation was fraught with danger and difficulty. Apparently he did not wait for the dust to settle.

The Effect on the Status of Tibet

The Chinese expeditionary forces reached Lhasa in September, 1728—two months after the surrender of the triumvirate. Jalangga and Mailu, the second in command, together with Seng-ko and Mala, constituted themselves as a high court of justice and indicted the three ministers on the charge of having acted against the orders of the Emperor. After a long-protracted trial, the two ministers, Ṅa-p'od-pa and Lum-pa-nas, were put to death by the "slicing process" together with fourteen other sentenced men who were either strangled or decapitated.[78]

As the father of the Dalai Lama was involved in the outbreak and the court of the young pontiff was the center of all intrigue and mischief, the imperial high command decided to remove the Dalai Lama from Lhasa and eventually sent him to Ka-ta, notwithstanding the supplications of the Panch'en Lama, P'o-lha-nas, and all the foremost dignitaries of the Church.[79] Later it was explained in Chinese official documents that the Dalai Lama was brought there in order to protect him against the threatened Dzungar raid.[80]

The Emperor now fully realized that his well-meant policy of withdrawing the troops and leaving the Tibetan Government without control had turned out to be a complete failure. He decided to entrust all temporal authority to P'o-lha-nas, who was appointed provisionally to supervise both U and Tsang with two cabinet members recommended by him, and who was given the title of *beise* by a most gracious rescript. The Panch'en Lama was asked to come to Lhasa. According to Tibetan sources, he was presented with an imperial edict granting to him theocratic control over Tsang and western Tibet as far as the Kailasa, of which he accepted only three districts, namely, Lha-rtse, P'un-ts'ogs-gliṅ, and Ṅam-riṅs.[81] This marks the creation of the Panch'en Lama's political importance as some sort of balance against that of the Dalai Lama.

In the matter of imperial supervision of the Tibetan Government, there was a return to the administrative ideas of the Emperor Shêng-tsu. Seng-ko and Mailu were appointed as Amban or Residents at Lhasa and Shigatse, each with one thousand troops drawn from the Szechwan and Shensi provinces.[82] It was later stipulated that the Residency thus created should in principle have its occupants changed every three years. The institution lasted until the end of the Ch'ing dynasty[83] except for a minor change in its organization in the beginning of 1911.[84] A strong garrison of one thousand men from Yünnan was left at Chamdo to secure the communications.[85] Ba-t'ang and Li-t'ang were formally placed under the administration of Szechwan while Chung-tien and Wei-hsi were placed under that of Yünnan.[86]

The two Residents set to work on the military organization of the country and ordered the training of an efficient and reliable army which in due course would be able to take over most of the duties now imposed on the Chinese occupation troops. P'o-lha-nas gladly supported their effort in this direction. He soon re-established law and order and reorganized the postal stage system on a sound basis. By cleverly exploiting the dissensions in Bhutan, he succeeded with a minimum of effort in imposing his suzerainty on that country. Because of this success he was promoted to the rank of *beile* and his elder son was granted the title of duke.[87] The suzerainty over Bhutan was formally assumed by the Emperor himself.[88]

In 1731-32 there was a threat from the Dzungars.[89] They, having recovered under the able leadership of Chewanlaputan's son, Ts'e-rin, defeated a combined army under Marshall Furdan in July, 1731. It was feared they would make trouble in Tibet. P'o-lha-nas demonstrated his loyalty to the Emperor and earned a new favor, the granting of full judicial power in Tibet,[90] and a seal of office confirming the functions entrusted to him provisionally in 1728.[91]

In 1734 the Dzungars, after being defeated by Ts'e-reng, captain-general of the League of the Sain-noin Khanate, sent a mission to the Peking court to ask for peace, which was granted. The Dzungar menace was for the moment removed. The Dalai Lama's father, who had been summoned to Peking and who had given to the Emperor assurance never again to meddle with Tibetan politics,[92] was no longer an element of disturbance. The Emperor then issued a rescript and dispatched the seventeenth son of the late Emperor Shêng-tsu, named Yün-li and known also as Prince Kuo,[93] to Ka-ta to notify the Dalai Lama of the Emperor's assent to his return to Tibet. After having received the rescript, the Dalai Lama replied with an address of heartfelt thanks and of full submission to his imperial protector. In September, 1735, escorted by 500 Chinese soldiers, he returned to the Potala.[94]

Tibet, under P'o-lha-nas's efficient administration, was peaceful and prosperous. His small cabinet underwent an expansion. Pandita, nephew of K'an-c'en-nas, and Pu-lung-tsan were appointed by the Emperor as ministers, or bKa'-blon. He himself was shown a high mark of favor by the Emperor Kao-tsung who succeeded to the throne in 1736, by the granting of the title of *Chün-wang,* or prince of the second class, in January, 1740. This, merely a rank in the imperial peerage, was taken by Tibetans to mean "king," and he became known in Tibet as Mi-wang, or Mewan as written by Bogle.[95] Since his power was practically absolute and the authority of the Dalai Lama was in abeyance, Petech calls him the first Tibetan king after the tragic end of the last Tsang ruler in 1642.

The Residents, who played an active role in the first years of their installation, apparently became mere informers to the Emperor on the doings of the "king." The decline in authority of this office was due partly to the frequent changing, if not the deteriorating quality, of the occupants and partly to the fact that since 1734 one post remained vacant and thus there was only one Resident stationed at Lhasa during the following year. Another fact that must have had some bearing also was the withdrawal of three-fourths of the garrison forces in the autumn of 1733,[96] leaving only 500 men at the disposal of the Resident.

The Emperor, however, was quite content with P'o-lha-nas, who repeatedly demonstrated his full loyalty to his protector.[97] The court of Peking had another channel for keeping itself informed of what had been going on in Tibet, that is, through the tribute missions sent by the Dalai Lama and the Panch'en Lama on alternate years and the envoys of P'o-lha-nas sent along with those of the Dalai Lama.[98] Imperial control on the spot may have slackened, but the shadow of supervision was always there. As described by Petech,[99] out of political necessity P'o-lha-nas made himself the tool of the court of Peking. It was absolutely out of the question for Tibet to have a policy of its own. Imperial supervision was too close, and Tibet had no material force of its own to throw on the scales, except for the great religious influence of the Yellow Sect, which was not under P'o-lha-nas's control.

When P'o-lha-nas was approaching the end of his life, the Emperor ordered him to recommend one of his two sons to inherit his title and his ruling powers. He chose the younger son, Gyurmed-namgyal, and passed over the heir-apparent, the duke of mKa'-ris, because of his bad health. At least this is the reason he reported to the Emperor; actually he made the decision out of a stronger affection for his younger son.[100]

Events Leading to the Third Expedition

P'o-lha-nas died on March 12, 1747. The Emperor when informed wrote at once to Fuch'ing, the Resident at Lhasa, approving of Gyurmed-namgyal's succession[101] but expressing his doubts on the latter's ability to maintain the strong government of his father. He told Fuch'ing to watch the new ruler and report on his capabilities and intentions.[102]

This ambitious young man soon felt the inconvenience caused by the presence of the Imperial Garrison Force and the Resident. He appealed to the Emperor for the withdrawal of the imperial troops, assuring him of his loyalty and of his ability to maintain order. His request was granted; 400 soldiers were recalled to China, and only a small personal escort of 100 men remained with the Resident.[103]

Gyurmed-namgyal was on bad terms with his minister and brother-in-law Pandita. His relations with the Dalai Lama, rather strained during P'o-lha-nas's last months, now went from bad to worse.[104] His petition for permission to send some lamas to those regions which had been taken under direct imperial administration during the K'ang-hsi period of rule (the reign of Shêng-tsu) aroused the suspicions of the Peking court.[105] Yet the Emperor decided to overlook Gyurmed-namgyal's inconsiderate behavior on account of his youth and inexperience, and of his father's merits.[106] He appointed another Resident to fill the long-open vacancy so as to reinforce his observation posts.[107]

The situation worsened step by step. Gyurmed-namgyal murdered his elder brother without letting the latter receive the Emperor's summons to Lhasa to be judged by an imperial arbitrator.[108] He then intrigued with the Dzungars and planned an uprising to overthrow the imperial authority.[109]

The Residents reported the preparations for revolt to the Emperor who at first did not believe the report, as he thought there was no cause for an open rebellion,[110] and therefore he denied his approval to a proposal to increase the Lhasa garrison.[111] Later the Residents were told to investigate the matter carefully and exercise great prudence.[112] Permission was at last reluctantly given them to act as circumstances required.[113]

Before the arrival of the Emperor's final answer, the situation became so serious that the two Residents took the responsibility of killing the conspirator at the Residence to which Gyurmed-namgyal had gone at their invitation. They were themselves soon murdered by the dead man's followers. All this occurred on November 11, 1750.

It is noteworthy that during the riot the Dalai Lama first sent his secretaries to the spot to argue with the mob and to dissuade it from violence. He then caused a proclamation to be posted on the walls and pillars of Lhasa, in which he announced that Gyurmed-namgyal had been justly executed for his crimes, and threatened with punishment by the Emperor anyone who dared lay hands on the Residents. At last the Dalai Lama himself came out of the Potala and addressed the mob. But the mob, instigated by the followers of Gyurmed-namgyal, shouted down the Dalai Lama, tore away the posters of his proclamation, and went so far as to turn their weapons against his sacred person, compelling him to take refuge in the Potala. The Residence was then surrounded and set on fire, and the two Residents, Fuch'ing and Labdon, defended themselves to the bitter end. Forty-nine out of the 100 guards were killed, together with their commanding officers and seventy-seven Chinese civilians. The military paymaster's office was looted with the loss of 85,000 taels.[114]

The Emperor was enraged and ordered the governor-general of Szechwan, Ts'e-rin, to proceed with a large force and quell the revolt. In the meantime order was restored through the joint efforts of the Dalai Lama and Pandita. The latter soon succeeded in hunting down the rebel leader Blo-bzan-bkra-śis and his accomplices, who fled from the town trying to effect their escape to Dzungaria. The greater part of the treasure looted from the military paymaster's office was recovered. The Emperor then ordered Ts'e-rin to march to Lhasa with only 800 men who reached their destination after what was actually only a military promenade like the previous 1728 expedition. Before his arrival the newly appointed Resident Bandi took over from Pandita the persons of Blo-bzan-bkra-śis and twelve other rebel leaders, questioned them, and sentenced them to death.[115]

Changes in the Status of Tibet after the Third Expedition

Advantage was taken of the presence of the punitive troops to secure the final pacification and submission of Tibet. The Emperor adopted the policy of a wide distribution of administrative authority and considered the time opportune for a new approach.[116] He abolished the office of temporal ruler and invested secular power in the hands of four ministers who constituted a reorganized bKa'-blon under the leadership of the Dalai Lama who thus became for the first time a temporal ruler. Provincial governors were to be appointed by the Dalai Lama acting on the advice of the ministers in agreement with the Resident. The provincial commanders responsible for the military defence and the maintenance of law were to be appointed by bKa'-blon, but they were to hold an imperial commission.[117]

Petech thinks that in all these proceedings the sovereignty of the Dalai Lama was always understood, but nowhere expressly affirmed in the Chinese documents.[118] He tells us of the complete eclipse of the Dalai Lama from 1706 to 1720, his exile to Ka-ta and deprivation of all temporal authority, and that after his return in 1735, up to the eve of the 1750 incident, he had absolutely no political power and was strictly limited to his religious functions.[119] He also informs us from Tibetan sources that at the end of the civil war of 1727-28 the Dalai Lama had to ask P'o-lha-nas for permission when he wished to retire from the Potala to aBras-spuns monastery and it was agreed that he should leave with four attendants and his father with three, accompanied on the way by 2,000 monks.[120] At the same time he tells us that "the donation of Gushi Khan to the fifth Dalai, unrecognized by the Chinese, lapsed in 1717-20," that "the year 1710 saw the formal proclamation of the Chinese protectorate" over Tibet, by granting the Dalai Lama a sealed document of investiture,[121] and that "when the Chinese installed the seventh Dalai Lama in Lhasa (1720), they completely ignored his theoretical rights."[122] The writer wonders where Petech draws the inference that the sovereignty of the Dalai Lama was always understood.

After all, the Dalai Lama's authority, even if it resembled or suggested sovereignty, was given by the Emperor. Three ministers were chosen by Ts'e-rin and his colleagues; they already held their ranks of bKa'-blon and duke, or *taiji,* by imperial grants. The fourth member representing the interests of the Yellow Sect was recommended by the Dalai Lama according to Ts'e-rin's report,[123] while the Tibetan sources given by Petech[124] record that he was selected by common agreement of the three bKa'-blon, on the proposal of the Dalai Lama. They were all, however, subject to the sanction of the Emperor. In his edict to the bKa'-blon the Emperor told them to obey and honor the Dalai Lama and whenever important questions arose to inform the Dalai Lama and the Residents, follow their directions, and act accordingly.[125] Here we see clearly where the power lies that determines and controls the government in the final analysis.

The nonexistence of the so-called Dalai Lama's sovereignty can be further attested from the Emperor's refusal to grant the Lama's request to appoint Pandita as *Chün-wang,* or ruler. Pandita was ordered by the Residents Fuch'ing and Labdon, immediately after they had killed Gyurmed-namgyal at their Residence, to take the reins of government. Apparently he failed to rise to the occasion. Two days after the riot the Dalai Lama appointed him administrator of the realm, to carry on the government until the arrival of imperial officials and troops.[126] But the Emperor, who was displeased with Pandita's failure to rescue the Residents, and who had for a moment even the intention of killing him in case he should show any sign of being unruly,[127] turned down the Dalai Lama's request and firmly refused to sanction his promotion.[128] The Emperor later decided to retain Pandita in the new bKa'-blon, but ordered Ts'e-rin and Bandi not to allow him any influence in the choice of other members of the bKa'-blon.[129] Had the Dalai Lama possessed any "understood" sovereignty, the Emperor would have gracefully yielded to this *fait accompli* in the form of a reward for Pandita's quick arrest of the rebel leaders.

Aside from the reorganization of the administrative machinery, the Emperor paid special attention to the establishment of a permanent garrison in Lhasa and a dispatch service under direct imperial management. The strength of the garrison was fixed at 1,500. A new schedule was approved for the distribution of the imperial garrison in the troubled and strategically important boderland between Tibet and Szechwan.[130] The Tibetan authorities were ordered to sever all communications with the Dzungars. The periodic tribute-missions of the Dalai Lama and of the Panch'en Lama to Peking were regulated by the old practice.[131]

The position of the Residents was consolidated. Besides commanding the garrison and having exclusive charge of the mail service, their advice had to be taken by the bKa'-blon on every important affair. This gave them a broad right of supervision. But they were ordered by the Emperor to leave the routine and trivial matters in the hands of the bKa'-blon as usual,[132] and were given only "limited right to take part in the government."[133] In fact, as stated by George Bogle on December 5, 1774, they seldom interfered in the management of the country. Bogle's general report written in the next year has this to say:

> The Emperor of China is acknowledged as the sovereign of the country; the appointment to the first offices in the State is made by his order, and in all measures of consequence reference is first had to the Court of Peking, but the internal government of the country is committed to natives. The Chinese in general are confined to the capital, no tribute is exacted, and the people of Tibet, except at Lhasa, hardly feel the weight of a foreign yoke.[134]

Not all the above-mentioned measures proved a success. The bKa'-blon abused its power and its administration was corrupt, while the Dalai Lama spent his time in meditation or in the performance of religious ceremonies, leaving his brother and retinue a free hand to do whatever they wished for their own benefit.[135] The Residency, as noted by Emperor Kao-tsung, "eventually became non-existent." As before, reform had to wait for another military campaign to create an opportunity for it. Such an opportunity was afforded by the Gurkha invasion.

Events Leading to the Conquest of Nepal

In 1780 the Panch'en Lama went to Peking to take part in the festivities on the Emperor Kao-tsung's seventieth birthday, and did an unprecedented thing—kowtowing instead of kneeling on coming into the presence of the Emperor, thus signifying his deference to the throne.[136] During his stay he contracted smallpox—a disease which is dreaded to this day in Tibet—and, in the language of Buddhism, "entered upon the perfection of repose." When his remains were solemnly taken back, one of his brothers, Chumba Hutukhtu, who was in charge of the treasury (Shangshang), appropriated all the precious gifts presented by the Emperor and other patrons to the deceased without sharing them with another brother, Dza-marpa, who, strange to say, was a lama of the Red Sect. The latter was so infuriated that he went to Gurkha (Nepal, under Gurkha rule since 1769) and instigated the Gurkhas to invade Tibet.

In 1788 [137] a Gurkha army entered Tibet and occupied three districts under the pretext of protesting against frauds by the Tibetans, who had, they alleged, mixed their exports of salt with earth, and also against the excessive duties levied on Gurkha goods.[138] The native forces proved no match for the invaders. The Emperor sent his aide-de-camp, Pachung, who was conversant in Tibetan, and two other generals to reinforce the Tibetan armies. Instead of fighting the Gurkhas, the imperial generals induced the Tibetans to make a secret arrangement with the Gurkhas, promising to pay them annually a big sum and thus buying them off.[139] They then reported to the Emperor that the Gurkha chief wished only to send a tribute-mission to China and that they had settled the little frontier incident without the loss of a single soldier.

But the failure of the Tibetans to pay the money brought the Gurkhas back, and there was another war in 1791. The timid Resident Pao-t'ai moved the Panch'en Lama, then a child of ten, to Anterior Tibet and even suggested moving the Dalai Lama to Sining.[140] Chumba, the treasurer, fled with his fortune, and some leading lamas of Tashi-lhunpo made a false statement to the effect that the goddess, Marici appealed to, had advised non-resistance. That shattered the morale of the natives, and the invaders easily captured Shigatse and looted Tashi-lhunpo.[141]

The Imperial Government, kept in ignorance of what had been happening, received information of the situation after the Gurkhas were masters of Ulterior Tibet. It organized an expeditionary force immediately. Meanwhile, the Gurkhas had sent their booty home and retreated slowly towards Nieh-la-mu (Nie'lan) and Ting-chieh,[142] having learned of the approach of the Chinese army. The latter, under the able command of the Manchu General Fu-k'ang-an, hurried to Tibet by way of Kokonor in the depths of winter. In the battle that followed the Gurkhas were badly defeated. After several further sharp engagements the imperial forces reached within one day's march of the enemy's capital.

Fearing the loss of the seat of government, apprehensive that his neighbors, Sikkim and Bhutan, aroused by Chinese agents might fall upon him to revenge his former invasions, and failing help from the British,[143] the Gurkha ruler sued repeatedly for peace, which was granted on rather humiliating terms. The Gurkhas undertook to restore all their plunder and to send a tribute-mission every five years to Peking. It was stipulated that Nepal's tribute status was to be like that of various other dependencies of China, such as Korea, Annam, Siam, and Burma.[144] Nepal faithfully observed this obligation until 1908, only three years before the fall of the Ch'ing dynasty.[145] An inscribed stone slab was erected in Lhasa in memory of the conquest. Its inscription is given in the appendix to Sir Charles Bell's book, *Tibet, Past and Present.*

Exercise of Full Chinese Sovereignty in Tibet

After rescuing Tibet from the Gurkhas, the Emperor found the time was ripe to reform the whole administration of Tibet and to take effective control of the reins of government in order to preclude the need of further repetition of expensive expeditions. On the recommendation of Fu-k'ang-an, the Residents, one stationed at Lhasa, the other at Shigatse, were given the same rank as the Dalai Lama and the Panch'en Lama. The bKa'-blon, which was largely responsible for the corrupt state of affairs, was deprived of most of its power, and the Tibetan officials, both lay and ecclesiastical, were ordered to submit to the Residents' decision in all questions of importance.[146] The Dalai and Panch'en were not given the right to memorialize the throne, but were authorized only to "report to the Residents and ask their orders."[147]

Formerly the Residents—to use the words of Emperor Kaotsung—had been men of mediocre abilities and contented themselves with being figureheads. They had considered the office as merely a steppingstone to promotion[148] or as a miserable post to be lived through somehow. Now that the Residents were placed upon a footing of equality with the governor-general of the adjacent province of Szechwan, more care was taken in selecting them. Moreover, a much larger staff with commissioners and agents was set up.[149]

The Residents were made responsible also for frontier defenses and the efficiency of native levies. A regular indigenous army of 3,000 men was established under imperial command and given regular pay. Besides, 1,000 Mongolian and 1,000 Chinese troops were stationed in Tibet.[150] From this time on "the Manchou Minister Resident at Lhasa," as remarked by Sir John Davis, first British Minister to China, "in fact, rules Tibet on the part of the Chinese Emperor."[151]

Looking at the status of Tibet from the judicial angle, we find imperial justice was once again exercised right after the military campaign as on the three previous occasions. Sandzin-panyur, a member of the bKa'-blon and a son of Duke Pandita, had arranged the peace terms with the Gurkhas at the time of the latter's first invasion, without the sanction of the Imperial Government. Captured by the Gurkhas in 1791 and released only after military pressure had been exercised by the Imperial Army, he was sent under custody to Peking for trial and subsequently dismissed from his cabinet post.[152] The property of Sonomuwangchale, another member of the bKa'-blon whose corruption in charging high commissions and extra levies in trade with the Gurkhas was responsible for the Gurkha-Tibetan conflict and who committed suicide when his misdeed was made known to the Emperor, was confiscated by an imperial order and his heir was deprived of the right to inherit his title. Also confiscated and given to the treasury for the expenses of the newly established native army were the properties of Dza-marpa and Chumba. The former escaped capital punishment as he had died of illness in Nepal before the conclusion of the campaign.[153]

Measures were adopted to improve the economic condition of the people—a necessity that the Buddhist world had very often neglected. The money coined by the Gurkhas, which had been the source of trouble between Nepal and Tibet, was declared illegal and suppressed;[154] a new uniform currency bearing the title of the Emperor was issued by the Tibetan treasury and a mint with Chinese experts was established.[155]

As to foreign trade, regulations were issued to fix the period during which transactions should be carried out, the number of merchants who were to enjoy the right to trade, and the routes that the caravans were to take. Everyone engaged in foreign trade was required to produce a passport and submit to examination by the frontier guards, who reported to the Residents. Import duties in kind were regulated and attempts at evading the payment of the duties were to meet with heavy punishment.[156]

Taxation was reorganized and the financial administration reformed with a view to establishing equilibrium in the finances and suppressing corrupt practices. The Residents were invested with the power to examine the revenue and expenditure. The treasuries of the Potala and Tashi-lhunpo were both placed under the supervision of the Residents,[157] but the latter were forbidden to interfere with the funds assigned to the Dalai and Panch'en Lamas for their personal and official use.

A general reform of the administration was carried out. The number and pay of both lay and ecclesiastical officials were put upon a regular basis. The duties of each official were defined. Excepting those of minor rank, all were to be selected by the Dalai or Panch'en Lamas in conjunction with the Residents. The members of the bKa'-blon were to be appointed by decree from Peking on the recommendation of the Residents.[158]

As foreign elements had been responsible for trouble in the past, measures were taken to limit intercourse between Tibetans and foreign peoples. All communications with neighboring states such as Nepal, Bhutan, and Sikkim were to be through the Residents. Even communications addressed to the Dalai and Panch'en Lamas were to be made known to the imperial representatives. In fact, replies to the chief of Nepal when he sent a mission to tender his apology to the Dalai and Panch'en Lamas were drafted by the Residents, and Resident Ho-lin told the young Dalai Lama what to say when receiving the Nepal envoy.[159] Nor were members of the bKa'-blon allowed to communicate directly with the outside world. Letters addressed to them were to be submitted to the Residents and the Dalai Lama; and replies were to be sent only with their approval. Even the missions sent by the princes of Mongolia and Kokonor in connection with religion were to be sanctioned by the Residents in advance. Foreigners crossing the frontier were to be subjected to careful examination by the outposts and could enter Tibet only after securing a permit. Lamas and pilgrims leaving the territory had to carry passports.[160] The boundaries with Nepal, Sikkim, and Bhutan were clearly demarcated. Damaged frontier marks were rebuilt and those that had been obliterated replaced.[161]

Finally, special marks of favor were conferred on the Dalai and Panch'en Lamas, though stern measures were taken to rid the bKa'-blon of the influence of the Dalai Lama's relatives[162] and retinue, and a decree was issued to discontinue the practice of selecting a lama to represent the interests of the Church in this highest administrative organ. Instead the vacancy was to be filled by a layman.[163] Immense quantities of grain and huge sums of money were sent to Ulterior Tibet to relieve the poor. All demolished houses were rebuilt for them by the government. All refugees were moved back to their rebuilt homes and assured of peaceful occupation. The taxes of the whole of Tibet were either exempted or reduced by half for one year, and the compulsory transport service which made thousands of people abandon their homes was regulated, greatly reducing the burden of the masses.[164]

How far these regulations were to be put into practice depended upon the ability and honesty of the Resident and his subordinates. They were calculated to remove the causes of unrest. By the measures that were introduced the Imperial Government secured control of the key positions in Tibet without attempting to interfere with the daily life of the people.

W. W. Rockhill, who had the unique fortune of being a scholar of Tibetan and serving as United States Minister to China, on concluding his study of Tibet's relations with China from 1644 to 1908, made the following remark,

> The preceding study . . . has, I trust, made clear the real nature and the extent of the autonomy enjoyed by Tibet for the last hundred and fifty years, and with which the Tibetans are, I believe, perfectly satisfied. There has been no claim raised by them for total or even greater independence of China, no wish to deprive themselves of the aid and guidance of China, no dissatisfaction with the reforms of 1793, which were well suited to the requirements of the country and the customs of the people.[165]

Sir Charles Bell,[166] referring to present-day Tibet, said, "Among the peasantry too we hear from time to time of those who express a wish that the Chinese would return." It may be inferred from that statement that the Tibetans cherish the memory of the above-described measures. It was due only to the folly and arrogance of the Manchus in later times, the weakness of their military forces, and the intrigues of foreign powers that Tibet drifted gradually away from its traditional position in the polity of China.

Ch'ing-shih kao,[167] in describing the new status of the Residents who were given direct participation in the Tibetan government, and the measures putting the native army under imperial command and creating a uniform currency under Chinese supervision, called forth the remark that full Chinese sovereignty had been established over Tibet. The writer of this study thinks that another innovation, viz., the change in the method of choosing the Dalai and Panch'en Lamas and other great ecclesiastical dignitaries of Tibet and Mongolia, as stipulated in an edict of the Emperor, demonstrated even more clearly where lay the supreme political power in the final analysis.

Hitherto, the succession to these high ecclesiastical offices had been decided according to the belief that, on the death of a high lama, his soul took life again in the body of an infant born soon after. This system had apparently been honestly worked in the earlier years of Lamaism, as the first five Dalai Lamas had been found in different districts and some of them belonged to poor and obscure families. The selection of the infant was in the hands of the invokers of oracles, and an ambitious family was naturally tempted to bribe the invokers of oracles to select an infant that had been born to it. That corruption eventually developed under the system was sufficiently proved by the fact that successive occupants of the high offices (Dalai, Panch'en, and Hutukhtus) had been selected from ruling or aristocratic families. In fact, several holders of the offices even came from one family. The eighth Dalai Lama and the seventh Panch'en Lama were said to be first cousins.[168] The sixth Panch'en Lama and Chumba Hutukhtu were brothers. Facts like these, coupled with the Gurkha invasion, constituted the case for a reform.

The system was finally discredited on the death of the Grand Lama Cheptsundampa (Jebtsun-damba Hutukhtu), the Patriarch of Urga. It was then announced that the soul of the deceased lama had taken refuge in the womb of the Princess T'ushit'u Khanate, who was *enceinte* at the time. It so happened that the princess gave birth to a female child, who was, of course, disqualified from succeeding to the office.[169]

Following upon the victory over the Gurkhas, the Emperor in 1792[170] ordered that the successors of the Dalai and Panch'en Lamas and other high ecclesiastical dignitaries were to be selected by the drawing of lots, should there be more than one claimant. Next year he had a golden urn made for this purpose and sent it to Lhasa under the custody of a high officer of the Imperial Guards. He proclaimed that henceforth selection should be made among the children reported as likely to be the reembodiment, and that the name and the date of birth of each should be written upon a slip which should be placed in the urn. The Dalai Lama in company with the Resident was to draw a slip in the presence of all the people and the one thus drawn was to receive patents of investiture from the Imperial Government.

Some Western writers have interpreted the reform as only a device by which the Emperor was enabled to prevent the selection of men who were distasteful to him or inimical to Chinese authority in Tibet. The insinuation is not warranted because the drawing of lots was resorted to only when the succession was disputed. For instance, in the case of the ninth and the thirteenth Dalai Lamas, the Emperor, by special decree, suspended the drawing of lots, because there was but one claimant.[171]

Had the Emperor been actuated by dishonest motives in imposing the reform, he would have retained the old system, because by the simple device of bribing or intimidating the invokers of oracles, he could have secured the selection of his own nominees to the offices. The drawing of lots was, to say the least, less liable to be controlled or influenced by the Emperor.

Moreover, the real motive of the Emperor can be easily seen. The new system added to the moral authority of the Emperor in Tibet and deprived the offices of Dalai Lama and Panch'en Lama of their character of self-regulating autonomies. The change also implies a subordination of Church to State and shows the source of supreme political power.

Imperial Authority on the Decline

After the abdication of the great Emperor Ch'ien-lung (posthumously known as Kao-tsung) in 1796, and his death in 1799, the Manchu dynasty gradually declined in power under a succession of weak emperors. The editors of the *Ch'ing-shih kao* blamed Ch'i-shan (Ki-shen), the Resident from 1843 to 1847 [172] for the loss of the power to control the purse of Tibet and its army, as he submitted to the throne and secured its approval of a new regulation of 28 articles, which suspended the supervision of the treasury and did away with the practice of training the native troops by Manchu or Chinese officers.[173] Indeed, his policy must have hastened the deterioration of the imperial position in Tibet. But the latter could not have been avoided when the court found itself in the situation described in the following paragraphs.

Imperial authority in Tibet, despite the weakening effect on the prestige of the office of the Resident caused by the misconduct of its earlier occupants Ts'e-pa-k'e (1804-5) [174] and Wên-kan (1820-23),[175] was still maintained up to 1840 as shown in the record of the punishment of a bKa'-blon and a high ecclesiastical official in that year by a decree of the Emperor at the suggestion of the Resident.[176] But as soon as the first Anglo-Chinese war, otherwise known as the Opium War, broke out, the imperial position in Tibet, as a result of being deprived of the usual facility to get reinforcements from Szechwan and other neighboring provinces, became so weakened and so exposed to danger that more reliance had to be placed on the Tibetan troops, who were consequently given better weapons.[177]

In 1841, while the Anglo-Chinese war was going on, the tribesmen of La-ta-k'e (Ladakh) in collaboration with the "Sen-pa savages" invaded Tibet and occupied more than 1,700 *li* of the Tibetan territory.[178] As the Manchu Court was then utterly ignorant of the geography of India,[179] the source and the location of the invading force given by *Shih-lu* cannot be taken for granted. What is meant by "Sen-pa savages" is presumably the Dorga force of 5,000 men under Zorawar Singh who invaded western Tibet from Kashmir.[180] The Emperor dispatched 1,000 soldiers from Ulterior Tibet and 300 soldiers together with 1,000 militia from Lhasa and its vicinities to engage the enemy,[181] and further reinforced this army with 500 soldiers.[182] All these were Tibetans. Though the Resident and his deputy got the credit for the ensuing victory,[183] it was the Tibetan troops under the command of a bKa'-blon who inflicted a crushing defeat on the invaders and recovered all the lost territory.[184]

While the Tibetan troops were gaining in strength, the Imperial Garrison Force deteriorated both in quality and in discipline. Its soldiers were sent mostly from Szechwan to serve garrison duty of three years. While they were in Tibet, many cohabited with Tibetan women and then left behind children who had to live on the army. The payroll of the garrison force made no provision for these sons of illegitimate birth. The only way open to the garrison command was to enlist the boys in the army and have their names on the payroll, even if they were unfit for military service. In 1844 the Emperor was surprised to find from the Resident Ch'i-shan's report that almost 30 percent of the garrison forces were these fatherless boys whose mother tongue was Tibetan. He proclaimed some restrictions on future recruitment, but nothing was recorded in *Shih-lu* that showed any real improvement of the situation.[185]

The Chinese defeat in her first war with a Western power cost the Manchu regime even more heavily in prestige than in material losses, including the cession of Hong Kong and an indemnity amounting to a total of twenty-one million dollars. The Emperor soon realized his precarious position in Tibet for whose hold he had relied more on his inherited prestige than on his actual force on the spot. He saw, however, no immediate danger of an open revolt from within, though there had been demonstrations of disobedience by lamas of a leading monastery toward his incapable, if not grasping, Resident Meng-pao (1839-42).[186] It was rather a possible invasion from without that gave him cause for anxiety. Indeed, he demonstrated once more his authority in depriving the powerful No-men-han, A-wang-cha-mu-pa-lo-ts'u-lo-ch'i-mu, who acted as regent during the Dalai Lama's minority, of his titles and in confiscating all his property.[187] But even in taking this action he was afraid that the followers of the No-men-han might entice foreigners to make trouble, and cautioned the Resident to restrain them and to adopt preventive measures.[188]

The Emperor's fear of trouble from without was more pronounced in his instructions to the Resident regarding the treatment of Nepal.[189] He must have seen the writing on the wall when the English raised the issue of fixing the boundary of, and establishing trade with, Tibet in January of 1847.[190] We shall see in the following chapter how this issue unfolded itself and eventually affected the status of Tibet. Even in this early stage, we find that the Emperor was already worried about the noncompliance of the Tibetans on the frontier when he ordered the bKa'-blon to urge them to move inward in order to avoid a clash with the penetrating British power.[191] The Emperor's words in the imperial edict showed unmistakable signs of the weakness of his position in Tibet.[192]

Before long, trouble did come from Nepal whose peace with Tibet had been maintained only by a strong intervening imperial power. In 1855, Gurkhas invaded Tibet again under the pretext of alleged ill-treatment of their subjects. The Tibetan army was repeatedly defeated. The Imperial Government, therefore, ordered the general stationed in Szechwan to proceed with his army to the aid of the Tibetans. The threat of armed intervention by the Emperor led Nepal to come to terms with Tibet in 1856. Tibet agreed to pay annually a sum of money to the Gurkhas and to grant them free trade. The Gurkhas, in return, agreed to restore the occupied territory and evacuate their troops. Apparently neither the Nepalese nor the Tibetans were fully aware of the weakened position of the Peking Court; both agreed to acknowledge allegiance to the Great Emperor of China.[193]

Meanwhile the Taiping Rebellion was in full swing. Four years later China was again humiliated in a war with England and France, and Peking was invaded by the combined forces of the two countries. Attacked from without and torn by internal dissension, China was no longer able to maintain a firm hold upon affairs in Tibet. During the Nepal affair, we see already the weakness of the imperial position, although it was not known to the Nepalese. In a report the Resident informed the Emperor that the native troops remained unmobilized in spite of his repeated orders.[194] In two edicts the Emperor told his representative on the spot that he could hardly afford the expense of sending troops from China Proper, and that he was short of both manpower and money to cope with home rebellions.[195]

Later, in 1864, when the rebellion of the chief of Nyarong broke out, the Imperial Government had to rely upon native troops to suppress it. With both hands full of trouble at home, the Emperor wished only to see a compromise reached among the native tribes so that the interrupted dispatch service could be resumed. At first he ordered the Tibetan native army to withdraw[196] and then he learned from the Resident that these troops were successfully engaging the rebels and that his order could not be executed.[197] This shows that he was poorly informed and not in a position to control the situation. Under these circumstances he could only leave the Tibetan native troops and the local tribes to fight among themselves[198] and to express his sanction when the former had repeatedly won some decisive battles.[199] Some Chinese troops from Szechwan joined in the final stage, and throughout the whole campaign the Chinese commissioner at Tach'ienlu, Shih Chih-k'ang, rendered valuable service in bringing about the victory. But the brunt of the campaign was borne by the Tibetans, and the reconquered territory was therefore handed over to the Dalai Lama as a favor in 1865.[200] In other words the Imperial Court confirmed the actualities of the situation—that real power had passed to the Dalai Lama's hands.

By 1864 the Taiping Rebellion had been suppressed after fourteen years of hard fighting. As contemporary symptoms of a political breakdown, the Mohammedan subjects in Sinkiang, Kansu, and Yünnan rose in revolt. Order was restored only after years of patient and energetic military operations which, in the case of Kansu and Sinkiang, lasted over a decade. Floods, droughts, and locusts befell the country in 1876. Famine in Shansi and other provinces between 1876 and 1878 added to the already long list of calamities.[201] In 1894 war with Japan became unavoidable, and China was defeated. After that she was confronted with the threat of partition[202] by foreign Powers.

Meanwhile, at court, intrigues were increasing, and the struggle between advocates of reform and the conservatives was threatening to lead to a *coup d'état.* The Dowager-Empress, who backed the latter, was triumphant. The conservatives made her connive with the Boxers, and an antiforeign movement was organized in North China. As a result a force of eight countries combined to attack China and invade the capital, and the dynasty was once more humiliated. The protocol then signed (1901) imposed a crushing indemnity and the Imperial Court had perforce to accept such terms as were offered.

These events struck a fatal blow at imperial prestige in Tibet, while the situation of Tibet itself had been going from bad to worse. As we shall see in the next chapter, the menace of British encroachment was aggravated by Russian activities. The British influence was felt by Tibetans especially after the recognition by the Imperial Court of the British protection over Sikkim in 1890. The Tibetan authorities for a time entertained the hope of relying upon the Russian Tzar rather than on the Emperor of Peking.[203] Under these circumstances even a capable Resident working hand in hand with a helpful governor-general of Szechwan could hardly salvage much of the imperial authority.

In fact, as was remarked by Ting Pao-cheng, the governor-general of Szechwan from 1876 to 1885, in his memorial to the throne, the control of the Tibetan administration had been relaxed since the last years of the Hsüan-tsung reign (1821-50), and the Tibetan civil service had become a separate body, no longer subordinate to the imperial institution.[204] During the last decades of the Ch'ing dynasty all the occupants of the Residency, with the exceptions of Wên-shih (1886-88)[205] and Shêng-t'ai,[206] were either grasping or incompetent[207] or both. The corruption of the imperial institution from the Resident downward was bared by Chang Ying-tang[208] in his memorial to the throne. For example, a Resident usually took bribes of no less than twelve thousand taels in recommending one bKa'-blon, and several hundreds or several thousands of taels in appointing a Tibetan official or officer in accordance with his rank. The retinue of a Resident was full of persons dishonorably discharged from former services or with criminal records. A treasurer at Ching-hsi had to bribe the Resident annually with three thousand taels. Most officials in charge of various treasury and supply offices expropriated official funds to the extent of tens of thousands of taels in a single case. Naturally, they commanded no respect from the Tibetans and could not enforce regulations or administer justice.[209]

As a result of the conditions described above, real power gradually passed into the Dalai Lama's hands. This explains also why in 1883,[210] when a dispute arose between Nepal and Tibet as a result of an attack upon eighty-three Nepalese merchant families by a mob in Tibet, the Resident could offer only his good offices and send a commissioner to the spot as a mediator.[211] A settlement was reached in the next year. The Tibetans agreed to pay a considerable sum of money as an indemnity, more than one-third of which was covered by a loan drawn from the Szechwan treasury.[212]

The transfer of the real power to the Dalai Lama can be more clearly seen from the handling of the internal affairs of Tibet. In 1880, trouble again broke out in Nyrong. The Tibetan magistrate So-k'ang-se backed the rebellious tribesmen to defy the imperial authority. Though the rebellion was suppressed by an imperial force, the Resident had to ask the Dalai Lama to replace So-k'ang-se with another Tibetan magistrate. This the latter accordingly did.[213] Sixteen years later, the Tibetan magistrate of Nyrong openly defied the imperial authority by extending his jurisdiction to the neighboring tribes. This time the Tibetan authorities refused to comply with the imperial order to have the magistrate replaced.[214] Lu Chuan-ling, governor-general of Szechwan then resorted to force and occupied the whole of Nyrong. In spite of his repeated requests to take back Nyrong from the Dalai Lama and incorporate it under his jurisdiction, the Emperor finally decided in favor of the commander-in-chief of the Manchu garrison forces in Szechwan Kung-shou's memorial and ordered the withdrawal from Nyrong and the return of the latter to the Dalai Lama.[215] In 1902, though the Dalai Lama still observed the formality as a nominal respect to the Emperor and recommended two candidates for successor to the magistrate of Nyrong who had been promoted to bKa'-blon, he could order the first candidate to proceed to the post and take office only to be confirmed by an imperial edict.[216]

The helpless position of the Resident in facing the British advance demonstrates further the decline of the imperial authority. As pointed out in Lu Chuan-ling's memorial to the throne sent in the spring of 1896, the Resident K'uei-huan and the deputy No-ch'in could not get transport from the Tibetans, nor Tibetan officials to accompany the trip, when they intended to dispatch someone to demarcate the frontier with the British.[217] In 1902 the Resident Yü-kang and the deputy An-ch'eng experienced the same difficulty. They found the situation so untenable that they begged the Emperor to relieve them from their posts.[218]

Meanwhile, the Dalai Lama was concentrating the power in his own hands. In 1900, he killed his own tutor Demo Hutukhtu who had been in power up to 1895 and who had always enjoyed the confidence of the Imperial Court.[219] After the Boxer catastrophe, he and the Tibetan officials listened to the Resident's advice only when it was acceptable to them, and orders, regulations, and treaties which were distasteful to them were utterly disregarded.[220] The nominal authority of the Emperor, however, continued to be acknowledged. A Japanese writer, Ekai Kawanguchi, who was in Tibet at the time, has described the holding of a service of prayer for the victory of China, the safety of the Emperor in the Boxer War, and the salvation of the country.[221]

In 1904 Japan, which had made an alliance with Great Britain in 1902, declared war upon Russia and the fighting took place in the dynastic homeland of Manchuria. In the same year an armed mission was sent by the British into Tibet, and Lhasa was forced to open its gates to foreign troops.[222] As explained later, a treaty was signed in 1906 between the Imperial Government and Great Britain under which the Court gave its sanction to the Lhasa Convention, which had been dictated to the Tibetans by the British commander in the absence of the Dalai Lama, although not a single Manchu or Chinese signature was attached to it. Under the treaty Great Britain formally recognized China's rights in Tibet, and China paid the indemnity on the latter's behalf.

China Attempts to Resume Full Sovereignty in Tibet

Roused by the British advance upon Lhasa in 1904 and alarmed at the terms forced upon Tibet, the Imperial Government felt the necessity of entrenching itself there more firmly. Feng-chien, the Deputy Resident, was instructed to proceed to Tibet with a view to curtailing gradually the powers of the native rulers and bringing the territory under the more direct control of the Imperial Government. He took up his residence temporarily at Ba-t'ang and began to carry out reclamation work and mining operations. These activities caused unrest among the superstitious natives and his arrogance in interfering with the authority of the lamas, together with the harshness of his measures, led to an open revolt. His troops were quite insufficient to quell the outbreak, and he was killed by the rebels.

The Imperial Government was prompt in taking punitive measures. Under the able leadership of Chao Erh-feng, its troops conquered Ba-t'ang and the adjoining district in the summer of 1906. The Resident, Lien-yü, who had been waiting for Chao to open the road, was now able to proceed to his post. Chao was granted honors and created a frontier high commissioner. He abolished the rank of native chief and appointed Chinese magistrates in their places, introduced new laws limiting the number of lamas and depriving monasteries of their temporal power, and inaugurated schemes for having the land cultivated by Chinese immigrants.[223]

In 1908 Chao was appointed Resident and ordered, together with Lien-yü, to investigate local conditions and prepare plans for comprehensive measures in Tibet. He conquered another important district called De-ge in the autumn of 1908 and the districts of Chamdo, Draya, and Markam in the following year. Meanwhile, a comprehensive scheme for the development of Tibet was worked out. It covered military training, reclamation work, the spread of education, the encouragement of trade, and the general improvement of administration. How far these measures impressed the people, in spite of the difficulties and opposition that they naturally encountered, can be fairly gauged from the words of Sir Charles Bell:

> It may be freely conceded that China's work in Tibet had its own good points. The Chinese officials of the modern school, who came in now, lessened the bribes taken by the Tibetan officials from the poorer classes, and in ordinary nonpolitical cases gave straighter jus-

tice than that dealt out by the Tibetan magistracy. There was no doubt some foundation for the Amban's claim that the poorer classes in Tibet were in favor of China.[224]

In a meeting of the Royal Central Asiatic Society held in London, in March, 1924, the speaker, Brigadier-General M. E. Willoughby, an old China Hand, and Sir Francis Younghusband, who forced open the Lhasa gate, both praised Chao Erh-feng's work.[225] Sir Eric Teichman, who spent a number of years as British consular officer at Tach'ienlu, made the comment that "Chao Erh-feng's justice and fair dealings are remembered today in Eastern Tibet as well as his severity." [226]

In February, 1910, the Imperial Army marched from Chamdo into Lhasa. The Dalai Lama, newly returned from Peking with the additional title of "Loyally Submissive Vicegerent," [227] was having difficulty with the Resident, Lien-yü. He was greatly disturbed by news of the farreaching measures Chao had carried out in eastern Tibet, especially the curtailment of the power of the monasteries and the restrictions on lamas. Failing to come to an understanding with the imperial authorities in Lhasa, he fled before the Imperial Army arrived and became a guest of the Government of India. On the recommendation of Lien-yü, the Chinese Government immediately issued a decree depriving the Dalai Lama of his titles.[228] The Chinese Government soon found out the error it had thereby committed, and an effort was made to secure the return of the Dalai Lama to Lhasa, but it proved futile.[229]

In 1911, as a result of the revolution, the Manchu dynasty was overthrown and China became a republic. The Chinese soldiers in Lhasa were originally soldiers of fortune hastily enlisted in Szechwan, with many belonging to the Ko-lao-hui, a secret society composed of both national revolutionists and hoodlums. Since their arrival they had been suffering from the high cost of rice, their staple food, whose market price in Tibet was three times higher than it was in Szechwan. Their insufficient pay was also in arrears. They mutinied on hearing of the events at home. At first they looted only the treasury and the mint. But their call to other units stationed at outlying points to join their intended homeward march brought to Lhasa more mutinous soldiers whose plunder on the way and in the capital aroused widespread ill-feeling among the Tibetans.

After that the situation became fluid; personal feuds and political dissensions made the Chinese position in Tibet entirely untenable. For a time the commander Chung-yin, a Manchu,[230] together with some royalists, made an attempt to restore order and discipline by making a false proclamation that the revolution in China Proper had been suppressed. Later, when the news of the establishment of the Republic reached Lhasa, a council and a new form of administration modeled after other provinces were set up, but there were no funds for their maintenance. Desperation drove the new government to attack the rich Sera monastery and thus brought on hostilities with the powerful Tibetan Church. The failure of this risky measure brought the downfall of the new government. Lien-yü, who had been held for a short time at Tashi-lhunpo as a hostage by mutinous soldiers,[231] and later was made an administrative advisor to the new government, was now asked by them, after several months of hard fighting, to make an arrangement for restoring peace. In the meantime the Dalai Lama came back from India and helped to bring about the armistice. The Nepalese agent also rendered valuable service in this connection. It was agreed that only sixty soldiers were to remain as a bodyguard of the Resident, and Chung-yin was to leave Tibet[232] with the rest of the Chinese troops, who were to be disarmed, and their weapons stored in Lhasa monastery and sealed by both parties. For our study of the status of Tibet, it is interesting to note that the Tibetans agreed to the restoration of the *status quo ante bellum* in regard to the Residency and other commissionships. The fighting between the Chinese soldiers and the Tibetan levies was not at all exclusively motivated by national feelings. The Drespung, Yuncheng, and Demo monasteries did their best to help the Chinese with provisions. The last named (Ten-gye-ling monastery) fought openly for the Chinese,[233] while the Chinese Colonel Hsieh Kuo-liang and three other Chinese officers fought on the side of the Tibetans. In fact, expediency was the determining principle and everything was in a state of confusion.

At the time when the last item of the armistice was to be carried out and the Chinese troops were being disarmed and making preparations for departure, the new republican government suddenly appointed Chung-yin to take the place of Lien-yü as high commissioner. Chung-yin was *persona non grata* to the Tibetans, who tried to persuade Lien-yü to remain. As soon as the latter had left, the Tibetans attacked the forces of Chung-yin, which fought bravely and held out for two months until they were at last conquered by starvation.[234] Through the effort of the Nepalese agent, it was agreed that all Chinese soldiers should leave by way of India, while the Tibetan authorities undertook to provide them with transport facilities, and to protect Chinese civilians if they chose to stay. This time the Tibetans refused to let any Chinese official organization remain, not to mention the once powerful Residency. On January 6, 1913, Chung-yin and the last remnant of his troops marched out of Lhasa.[235]

CHAPTER IV

TIBET AS A BUFFER STATE

WE HAVE SEEN the vicissitudes that led the Imperial Government from a position of nominal suzerainty to the exercise of full sovereignty in Tibet. Up to the latter part of the nineteenth century, Sino-Tibetan relations were not affected by world politics. To the Chinese, Tien-hsia was still their traditional conception of the world, while to the Tibetans the world was a myth in their Buddhistic canons. But they were soon to feel the impact of the West.

Early Contact with the West

Tibet was not a forbidden land from the outset. It was recorded by William de Rubruquis that a goldsmith from Paris, Guillaume Boucher by name, whom he met at Karakorum, had resided at the gold mines of "Bocol" in northeast Tibet in the middle of the thirteenth century.[1] For some time it was believed that Friar Odoric of Pordonone had visited the city of Lhasa in the fourteenth century,[2] but in fact, as proved by Berthold Laufer,[3] "he had never traversed Tibet proper, has never been at Lhasa." The first Europeans actually to cross the Himalayas were Antonio Andarade and Manuel Marques, two Portuguese Jesuits, who arrived in the beginning of August, 1624, and founded a mission at Tsaparang in western Tibet;[4] and the honor of being the first Europeans to have entered Lhasa fell upon two other Jesuit missionaries, Frs. Gruber and d'Orville, who spent two months there in 1661 on their way from China to India.[5] These early missionaries, we may assume, came to this hidden land for the purpose of propagating their faith. Their short-lived missions could hardly have affected the outlook of the Tibetans and had practically no bearing on the status of Tibet. But we shall see that before long, "grasping merchant and murderous machine gun followed the missionaries' trail" [6] and brought the Tibetan status to an entirely different phase.

Futile Efforts of the English to Open Tibet

The impact of the West, so far as Tibet is concerned, was not felt until 1768, when the Court of Directors of the East India Company recommended the obtaining of intelligence regarding whether or not cloth or other European commodities could find a market in Tibet and West China by way of Nepal.[7] This step was taken when Harry Verelst was governor of Bengal; but his successor, Warren Hastings, is usually given the entire credit for conceiving and initiating the idea of trade between Bengal and Tibet.[8]

It was for this commercial reconnaissance that George Bogle was sent to Tibet by Hastings in 1774, though ostensibly he was sent "on the justifiable plea of paying a proper tribute of respect in return for the advances which had been made by the Lama." [9] Here we must point out that the advances made by the Panch'en Lama were for the purpose of mediating between the English and the Bhutanese while the latter, his vassal subjects,[10] were suffering from an unprovoked aggression by the former. As remarked by Cammann,[11] Hastings entered the war under the pretext of helping the wronged ruler of a weak state to regain his rightful position, but he privately admitted in correspondence that his purpose was to gain possession of Cooch Behar for the Company. So it was the English who made the first advance when their troops invaded a state under the suzerainty of Tibet. In other words, the impact of the West was imposed on the Tibetans without choice from the very beginning.[12]

This first English mission failed to procure permission to trade in Tibet. It was prevented from crossing to Lhasa from Tashilhunpo because of the hostile attitude of the Regent. The government at Lhasa, as Bogle wrote in his general report, considered him "as sent to explore their country, which the ambition of the English might afterwards prompt them to invade, and their superiority in arms render their attempt successful." [13] It is worth noting that Bogle was told by the representatives of the Regent who came down to see him that the Regent "would do everything in his power, but that he and all the country were subject to the Emperor of China." The reference to the Emperor's ultimate authority made Bogle exclaim: "This is a stumbling block which crosses me in all my path."[14]

Despite the great setback suffered from the sudden deaths of Bogle and the Panch'en Lama to his plan for promoting and extending the Company's trade with Tibet, Hastings was not daunted. In 1783 he sent his kinsman, Lieutenant Samuel Turner, to Tashi-lhunpo under the pretext of presenting his respects to his old friend the Lama in his new reincarnation. This second mission accomplished no more than cementing already existing relations with the authorities of Tashi-lhunpo. Turner, like Bogle, could not proceed to Lhasa to try to obtain permission for free intercourse between Tibet and Bengal. But his report on Tibetan trade was far more detailed and comprehensive than Bogle's and he obtained a clearer idea of the complex elements involved in Tibetan politics which would be very useful for the Company's enterprise.[15] Though he had the advantage of not dealing with the same Regent at Lhasa who had plagued Bogle, he realized, as had Bogle, that the power of the court at Peking and of the new Regent was an insurmountable barrier to any permanent negotiations at that time. He found that the Tibetans had the greatest awe of the Emperor, of his Residents and other officials, and of the Lhasa Regent.[16]

Less than one year after Turner's return, Hastings resigned and left Calcutta for England. But the question of how best to establish trade relations between the Company and Tibet remained a live issue. In March, 1786, the Directors declared that a very beneficial commerce with Tibet—both in Indian and British goods—ought to be practicable, and that from it Bengal would receive a much needed supply of gold.[17]

In the preceding chapter, mention was made of British help not being forthcoming when the Gurkhas were being beaten by the Chinese imperial forces. In this Sino-Nepalese war, we can already see the complications of an international situation hitherto unknown in this remote region. The Gurkha Rajah, at the time when the Chinese armies sent to the rescue of the Tibetans were approaching, suddenly signed on March 1, 1792, a commercial treaty[18] with his old enemies, the English, after having stalled off their representative for some time. Cammann suspected that Jonathan Duncan, the Company Resident in Benares, had held out to the Rajah some hope of assistance in his Tibetan campaign in exchange for the commercial treaty which he had worked so hard to obtain.[19] In fact, a few months later, when he had sustained numerous defeats in Tibet and the Chinese forces were at the heels of his fleeing army, the Rajah wrote repeatedly to Lord Cornwallis, the successor of Hastings, asking for ten cannon, together with ammunition, and ten young Europeans who would understand how to manage artillery.[20]

To this request Cornwallis sent a reply on September 15, the day on which Duncan's report on the repeated defeat of the Nepalese reached Calcutta. He pointed out in the reply that it was especially necessary to adhere to the policy of noninterference, because the Company had interests in China, and could not afford to send aid against a dependency of hers. He closed by offering to assist in mediation, and by the end of the month he had actually sent for this purpose an envoy, Colonel Kirkpatrick, who arrived at the Nepalese capital when the war had been over for several months.[21] Here we find documentary evidence to show that the English recognized Tibet as a dependency of China as early as 1792.

Lord Cornwallis was also approached by the other party of the armed dispute. Marshall Fu-k'ang-an, the Commander-in-Chief of the imperial forces, wrote him on March 31, 1792, asking him—just as he asked the rulers of Bhutan and Sikkim—as a neighbor of the Gurkhas, to help the Chinese punish the invaders.[22] The Dalai Lama and the Panch'en Lama, too, each sent him a letter (that of the former being written in Tibetan, that of the latter in Persian) urging him not to help the Rajah who would ask for English aid, and requesting that if any fugitive Gurkha chieftain should fall into his hands, he should seize him and deliver him up to the Emperor of China, or at least prevent him from returning home.[23]

To these letters Lord Cornwallis replied, explaining that the Company could not interfere in disputes between foreign powers except when self-defense or wanton attacks obliged them, and offering to help mediate in the quarrel as soon as the season permitted.[24] His proposal to mediate got a response only from the Panch'en Lama, who told him that there was no point in going to the trouble of sending an agent to the Gurkha Rajah because now the latter had also become a dependent of the Emperor of China, and within the Empire there was no reason for dispute.[25]

In spite of Lord Cornwallis's declaration of neutrality, Marshall Fu-k'ang-an, according to Lord Macartney, suspected that the English had aided the Gurkhas.[26] Members of the Macartney Mission, while on their way to Peking by boat up the Pei Ho, in the summer of 1793, found that the reason for their being watched with an unexpected degree of suspicion was that the English were suspected of having given aid to the Gurkhas in the recent war.[27] This belief on the part of the Chinese was, as remarked by Earl H. Pritchard,[28] a serious impediment to the Macartney Mission.

At the suggestion of Lord Macartney a letter from the King of England was sent to Peking in 1795 and reached its destination early in the following year. This told the Manchu Court how the English had attacked the Gurkhas in the rear and urged them to submit to the imperial forces. The Emperor, Kao-tsung, wrote a cold formal reply, explaining that his Marshal, Fu-k'ang-an, had defeated the Gurkhas unaided and that the English had received the wrong story about the war.[29] The noted Chinese historian Wei Yüan mentioned this communication in his *Shêng-wu-chi*[30] with a remark that, "till so told by the English envoy, the Court was not aware that the Gurkhas were facing some trouble on their southern frontier while they were being beaten by the Chinese forces."

The English tried to open Tibet not only from India but also from the other end through Peking. In the spring of 1787 Lieutenant-Colonel Charles Cathcart, M.P. and Quartermaster-General to the Company's army in Bengal, was asked by the English Government to serve as envoy on England's first mission to China. In his preliminary proposals to Henry Dundas, who was acting head of the Board of Control for India, Cathcart said that he wanted to take with him as his private secretary Captain Patrick Alexander Agnew. If the reception should be especially favorable, Agnew was to return to India by way of Tibet with proposals for the opening of commercial relations between the latter and Bengal.[31] Cathcart, however, died enroute on December 21, 1787, and the mission was forced to return home.[32]

In 1811, Thomas Manning, a scholar of Chinese with some medical knowledge, which he learned in six months in a London hospital,[33] achieved the distinction of being the first Englishman to reach Lhasa and have an audience with the Dalai Lama.[34] Whether he had been provided with all facilities by Lord Minto, the Governor-General of India, as pointed out by Taraknath Das,[35] or had been left entirely to his own resources without official recognition of any kind, as remarked by Markham,[36] he did not and could not accomplish anything of political consequence.

Later in the 1840's, Sir John Davis, as the first British Minister to China, tried again to get China to open Tibet to trade.[37] As he himself wrote,[38] Lord Harding, the Governor-General of India, engaged the services of His Majesty's plenipotentiary in China to communicate with Kiying, the Grand Secretary of the Court. The latter replied that "trading with Tibet would not be in conformity with the Maritime treaty, as it is not included in the Five Ports." Though Kiying later admitted that the traders on the Indian frontier[39] might carry on a commerce entirely different from that of the English merchants at the Five Ports of China, and promised to transmit faithfully to his sovereign the whole tenor of the correspondence, Sir John's effort was after all made in vain.

As the English had been trying to open Tibet, it was only natural that in 1876, by which time England was free to impose terms which had to be accepted without demur by China, her minister, Sir Thomas Wade, inserted in the much criticized[40] Anglo-Chinese Chefoo Convention a separate article providing for proper protection for a British mission of exploration from China to India, or from India to China, via Tibet.[41]

Tibetan Reaction to the Approach of the British

Now let us see what reaction the Tibetans had to this provision. Mention has been made earlier of Bogle's having been suspected by the Tibetans "as sent to explore their country." When told of his coming, the Regent of Lhasa wrote to the Panch'en Lama to refuse admittance to him, saying that the English "were fond of war; and after insinuating themselves into a country, raised disturbances and made themselves masters of it." [42] Later events in Nepal, Bhutan, and Sikkim, as related below, seemed to confirm their fears.

NEPAL

In 1814, Gurkhas attacked three police stations in Butwal—a disputed territory which they had conquered but which was regained by the British without open hostilities. The Marquess of Hastings answered with a declaration of war, and himself planned a campaign to attack simultaneously at four different points. On account of the brilliant qualities of the Gurkhas as soldiers and the British troops' lack of knowledge of the geographical difficulties of the mountainous region, the British at first met with reverses. It was not until November of the next year, when there was no hope of further resistance, that the Gurkhas were forced to sign a treaty at Sagauli. But the Nepalese Government hesitated to ratify the treaty and hostilities were resumed.[43]

After another defeat in a decisive battle fought at Makwanpur, close to their capital, on February 28, 1816, the Gurkhas ratified the treaty. By its terms they gave up their claims to places in the lowlands along their southern frontier, ceded to the British the districts of Garhwal and Kumaon on the west of Nepal, withdrew from Sikkim, and agreed to receive a British Resident at Katmandu. The British now obtained sites for important hill stations and summer capitals such as Simla, Mussorie, Almora, Ranikhet, Landour, and Naini Tal; and also greater facilities for communications with the regions of Central Asia. By a treaty with the Rajah of Sikkim, signed on February 10, 1817, a tract ceded by the Nepalese was given to him. This not only showed favor to a protégé but also created a strategically advantageous position for the British by setting a barrier between the eastern frontier of Nepal and Bhutan.[44]

BHUTAN

In 1826 the British annexed Assam and brought the territories of Bhutan into contact with British possessions, in consequence of which constant friction arose regarding the border. For strategic reasons the British authorities wanted to secure control over the rich and fertile Duras (passes) between the two states. They took over some of the Duras and paid the Bhutanese an annual subsidy,[45] thus creating widespread ill-feeling among the Bhutanese and giving rise to what John Claude White called "constant aggressions committed by the Bhutanese on our frontier."[46] In 1865, under the pretext of avenging the insults inflicted upon Ashley Eden, the British envoy, a large-scale campaign was carried out. The Bhutanese after several months of successful resistance were forced to conclude a treaty on November 11 at Sinchula, known by the Bhutanese as the Ten-Article Treaty of Rawa Pani. Under its terms Bhutan ceded Athara Duras, a narrow strip of territory lying at the foot of the hills, to the British who also retained possession of the Assam and Bengal Duras; while the Eastern Duras, lying east of the Sanko River, was incorporated with the Goolpara and Kamrup districts of Assam. It also agreed to arbitration by the British Government in all disputes between the Bhutan Government and the Chiefs of Cooch Behar and Sikkim. In return Bhutan was to receive from the revenues of the Duras an annual sum beginning with Rs 25,000 and later increasing to Rs 50,000 on fulfillment of the conditions of the treaty.[47]

SIKKIM

In 1834-35 another internecine strife broke out between Nepal and Sikkim. Captain Lloyd was sent by the Indian Government to interfere. He obtained a grant of a strip of territory including Darjeeling, whose value as a sanatorium he had discovered during a similar mission in 1826. In 1849, after the representative of the British Government had been captured but released, and Doctors Hooker and Campbell had been maltreated while traveling in Sikkim, the Terai, which had been restored to Sikkim in 1817, and other territory amounting to 1,676 square miles were seized as a punishment.[48] This naturally led to further trouble. Finally, after a military expedition to Tumlong, the capital, the treaty of 1861 was enacted.[49] By this treaty the Government of Sikkim, among other obligations, agreed to refer any disputes or questions between its people and those of neighboring states to the arbitration of the British Government and to abide by its decision, and the whole military force of Sikkim would afford every aid and facility to British troops when employed in the hills. Article 19, in which the Government of Sikkim engaged not to lease any portion of its territory to any other state without the permission of the British Government, shows still more clearly the status to which Sikkim was reduced.

These events in their neighboring states must have deeply impressed the Tibetans. What had happened in Sikkim and Bhutan especially would not and could not pass without being noticed by them, as these two states were then closely linked with Tibet by religious as well as political ties. Even Ashley Eden, the British Envoy and Special Commissioner to Sikkim, acknowledged in his dispatch to the Secretary of the Government of Bengal (dated April 8, 1861) that "Nepal is tributary to China, Tibet is tributary to China, and Sikkim and Bhutan are tributary to Tibet."[50] Bhutan, "of the same race and religion as Tibet,"[51] had been under the Tibetan suzerainty since the P'o-lha-nas days.[52] Sikkim was originally under Tibetan rule. Its ruler was little more than an official of the Tibetan Government, and even today its ruler and most of its leading men are still Tibetan.[53] The Tibetans must have drawn from their fate a reference if not a lesson.

In view of these facts, and also of Sarat Chandra Das's clandestine entry into Lhasa and his surreptitious explorations,[54] it is not surprising that the Tibetans raised strong objections to a proposed British Mission to Tibet in 1885. In that year Colman Macaulay, a secretary of the Government of Bengal, obtained Chinese assent to conduct a mission to Lhasa in accordance with the separate article of the Anglo-Chinese Chefoo Convention.

Imperial power was by this time at a low ebb. Having just been defeated in a war with France and having lost another vassal state, Annam, the Peking Government could not evade its obligations under the Chefoo Convention. Nor was it in a position to force the Tibetans to accept this foreign mission, its weakness having been made known to the Tibetans in the settlement of their dispute with the Nepalese in the previous year.[55] Besides, as Chinese policy in Tibet had been one of exclusion, forbidding the Tibetans to communicate directly with their neighboring countries,[56] it would have been awkward to force the superstitious

Tibetans to admit Macaulay's Mission of exploration and investigation of their minerals, even if it had possessed authority and power to do so.

The Chinese Government's dilemma was soon solved by giving to the British a new and greater concession. In the next year (1886), China signed a convention with them, recognizing the latter's annexation of her vassal state, Burma, in order to secure the provision of Article IV which reads: "Inasmuch as inquiry into the circumstances by the Chinese Government has shown the existence of many obstacles to the Mission to Tibet provided for in a separate article of the Chefoo Agreement, England consents to countermand the Mission."[57]

Events Leading to the British Expedition

The Tibetans, ignorant of this convention, mistook the British withdrawal of the Macaulay Mission as a sign of weakness. They crossed the Jeylap La and built a fort at Lingtu in Sikkim to block the latter's communication with India. They persuaded the ruler of Sikkim to move his seat to Tibet as he had formerly done. This, however, was apparently contrary to Article 22 of the Anglo-Sikkimese Treaty of 1861, which provided that he should move the seat of his government from Tibet to Sikkim and reside there for nine months in the year. But the ruler took the Tibetan's advice and joined the anti-English front. According to the British, the Tibetans violated the sanctity of Sikkim and challenged British authority as the suzerain power; while the Tibetans believed that they were acting within their rights inside their own dominion, and considered the establishment of the British protectorate over Sikkim as a clear usurpation of their jurisdiction. After all, their action cannot be simply interpreted as "an 'inexplicable invasion' into the protected state of Sikkim" as some English and Indian writers assert.[58]

In March of 1888, British forces under General Graham drove the Tibetans out of Lingtu and took up a position at Gnatong. The Tibetans made two other attacks in the autumn. They were again driven back after having sustained heavy losses, and the pursuing British troops entered the Tibetan Chumbi Valley. The Peking Government was then stirred to action. It ordered its Resident in Lhasa to stop the Tibetans from further adventure and to try to effect a settlement.[59] The British found the expedition too expensive to maintain and were eager to secure Chinese recognition of the protectorate over Sikkim. Of course, they also took into consideration the improvement of trade which would result from the demarcation of the frontier and the restoration of peace.

Because of Peking's refusal to recognize the claim that Sikkim had been a British protectorate ever since 1861, one year's desultory negotiation passed without a settlement. The British lost their patience and proposed to close the incident without insisting upon a specific agreement.[60] The Chinese, fearing that leaving the matter in abeyance might usher in future trouble not only from the British but also from the Russians,[61] decided to give in. An agreement was finally signed on March 17, 1890, by the Governor-General of India, Lord Lansdowne, and the Resident Shêng-t'ai, in Calcutta. Besides sanctioning British control over the internal administration and foreign relations of Sikkim, the treaty stipulated that the water parting of the Teesta River should form the boundary between Sikkim and Tibet.[62]

Regarding the unsettled questions mentioned in Articles 4, 5, and 6 of this treaty, further negotiations went on between the Chinese delegates, Huang Shao-hsun and Ho Chang-yung, and James H. Hart, on the one hand, and the British delegate A. W. Paul on the other. A compromise was at length reached and the Regulations regarding Trade, Communication, and Pasturage were signed in December, 1893. The chief provisions established a trade mart at Yatung, eight miles on the Tibetan side of the frontier, and the practice of extraterritorial jurisdiction in the event of trade disputes arising between British and Chinese or Tibetan subjects in Tibet.[63]

The Treaty of 1890 and the Regulations of 1893 gave the British subjects in Tibet various privileges which were not to be reciprocally enjoyed by the Tibetans in Sikkim. It was further stipulated that the Tibetans in exercising their customary right of grazing cattle in their former vassal state would have to abide by such regulations as the British Government might from time to time enact. To these provisions it was only natural that the Tibetans raised the gravest objections.[64]

The Tibetans refused also to countenance the delimitation of the Sikkim-Tibet frontier as provided in Article 1 of the Treaty of 1890. They pointed to the ancient marks or *ao-po* erected in 1794 as evidence to show that some original Tibetan territory had been marked off as being on the side of Sikkim.[65] They blamed the imperial delegate for his arbitrary decision without their concurrence, and went so far as to destroy the new boundary pillars erected by Mr. White, the Political Officer in Sikkim, at the Jeylap La and Donchuk La. Even Lord Elgin, the Viceroy of India, conceded that to this disputed region Tibet had a "reasonable" claim,[66] and both the Chinese and British authorities once tentatively agreed to demarcate as the Tibetans insisted, provided the latter let the customs house be removed from Yatung to Rinchingong.[67] The Tibetans, being reluctant from the beginning to open Yatung, and having "prevented Yatung from becoming a trade mart in anything but name," [68] naturally refused to give trading facilities in a place deeper within their frontier.[69] Furthermore, the new Viceroy, Lord Curzon, attached as an additional condition for his concession to the demarcation issue, the right to trade as far up as Phari. This demand sealed the fate of any possible agreement.[70]

As early as 1895 the Tibetan commissioner on the frontier question, Tchedonay Tenzing Wangpu, made a statement to Mr. White that the Tibetans did not consider themselves bound by the Convention with China, as they were not a party to it.[71] This position they still maintained when Mr. White reported to the Government of Bengal in the December of 1898.[72] But the British on the one hand still maintained that there was some prospect of exchanging their territorial claim for some concession in regard to trade. The Tibetans, on the other hand, as Mr. P. Nolan, the British Commissioner, remarked in an official communication dated May 4, 1890, "value their isolation more than these pastures, and would not exchange the first for the second." [73]

Lord Curzon's Altered or Forward Policy

In the meantime China's position in Tibet was further weakened by her defeat in war with Japan and the insurrection of her large Moslem population on the route between Lhasa and Peking.

The Chinese officials in Tibet, as Mr. P. Nolan reported on November 24, 1895, "sincerely desired to see the Convention carried out,"[74] but they had no means of making the Tibetans toe the line. It was under these circumstances that Lord Curzon secured in December of 1899 approval of his new course of action—to open direct negotiations with the Tibetans[75]—and formulated in January, 1903, his "altered policy," otherwise known as the "forward policy"—"to cover not merely the small question of the Sikkim frontier, but the entire question of our [British] future relations, commercial or otherwise with Tibet."[76]

The British, having decided to eliminate the Chinese factor in the controversy, made various attempts to open direct negotiations with the Tibetans. The Government of India, after having unsuccessfully tried the Sikkim route, contemplated dispatching a suitable emissary to Lhasa through Yünnan, or through Nepal, or by way of Ladakh; but its efforts were of no avail. They tried as a last resort to send a letter addressed by the Viceroy to the Dalai Lama. The first agent dared not, in the face of the regulations against the intrusion of foreigners into Tibet, send it to Lhasa,[77] and the second agent, who was in the service of the Dalai Lama, brought back the letter with the seals intact, giving the explanation that the Dalai Lama refused to accept it on the ground that he was bound by agreement not to correspond with foreign governments without consulting the Council of State and the Chinese Resident.[78] It is obvious that the British efforts were not frustrated by the regulations which the Chinese Residents were no longer in a position to enforce; it was rather deep-rooted suspicion of the British on the part of the Tibetans that doomed these efforts to failure.

When all these attempts failed, Lord Curzon, in February, 1902, called it "the most extraordinary anachronism of the 20th century that there should exist within less than 300 miles of the borders of British India a state and a government with whom political relations do not so much as exist, and with whom it is impossible even to exchange a written communication."[79] Now he talked about political relations, called Tibet a state, and the Dalai Lama a *de facto* as well *de jure* sovereign of the country: the issue was no longer a matter of mere trade and frontier relations between Sikkim and Tibet.

In the next year—one year after the conclusion of the Anglo-Japanese alliance, the primary motive of which was the protection of the interests of the two parties in the Far East, in China, and in Korea—the ambitious Viceroy of India, in his letter of January 8, 1903, to the Secretary of State for India, spoke of "Chinese suzerainty over Tibet as a constitutional fiction—a political affectation which has only been maintained because of its convenience to both parties." [80]

This often-quoted remark of Lord Curzon on the status of Tibet requires some comment. Mr. Joseph H. Choate, United States Ambassador to Great Britain, was instructed in June, 1904, to acquaint the British Foreign Office with the State Department's views on the British expedition. His instructions took strong exception to the official references of the Indian Government to Chinese sovereignty over Tibet as a "constitutional fiction" and a "political affectation," and stated that Great Britain had three times, in the Chefoo Convention of September 13, 1876, in the Peking Convention of July 24, 1886, and in the Calcutta Convention of March 17, 1890, recognized Chinese sovereignty by negotiating with the Chinese Government on questions relating to Tibet, and since then the Chinese had waived none of their sovereign rights.[81]

In fact, Lord Hamilton, the Secretary of State for India, in reply to the above-mentioned letter of Lord Curzon, though he did not repudiate categorically the latter's remarks, had these words in his instructions which shed some light on the actual status of Tibet: "His Majesty's Government cannot regard the question as one concerning India and Tibet alone. The position of China in its relations to the Powers of Europe, has been so modified in recent years that it is necessary to take into account those altered conditions in deciding on action affecting what must still be regarded as a province of China." [82]

Six months after Lord Curzon wrote that letter, the British delegates, Mr. White and Colonel Younghusband, handed to the Tibetan official, in the presence of the Chinese delegate, Ho Kuang-hsieh, at Khamba, a memorandum written in Tibetan [83] in which the British told the Tibetans that "elsewhere within the Chinese Empire, British subjects are allowed to carry on trade without any obstruction; Tibet as a dependency of the Empire, has been the only place that made obstacles to trade ever since 1886." [84] Here the British, instead of describing the Chinese sovereignty over Tibet as a "constitutional fiction" and a "political affectation," admitted again that Tibet was a dependency of the Chinese Empire. Their contradiction can be easily explained by borrowing Lord Curzon's words, "because of its convenience."

In order to justify his forward policy Lord Curzon brought up the issue of the Russian menace. Ever since the fourth decade of the nineteenth century, British and Russian interests clashed on another threshold of India—Afghanistan.[85] From 1871 to 1888 the famous Russian officer and explorer N. M. Prjivalsky explored Mongolia and northern Tibet. In 1899-1901 his assistant P. K. Kozloff headed a team to explore Tibet under the auspices of the Russian Geographical Society. During this period other Russian explorers like Sosnoffsky (1872, 1874-75), Kropotkin (1876-77), Ivanoff (1883), Bendersky (1883), and Grombchevsky (1889) explored the Dzungar, Tien Shan, Pamirs, and Karakoram regions.[86] On the British side, the well-known Survey of India started its work in 1842 which was extended to Kashmir in 1860. Following the footsteps of W. H. Johnson (1865), Martin Conway (1892) contributed valuable geographical knowledge of the mountainous route from Kashmir to Tibet. In 1896-97 H. H. P. Deasy surveyed northwestern Tibet up to Sinkiang and went as far as the upper valley of the Yarkand River. Among the British explorers, in addition to the above-mentioned Sarat Chandra Das, Nain Singh (Pundit) came to Lhasa in 1866 and 1874, Kalian Singh came to Shigatse in 1868, and Kishan Singh entered Tibet in 1871, 1874, and 1878, and visited both Shigatse and Lhasa. In 1891-92 H. Bower, another noted British explorer, traversed Tibet from Leh to China Proper.[87] The roads of these British and Russian explorers crossed each other in Tibet and Sinkiang; and thus, the Russian menace became a familiar topic to the British public, even had there been no conflict of interests elsewhere.

Despite these explorations and survey activities and her interests in trade, especially the trade in silk,[88] Russia's chief connection with Tibet was through her Buriat subjects who were followers of the Yellow Sect. In August, 1901, owing to the visit of certain Lamas from Tibet to Russia, Sir C. Scott, the British Ambassador in Petersburg, was instructed by the Marquess of Lansdowne to inform Count Lamsdorff, the Russian Foreign Minister, that "His Majesty's Government could not regard with indifference any proceedings that might have a tendency to alter or disturb the existing status of Tibet." The latter assured the British Ambassador that the visit was "chiefly concerned with matters of religion, and had no political or diplomatic object or character."[89]

A year later, "the British government believed that Russia was making a secret treaty to help China against those who were pressing her from different directions" and that "Russia was to receive Tibet in return for her services."[90] In September, 1902, Sir E. Satow, British Minister in Peking, was instructed to intimate, and did intimate, to the Peking Government that "should any agreement affecting the political status of Tibet be entered into by China with another power, His Majesty's Government would be compelled to take steps for the protection of British interests."[91] The Peking Government strongly denied that there was any such secret compact regarding Tibet.[92] In spite of the above-mentioned Russian assurance and Chinese denial, however, the British authorities in India were still of the opinion that their "vastly greater interests in Tibet clashed all along the line with those of the Muscovite."[93]

Mention has been made above of a meeting at Khamba in July, 1903. To use the words of Lord Curzon, "the Tibetans who were in occupation of the Giaogong plateau were directed by Mr. White to withdraw beyond the frontier, and our [the British] right to insist upon the observance of the boundary laid down by the Convention of 1890 was clearly asserted."[94] The Chinese Government for their part, while complaining to the British authorities about Mr. White's breaking down the barrier in the Na Chin Pass with a force of over 100 troops without any previous notice, thought it an opportune moment to reopen negotiations, and therefore named Ho Kuang-hsieh as its delegate in July, 1902.[95] By making this overture, as clearly seen by the Secretary of State for India, "China . . . implicitly accepts responsibility for the affairs of Tibet."[96] Lord Curzon, however, regarded the "Chinese proposal for a conference as affording an excellent opportunity for pressing forward and carrying out" his altered policy. He suggested the attaching of a condition that the conference should take place not upon the British frontier but at Lhasa, and that it should be attended by a representative of the Tibetan Government who would participate in the proceedings.[97]

Later, Lord Curzon thought it politic to name Khamba instead of Lhasa as the meeting place. He did this, apparently in consideration of international complications. Russia had made it clear to the British that they could not remain indifferent to any serious disturbances of the status quo in Tibet, saying they regarded Tibet as "forming a part of the Chinese Empire, in the integrity of which they took an interest."[98] Lord Curzon had taken into consideration also the lack of enthusiastic support on the part of the Secretary of State for India, who told him that "it would be premature to adopt measures so likely to precipitate a crisis in the affairs of Tibet"[99] as those the Viceroy had proposed. For the Khamba meeting, however, Lord Curzon demanded that "the Chinese delegates should be accompanied by a duly accredited Tibetan representative of the highest rank whose authority to bind the Tibetan Government is absolute and unquestioned."[100]

As to the scope of the negotiations, the Chinese were under the impression that Mr. White was probably proceeding to the frontier in the vicinity of Giaogong "with the object of discussing some frontier matters locally,"[101] while on the part of the British, even the Secretary of State for India presumed that "it will . . . be necessary to include in scope of negotiations the entire question of our future relations with Tibet, commercial, and otherwise";[102] but eventually he decided that the negotiations should be restricted to questions concerning trade relations, the frontier, and grazing rights, and that no proposal should be made for the establishment of a Political Agent either at Gyantse or at Lhasa as Lord Curzon had suggested.[103]

Since January, 1903, the Chinese Delegate, Ho Kuang-hsieh, had been waiting at Yatung, the trade mart on the frontier. On April 6 the Chinese Resident wrote to Lord Curzon in the following words: "Mr. Ho, who has now been at Yatung over three months, has petitioned me to the effect that during his enforced stay at Yatung he has on several occasions communicated with Mr. White and urged him to begin the discussion of affairs without delay, but failed to elicit any satisfactory reply. Also, Your Excellency has failed to vouchsafe any reply to my dispatch dated 28th November last year, and I feel much concerned in consequence. . . . I venture to beg an early reply." [104]

The Chinese, of course, had no idea that Lord Curzon was planning some "more practical measures with a view to securing commercial and political facilities," and the British Government was seeking for clarification of the Russian attitude, and waiting for a more opportune moment and "a better position to decide the question." [105] Lord Curzon always blamed the Chinese authorities for their procrastination. He may have been justified in his accusation on previous occasions, but this time, to use the words of Sir E. Satow, the British Minister in Peking: "The Chinese Government is really desirous of seeing the matter brought to a satisfactory conclusion." [106]

Dispatch of the British Armed Mission

On June 3, 1903, Lord Curzon wrote to the Chinese Resident at Lhasa notifying the latter of his momentous decision,[107] and on the same day he dispatched Colonel Younghusband, a noted explorer, and Mr. White, the Political Officer in Sikkim, to proceed to Khamba [108] with an armed escort of 200 men to be supported by another 300 men who would bring the ordnance reserve ammunition for the escort.[109] Mr. Scott calls this "mission to Khamba" a deliberate violation of the Convention of 1890, carried out with a high-handed disregard for the elementary principles of international law." [110]

As a matter of fact, Mr. Ho, the Chinese delegate, wrote to Mr. White to say that "we are, and have been, quite prepared to proceed to such place as may seem to His Excellency the Viceroy more desirable for the better discussion of the points at issue." The Chinese Resident wrote to Lord Curzon to say that "I . . . trust that Your Excellency will, without further loss of time, depute someone to discuss matters. The Deputy appointed by Your Excellency can either come to Yatung, or the Chinese Deputies will proceed to Sikkim, or other such places as may be decided on by Your Excellency." [111] Neither Mr. Ho nor the Chinese Resident had the least idea that the meeting place of a conference which was to "open negotiations . . . for the fulfillment of treaty obligations,"[112] would not be limited by the terms of the very treaty which recognized their rights to exclude Europeans from Tibet, with Yatung the only exception.

From the moment that the armed mission began to approach the frontier, both Tibetan and Chinese representatives continued their protests against the invasion. On June 15, 1903, the Chinese Frontier Commissioners sent a telegram to Mr. White requesting the British Commissioners not to proceed across the frontier fixed by the 1890 Convention, and stating that Khamba, being on the Tibetan side of the frontier, was an unsuitable rendezvous.[113] Nevertheless, Mr. White arrived with a full escort at Khamba on July 7, and Colonel Younghusband arrived there twelve days later.[114] On July 22 the Commissioners met. The Tibetan officials raised objections not only to holding negotiations at Khamba but also to the size of the British escort. They refused to receive any written communications from the British delegates, and when the latter asked them to report what had been said to their government, they replied they could not even do that much, and that they could make no report at all unless the British mission went back to the frontier at Giaogong, which was the place at which they meant to discuss matters.[115]

When the Chinese learned of the forthcoming armed mission, the Resident took action with a view to deterring the Tibetans from showing hostility to the English on their arrival. He admonished the bKa'-blons in person, telling them not to be obstinate as before, but to discuss matters with the mission on the basis of reason, and warned them that "if hostilities once begin, the horrors of war will be more than one can bear to think upon, and even the mediation of the Imperial Resident will be of no avail."[116] Fearing an attack, this extraordinary "commercial mission" was "strongly entrenched in the open with Maxim guns and perfectly ready."[117] But though large numbers of Tibetans were gathering along the lines of further advance, no attack was made upon the camp or upon the individual officers as they freely explored the neighborhood.

On July 29, a deputy from the Panch'en Lama called upon Colonel Younghusband "to demand the reason for his armed presence . . . and to request . . . immediate withdrawal" of the mission. This shows that in spite of the "considerable friction between the Shigatse and Lhasa people," the Tibetans were unanimous in demanding the withdrawal of the armed mission "across the frontier, or to Yatung, which was the place fixed for meetings of this kind." [118] The impasse dragged on. By the end of August Younghusband entered these words in the Political Diary of his mission: "Their present policy is one of passive obstruction. They have made up their minds to have no negotiations with us inside Tibet; they will simply leave us here." [119]

In the meantime a pretext for further advance was found. Two men had been sent out on July 18 by the British to spy out the land and were stopped by the Tibetans who sent them to Lhasa.[120] In reporting the incident to his home government Lord Curzon wrote:

> The most conspicuous proof of the hostility of the Tibetan Government and of their contemptuous disregard for the usages of civilization has been the arrest of two British subjects from Lachung at Shigatse, whence they have been deported to Lhasa, and it is credibly asserted, have been tortured and killed.[121]

As a matter of fact, the men were released nine months later at Lhasa, on the insistence of the Chinese Resident, without prompting from Colonel Younghusband, and were found to be safe and sound. A medical examination by the physician of the British Mission reported they were "in excellent health" and had been "well fed, showing no sign of ill treatment beyond imprisonment." In the meantime their imaginary sufferings served a useful purpose. After having made what Scott called "the old *civis Romanus sum* appeal," [122] Lord Curzon secured approval for the occupation of the Chumbi Valley; and then, under the pretext that a rupture of negotiations had taken place, while in fact negotiations could hardly be said ever to have begun, he eventually secured the sanction of the new Secretary of State for India, Mr. Brodrick, for an immediate advance to Gyangtse with reinforcements under the command of Brigadier-General MacDonald.[123]

On the way, at Geru, where the Tibetans had built a wall of loose stones across the valley, "a ridiculous position" was created with "Sikh and Mongol swaying backwards and forwards as they wrestled for the possession of sword and matchlock," when the former was ordered to disarm the latter forcibly. Then somewhere in the swaying mob a shot was fired, and a massacre, not a battle, followed, as a result of which at least 628 Tibetans were left on the field killed and wounded, and 222, including some slightly wounded, were taken prisoner. On the British side one war correspondent, Mr. Candler, was dangerously wounded, and one officer seriously wounded, and in addition two native ranks were wounded severely and eight slightly.[124]

At Yatung, Colonel Younghusband had given a pledge to the Tibetan general in these words: "We are not at war with Tibet, and unless we are ourselves attacked, we shall not attack the Tibetans."[125] Now the Tibetans were blamed for having made an unprovoked attack upon a peaceful "commercial mission," and henceforward in the dispatches, it was no longer "the Tibetans" but "the enemy."

On April 11, the "mission" arrived at Gyantse with 190 Tibetan corpses marking the trail of the British advance between Geru and Gyantse, not to count those who crawled away to hide their agonies and who died afterwards from their wounds. Younghusband reported to his government on that day that "General MacDonald has brought the mission here without loss of a single man, having only three wounded."[126]

The "mission" remained at Gyantse for three months endeavoring to open negotiations and being met with the stereotyped demand to return to the frontier. The Tibetans explained that they had to wait for the representatives of the three great monasteries for consultations before any reply could be made. To Younghusband this was not a good excuse, and he soon proposed the advance to Lhasa because the "psychological moment" had arrived and he was sure that by carrying the Chinese Resident with him he could probably manage this advance without further fighting, or, at any rate, without a serious collision.[127] Lord Curzon then pressed upon his home government the suggestion "that some definite limit of time should be imposed," and that a further advance toward Lhasa should be sanctioned to be effective after the lapse of the time limit.[128]

June 25 was named as the last day of grace allowed to the

Tibetans for opening negotiations. Later, the time limit was extended for five days, due to reports about the departure of Tibetan delegates from Lhasa.[129] No negotiations, however, took place or were expected at the eleventh hour. The Tibetan delegates sent by the Dalai Lama had not had credentials with them, and Younghusband considered himself unable to deal with them, in spite of the assurances given by "so staunch a friend of the British Government," Tongsa Penlop of Bhutan, that the Tibetans were really eager to negotiate.[130] In the meantime, another reinforcement consisting of eight companies of infantry, one mule corps, and four guns were called up from India. On July 14 the mission set out for the last stage of the advance.

On the 20th, Younghusband reached Negartse. Once more Tibetan delegates appeared on the scene and begged the British to return—this time not to the frontier, but to Gyantse for negotiations.[131] Younghusband refused to comply with their request and led his mission towards the Tibetan capital, meeting practically no further opposition. On the 24th the Tibetan National Assembly[132] communicated with Younghusband, promising to negotiate, but requesting the British not to proceed further. Younghusband refused.[133] Three days later, at the Chaksam ferry, several Tibetan delegates again called on Younghusband with a letter from the Dalai Lama himself and requested the mission not to come to the holy city. They argued that if the British went to Lhasa, the religion would be so violated that the Dalai Lama might die. Again Younghusband refused.[134]

As late as the afternoon of August 2, at Camp Tolung, the Ta Lama, the Tsarong Shappé, a Chinese official deputed by the Amban, the Abbot in private attendance on the Dalai Lama, a secretary of the council, and the Abbots of the three Lhasa monasteries visited Younghusband and repeated the usual requests that the British should not go to Lhasa. The latter reiterated his statements that "we must go there."[135] Here the reader should be reminded of three facts in this connection: (1) The Secretary of State for India, replying to a question on July 27, told the House of Commons that "there is nothing to prevent negotiations taking place at any point on the march to Lhasa if competent negotiators appear."[136] (2) But three months before, on April 22,

Younghusband had officially recommended to Lord Curzon and the latter had duly transmitted to the home government that "negotiations should take place at the capital instead of at the half-way house."[137] (3) And Lord Curzon reported to the Secretary of State for India on July 10 that Younghusband had been instructed: "Should Tibetan delegates appear after he has started, he is to explain our terms to them, to warn them . . . and to invite them to accompany the advance of the Mission"; and he again reported on July 18 that "Younghusband, before making a further diplomatic move, is awaiting definite advances on their part . . . . In any case, however, the Mission will not postpone its advance."[138]

Lhasa Reached and a Convention Imposed

On August 3, Lhasa was reached.[139] The Dalai Lama was reported to have fled to the north, and the government heads shifted responsibility. According to a report by a correspondent of the London *Daily Chronicle*, "the expedition has looted monasteries, and for weeks past, bales of plunder have been coming over the passes into India. Their contents have brought joy to the officers' wives and friends whose houses in the hill stations began to look as some of them looked after the sack of Peking four years ago [during the Boxer uprising]."[140]

The Chinese Resident, Yu-t'ai who had been prevented from meeting the British Commissioner before the latter's arrival at Gyantse by the Dalai Lama's insistence on British withdrawal to the frontier,[141] now called on Younghusband immediately and expressed his readiness to assist in arranging an agreement.[142] During the return visit the next day, Younghusband asked him to get the Tibetans to depute two or three representatives, which he readily promised to arrange.[143]

Yu-t'ai, in spite of all the difficulties he must have had with the Tibetans, could have gone to meet the British mission before its advance to Lhasa, if not before its arrival at Gyantse. Lack of transport was only a pretext. Nor was the Dalai Lama's insistence on British withdrawal an insurmountable difficulty or a prerequisite condition. It was rather his cowardice that prevented him from shouldering a responsibility on behalf of the Imperial Court or doing something for the Tibetans when he was most needed. In his telegraphic report to the Wai-wu-pu, this Manchu official expressed his hope for a favorable turn in the situation if the Tibetans should meet another great defeat at the hands of the British.[144] For him it did not require any effrontery to tell Younghusband that he had no authority to get the transport to proceed beyond Lhasa so as to serve as an excuse for his dilatoriness and inaction.[145] Apparently he entertained the queer idea of utilizing the British military might to reassert his lost authority in Tibet and therefore he did the best he could to collaborate with Younghusband. Actually, he played into the latter's hands.

Since it was no longer a negotiated peace but a dictated one, there remained only the question of the drafting of terms to be imposed upon the helpless Tibetans. If Lord Curzon's mission had so far had any real fight at all, he himself was about to put up a harder fight with his own home government on this question. His policy was one of complete political domination. He was resolved upon securing a solid and permanent footing in Tibet; but his home government, on the other hand, had to examine his proposals from the wider point of view of the relations of Great Britain to other powers, both European and Asiatic. When the home government sanctioned the advance of the mission to Gyantse, it wanted to avoid international entanglement, since the world situation was tense and the Russo-Japanese war was in the offing. Sir Ernest Satow, British Minister in Peking, was instructed to explain to the Chinese Government the reason for sanctioning the advance of the British Mission.[146] Lord Lansdowne assured Russia that the British Government had not any intention of annexing or even permanently occupying Tibetan territory and reiterated that Great Britain's sole object was to obtain satisfaction for the affront which she had received from the Tibetans.[147] Again when it sanctioned the advance to Lhasa, it informed the Peking Court of its decision and Sir C. Hardinge was instructed to repeat to the Russian Government the previous assurances and to add most emphatically that "so long as no other power endeavors to intervene in the affairs of Tibet, [the British] will not attempt either to annex it, to establish a protectorate over it, or in any way to control its internal administration."[148]

Lord Curzon knew pretty well the position of his home government. He was too wise to defy openly the instructions of the Secretary of State for India; but as there are more ways than one that lead to Rome, he skillfully entangled Mr. Brodrick in long and devious arguments, and trapped him into loose and unguarded amplifications of his originally definite and precise statements.[149] Since he was told that the advance of the mission should not be allowed to lead to occupation or to permanent intervention in Tibetan affairs in any form,[150] he calculated that there surely could be no objection to forbidding the Tibetans to have any relation with any other foreign power without British consent.[151] His home government stated clearly in the instructions that they were not prepared to establish a permanent mission in Tibet and neither at Lhasa nor elsewhere was a Resident to be demanded.[152] He was, however, sure that there could be no objection to retaining for the trade agent at Gyantse the privilege of "proceeding to Lhasa as occasion may require to discuss matters with the Chinese Amban or with the high officials of the Dalai Lama." [153] In his eyes, Chumbi Valley "lies to the south of the main watershed, and is Indian rather than Tibetan in character"; so it might be considered as separate if evacuation had to be effected in accordance with the instructions. And if the home government was pedantic enough to regard the Chumbi Valley as coming within the scope of its pledge to Russia not to annex Tibetan territory, there could be no harm in "reserving to ourselves the right to contract such communications as roads, railways, telegraphs, etc." [154]

As to the indemnity, Mr. Brodrick laid down clearly in his final instructions that the sum to be demanded should not exceed an amount which, it was believed, would be within the power of the Tibetans to pay, by installments, if necessary, spread over three years, and that the occupation of the Chumbi Valley as security for the indemnity and the newly opened trade marts would continue till the payment of the indemnity had been completed, or the marts opened effectually for the space of three years, whichever was the latest.[155] Here Lord Curzon decided to take the bold step of disregarding the instructions and confronting the Secretary of State with a *fait accompli*.

On September 1, Younghusband with the whole staff, all in full-dress uniform, rode through the city to the Chinese Residency. The Chinese Resident thereupon summoned the Shappés [156] who took their seats on stools in the centre of the room. Most of the members of the Tibetan National Assembly then present in Lhasa also came in and were huddled into the corners. Younghusband then arose and presented the final draft of the treaty in English, Chinese, and Tibetan to the Resident, who then handed the Tibetan copy to the Shappés.

Its leading provisions were:

1. The government of Tibet engaged to respect the Anglo-Chinese convention of 1890 and to recognize the frontier between Sikkim and Tibet as defined in Article I of the said convention. (Article I)
2. In addition to Yatung, two fresh trade marts were to be opened at Gyantse and at Gartok. (Article II)
3. The Tibetan Government undertook to levy no dues of any kind other than those provided for in the tariff to be mutually agreed upon. (Article IV)
4. An indemnity of half a million pounds—equivalent to rupees seventy-five lakhs—was to be paid by the Tibetan Government in installments. The Chumbi Valley was to remain in British occupation until the payment was completed. (Articles VI and VII)
5. The Tibetan Government agreed to raze all forts and fortifications and remove all armaments which might impede the course of free communication between the British frontier and the towns of Gyantse and Lhasa. (Article VIII)
6. Without British consent no Tibetan territory was to be ceded, leased, etc., to any Foreign Power, no concession for roads, mines, etc., was to be given, and no Tibetan revenues were to be pledged to a Foreign Power or to any of its subjects. No such Power was to be permitted to intervene in Tibetan affairs, or to send Agents to Tibet. (Article IX) [157]

Then with the permission of the Resident, Younghusband addressed the members of the National Assembly, telling them that he was prepared to explain any point in the final draft which they did not understand, but that he could not further discuss the terms and that they were given only one week within which they might receive explanations and think matters over.[158]

On the sixth day the treaty was signed in the presence of the Chinese Resident in the Audience Room of the holy Potala.[159] Younghusband nearly persuaded the Chinese Resident to attach his signature. Yu-t'ai might have done so but for the instructions of the Wai-wu-pu, which not only refused to give sanction but admonished him for having let the Tibetans enter into such a questionable agreement with the British.[160] The signed document had only one modification: The payment of the indemnity was distributed over seventy-five years instead of three, as would be the occupation of the Chumbi Valley which, under the terms of the final draft as well as of the signed convention, was to be continued till the full amount of the indemnity had been paid.[161]

When the ceremony was concluded, Younghusband addressed the Tibetans, saying that "we were not interfering in the smallest degree with their religion, we were annexing no part of their country, we were not interfering in their internal affairs, and we were fully recognizing the continued suzerainty of the Chinese Government. We merely sought to insure that they should abide by the treaty made on their behalf by the Amban in 1890." [162] In his report to the Government of India, Younghusband spoke of the convention as defining the boundaries, placing British trade relations upon a satisfactory footing, and giving the British the right to exclude any foreign influence if they should so wish, and containing an acknowledgment from the Tibetans that an indemnity was due for the insults shown them. In addition, he procured one passport for a party to proceed from Gyantse to Gartok to open a trade mart there, another for a party to proceed down the Brahmaputra to Assam, and a third for Mr. Wilton to return to Chengtu by way of Tach'ienlu. Furthermore, he procured from the Bhutanese Government permission for the construction of what was hoped to be the principal road piercing the Himalayas throughout their entire length.[163]

From the point of view of our subject, we should go beyond these diplomatic utterances and see what change the provisions of the treaty brought to the status of Tibet. It is obvious that the provisions of the treaty, if accepted as drawn, would have made Tibet a British protectorate in the true sense of the word.[164] Not to mention the restrictions on her foreign relations and defense; the uses that could be made of the right of the trade agent at Gyantse to visit Lhasa; the collection for 75 years of an annual tribute which might give occasion for interference in the affairs of Tibet; [165] and the military occupation of the Chumbi Valley, "the key to Tibet," "the only strategical point of value in the whole northeastern frontier from Kashmir to Burma," which would give the British "a clear run into Tibet" [166]—just the indemnity of five hundred thousand pounds (equivalent to rupees 75 lakhs) alone would have reduced Tibet to a state of financial vassalage to British India for three generations.

Such a sum was not within the power of the Tibetans to pay—a fact which Younghusband at first admitted [167] and which was clearly shown by the opinions expressed in this connection by the Chinese Resident and the Panch'en Lama.[168] And to fix such a sum was diametrically contrary to the instructions of his home government. Yet Younghusband was bold enough to impose the crushing burden on the Tibetans and to allow the payment to be distributed over seventy-five years, while retaining without modification the proviso that the Chumbi Valley was to be occupied as security till the full amount had been paid.

The Convention Amended in Deference to London Authority

Mr. Brodrick, on learning the contents of the signed Convention, pointed out to Lord Curzon the difficulty presented by the amount of indemnity, especially when the provision for its payment was read in connection with Article VII, the effect being that the British occupation of the Chumbi Valley (which had been recognized in the convention of 1890 and the trade regulations of 1893 as Tibetan territory) might have to continue for 75 years. He called this inconsistent with his instructions and with the declaration of His Majesty's Government as to withdrawal. Three days later he told the Viceroy that the home government "felt it highly undesirable that a term should be fixed for payment of indemnity which would have the effect of throwing the burden on future generations and of relieving from any immediate sacrifice the monasteries and those to whom the present troubles are due," and that they did not wish that indemnity should take the form of what would be regarded as a permanent tribute. Brodrick therefore authorized a reduction of indemnity from 75 lakhs to 25 lakhs of rupees, i.e., one third of the original amount and a revision of the provision in connection with the occupation of the Chumbi Valley.[169]

His instructions reached Younghusband on the eve of the latter's departure from Lhasa and no action was taken. Lord Curzon had intended to ask the Tibetans to agree to the establishment of an additional trade mart in eastern Tibet and to other concessions such as survey, new trade regulations, and lien on customs, as a bargain for indemnity remission.[170]

Finally, Mr. Brodrick, in reply to Lord Curzon's further explanation, told him bluntly that in regard to the indemnity Younghusband's convention had been framed in defiance of express instructions and "we cannot accept the situation created for us by our representative's disobedience to orders." He agreed to Lord Curzon's suggestion to have a declaration appended to the ratified convention to give effect to the reduction of indemnity, but insisted that "it should be so worded as to maintain the stipulation providing that, as security for fulfilment of provisions as to the trade marts, the Chumbi Valley is to be occupied until the marts have been opened effectively for three years." As regards the subsidiary agreement giving the Trade Agent at Gyantse the right of access to Lhasa, he decided to disallow it, as the home government regarded the agreement as unnecessary and as inconsistent with the principle on which their policy had throughout been based.[171]

Thus the Secretary of State won the battle at last. He won it with the support of Parliament. As early as July 13, 1903, Mr. Weir asked in the House of Commons whether the Government of India contemplated the dispatch of a commissioner to Tibet,[172] whereupon the Tibetan expedition seized the attention of the members of Parliament. Lord Curzon was often under fire. Lord Reay in the House of Lords assailed the Viceroy's policy as embodied in the letter dated January 8, 1903,[173] point by point. He held that the proper method of communication was with the Chinese authorities and called Curzon's phrase "constitutional fiction" an "extraordinary expression." He added: "This strikes me as an extremely impolitic assertion that a situation which our government had always recognized, which is founded on law, history and tradition should be considered a constitutional fiction—extremely impolitic when we realize what suzerainty means to us in India." He further pointed out that "far from looking upon the suzerainty as a constitutional fiction, the home government looked upon Tibet as a province of China." [174]

The Marquess of Ripon, who had been both Secretary of State for India and Viceroy of India (1880-84), called Lord Curzon's forward policy in India dangerous and unwise and told the House of Lords that the value of trade with Tibet was not much and it was unjust to attempt to advance and develop commerce by the agency of force. He was certain there was no European Power unwise enough to invade India through Tibet, over the highest mountains in the world, and maintained that the British Government should "not give an opportunity to any other Power to say that we are interfering with China or threatening the independence of any portion of her country." [175]

The Earl of Rosebery, who did "not think there is anything in the Papers which really justifies the dispatch of this expedition," sarcastically remarked that "the first hundred pages or something like that of this Blue-book are devoted entirely to the desire and ambition of the Indian Government to impose the drinking of Indian tea on a people which prefer Chinese tea." [176] He was of the opinion that "there is little or no commerce to be got out of Tibet" and he doubted that the expedition took place with the authority of the Chinese Government, as the latter had with such anguish pressed on the British Government the abandonment of the Macaulay expedition in 1885. He called the sanction of the advance of the mission to Gyantse, "the surrender of His Majesty's Government to the Viceroy," "in deference to the strong and energetic impulsion of Lord Curzon." [177]

There were no less heated debates in the House of Commons. For example, Mr. Gibson Bowles, who "did not believe that the results of the expedition would have a beneficial effect on Imperial interests and Imperial trade," told his fellow M.P.s that "Lord Curzon was a military and strategically-minded man and . . . it was to him that this Tibet expedition was due; it was his intention to take into India an unconquered border for political purposes."[178]

When the Curzon-Brodrick difference and the terms which Younghusband had imposed on the Tibetans were brought up, the Parliament showed even more indignation. In the House of Lords Earl Spencer attacked the terms by which the British Government were to occupy an important part of the country for seventy-five years, as contrary to the spirit and the letter of British assurances to the Chinese and Russian Governments. He thought that "if anybody is to blame, it is rather the Government of India, who differed from the Home Government, than Sir Francis Younghusband."[179] Simultaneously in the Lower House, Sir H. Campbell-Bannerman said that he gave the Secretary for India full credit for refusing to ratify the arrangements made at Lhasa; "but," he added, "it would have been better still if the Government had put down their foot earlier. Knowing the objective of the Indian authorities, and being strongly opposed to it, they yet suffered themselves to be goaded into proceedings which brought damage to the prestige of the country and involved the massacre of unarmed men." He thought it was not Colonel Younghusband's fault and asked the censure to be carried higher to the principal.[180] Mr. Gibson Bowles described Lord Curzon as "a very ambitious Viceroy, who, when he saw all the world annexing territory, said—'I will go one better; I will annex not territory, but the incarnate Buddha; I will have a divinity in my service. This is what I will do for my country.' " He believed that there was no doubt that it was with Lord Curzon's knowledge and acquiescence that this "defiance" of the authority of the home government by Colonel Younghusband had been carried on, and he thought that "the hard words defiance, disobedience, and disregard of authority might more properly have been applied to the Viceroy than to the able and gallant officer who conducted the expedition."[181]

With hostile criticism not confined to the opposing minority party in Parliament, Lord Curzon could have no *locus standi* from which he might defy the Secretary of State. The amendment made at the time of ratification was the only way to patch up the open breach.

The New Status Created by the Lhasa Arrangement

Now let us put aside the legal aspect and see what status was created for Tibet by the Lhasa arrangement in its amended form minus the subsidiary agreement. In reviewing the settlement arrived at in Lhasa, the Secretary of State for India explained to the Viceroy the object of British policy in his letter dated December 2, 1904. Unlike a similar letter written almost four months before in which he reiterated the importance of "considering the question, not as a local one concerning India and Tibet alone, but from a wider point of view of the relations of Great Britain to other powers, both European and Asiatic, and as involving the status of dependency of the Chinese Empire,"[182] this time he spoke of His Britannic Majesty's Government only as one "who have more immediately before them the interests of the British Empire as a whole." This shift of emphasis was probably due to the progress of the Russo-Japanese war, since by this time Japan, Britain's ally, had won some decisive battles both on land and on the sea; thus the Russian threat was being reduced.[183]

In this review the Secretary of State for India expressed his satisfaction in these words: "If the Tibetan Government had become involved in political relations with other Powers, a situation of danger might have been created on the frontier of the Indian Empire. This risk has now been removed by the conclusion of the Convention." According to his authoritative opinion, the object of the British policy was that "British influence should be recognized at Lhasa in such a manner as to exclude that of any other Power, and that Tibet should remain in that state of isolation from which till recently she has shown no intention to depart and which has hitherto caused her presence on our frontier to be a matter of indifference to us." "We have aimed," he further explained, "at affecting this result, not by establishing a resident at Lhasa, but by obtaining the consent of the Tibetan Government to a Convention by which they undertake neither to receive the Agent of any foreign Power nor to grant concessions or assignments of revenue to the subject of any foreign Power without the previous consent of the British Government."[184]

In other words, the British Government intended to make, and in fact did make, Tibet a buffer state, as a result of the armed mission. The increasingly favorable situation of the world and her own strength made Great Britain feel well disposed to leave Tibet in that state of isolation. After all, as Lord Cranmore and Browne once proudly said in the House of Lords, "Do not let us forget that if we abstain from interference in the internal affairs of Tibet, it is only on the condition that similar abstention is practised by other Powers, and that, should occasion arise, where Englishmen have been once, there they can go again."[185]

But how about the effect of this new status on Sino-Tibetan and Sino-British relations? Mr. Labouchere, a member of the British Parliament, asked the Secretary of State for India some questions which are pertinent to this study: "What is our precise position toward China in regard to Tibet; is Tibet an independent kingdom or is it a portion of the Chinese Empire; has the representative of China in Tibet full powers from his Government to enter into a treaty with us; and if so, would the treaty be valid before being ratified by the Chinese Government in Peking; or have we—assuming Tibet to be a dependency of China—obtained any assurance from the Chinese authorities that if we sign a treaty with Tibet such a treaty would be binding on China?"[186]

The answer of Mr. Brodrick was rather evasive. He said only: "For information regarding the status of Tibet, I must refer the honorable member to the Bluebook. The negotiations will be conducted jointly with the Chinese Amban and the Tibetan representatives. The Chinese Government has been kept duly apprised of the action of His Majesty's Government in Tibet, and the Chinese Amban at Lhasa expressed to Colonel Younghusband, on his arrival at Gyantse, his readiness to negotiate."

Indeed, negotiation, if there was any such thing, was conducted jointly with the Chinese Resident and the Tibetan representatives. The terms, based on telegraphic instructions, were first given and explained orally to three of the Resident's secretaries, and the written reply of the Tibetans to them was unofficially sent by the Resident to Mr. Wilton,[187] a British Consular officer in

Szechwan temporarily attached to the mission. The second reply of the Tibetans was also submitted to the Resident, who handed it to Younghusband during a visit on August 19. Later a letter agreeing to all the British terms, except that regarding indemnity, was handed to the Resident and a written assurance from the Tibetans accepting the ninth clause—the very clause that made Tibet a buffer state if not a zone of British interest—was also handed to Younghusband through the medium of the Resident.[188]

But since the Tibetans had very little say in the matter, and were not allowed to have any of their way,[189] there was practically no negotiation as the word is understood in diplomatic practice. As we have seen above, the Tibetan representatives were selected by the Resident at the request of Younghusband. It was in the presence of the Resident and at his official Residency that the final terms were dictated to the Tibetans, and the final draft of the treaty was handed to them through the Resident.

Though Lord Curzon regarded "Chinese suzerainty over Tibet as a constitutional fiction," Younghusband found it necessary to rely upon the collaboration of the Chinese Resident to effect a settlement of some sort. We find ample evidence in his dispatches pointing to that reliance. He came forward, together with the Resident, to ascertain from the Tibetans precisely what they did agree to, point by point, once it was clear that the Tibetans were trying to cause dissension between the Resident and himself.[190] He told the Resident that "nothing could be got out of these Tibetans except by pressure . . . and it would be much more satisfactory if the needful pressure could be put on by the Amban," and, in fact, "after pressure from the Amban . . . the Shappés were distinctly more subdued."[191] He showed Ti-Rimpoche, the Acting Regent, special attention, "as the Amban recognises him as principal in these negotiations."[192] He reported to his government that Ti-Rimpoche "with the Amban's consent, commenced to use the seal left by the Dalai Lama."[193] This shows the authority which the Resident still retained over the Tibetan Government even when under foreign military occupation. It is all the more significant that in his "report of the circumstances under which the Convention between Great Britain and Tibet was signed," Younghusband wrote: "In deference to the wish of the

Amban, I did not insert the words 'Regent of Tibet' after Ti-Rimpoche, as he has not yet been officially recognized as such by the Chinese Emperor." [194]

In the meeting to arrange final details and formalities regarding the signing of the Convention, Younghusband commenced by asking the Resident whose name he should enter in the Convention in the place of the Dalai Lama's name, and the latter's reply, "Ti-Rimpoche's," was adhered to by the Tibetans. As to the place to be selected for signing the Convention, Younghusband insisted on the Potala Palace. When the Tibetans murmured their objections, the Resident told them the matter was settled and did not admit of further discussion. Even to inspect the Palace for choosing the most appropriate room for the ceremony, Younghusband asked the Resident to have Chinese and Tibetan officials deputed to accompany his officers.[195] Indeed, as he wrote in his book *India and Tibet*,[196] he worked throughout with the Chinese Resident, and never directly with the Tibetans to the exclusion of the Chinese.

In the address delivered at the close of the ceremony as mentioned above, Younghusband told the Tibetans that "the British Government fully recognized the continued suzerainty of the Chinese Government." The Resident showed special pleasure when these words were translated to him. Younghusband then turned to the Resident and thanked him for the help he had given him in making the Convention.[197]

Younghusband knew how to win the collaboration of the Resident. He explained to the Tibetans in his presence that by Clause IX the British "had not the least desire to supplant China in the suzerainty of Tibet . . . and China was not included in the term 'Foreign Power,' " and later he addressed a note to the Resident confirming the exclusion of China from the term "Foreign Power" and the right of Chinese merchants to the trading marts.[198] When Ti-Rimpoche in another interview dwelt upon the impossibility of paying what he considered too heavy an indemnity and told Younghusband that the British were putting on the donkey a greater load than it could possibly carry, the latter replied that he was not asking the donkey to carry the whole load in one single journey. Ti-Rimpoche laughed and asked what would happen if the donkey died. Younghusband said, "I should ask the Amban to see that the donkey was properly treated so that there should be no fear of its dying." [199]

This could be interpreted not only as a recognition of the Resident's position and authority, but also as the imposition on him of a responsibility. Indeed it was rather the latter that Younghusband took into account. As early as August 10, he paid a visit to the Resident and "impressed upon him the responsibility which lies on the Chinese Government to make the Tibetans conclude a settlement." [200] On being told that the Resident was instructed by the Chinese Government not to sign, he addressed him a note holding China responsible for any difficulty arising in the enforcement of the Convention.[201] At Gyantse, in April, he thought of carrying the Amban with him, now that he had succeeded in carrying him to the point that served his essential, if not full, purpose.[202]

In fact, the collaboration with the Chinese Resident, which the Government of India had in mind and which Younghusband carried out, was on a larger scale than the signing of the Convention. In a letter to the Secretary of State for India, dated June 30, 1904, the Government of India expressed the "hope to be able, with the help or assent of the Chinese authorities, to establish a new Government with whom we could negotiate, and to secure the cooperation of the Chinese Amban in the appointment of a Regent." [203]

Younghusband was, of course, fully aware of the difference it would make when the Convention originally drafted for signature by him and the Dalai Lama [204] was signed by Ti-Rimpoche in the latter's place. The Dalai Lama, according to Lord Curzon, "was a *de facto* as well as *de jure* sovereign of the country." [205] Ti-Rimpoche told Younghusband that he thought the Dalai Lama ought to be present to make a settlement with the British, and Younghusband replied that he wished the Dalai Lama to affix his seal in his presence.[206] But the Dalai Lama fled not only before the arrival of Younghusband's armed "Mission" but before the arrival of Ti-Rimpoche, whom he had hastily summoned. He communicated with people in Lhasa while on his way and wrote to the National Assembly, saying that the "English are very crafty people" and warning them to be careful,[207] but never did he issue a full power or definitely authorize anyone to sign the Convention which imposed so heavy an obligation on his people and which even changed the status of his dominion. Even had he done so, it would still be a question of "incapacity arising from status." [208]

The fact that both the Chinese Resident and the Tibetan authorities sent messages to the Dalai Lama asking him to return [209] shows clearly the importance of his presence. Younghusband, at the moment of dictating his terms to the Tibetans at the Residency, still found it necessary to ask the Resident, "is there any chance of the Dalai Lama returning in time to conclude the Convention with me?," though he had previously reported to his government in these words: "People of all ranks sincerely trust he has gone for good and we have no reason to regret his departure, for a perfectly satisfactory settlement can be made without him in a manner suggested by the Amban. His departure is not regretted by Tibetans, and it would not prove prejudicial to our interests." [210]

Younghusband must have worried about the consequences of the Dalai Lama's return and feared that he might be able to upset the Convention. He reported the opinion of Tongsa Penlop of Bhutan and that of the Nepalese representative on this point; [211] but it seemed that his worry was not allayed by their consolatory opinion. Something still had to be done. He told the Resident that "the Dalai Lama should certainly either come back or abdicate; and if he remained away at this important juncture, the assumption would be that he renounced the function of government." He gladly forwarded to Peking via Gyantse a telegram which the Resident asked him to have dispatched as quickly as possible and which contained the recommendation to the Emperor to denounce the Dalai Lama. He said to the Resident that he would do this service for him and "considered he was acting with great wisdom in denouncing the Dalai Lama, for it was he who had brought all this trouble upon his country and he deserved to suffer for it." No doubt Younghusband must have been happy to hear from the Resident that the effect of his denunciation would be to reduce the Dalai Lama to an ordinary man or a common monk, and that the Panch'en Lama would be summoned to Lhasa with a view to making him head of the whole Tibetan Church.[212] Here we should be reminded of the long-standing friendship between the Government of India and the Panch'en Lamas of Tashi-lhunpo, established since George Bogle's mission in 1774, and of "the friendly relations which Colonel Younghusband was able to establish at Khamba Jong with ecclesiastical envoys from the Tashi (Panch'en) Lama of Shigatse (Tashi-lhunpo)." [213]

As a result of this telegraphic recommendation,[214] the Dalai Lama was temporarily deprived of his rank and in his place was appointed the Panch'en Lama. The writer considers that Sir Francis Younghusband should be given every benefit of the doubt and no criticism should be based on conjecture. But it is significant that when he replied to his government's enquiry as to whether there were precedents for the degradation of the Dalai Lama by the Chinese Emperor, or for the assumption of his place by the Tashi Lama, he should have included these words: "The fact that I endeavoured to induce the Dalai Lama to come in is well known to Buddhists here, and they are also aware that, after he had definitely fled the country, it was on the initiative of the Amban that he was denounced." He added: "I personally consider the denunciation a very politic step. It also has the approval of Tongsa Penlop and the Nepalese." [215] We can well imagine how deeply he was involved in the matter and the extent to which he collaborated with the Resident.

Chinese Adherence to the Lhasa Convention

After all, in spite of the impressive show put up at the Potala Palace and the "perfectly satisfactory settlement," the fact remains that neither the Chinese Resident nor the Tibetan representative had full power to enter into a treaty with Younghusband. The British Commissioner brought back with him a "Convention" signed only by a miscellaneous assortment of all the officials and ecclesiastics he could lay hands on in Lhasa. As Scott put it, "their worthless signatures and seals are all duly attached to the 'Convention' in imposing array, but they have no more binding effect than if the Archbishop of Canterbury and the Chairman of the London County Council were to sign a new treaty with

France." Scott said that the device Younghusband had adopted "would not stand examination in any impartial international tribunal."[216] It was a device to get the Chinese Amban to proclaim the temporary deposition of the Dalai Lama and then set up a temporary government of his own.

Thus the new status of Tibet as a buffer state created by the Convention was without legal foundation unless some sort of formal agreement could be reached to make it binding on China, whose continued suzerainty over Tibet the British declared they fully recognized. In short, the Lhasa arrangement was made by the agency of force. The only validity that the Convention had was derived from the continued exercise of force. The queer and undefined status created was well illustrated by two items at the end of the Blue Book, Cd. 2370, which could not be more fittingly concluded by anything else. The one was a letter addressed by the Nepalese Prime Minister to the four Kazis (bKa'-blons) at Lhasa which was "written in the hope that it may assist in the due observance of the terms of the treaty recently signed between the British Government and Tibet, and the spirit and intention which has prompted it," and which contained the following remarkable passage:

> . . . you must not forget that the very existence of Tibet as a separate nation depends upon your religiously carrying out the terms of the treaty, and scrupulously avoiding any occasion of friction with the British Power.[217]

The other was a notice posted by the Chinese Resident in Lhasa denouncing the Dalai Lama while the British armed mission was still in the city (dated September 10, 1904, three days after the signing of the so-called convention or treaty). In the notice the Resident started by saying, "For more than 200 years Tibet has been a feudatory of China," and ended with these words:

> In future, Tibet being a feudatory of China, the Dalai Lama will be responsible for the yellow-cap faith and monks, and will only be concerned slightly in official matters, while the Amban will conduct all Tibetan affairs with the Tibetan officials and important matters will be referred to the Emperor.[218]

Here we see that the Chinese Government, maintaining its traditional position, did not feel itself bound in the least by the newly created status of Tibet. China rightfully maintained that she was not included in the term "Foreign Power" as provided in the Clause IX of the Convention. As we have already seen, she made a great effort afterwards to reassert her full sovereignty in Tibet.

The British Government saw clearly the necessity of Chinese adherence to the Convention. On August 17, Younghusband called on the Resident and handed him a draft of the Proposed Adhesion Agreement intended to register Chinese sanction of the Convention without modifying any of its terms.[219] Two days later he reported that the Resident raised no objection to the form of it. He explained to the Tibetans on August 31 that "the Chinese suzerainty was *fully* recognized in the Proposed Adhesion Agreement."[220] But, as mentioned above, the Wai-wu-pu telegraphed to the Resident instructing him not to sign it.[221] T'ang Shao-i (Tong Shao-yi) was then appointed to proceed to Tibet to investigate and conduct affairs.[222] Since the British "Mission" had left Lhasa without an Adhesion Agreement, and the weak Peking Government could not resist the pressure of the British, T'ang was then reappointed Minister to the Court of St. James and instructed to proceed to Calcutta instead, in order to negotiate with the Government of India. The Viceroy was named to conduct the negotiations on behalf of the British Government.[223]

T'ang arrived at Calcutta in February, 1905, and shortly afterward negotiations began.[224] The British delegate at first insisted on the acceptance by China of the proposed Adhesion Agreement which Younghusband had handed to the Chinese Resident at Lhasa, while T'ang insisted on redrafting Clause IX of the Lhasa Convention in order to clarify the British position in regard to Tibet and to safeguard Chinese sovereignty.

It was on the question of Chinese sovereignty or suzerainty over Tibet that the issue centered. T'ang, citing as evidence the investiture of the Dalai and Panch'en Lamas, the appointment of bKa'-blons and local Tibetan officials by the Chinese Court, and the supervision of the native troops by the Imperial Resident, maintained that Chinese sovereignty in Tibet should be recognized. Facing British opposition to the mention of sovereignty, he later proposed the insertion in Clause I of the recognition by the British of the original and the existing rights enjoyed by the

Chinese Government in Tibet and the amendment of Clause IX to the effect that the Chinese Government should be the sole intermediary in all communications between India and Tibet.[225] But the British Government could agree only to the recognition of Chinese suzerainty in Tibet and would "abate nothing to their right to enforce the fulfilment of the terms of the Lhasa Convention by such means as may be found convenient," although, by seeking Chinese adherence, they intended to secure Chinese help in the execution of the Convention and wanted to be relieved of the pain of enforcing it alone.[226]

Being unable to break the ensuing deadlock, T'ang asked leave to return home. In September, his request was granted and his secretary Chang Ying-tang was appointed to go on with the negotiations.[227]

Then the Chinese Government communicated to Sir Ernest Satow, the British Minister at Peking, "an Imperial Decree commanding that the indemnity in consequence of the British military expedition shall be paid by the Chinese Government on behalf of Tibet." This move, according to the British Minister, was "intended to force the hand of the Indian Government and to induce them to accept an arrangement which the Chinese Government could afterwards quote as a precedent in other matters." [228]

The British Government maintained that the indemnity was required of the Tibetans, partly as a punitive measure and partly in order that by the annual payment of the necessary installments they should formally recognize the binding nature of the obligations entered into by them towards the British Government. Should Tibet be released from such a burden, that fundamental purpose would be lost. At the same time, they believed that the Chinese Government made such a move "with the object of re-establishing their theoretical right to supremacy over the Tibetan Government," as well as from the fear that British troops would remain in the strategical Chumbi Valley for a long time in case of default of payment by the Tibetans. They therefore replied that "unless China adheres to the Convention in the form in which it is now presented," the proposed arrangement of payment on behalf of Tibet could not be entertained. For, in the eyes of the British Foreign Office, acceptance would be tantamount to admitting the intervention of China in relieving Tibet from this portion of her obligations while avoiding all responsibility for any other portion of the Convention.[229]

Since the British delegate had not only maintained his original position, but even pressed Chang either to accept the proposition or drop it altogether, the negotiations made no progress. At last, Chang, at the breakup of the meeting, announced that the reason for the suspension was the uncompromising attitude of the British delegate.[230]

Negotiations were, however, soon to be resumed between Sir Ernest Satow and T'ang at Peking. The change of government in London with the Liberals in power gave them a better prospect of success. In the meantime, the first installment of the indemnity was due and the Government of India notified the Tibetans that they desired it to be paid on January 1 at Gyantse. The Viceroy was of the opinion that annual payment by Tibetans in Tibet, even though China should provide the money, would be preferable, from the point of view of the local political effect, to payment of a lump sum by China direct.[231] Ti-Rimpoche in reply stated that he learned from the Resident that the question of payment of the indemnity was to be the subject of discussion with China and a month later the British were informed by the Lhasa authorities that under orders from the Emperor of China, Sechung Shappé was being deputed to Calcutta where he was to receive the amount from Chang and pay the Government of India there.[232]

The Viceroy took the nonpayment resulting from China's action as placing the British in an advantageous position in further negotiations that might be undertaken with the Chinese Government, and the British Foreign Secretary thought that a refusal to accept payment was likely to make the Chinese Government adhere to the Lhasa Convention.[233] The Government of India believed that the suggestion that the whole indemnity should be paid in three installments instead of twenty-five annual installments of one lakh each was a Chinese device having for its object the weakening of the British position in Tibet, but the Secretary of State for India, Mr. Morley, "while recognizing that certain advantages have been supposed by some to arise from the political point of view in maintaining [the British] hold over the Tibetans for the full period of twenty-five years," was of the opinion that such advantages would be altogether outweighed by the relief from the necessity of enforcing a direct annual tribute for so long a period.[234]

So when the Adhesion Agreement was signed in Peking on April 27, 1906, the British Government immediately consented not only to let China pay the whole indemnity for Tibet but also to pay it in three installments.[235] And later when the last installment was paid by China in January, 1908, the evacuation of the Chumbi Valley was effectively carried out on February 8.[236] From the point of view of our subject, it is interesting to note that in paying the third installment, the Chinese Government wanted the check to be handed over by Chang instead of by the Tibetan Shappé, and the British Government saw in it "firm determination that Chinese sovereignty over Tibet, to the exclusion of all local autonomy, shall be indicated and that direct communication of all kinds between [British] officials and Tibetans shall be prevented." It was only after a representation made by the British Minister under instruction from his government to warn the Wai-wu-pu of "the serious consequences" and effectual delay of the transfer of authority in the Chumbi Valley, that the Chinese Government agreed to having its check delivered by the Shappé on January 27.[237]

As to the terms of the Adhesion Agreement, here is the official explanation on the part of the British Government given in reply to questions put both in the House of Lords and in the House of Commons on May 1 and 2, 1906, respectively:

It secures the adhesion of China to the Convention established with Tibet in 1904. It does not alter the arrangements arrived at under the Convention of Tibet as confirmed by the Government of India. It contains an engagement on our part not to encroach on Tibetan territory nor to interfere in the government of Tibet, the Government of China undertaking on their part not to allow any foreign State to interfere in the government or internal administration of Tibet. It also states that we do not seek for ourselves any of the concessions mentioned in Article IX of the Convention of Tibet which were denied by that Article to any other State or to the subjects of any other State. It does not alter the amount of the Tibetan indemnity in any way.[238]

From the above, we have seen that the new status of Tibet as a buffer state was now more clearly defined. The Adhesion Agreement gave sanction to the Lhasa Convention and made China share with Great Britain the burden of securing the due fulfillment of its terms. In other words, the fatherless child born of the rendezvous between Younghusband and a miscellaneous assortment of all the officials and ecclesiastics he could lay hands on in Lhasa was hereby legitimized.

Let us see then what consolation China could derive from the new agreement. Whether the British Government would still regard Tibet as China's province[239] or only recognize China as the suzerain of Tibet, the fact that they sent a military expedition to Lhasa without consulting China beforehand had already imperiled her position, whatever it may have been.

A year after the signing of the Lhasa Convention, and while the Adhesion negotiation was going on, the Government of India asked the Panch'en Lama, whose office had been closely associated with that of the Viceroy since the days of Warren Hastings, and who was now acting as the spiritual head of the whole of Tibet, to make a journey with the "primary object . . . to enable him to be present in Calcutta during the visit of the Prince of Wales." According to the explanation of the Viceroy to the Secretary of State, the "invitation to the Lama was complimentary."[240] But according to the letters of the Lama to the Resident, he was forced by the British Trade Agent at Gyantse, Captain O'Connor, to take the journey in spite of his plea that he dared not leave his country without the sanction of the Chinese Emperor.[241] The Chinese Government was greatly alarmed, fearing that this journey might further imperil its position. Being unable to stop the British-escorted Lama on the way, it addressed a semi-official note to the British Minister at Peking asking him to inform the Indian Government that it "will refuse to recognize any agreement which the Lama may make should he, on his visit to India, discuss any business matter."[242] The whole incident lays bare the helplessness of the Chinese Government.

Now, by signing the Adhesion Agreement, China's imperiled

position was saved. The British Government formally acknowledged China's rights in Tibet. China's payment of the indemnity for the Tibetans not only reestablished her right to supremacy over the Tibetan Government, but also created renewed friendly feelings among the Tibetan people. With Russia definitely excluded and the British tied to a self-denying clause, the way was paved for her to consolidate her power in Tibet. In fact, as already described, for a time she resumed full sovereignty and ruled Tibet through the Lhasa Government which was brought under her control during the absence of the Dalai Lama.

To consolidate her position further, China took steps to forbid direct communications between the British and the Tibetans in commercial transactions at trade marts and appointed Chinese instead of Tibetans as diplomatic and commercial representatives at these trade marts. Chang Ying-tang, who was then in Lhasa to make a general investigation and undertake local reforms, took the view "that virtual recognition of Chinese sovereignty over Tibet was involved in the signature of the Adhesion Agreement, and that 'Chinese authorities in Tibet' should consequently be the interpretation placed on the phrase 'Tibetan Government' wherever the latter occurs in the Lhasa Convention." [243]

There was much British opposition to China's assertive policy in Tibet and numerous representations were made to the Chinese Government against what the British considered a change of the status quo in Tibet. But after all, as the British Secretary of State for India admitted in a letter to the Foreign Office, "the principle has been recognized that provided nothing is done either by the Tibetan or Chinese authorities to impair those privileges secured to Great Britain by the Lhasa Convention of 1904 and the Peking Convention of 1906, the British Government are precluded by the terms of the Convention from interfering, even if they had the desire to do so, with Chinese action in Tibet." [244]

Trade Regulations Signed by Anglo-Chinese Plenipotentiaries and the Tibetan Delegate

Considerable friction had developed between the Chinese officials on the Tibetan frontier and the British authorities regarding the questions of direct dealings between British and Tibetan officers and merchants, the appointment of Tibetan officials to trade marts, and the interpreting of previous treaties.[245] In consequence, both Great Britain and China deemed it necessary to negotiate new trade regulations to replace those of 1893, provision for which had been made in Article III of the Lhasa Convention.

First of all, the question of Tibetan representation called for a settlement. The British Government notified the Wai-wu-pu that according to Article III of the Lhasa Convention, the Tibetan Government undertook to appoint fully authorized delegates to negotiate with the British Representatives concerning the amendment of the Regulations of 1893.[246] Peking agreed that Tibet should depute a Tibetan, but wished that the action of the Tibetan Representative be subject to the approval of the Chinese delegate.[247] This point was finally won, and the Preamble clearly laid down that "the high authorities of Tibet [not the Tibetan Government] have named as their fully authorized Representative, to act under the directions of Chang Ta-jen and take part in the regulations, the Tsarong Shappé, Wang Chuk Gyalpo."[248]

In an official dispatch from the Under-Secretary of State, India Office, to the Under-Secretary of State, Foreign Office,[249] we find these words: "A comparison of the British and Chinese drafts of the proposed Regulations show that the points at real issue in the Regulations are not only those of political status involved in the wording of the Preamble, but practical commercial questions of great complexity and inherent difficulty, such as that, for instance, to which the Government of India draws special attention, of the terms under which Indian tea is to be admitted into Tibet."

After having gone through "difficult and troublesome negotiations," the agreement was signed on April 20, 1908, at Calcutta. Ratifications by the Chinese and British Governments were exchanged on October 14 of the same year.[250] The Regulations stipulated that the administration of trade marts should remain with the Tibetan officers, under the Chinese officers' supervision and directions. Direct relations between local Tibetan officers and the British trade agents were established. Even in cases of disagreement between them, China was not to decide. Her Resident was to be notified, but the settlement was to be effected by the Government of India and the Tibetan high authorities at

Lhasa. Only when questions could not be decided by agreement between the high Tibetan and Indian authorities was China invited to arrange with Great Britain for a settlement (Article III).

In the event of disputes arising at the marts between British subjects and persons of Chinese and Tibetan nationality, they were to be adjudicated by a personal conference between the British trade agent at the nearest mart and the Chinese and Tibetan authorities of the Judicial Court at the mart. Where there was a divergence of views, the law of the defendant's country should prevail. In any such mixed cases the officer or officers of the defendant's nationality should preside at the trial, the officer or officers of the plaintiff's merely atending to watch its course. All questions regarding rights, whether of property or person, arising between British subjects were to be subject to the jurisdiction of the British authorities. British subjects who committed any crime at the marts, or on the routes to the marts, would be handed over by the local authorities to the British trade agent at the mart nearest to the scene of offence, to be tried and punished according to the laws of India (Article IV).

Great Britain agreed to relinquish her rights of extraterritoriality only when the Tibetan authorities, in obedience to the instructions of the Peking Government, had demonstrated a strong desire to reform their judicial system and to bring it into accord with that of Western nations, and to relinquish them only when "such rights are relinquished in China, and when she is satisfied that the state of the Tibetan laws and the arrangements for their administration and other considerations warrant her in so doing" (Article V). The Regulations in general and this article in particular manifested the British genius for safeguarding their self-interest.

There are some further provisions which have a bearing on the status of Tibet. Great Britain announced her readiness "to consider the transfer to China of the telegraph lines from the Indian frontier to Gyantse when the telegraph lines from China reach that mart, and in the meantime Chinese and Tibetan messages will be duly received and transmitted by the line constructed by the Government of India" (Article VI). She would also consider the abolition of her trade agents' couriers "when efficient arrangements have been made by China in Tibet for a postal service" (Article VIII). She undertook to withdraw the trade agents' guards at the marts and to station no troops in Tibet, so as to remove all cause for suspicion and disturbance among the inhabitants, when China had fulfilled her obligation to arrange effective police measures at the marts and along the routes to the marts (Article XII). "British officers and subjects, as well as goods, proceeding to the trade marts must adhere to the trade routes from the frontier of India. They shall not, without permission, proceed beyond the marts, or to Gartok from Yatung and Gyantse, or from Gartok to Yatung and Gyantse, by any route through the interior of Tibet; but natives of the Indian frontier who have already by usuage traded and resided in Tibet elsewhere than at the marts shall be at liberty to continue their trade in accordance with the existing practice, but when so trading or residing they shall remain, as heretofore, amenable to the local jurisdiction" (Article IX).

In spite of long and strenuous efforts made by both parties, certain topics were not settled and had to be reserved for subsequent consideration. They were questions relating to extradition, the appointment of Chinese trade agents with consular privileges at Kalimpong near the Sikkim and Indian frontier, across which half the entire trade between Tibet and India passes,[251] the levy of custom duties, and the importation of Indian tea to Tibet,[252] to which, as mentioned above, the Government of India drew special attention.

The main difficulties that prevented their settlement arose from the lack of any clearly defined status for Tibet in her relations with Great Britain and China. Had the British, or rather the Indian Government, still regarded Tibet as a province of China, as the Secretary of State for India had once maintained,[253] or had they looked upon Tibet as an independent country, as Lord Curzon once had a mind to do, and refrained from making her virtually their protectorate, these questions would have been easily settled in one way or another.

As an illustration of the confusion, the question of importing Indian tea into Tibet may be considered. It involved depriving the Chinese Government of an annual income of more than one hundred thousand taels of tea duty collected at Tach'ienlu alone, if the China tea market in Tibet were taken over by Indian tea. The transport cost of Indian tea by rail up to the frontier would be far less than that of China tea, more than 90 percent of the latter's market price in Tibet being usually paid for transport cost. It also involved the deprivation of a huge revenue to the Tibetan Treasury which annually advanced to the Tibetan and the Chinese tea merchants great quantities of local currency at a very high interest rate. Further there was the existence of several tens of thousands of Tibetan coolies who made their living on the transportation of China tea from the Szechwan Province.[254] This conflict of interest could have been solved had it not been further complicated by the lack of any clearly defined status for Tibet. The Indian Government on the one hand was opposed to the conversion of the trade marts in Tibet into the same type of treaty port as then existed in China Proper, "whereby," in their opinion, "objects of their policy in Tibet would be entirely defeated."[255] But on the other hand, they argued that Yatung, also a trade mart, should be considered a treaty port of China, where Indian tea ought to be subject to 5 percent (ad valorem) duty only.[256]

Tibet's Buffer State Status Confirmed by the Anglo-Russian Convention

Externally, Tibet's status as a buffer state could not be secured unless there were a written agreement to bind Russia to the recognition of such a status. The Adhesion Agreement signed between Great Britain and China in 1906 made the Tibetan status as a buffer state more clearly defined, but not more secure, as China Proper itself was subject to partition into zones of influence and her adherence did not change the international picture in the least. Indeed, Mr. Brodrick, the Secretary of State for India, told the members of the House of Commons: "The negotiations have to take place with the Suzerain Power."[257] But, in fact, China by then, had been written off as a Power.

As he had done on previous occasions, Lord Curzon, in defending his forward policy, conjured up the old bugbear of Russian intrigue, though he was aware that "the Russian border nowhere even touches that of Tibet and that the nearest point of Russian territory is considerably more than a thousand miles short of the Tibetan Capital."[258] Besides, as pointed out by the Marquess of Ripon in the House of Lords, there was no European power or any power in its senses, silly enough to invade India through Tibet, over the snow-clad "roof of the world."[259]

The much-talked-of visits of Dorjieff,[260] the tutor of the Dalai Lama, to Russia and his audience with the Tzar were explained by the Russian Foreign Minister to the British Ambassador as a religious mission "with the object of making money collections for his Order from the numerous Buddhists in the Russian Empire," having no political or diplomatic object or character, and the British Government received this assurance with satisfaction.[261] Further, the Russian Ambassador, Count Benckendorf, officially assured the Marquess of Lansdowne, the British Foreign Secretary, that "there was no Convention about Tibet, either with Tibet itself or with China, or with anyone else, nor had the Russian Government any Agents in that country, or any intention of sending Agents or Missions there." Again the British Government accepted with confidence Russia's official assurance and regarded the satisfactory nature of these pledges as having "modified the apprehensions that had been felt as to the establishment at Lhasa of foreign influences incompatible with our interests" (the words of the Secretary of State for India).[262] Yet, despite all this, as a member of the British Parliament said in the House of Commons, "the whole Blue-book [he referred to Cd. 1920] showed that a fear of Russia was at the bottom of the business,"[263] and this fear did not abate notwithstanding the repeated assurance given by the Russian Foreign Minister, Count Lamsdorff, in June, 1904.[264]

The reason for this persistent fear of Russia can be best explained by the statement of A. J. Balfour, the British Prime Minister and First Lord of the Treasury, made in the House of Commons:[265]

> I admit everything that has been said as to the impossibility of invading India by way of Tibet. . . . But that does not alter the fact that though no army is likely to penetrate our northern frontier from Tibet, it would be a serious misfortune to the Indian Government and a danger to our northern frontier, should Tibet fall under any European influence other than our own.

There seems to be no reason to doubt the remark made by Oscar Crosby, who in 1903 traveled in Tibet and Turkestan, that British state dispatches did make vague, one-sided statements to the effect that some Tibetans relied upon "another power" for protection, and made these accusations serve as the excuse for their attack upon Tibet and for executing the extremist policy of empire-stretching.[266] Nevertheless, from a Russian source we find evidence that the British fear was not altogether unfounded. For example, on March 1, 1903, General Kuropatkin, Russian Minister of War, noted in his diary: [267]

> I told Witte that our Tsar has grandiose plans in his head: to capture Manchuria for Russia and to annex Korea. He is dreaming also of bringing Tibet under his dominion.

Besides, the Russians never consented to letting the British have a free hand in Tibet. When they gave the above-mentioned clear-cut pledges to Great Britain, they made it plain that though they "had no designs whatever on Tibet, they could not remain indifferent if the status quo were seriously disturbed, in which case it might be necessary for them to safeguard their interests in Asia, though even then the measures they might be compelled to take would be elsewhere, as Tibet was in any contingency outside the scope of their policy ['ne viserait le Thibet en aucun cas'], and they had no desire to interfere in its affairs. They were interested in the integrity of the Chinese Empire, of which they regarded Tibet as a part." [268] From this, it may be seen that Great Britain and Russia did not entirely see eye to eye, and a pact was needed to reconcile their interests.

The difficulties in the way of a rapprochement between Great Britain and Russia, especially in the light of their greater conflict of interests elsewhere in the world, were serious enough to make it seem impossible. Fortunately for their chances of reaching an agreement, the way was paved by the Anglo-French *Entente Cordiale* of 1904, which "had removed England's principal fear of Russia as 'the ally of France' and cleared the way for England to deal with her as 'the invader of India.'" [269] The success of the British expedition in Tibet must have convinced Russian leaders that they were not in a position to compete with the British there, owing to the immense geographical barriers. Moreover, Russia's position in the world had so changed since her disastrous defeat in the war with Japan that she could take no effective part in the critical events of the following years. Weakened by war and torn by increasing acts of terrorism, she was no longer a serious threat to the vital interests of the British Empire.[270]

There were two further facts that rendered the accomplishment of an Anglo-Russian rapprochement somewhat easier. One was the granting of a constitution to Russia by the Tzar and the opening of the First Duma (March 5, 1907), despite its subsequent suspension. This fact made it easier for a Liberal Government, which held office in Great Britain after 1906, to hold out the hand of friendship. The second fact was the loss of English influence at Constantinople and the gravitation of the Porte toward Germany—a fact that had been evident in the confidential reports of the British agents at Constantinople since about the year 1890.[271] Above all, it was the serious German threat, especially her growing navy, that made it possible for the traditional rivals to form a common front, although in the beginning the German Government did regard the Anglo-Russian rapprochement with benevolence and accepted Sir Edward Grey's explanation that they were not making a ring against Germany.[272]

Sir Charles Hardinge succeeded in laying the foundations for the Anglo-Russian negotiations, but he was soon appointed Permanent Under-Secretary at the Foreign Office. Sir Arthur Nicholson succeeded him as the British Ambassador to St. Petersburg. On June 6, 1906, only nine days after his arrival at the Russian capital, and the day after the presentation of his letters of credence, he opened formal negotiations. He proposed to M. Isvolsky, the Russian Foreign Minister, that the scope of the negotiations should be restricted to a matter-of-fact treatment of the respective British and Russian interests in certain specific regions and that the discussion should begin with the question least likely to lead to controversy. Consequently, the question of Tibet received attention first.[273]

The Tibetan problem in itself was simple enough. The British wished to keep Tibet as a buffer state immune from penetration by either power, and they were prepared to abandon the position implied in the Younghusband Convention if Russia would agree to regard Tibet as a zone forbidden to her agents and her infiltration. But Nicolson was instructed to obtain also a full recognition of the British predominant position and an engagement on the part of Russia to abstain from any interference, direct or indirect, in the affairs of Tibet.[274]

In the first instance, Isvolsky seemed to be troubled by the British demand for special interests in Tibet. In the course of negotiations three main difficulties arose. The Russians were unwilling to accept the British formula by which the British claimed a predominant position in regard to the external affairs of Tibet. They were unwilling also to renounce the right of sending Buddhist pilgrims and scientific missions to Lhasa. And they objected to the British occupation of the Chumbi Valley. These difficulties were met in a conciliatory spirit and the reluctant compromise was embodied in a Convention which is a masterpiece of drafting.[275]

The Tibetan negotiations proved the simplest of the three subjects of discussion, the other two being related to Afghanistan and Persia. By January 15, 1907, they reached a stage where only a few final touches were required. The whole Convention was signed at the Russian Foreign Office on August 31.[276] In conducting these negotiations the British may have faced more difficulty from their own Government of India than from the Russians. In a letter from the British Foreign Minister, Sir Edward Grey (later Viscount Grey of Fallodon), to the Prime Minister, announcing the conclusion of the Agreement, we find these words:

> But without Morley we should have made no progress at all, for the Government of India would have blocked every point and Morley has removed mountains in the path of the negotiations.[277]

In the preamble of the Convention, both the suzerain rights of China in Tibet and the special interests of Great Britain in the maintenance of the status quo in the external relations of Tibet, by reason of her geographical position, were recognized. Both parties pledged themselves to respect the territorial integrity of Tibet and to abstain from all interference in its internal administration. They engaged not to enter into negotiations with Tibet except through the intermediary of the Chinese Government. Direct relations between the British Commercial Agent and the

Tibetan authorities were, however, not subject to the provision. The British as well as the Russian Government undertook not to send a Representative to Lhasa. Though the Buddhist subjects of the two contracting countries might enter into direct relations on strictly religious matters with the Dalai Lama, neither government was to allow those relations to infringe on the stipulations of the Convention. They also undertook not to seek or obtain, whether for themselves or their subjects, any concession for railways, roads, telegraphs, and mines, or other rights in Tibet. Nor should any part of the revenues of Tibet be pledged or assigned to them or to any of their subjects.

In an annex Great Britain reaffirmed her declaration as to the evacuation of her forces from the Chumbi Valley. In an exchange of notes both parties expressed their desire that for a period of three years no scientific mission should be allowed to enter Tibet, unless by previous agreement, and promised to consult each other at the expiration of the term of three years. Curiously enough, they agreed to approach the Chinese Government with a view to inducing them to accept a similar obligation for a corresponding period,[278] yet the latter, not being a party to the Convention, were not consulted at all in the course of the negotiation whose object was to conclude a Convention applicable to a part of China's territory—Tibet.

The Convention was not published till September, 1907. It was favorably received by the Russian press, which lauded its equitable character and noted that the withdrawal of Russian political influence in Tibet did not prejudice Russian interests.[279] In Great Britain a full blast of criticism did not burst until February, 1908. It was on February 6 that Lord Curzon launched a full-dress attack upon the whole Convention in the House of Lords. He called it the most far-reaching and most important treaty that had been concluded by the British Government during the past fifty years. But he held it to be unequal and unfair and named the Tibetan Convention an absolute surrender.[280] Similar strictures were made in the House of Commons ten days later.[281] The Convention was, however, ratified and it came into force.

According to Lord Grey, what Great Britain gained by the Convention was real, what Russia gained was apparent; [282] and in fact the British gave up what was of little or no practical value to them. In defending the Convention he wrote:

Our interests were so important and in such intimate contact in Asia that, without an understanding, there was bound to be friction increasing to the point of danger—a friction that was an increasing cause of weakness and insecurity to the position of the British Empire. . . . The cardinal object in these negotiations was to secure ourselves forever, as far as a treaty could secure us, from further Russian advances in the direction of the Indian frontier. Russia was to cease threatening and annoying British interests concerned with India. This had been a formidable diplomatic weapon in her hands. She was now, once and for all, to give it up. The gain to us was great. We were freed from an anxiety that had often preoccupied British Governments; a frequent source of friction and a possible cause of war was removed.[283]

The Anglo-Russian Convention's Effect on British-Russian Mutual Dealings and Respective Conduct

The Tibetan part of the Convention was faithfully observed by Russia.[284] Thus the status of Tibet as a buffer state was made secure both by letter and deed. In the following years Great Britain, being freed from the anxiety caused by Russia, was worried over a possible change of status quo caused by Chinese assertive measures in Tibet.[285] The Russians did not exploit this delicate situation in Tibet to their advantage. We find, instead, concerted action by Russia and Great Britain on several occasions.

In January of 1908, prior to his arrival at Peking, the Dalai Lama sent a Tibetan official with a complimentary letter to see the British Minister, Sir John Jordan, and to pay visits to the Russian and other legations.[286] He realized the weakness of the Chinese position and was eager to get some foreign support to facilitate his return to the Potala. The American Minister, W. W. Rockhill, went to see him at Wu-T'ai-Shan, a Buddhist center in Shansi Province, and passed a week with him.[287] So, too, did Colonel Mannerheim, later the hero of Finland, who was undertaking an 8,500-mile expedition across the whole continent of Asia at the invitation of the Russian Chief of Staff.[288] In the Japanese Foreign Office Archives, made available to the Library of Congress by the Occupation Authorities, the writer found a document showing that Sonyu Otani, Japanese Colonial Minister, also went to Shansi to see the Dalai Lama, and his secret visit led to what the Japanese called "Buddhistic Cooperation."[289] In November the Dalai Lama, then in Peking waiting to be received in audience by the Dowager-Empress, sent an emissary to pay visits to the British and Russian, as well as the United States, French, and German, legations. The Russian Minister, M. Korostovetz, thereupon consulted his British colleague as to what course to adopt. He expressed his desire for common action, to which the British Minister readily agreed.[290]

In March, 1909, Dorjieff went to Russia via Peking and once more had an audience with the Tzar. When the British Ambassador, Sir Arthur Nicolson, mentioned this to Russian Foreign Minister Isvolsky, the latter at once explained that the visit was for the purpose of soliciting His Majesty's sanction to the erection of a Buddhist temple in St. Petersburg, as there were a considerable number of Buddhist residents in the capital, and that nothing political was involved. The British Ambassador replied that he had no suspicions of any kind and that he only mentioned the audience of Dorjieff as an interesting incident.[291]

Further evidence of Anglo-Russian collaboration is shown in a telegram sent from the British Foreign Minister to Sir Arthur Nicolson on February 28, 1910. The latter was told that a copy of a memorandum explaining the state of affairs in Tibet, and the representations made at Peking by the British Minister, had been communicated to the Russian Ambassador in London. In the same telegram Nicolson was instructed to inform the Russian Foreign Minister of the contents of the reply of the Chinese Foreign Ministry which was being sent by dispatch.[292]

In the following two cases we see the effect of the binding force of the Convention not only on the mutual dealings of Great Britain and Russia but also on their respective conduct. We can well imagine what change might have been brought to the status of Tibet but for the Convention.

In December of 1910, greatly disturbed by a preliminary agreement signed by an American group of financiers undertaking a loan to China for $50,000,000 gold which would include a projected "Manchurian loan of 20,000,000 taels," the Russian Ministerial Council held an extraordinary meeting to discuss whether the moment was favorable for going to war with China in order to take possession of Manchuria in agreement with Japan.[293] Though the eventual annexation of northern Manchuria was admitted by all present to be "an imperative necessity," it was decided that considering the probable opposition of the United States and England, pressure rather than a war of annexation should be the policy for the time being. Eight days after the meeting Sazonoff wrote to the Russian Ambassador in London informing him of the plan for "putting pressure upon China in order to place China under obligation to leave the status quo in Mongolia unaltered and to take no military measures there," and asking his opinion about the question: "Can we rely in general, and under what conditions, on English support, should the plan . . . really be carried into effect?" In the dispatch Sazonoff added that the Russian Government would be disposed to withdraw their earlier objections to the British Government's sending "scientific expeditions" to Tibet,[294] in accordance with the notes exchanged at the time of signing the 1907 Convention.

In February of 1910, as mentioned in the preceding chapter, the Dalai Lama fled his country with pursuing Chinese at his heels. Before his departure, he sent officials to Calcutta to represent to the Viceroy his case in the trouble with the Chinese authorities. These Tibetan officials spoke freely at an interview with the Secretary of the Foreign Department concerning their apprehension of the Chinese and said that they looked for assistance to the British.[295] When the Dalai Lama passed through Yatung, he left with the British Trade Agent a report to be forwarded to the Viceroy in which he wrote: "I now look to you for protection, and I trust that the relations between the British Government and Tibet will be those of a father to his children."[296]

During a private interview with Lord Minto, the Viceroy, on March 14, the Lama appealed to the British authorities to restore Tibet's right of dealing direct with the British and to rid Tibet of Chinese troops as well as Chinese influence. He gave an account of his relations with Dorjieff, who, he said, was a purely spiritual adviser.[297] His ministers in Sikkim asked the British political officer that British officers with soldiers might be sent to Lhasa, to inquire into and discuss with the Chinese the current condition of affairs. They also proposed an alliance between India and Tibet under which each party would help the other on the same terms, as in an arrangement which they said existed between the Governments of India and Nepal.[298]

Facing such tempting requests made by the Tibetan refugees, the British Government might have exploited the situation to their own advantage. But they did not. According to the report of Count Benckendorff, the Russian Ambassador in London, to the Acting Foreign Minister in St. Petersburg, the British considered the Dalai Lama useless to serve their purpose, as he was a man lacking courage and energy and had very little influence over the Buddhist subjects of the British Empire. They also doubted his popularity at home.[299] No doubt, the Liberal Government in London must have considered this Tibetan appeal and the Dalai Lama's request to come to London from the wider point of view of Great Britain's relation to other powers and the world situation as a whole. But the official explanation to the Tibetan representation from the very beginning was that "treaty obligations with China and Russia preclude the British Government from interference in Tibet's internal administration."[300]

At the time when the Dalai Lama first approached the Indian Government before his departure from Lhasa, he already entertained the hope that both Great Britain and Russia would interfere in his dispute with the Chinese authorities. When, later, he was told that the British Government was not in a position to do so and that his proposed visit to London had met with a cold response, he wrote to the Russian Foreign Office expressing his wish to visit St. Petersburg by way of London and requesting the Russian Government either by concerted action with Great Britain or alone to urge China to restore his rights. If that could not be done, he added, he would like to ask that the dispute be submitted to an International Tribunal.[301]

Count Benckendorff reported to the Russian Acting Foreign Minister that he was fully convinced that the Indian Government had already been aware of the authentic and full contents of the letter and even knew the intermediary who had transmitted it. He suggested that the Russian Government should adopt a similar attitude toward the Dalai Lama and respond with the same explanation as the British did, that is, the Convention put them under an obligation that precluded all interference in Tibet's internal administration. As a gesture to show sympathetic understanding and friendly consideration, he further proposed to communicate the substance of the Dalai Lama's letter and the Russian reply to the British Government, as the Lama was taking asylum in British territory and the matter related to the internal affairs of Tibet.[302] In another dispatch the Russian Ambassador again urged the maintenance of solidarity with Great Britain in Asia, in face of the menace of German expansion, and warned against the effect of raising questions, less directly important to Russia, like that of Tibet.[303]

Of course, Anglo-Russian understanding concerning Tibet was not free from suspicion. In January, 1912, the Russian Consul-General at Calcutta was instructed to deliver a letter from the Tzar to the Dalai Lama. He approached the Indian Government to try to arrange for an interview. The latter told him that the Lama had already left India; but he learned from other sources that the Lama was still at Darjeeling. He went there secretly and the British, being greatly disturbed, sent a political officer to follow him. At last an interview was arranged, with this British officer acting as interpreter. The letter from the Tzar was only complimentary in character and the Russian Consul-General avoided anything political in his talk with the Lama.[304] Nevertheless, the Tzar's personal letter delivered in such a manner, at a moment when the situation in Tibet was undergoing a fundamental change as a result of the Chinese Revolution, must have had its significance.

But on the whole, Anglo-Russian collaboration in regard to Tibet was passably maintained. When the Dalai Lama was about to return to Tibet, the British Government kept the Russian Government informed of the date of his proposed departure and also of the following message of advice and farewell which the Government of India had been authorized to communicate to him:

> The Government of India wish the Dalai Lama a safe and prosperous journey, and hope that he has found his stay in India comfortable. The desire of the Government is to see the internal autonomy of Tibet under Chinese suzerainty maintained without Chinese inter-

ference so long as Treaty obligations are duly performed and cordial relations preserved between Tibet and India. They look to the Dalai Lama to do his best to secure the objects. The first essential is that there should be a cessation of internal discord and a restoration of order.[305]

The above message can be interpreted on the one hand as a pronouncement of the British intention to maintain the status of Tibet as a buffer state. But, on the other hand, it was no less a pronouncement of a change of the status quo comparable to that which the British Government had charged China with intending. Instead of abstaining from all interference in Tibet's internal administration, it defined the internal administration of Tibet as autonomy without Chinese interference.

CHAPTER V

TIBET UNDER THE REPUBLICAN REGIME

UP TO THE END of the Ch'ing dynasty, the Government of China never waived any sovereign rights in Tibet. Indeed, even on the eve of the revolution, they were arguing with the British Government over the rights they had exercised and claimed still to exercise, not only in Tibet, but also in Nepal and Bhutan.[1] They were then doing what the British Foreign Secretary and the British Secretary of State for India called "deliberately or actively making China's suzerainty over Tibet effective."[2]

When China was proclaimed a republic, efforts were soon made to regain control of Tibet. Seats were allotted to Tibet in the National Assembly and the five-colored national flag had the black bar to stand for Tibet. On April 12, 1912, President Yuan Shih-kai issued a proclamation declaring that Tibet, Mongolia, and Sinkiang would henceforth be regarded as on equal footing with the provinces of China Proper and as integral parts of the Republic.[3] He mobilized the troops of Szechwan and Yünnan provinces and appointed General Yin Chang-heng, Governor of Szechwan, as the Commander-in-Chief of the Expeditionary Forces with the object of retrieving the Chinese position in eastern Tibet[4] and raising the siege of the Chinese garrison at Lhasa.

Negotiations Leading to the Simla Conference

The British Government, being determined, as shown in their message of advice and farewell to the Dalai Lama, "to see the internal autonomy of Tibet . . . without Chinese interference," intervened in spite of the treaty obligations which precluded them from interfering with Chinese action in Tibet.[5] On August 16, 1912, Sir John Jordan, British Minister at Peking, having been instructed to take up the matter with the highest authorities of

China, had an audience with President Yuan Shih-kai and protested orally against Chinese military action towards Tibet, and against the alleged Chinese intention of converting the latter into a province. Yuan told him that no treaty provision forbade China to dispatch her troops into Tibet. The Chinese troops, he added, were only settling some frontier affairs at Li-t'ang, Ba-t'ang, and Chamdo, and no attempt would be made to convert Tibet into a province. He finally disclosed his intention to restore the titles of the Dalai Lama and let him return to Tibet to take charge of the situation. To this the British Minister readily agreed.[6]

The next day Sir John Jordan addressed a stiff and threatening memorandum to the Chinese Foreign Office in which he laid down the fundamental views of his government on the Tibetan question. While recognizing Chinese suzerainty over Tibet, the British Government were not prepared to admit the right of China to intervene in the internal administration of Tibet; they would not tolerate the maintenance of an unlimited number of troops either at Lhasa or in Tibet generally; they would demand a written agreement made on the foregoing lines as a condition of extending recognition to the Chinese Republic; and, in the meantime, all communications with Tibet via India must be regarded as closed to the Chinese and would be reopened only when an agreement had been concluded.[7]

The Chinese Government considered this memorandum a gross violation of their legitimate rights in Tibet as well as an infringement of the spirit and letter of the Anglo-Chinese Convention of 1906, and therefore made no immediate reply.

Meanwhile, British intervention met with unfavorable criticism from the Legation Quarter in Peking[8] and gave rise to public anger among the Chinese. Most representative of the latter was Dr. Wu Chao-chu's comment, which maintained that China's position was not one of suzerainty, but of actual sovereignty. Quoting Article II of the Anglo-Chinese Convention of 1906 to the effect that China undertook not to permit any other foreign state to interfere with the territory or internal administration of Tibet, Dr. Wu argued that China could never undertake the duty if she did not permit herself to do certain acts. Moreover, she was not included in "other foreign states," so that it was completely legal to adopt such policies as she saw fit with regard to Tibet. Otherwise, why should she have been allowed, Dr. Wu asked, the right of keeping the Chinese amban in Lhasa, and why had China been recognized as the proper official channel in dealings between the governments of India and Tibet?[9]

The Chinese Government, however, had to yield to the pressure of the British in face of internal difficulties as well as international developments. The central administration in Peking could hardly command the respect, not to say the allegiance, of many southern provinces. The conservatives, composed mainly of the militarists and bureaucrats of the old regime, and the revolutionists, known as Kuomintang, were but ostensibly reconciled. The expeditionary forces had initial successes and recovered many frontier districts; but they were facing stiffer and better organized resistance, while the ill-disciplined Chinese garrison troops at Lhasa were running short of both munitions and food and could not hold out much longer.

The international prospect was even more gloomy since Russia, the only power that could be expected to counteract any British action in Tibet, was herself engaged in carrying out her own design in Mongolia. On October 21, 1912, the Russo-Mongolian Agreement was signed in Urga. By this agreement the Russian Government made a virtual protectorate of a vast part of the Chinese territory which had a close religious tie with Tibet.[10] Besides, there were strong indications that similar action might be taken by other powers in their respective spheres of influence, especially the Germans in Shantung and the Japanese in Manchuria.[11]

Under these circumstances, President Yuan Shih-kai, who was negotiating a loan from the Quadruple (which soon became the Quintuple) Syndicate and other foreign financiers[12] in order to pay the army and meet the current expenses of the government, would certainly not give offence to the British, whose interests predominated in China. On August 31, 1912, he issued orders to General Yin to halt the expedition and eight weeks later he sent a telegram to the Dalai Lama informing him of the restoration of his titles.[13]

But the British still demanded a new agreement. When the Chinese Foreign Office asked the British Minister for a visa for an envoy who was being sent to take the patents of the restored titles to the Dalai Lama by way of India and Sikkim, the request was turned down. Later when the Chinese Foreign Office lodged a protest against the British construction of a route from Gyantse to Lhasa, the British Minister replied that his government could not discuss any matter concerning Tibet before a reply was received to the memorandum of August 17.[14]

The reply was finally made on December 23, 1912. The Chinese Government emphatically stated that they had no intention of converting Tibet into another province of China; their Tibetan policy was governed by the various pronouncements, as well as by the principle of the union of the five races into one family as provided in the provisional constitution; and that the preservation of the traditional system of the Tibetan Government was as much the desire of China as of Great Britain. The reply also asserted that the right of dispatching troops into Tibet was necessary for the fulfillment of the responsibility attaching to China's treaty obligations with Great Britain which required China to preserve peace and order throughout Tibet. But China never contemplated the idea of stationing an unlimited number of troops there. As to the British request that China should negotiate a new treaty, the Chinese Government argued that the existing treaties signed by the late regime had defined Tibet's status with sufficient clearness and that therefore there was no need to negotiate a new one. In addition, the Chinese Government expressed regret that the Indian Government should have closed all communications between China and Tibet via India, such an act being rarely resorted to except by nations at war. Finally, the Chinese Government regretted that Great Britain should threaten to refuse recognition of the Republic, and expressed the hope that an early recognition be accorded as such recognition would be of mutual advantage to both countries.[15]

In the meantime an important event gave both Great Britain and China cause for worry. It was reported in the press that on January 13, 1913, Dorjieff, acting as the Dalai Lama's agent, and equipped with the latter's credentials,[16] obtained during the Dalai

Lama's flight to Urga, signed a treaty on behalf of the Tibetan Government with Mongolia at Urga.[17] In the alleged treaty, both Tibet and Mongolia declared themselves free from Manchu domination, asserted their position as independent states, and declared themselves allies in view of their common religion (Articles II, III, and V). Each recognized the other's independence, and both agreed to work for the advancement of Buddhism and to assist each other against external and internal dangers (Article IV).

In chapter II mention was made of China's grand strategy to prevent Mongolia and Tibet from joining hands. This strategy had been in operation since the Han dynasty. Now, according to the press report, they had joined hands in an open rebellion which menaced the very existence of the trouble-ridden infant republic. Worse still, a treaty like this would certainly involve the two big powers whose respective designs in Mongolia and Tibet had always worried China. Great Britain also was concerned over the treaty, as it might give the Russians the advantage of extending their influence through the medium of Mongolian traders and pilgrims into Tibet; and a Russian influence in Tibet, as Sir Charles Bell asserted,[18] could not fail to endanger British and Indian interests. Great Britain had been crying wolf in regard to Tibet; this time she seemed to hear at least the distant footsteps of a bear.

The British intelligence service must have had beforehand some information of Dorjieff's renewed activities at Urga. This was indicated by the fact that the British Government found it so imperative to consolidate its own position in Tibet by concluding a new agreement. Sir John Jordan, being discontented with the Chinese reply, told the Chinese Foreign Office that if China should again refuse to take part in a meeting with a view to concluding a new treaty, his government would directly negotiate one with Tibet alone.[19]

It was under such pressure that the Chinese Government notified the British Minister of their readiness to discuss the Tibetan problem in order that all misunderstandings between the two countries might be avoided and a harmonious agreement reached.[20] Hence the Conference at Simla—a meeting initiated by the British Government and reluctantly agreed to by the Chinese.

The Simla Conference and Its Failure

Even before the opening of the conference, China had to yield on two points. She suggested that the meeting place be either Peking or London, while the British Government insisted not only that the meeting be held in India but also that the Tibetan plenipotentiary should participate on an equal footing with both the Chinese and British delegates.[21]

The Chinese knew pretty well the attitude of the British authorities in India toward Tibet. A meeting in India would without doubt doom their efforts to recover their position held at the time of Chao Erh-feng's conquests. It was because of his opposition to India as a meeting place that Wen Chung-yao, formerly Deputy Resident in Lhasa, refused to accept appointment as the Chinese delegate.[22] Chen I-fan (Ivan Chen), Special Commissioner for Foreign Affairs in Shanghai, was sent instead.

In the preceding chapter we saw the hard struggle put up by the Chinese plenipotentiaries to make the Tibetan delegate's position subordinate to their own during the negotiations of 1907-8 which terminated in the Trade Regulations.[23] In the preamble of that instrument it was clearly stipulated that the Tibetan representative was to act under the direction of the Chinese plenipotentiary, and Article III provided that the administration of the trade marts should remain with the Tibetan officers under the Chinese officers' supervision and direction. Now the Tibetan representative was to be regarded not as a delegate under the directions of the Chinese, but a plenipotentiary on an equal footing with his Chinese and British counterparts. The status of Tibet had indeed changed.

On October[24] 13, 1913, the tripartite conference was convoked at Simla with the British delegate Sir Arthur Henry McMahon in the Chair. The Tibetan delegate, Lonchen Shatra, having stayed for more than three months with Sir Charles Bell who had been sent to Gyantse to meet him, submitted a proposal consisting of six demands. Besides asking for independence[25] and indemnity as well as the right to denounce the Anglo-Chinese Convention of 1906, and to amend the Trade Regulations of 1893 and 1908, the Tibetan delegate insisted on the return to Tibet of all the land as far as Tach'ienlu and the extension of the Tibetan territory to include Kokonor. In this connection, let us quote the words of two British old China Hands to show the absurdity of the Tibetan claim. Sir John Jordan said at the Royal Central Asian Society in 1924:

> The Tibetans, in my opinion, have always been very unreasonable about the boundary, and have claimed a frontier right away to Tach'ienlu. No one could make me believe that Tach'ienlu and Batáng are not Chinese.[26]

Brigadier M. E. Willoughby said in the same meeting:

> By the way, I would here remark that the inclusion of Kokonor in our European maps in Tibet is somewhat misleading. Tibet, under the temporal control of the Dalai Lama, extends northwards only to the Dangla range separating it from Kokonor.[27]

The Chinese counterproposal consisted of seven items: [28] (1) It asked for a clear provision to the effect that Tibet should be regarded as an integral part of China; (2) China would undertake not to convert Tibet into a province; (3) Great Britain should undertake not to annex Tibet or any portion of its territory; (4) a Chinese Resident should be stationed at Lhasa with 2,600 soldiers, of whom 1,600 were to be posted in such localities as the Resident should see fit; (5) the foreign and military affairs of Tibet should be conducted under Chinese direction; (6) apart from contacts with the British Trade Agents as provided in Article V of the Lhasa Convention of 1904 (confirmed by the Adhesion Agreement of 1906), Tibet should not enter into negotiations or agreements with any foreign country except through the Chinese Government; and (7) the Tibetan boundary should be fixed at Giamda, a line once suggested by Fu Sung-mu after Chao Erhfeng's conquests.[29]

With two proposals so widely apart, there was no basis for agreement even after months of negotiation. On February 17, 1914, the British delegate, acting as a middleman, proposed the division of Tibet into two zones—Inner and Outer Tibet. At the end of March he submitted a draft convention and told the Chinese delegate to give a definite answer within one week. Should the answer be in the negative, the conference would be called off.

In view of the precedent set by the Russo-Chinese agreement in regard to Mongolia signed in November, 1913,[30] which divided Mongolia into Inner and Outer zones, the Chinese Government found it very difficult to reject the British demand. From there on, the arguments shifted to the delimitation of the boundary for Inner and Outer Tibet.

It is beyond the scope of this treatise to relate the details of the protracted haggling which on more than one occasion brought the conference to the verge of a breakdown. The Chinese, on the boundary issue alone, made four concessions on March 18 and 28 and April 3 and 20, respectively, while the British delegate made two amendments to his original draft on March 17 and 27.[31] According to China's last concession, the land north of Dangla Range should belong to Ch'inghai Province with the original boundary maintained; Ba-t'ang, Li-t'ang, and Atuntze should be regarded as a part of China Proper under direct Chinese rule; while the land east of the Salween River including Derge, Nyarong, and the territory of the Thirty-Nine Tribes should form a special district called Kang (Kham).

According to the first British amendment, the land northeast of the Jagchuka Range (in Ch'inghai, otherwise known as Kokonor), Chinchuan (in Szechwan), Tach'ienlu, and Atuntze (in Yünnan) would be put under direct Chinese rule; while Nyarong and De-ge should be turned over to Inner Tibet. Since the British insisted that for the sake of security of the autonomous Outer Tibet, no Chinese troops should be stationed within a distance of three hundred miles from Lhasa, they rejected the legitimate demand of the Chinese to demarcate at the Dangla Range, and proposed instead that only the land northeast of Surhan Budda Mountain and Amne Machin Mountain should be included in the province of Ch'inghai. In fact, all these places mentioned in the British amendment had long been under Chinese rule, and the jurisdiction of the province of Ch'inghai had always extended to the Dangla Range, as pointed out by Willoughby. In other words, the Chinese Government was expected to transfer, if not to cede, to Tibet, a considerable portion of the territory still under its full control[32] as if it had been defeated by the latter on the battlefield. No wonder that on the last point it refused to give in after having already made many humiliating concessions.[33]

The British Draft Convention consisted of eleven articles and seven exchanges of notes. China's suzerainty over the whole of Tibet was to be recognized together with the autonomy of Outer Tibet. Both Great Britain and China were to respect the territorial integrity of the country, and to abstain from interference in the administration of Outer Tibet (including the selection and installation of the Dalai Lama), which was to remain in the hands of the Tibetan Government at Lhasa. Into that region China would be forbidden to send troops, or civil or military officers, except a Resident at Lhasa with an escort of not more than 300 men. Nor was she to colonize it. In Inner Tibet China could maintain her administrative system, subject, however, to the proviso that the Tibetan Government in Lhasa was to retain its existing rights, including the power to select and appoint the high priests of monasteries, and to retain full control in all matters affecting religious institutions. Tibet would not be represented in the Chinese Parliament or in any other similar body. China would pledge not to convert Tibet into a province,[34] while Great Britain would engage not to annex Tibetan territory or station troops, or civil or military officers, nor to establish colonies in Tibet.

The special interest of Great Britain in the existence of an effective government, and in the maintenance of peace and order in the neighborhood of the frontiers of India and adjoining states, was to be recognized. The right of the British Trade Agent at Gyantse to have access to Lhasa, which the British Secretary of State for India once declared as "unnecessary and inconsistent with the principle on which the British policy has throughout been based,"[35] was now definitely stipulated in Article VIII, which provided that he could visit Lhasa even with his escort.

Other articles not only show the privileged position of Great Britain, but also affect the status of Tibet. Article VI provides that no less favorable treatment shall be accorded to British commerce than to the commerce of China or the most favored nations.

Article XI provides that in case of differences between the governments of China and Tibet in regard to questions arising out of this Convention, the aforesaid governments engage to refer them to the British Government for equitable adjustment. Further, Article V provides that the governments of China and Tibet engage that they will not enter into any negotiations or agreements regarding Tibet with one another, or with any other power, excepting such negotiations and agreements between Great Britain and Tibet as are provided for by the Lhasa Convention of 1904 and the Adhesion Agreement of 1906.[36]

It is especially significant that the understanding that Tibet forms part of Chinese territory should not be stipulated in the main text of the Convention and should only take the form of an exchange of notes.

Immediately after offering the second amendment (March 27), the British delegate declared that the general debates should come to a close. He stated that the results of the deliberations in the conference should be considered as the final agreement acceptable to all parties concerned. "Since the Tibetan delegate has already initialed the draft convention," he told the Chinese delegate, Ivan Chen, "and if the Chinese delegate refuses to do so, the British and Tibetan delegates will delete Articles II and IV which are primarily concerned with the interests of China, and forthwith sign it. In such a case, the two countries will not consult with China on matters concerning themselves."[37] Faced with such intimidation, Chen found no way open but to initial the draft.

The Chinese Government, upon receiving Chen's report, instructed him not to sign the formal instrument under any circumstances, and at the same time notified the British Minister at Peking that the other items contained in the draft convention could be accepted in principle, but the boundary arrangement most certainly could not be recognized.[38]

The British Minister at Peking then exerted great pressure by sending stern notes. The impotent Chinese Government made two further concessions, mainly on the boundary issue, which were rejected by the British.[39] As the Chinese delegate had already made it clear that he was instructed not to sign, the

British and Tibetan delegates affixed their signatures on July 3, 1914. A few weeks later World War I broke out and Tibetan affairs were thrown into the background.

Even before the signing of this questionable instrument, the British authorities in India had already taken the advantage of the conference to reap some fruits. Sir Charles Bell tells us that one of his duties was to negotiate with the Tibetan delegate the frontier to be established between Tibet and northeastern India, following a line eight hundred and fifty miles long, marked out on a map by the British delegate, Sir Arthur Henry McMahon. He was able to gain the Tibetan delegate's consent to the frontier *desired* by Sir Henry, which stands back everywhere about a hundred miles from the plains of India. Another duty of his was to negotiate a fresh trade treaty to govern commercial relations between India and Outer Tibet. "In this," he said, "as far as I can remember, I was free to follow my own ideas." [40]

It is noteworthy that soon after the breakup of the conference, the British Foreign Minister, the same Sir Edward Grey who had directed the Anglo-Chinese negotiations of 1906 to a successful conclusion and who had defended the Anglo-Russian Convention of 1907 before the Parliament,[41] told the House of Commons on July 10 that Chinese action in Tibet since 1906 had been most unreasonable and that the sole object of the new convention was to get China to agree to certain boundaries, and to restore her position in regard to Tibet as it existed prior to 1906. He expressed the hope that China "may still sign," and he added, "but if it does not, and resorts to an aggressive policy in regard to Tibet which disturbs the Indian frontier, the consequences must be disastrous to China." [42] These words, compared with his earlier utterances, as well as those of his predecessors and other former government spokesmen, reveal a change of British policy and therefore a change in the status of Tibet. Indeed, the dispensation of the political fortunes of eastern Asia, as remarked by Griswold, had become the private affairs of Britain and her allies.[43]

The reason that Sir Edward still hoped that China might sign was because the Chinese signature was necessary in order to make the new convention valid. The Chinese Government notified the British Minister and telegraphed London that it would not and could not recognize the Simla Convention even if it were signed by British and Tibetan delegates.[44] Here, the reader should be reminded of the provision in the Anglo-Russian Convention concerning Tibet of 1907 (Article II), that Great Britain as well as Russia engaged not to enter into negotiations with Tibet except through the intermediary of the Chinese Government.

It is known to every student of international law and relations that when negotiations are concluded and a treaty has been embodied in a proper form, it is only the completion of the first step in the making of a treaty,[45] and that confirmation and approval, manifested through ratification, is another step to be taken after the signing and sealing of a treaty, before the agreement becomes a binding one.[46] Credentials, however expressed, and notwithstanding the implication of full powers contained in the name "plenipotentiary," empower the representative to nothing more than to negotiate and to conclude provisionally.[47] As a rule, the representatives do not conclude a treaty finally, for all treaties concluded by such representatives are, in principle, not valid before ratification.[48]

In the present case the Simla Convention called for ratification as one of the steps to be taken before the contractual relationship could be perfected, and the Chinese delegate, Ivan Chen, did not even sign, he merely initialed it. Since "it is not apparent how a legal duty to ratify results from the mere signature of the instrument," [49] the writer wonders how Great Britain could regard "the convention as concluded by the act of initialling." [50]

The English authority on the law of treaties, McNair, says "the rule which obtained the widest . . . acceptance in the past is that ratification is required to give [a treaty] legal effect." He further speaks of "entry into force of treaties" as "the earliest date at which ratification takes place." [51]

Let us assume that the convention was duly signed and sealed. China still had the right to repudiate it. "International law clearly recognizes that there is no legal ground of complaint by one party if the other should repudiate the agreement signed in its behalf by its agents." [52] In the present case the Chinese Government was of the opinion that its delegate, Ivan Chen, had acted in excess of his power. His mission was confined to Tibet, but without asking for instructions he had initialed a draft convention which involved the territory of China Proper. His government claimed the right to denounce him, to recall him, and to disavow his action.

As the Simla Conference ended with the Chinese repudiation, Teichman was right in saying that "the Conference finally broke up in the summer of 1914 without an agreement having been reached."[53] It sounds incredible that the Indian Government under Pandit Nehru, as revealed by Ambassador Lo Chia-lun,[54] should have declared in its reply to the Chinese Government that it recognized only the validity of the Simla Convention of 1914. The Chinese Foreign Office had, on October 9, 1948, sent a note[55] to the Indian Embassy proposing revision of the Trade Regulations of 1908 in regard to Tibet, Article XIII of which provides an occasion for revision at the end of each successive ten years. The Indian reply was not made until March 22, 1949, when the Chinese Government was about to be evacuated from Nanking in face of the communist attack. The Chinese Government, however, still managed to send a note to the Indian Government through its embassy at New Delhi on November 18 (as the Indian Embassy in China could no longer be reached) in which it repudiated the Indian claim and denounced once more the so-called validity of the Simla Convention.[56]

Renewed Bargaining between Russia and Britain

The changed situation in Tibet brought renewed bargaining between Russia and Britain. According to the records in the Russian archives, Great Britain proposed revision of the Anglo-Russian Convention of 1907 concerning Tibet, in the spring of 1914. The Russian Foreign Office remarked in its file that "as the British proposal apparently amounted to converting Tibet into Britain's virtual protectorate, we should ask for compensation either in Afganistan or in Persia."[57] A few days later, the Russian Foreign Minister wrote to his minister at Peking informing him of Britain's proposal, which, he added, was intended to free her from the treaty restrictions and to give her a free hand in Tibet. "I promised in my reply," he went on, "to consider it but on condition that we should be given assurance beforehand that our wishes would be satisfied." The Russian Foreign Minister therefore asked his minister at Peking to suggest demands that should be made to the British in exchange. He called the attention of the latter to the fact that in the beginning Britain suggested a mutual recognition of the respective zones of influence—Mongolia to Russia, Tibet to Britain—to which Russia did not agree, as, it was then pointed out to Britain, Russia originally enjoyed freedom of action in Mongolia, while British action in Tibet was tied by the obligations under the 1907 convention.[58]

In reply to his foreign minister's enquiry, the Russian minister, Krupenski, suggested that Britain should recognize North Manchuria, Mongolia, and the western part of China as the special zones of influence of Russia, and that Britain should refrain from any interference when Russian designs in these zones were to be carried out. He suggested a Russian concession to Britain in regard to the Yangtse Valley should his proposed demand be considered excessive.[59]

In 1915 China faced a more immediate danger from her eastern neighbor, Japan, when the latter presented her with the Twenty-One Demands. She experienced a new humiliation and yielded to the Japanese ultimatum. From then on, she found it all the more necessary not to give the least offence to the wishes of Japan's ally, the all-powerful Great Britain. President Yuan Shih-kai (who also wished to win British support for his forthcoming, short-lived, imperial regime) therefore directed the Chinese Foreign Office to work out a compromise solution. The latter accordingly drafted a new proposal, and with the President's approval, handed it to the British Minister on June 28, 1915. The new proposal, besides two other items, made a further territorial concession in granting Chamdo to Outer Tibet on condition that the provision "Tibet is a part of China" should be included in the main text of the convention. The British Government at first agreed to make minor changes to the Simla draft, but finally refused to reopen negotiations. On August, the Chinese Foreign Office, instructed by Yuan Shih-kai, made another greater territorial concession which still failed to please the British.[60]

From 1916 on, China hardly had a single year without civil strife. Foreign menace, other than that of Japan, was temporarily alleviated because of World War I, but internal dissension went on with ever greater destruction. The authority of the central government extended not much further than the gates of Peking. The troops which had been left at the Tibetan border without care and provision were eventually reduced to a point where the British-trained[61] and British-equipped Tibetan army easily defeated them when their commander at Chamdo, P'eng Jih-sheng, acting on his own authority and without the sanction of the Chinese Government, deliberately provoked a resumption of hostilities in the autumn of 1917.

By the middle of the summer of 1918 the Tibetans, following their capture of Chamdo, Draya, Markam, Gonjo, and De-ge, were approaching Kanze and Nyarong in one direction and Ba-t'ang in another. At this juncture the local Chinese leaders on the frontier invoked the mediation of Teichman, the British Consular Agent stationed at Tach'ienlu and Markam, whose duty it was, according to his own account, to watch events on the border with a view to keeping the peace between the two parties pending a final settlement of the dispute by diplomatic means.[62] A truce was finally arranged by virtue of two documents signed in August and October, respectively, with Teichman acting as the middleman and witness.[63] By the end of 1918 the frontier regions had settled down with the Chinese remaining in control of Ba-t'ang, Li-t'ang, Nyarong, Kanze, and the area to the east of them, while the Tibetans retained Chamdo, Draya, Markham, De-ge, and the area further west. In this incident, the Tibetans made a successful show of force while British influence, now well established in eastern Tibet, was fully manifested in the arrangement of the truce.

Renewed Negotiations under British Pressure

From February of 1918 to the end of the year the British Minister at Peking, Sir John Jordan, pressed the Chinese Foreign Office at least nine times to begin negotiations for settling the Tibetan issue.[64] When World War I came to an end, the Chinese Government realized that they no longer had an excuse for putting off this knotty problem. In May, 1919, Teichman went to Peking to furnish Sir John with additional reasons for pressing the resumption of negotiations as the truce he had arranged in the previous year was to expire after one year's duration.

It will serve no purpose to give an account of the subsequent negotiations which in fact proved fruitless. There is, however, a point worth mentioning. On August 13, 1919, the British Minister, under instructions from his government, presented a counterproposal to the Chinese Foreign Office which suggested abandoning the attempt to divide Tibet into Inner and Outer zones and to place Ba-t'ang, Li-t'ang, Tach'ienlu, Dawn, Luho, Nyarong, and Kanze under direct rule as a part of China Proper, while the territory west of this area, including De-ge, was to be incorporated into autonomous Tibet. When he found the boundary thus proposed not acceptable to the Chinese, the British Minister suggested adding Gonchen, the gateway to Sining, then under Tibetan occupation, to the Chinese.[65] Here we see how freely Britain drew boundaries for Tibet and disposed of the territory to which they had no right whatsoever. From this we also see what the status of Tibet actually was.

The Chinese Government might have yielded to the latest British compromise proposal, which, besides the above-mentioned arrangement, was to create a non-military zone outside an autonomous Tibet, but with a status similar to the Inner Zone originally provided for in the Simla draft, to cover all the territory south of the Kuenlen Mountains and north of the Dangla Range. It was, however, prevented from doing so by a wave of strong opposition raised in the Parliament in Peking, voiced by the leaders of the local governments of Szechwan, Yünnan, Kansu, and Ch'inghai—the regions which were adjacent to Tibet and therefore had a keen interest in the matter—as well as by various civil organizations, when the British demands were made known to them by a circular telegram sent out by the Chinese Foreign Office dated September 5, 1919.[66] Popular opposition was greatly inspired and encouraged by current events in Mongolia where the autonomous Outer Zone was revoked by the Outer Mongolians as a result of the Soviet Revolution.

When the Chinese Foreign Office decided to suspend negotiations in the face of popular opposition, Sir John Jordan tried to bring the matter to a higher level; however, his appeal to the

Chinese Prime Minister and to the Chinese President was of no avail.[67] In January, 1920, he made another attempt to reopen negotiations, and suggested a conference at Lhasa to solve the problem, but he was soon recalled and left China in March.[68]

His successor, Sir Beilby Francis Alston, took up the issue in the spring of 1921. The Chinese Foreign Office prepared a countermeasure of seven points which repudiated the Simla draft as a basis for negotiation and showed a stronger stand than before. Since the Washington Conference was approaching, it did not heed the urging of the new British Minister,[69] intending to thrash out the Tibetan problem in the open. But when the Washington Conference was convened, the Shantung problem seemed so much more important both to the Chinese and the other powers that the Tibetan issue was not broached. It is significant from the point of view of our study that Tibet was alleged to have expressed the following opinion in regard to this conference:

1. It should not discuss Tibetan problems unless Tibet were represented. But, even if now invited, there would not be sufficient time to instruct and send a representative.
2. References would have to be made from time to time and America was much too far away for these.
3. They were unwilling to enter on negotiations unless Sir Charles Bell were present at them.[70]

As the issue failed even to appear on the agenda of the Washington Conference, efforts were again made to deal with it through ordinary diplomatic channels. In 1922 the Chinese chargé d'affairs in London informed the home government that Great Britain had formulated three conditions for its solution:

1. Tibet was to have complete control over its foreign affairs.
2. Great Britain was to have the right to construct the Indo-Tibetan Railway.
3. Absolute independence was to be given to Tibet in regard to internal administration.

In 1924, when the British Labor Cabinet was formed, the Chinese Foreign Office entertained the hope of settling the Tibetan problem with a Socialist government and formulated a ten-point measure.[71] But deteriorating internal conditions which reduced the central government in Peking to a government only in name prevented the measure from being carried out. A change of the situation in Tibet itself, as a result of the Panch'en Lama's flight to China Proper in December, 1923, also made the Chinese Government hesitate to take up the thorny problem with Great Britain, where a change of government in London did not necessarily mean a change in the policy of the Indian Government reformulated after the significant mission of Sir Charles Bell to Lhasa in 1920-21.[72] Thus the issue remained suspended with Tibet's status politically vague and legally undefined till the establishment of the National Government in Nanking in 1927.

The Panch'en Lama's Flight to China Proper

It may be recalled that in 1904, when Lhasa was under British military occupation, the Dalai Lama was temporarily deprived of his rank and in his place was appointed the Panch'en Lama as a result of the telegraphic recommendation made by the Chinese Resident Yu-t'ai and sent through Younghusband.[73] Though the Panch'en Lama declined this high honor, he nevertheless offered his complete support to the imperial authorities in Tibet during the period of the Dalai Lama's absence. In the winter of 1905 he was forced to accept the British invitation to visit India, the "primary object" of which was "to enable him to be present in Calcutta during the visit of the Prince of Wales." [74] The Dalai Lama, who already resented the Panch'en Lama's cooperation with the Chinese authorities in Tibet,[75] viewed the Panch'en Lama's visit to India as a means of soliciting British help to obtain independence from his rule.[76]

Upon his return to Lhasa in 1912 from exile in India, the Dalai Lama condemned the Panch'en Lama for not fighting the Chinese garrison troops who, as related in Chapter III, mutinied on hearing of the outbreak of revolution in the homeland. On the other hand, the Panch'en Lama, in his concern for the Buddhist conviction which forbade killing, viewed with great dissatisfaction the Dalai Lama's policy of allying himself with the British, and his associating with the idea of fighting and of ordering military opposition to the Chinese.[77]

In a word, the personal grievance which was caused by a ceremonial incident, or rather a protocol mistake, in 1902,[78] became a struggle for secular power in general and for the right to collect taxes and levies in the districts near Tashi-lhunpo in particular, at a time when the imperial domination was overthrown and the situation was further complicated by the British influence behind the scenes.[79] The suspicion and the misunderstanding between the two Grand Lamas increased at the instigations of their respective followers.[80] Toward the end of 1923, a rupture appeared in their relations when the Dalai Lama asked the Panch'en Lama to pay a huge amount of money and food held to have been in arrears. The Panch'en Lama, not being in a position to pay, and facing the prospect of having to go to Lhasa for a conference, fled from Tashi-lhunpo in disguise. After many months of hard traveling and months of delay caused by large numbers of pilgrims who came to pay their respects to him, he reached Peking in February, 1925, where he was given a state welcome.[81]

It must not be assumed that the Dalai Lama was pro-British while the Panch'en Lama was pro-Chinese.[82] They both tried to adjust themselves to the changing situation created by the British expedition and the Chinese revolution. They might have thought of taking advantage of the change and making the best of the situation, but neither was heartily pro-British.

The Dalai Lama Turning Strongly Away from Britain toward China

As mentioned before, the Russian Consul at Calcutta had an interview with the exiled Dalai Lama and handed to him a letter from the Tzar. Then he reported to his government that the Lama was not really pro-British.[83] In fact, "by 1925 the Dalai Lama was turning strongly away from Britain towards China." He appointed an official named Lung-shar as Commander-in-Chief of the Tibetan army. "Lung-shar was markedly anti-British.[84] Tsarong, former Commander-in-Chief, who was always very pro-British, lost most of his power and was subsequently degraded." Laden La, a British subject, born of a Sikkimese mother, and a former Superintendent of Police in Darjeeling, had been made Commissioner of Police for Lhasa in May, 1924, shortly afterwards gaining control of the administration of justice in the capital; but he was dismissed as a result of Tibetan public demand.[85] "In 1926, the English school at Gyantse was closed. At this time the British political authorities in Tibet started to establish a motor mail service between Pa-ri and Gyantse in order to quicken the mails, but the Tibetan Government forbade it." The Dalai Lama rejected the British plan for building up the water electric power, and telephone systems. Besides, he refused to accept the British plan for the joint development of the Tibetan mines.[86]

It is interesting to note that in May of 1932 the representative of the Dalai Lama in Nanking, Kung-chüeh-chung-ni, submitted to the Chinese Government a manifesto issued by the three leading monasteries of Lhasa to support his accusation of the Panch'en Lama and his protest against the latter's new title, and that the representative of the Panch'en Lama, Lo-sang-chien-tsan, immediately petitioned in his master's defence. Each side accused the other of having been pro-British.[87]

Nor should it be assumed that the Dalai Lama ever had the intention of severing relations with China altogether. In January and February of the first year of the Chinese Republic (1912), President Yuan Shih-kai and the Dalai Lama exchanged telegraphic communications the contents of which showed good will on both sides.[88] No communication from the Lama then or after ever claimed independence; it was only the Dalai Lama's demand for Chamdo, Markham, and the adjacent districts that prevented a proposed and agreed conference from taking place.[89] In 1918 the Dalai Lama chose three learned Lamas—one from each of the three leading monasteries—and sent them to Peking to fill teaching posts in Yung-Ho-Kung, the noted Lamaist temple in the capital. In 1920, the provincial government of Kansu sent a mission to Tibet which was given a hearty welcome by the Dalai Lama, and which, as remarked by Sir Charles Bell,[90] augmented Chinese influence in Lhasa. In 1921, the Dalai Lama again sent to Peking three learned Lamas, together with their respective disciples, and in the following year a higher Lama named Kung-chüeh-chung-ni, who was later sent back as the Dalai Lama's representative in Nanking, was dispatched to take charge of the religious affairs of the Peking temple.[91]

Aside from religious missions, the Dalai Lama sent Tun-chu-wang-chieh as his representative with messages and presents to Peking in 1922 and 1924, and the latter was received by Presidents Li Yuan-hung and Tsao K'un.[92]

In 1924 Brigadier-General M. E. Willoughby told the members of the Central Asian Society in London that to the best of his knowledge no vestige of Chinese control remained in central Tibet.[93] The writer has no reason to doubt his statement. Yet by the following year even Sir Charles Bell admitted that the Dalai Lama was turning strongly away from powerful Britain towards weak and divided China.[94] The writer suggests that the explanation for this is the absence of anti-Chinese and pro-British feeling on the part of the Dalai Lama; the existence of friendly, though rather sporadic, contacts between Tibet and China Proper as related above; and the historical "connection between Tibet and China based on contiguity and natural affinities" which Sir Charles Bell predicted is destined to remain.[95]

The turning away of the Dalai Lama from Britain towards China did not fail to impress favorably the Kuomintang which was about to win its anti-militarist cause under the banner of San-min-chu-i (that is, for nationalism, democracy, and people's livelihood). In 1928, a year after the establishment of the Nationalist Government in Nanking, the Panch'en Lama sent delegates to express his respects to the new regime, and at the same time put forward a request that the Chinese Government assume full charge of affairs in Tibet in order to save it from becoming a "second India."[96] It was mainly due to the Dalai Lama's inclination towards China that the authorities in Nanking decided to look upon the Lhasa Government as the proper channel for readjusting relations with Tibet.

The Chinese National Government's Effort toward Rapprochement

Thus, in 1929, the Chinese Government dispatched Miss Liu Man-ch'ing on a semi-official mission to Lhasa for the purpose of conveying to the Tibetan Government and people its good will and friendship and to make a report on conditions in that region.[97] Miss Liu was born in Lhasa in 1906 to a Chinese father and a Tibetan mother. She was brought as a girl to Peking for her education and graduated from a normal school. Because of her knowledge of both the Chinese and Tibetan languages, she was employed as an interpreter to the Commission for Mongolian and Tibetan Affairs in 1928. She volunteered for the mission and when accepted she soon started her arduous journey by way of Szechwan with only a small escort. On February 7, 1930, she reached Lhasa, where she received a warm welcome from the Tibetan Government and people.[98]

In her first interview with the Dalai Lama, Miss Liu took pains to explain the doctrine of the Kuomintang and the Government's plan for national construction and development. She also conveyed the deep concern of President Chiang Kai-shek over prevailing conditions in Tibet and his eager wish to see Tibet rejoin the family of the Republic as brothers. The Dalai Lama expressed his appreciation and showed unprecedented courtesy to the young lady by touching her head with his holy hand.[99]

During the last interview granted to Miss Liu on May 25, the Dalai Lama stated that the Chinese Government in the past had neglected Tibet and, what was worse, even regarded Tibet as a barren and worthless land. He went on to say:

> Since President Chiang had Tibet in mind and had sent you here shortly after the establishment of the new government to express concern for and sympathy toward Tibet, I am deeply touched and would like to ask you to convey personally my appreciation and gratitude which have been also expressed in my letter to him. I am looking forward to a day of mutual aid. What I expect most of China is real unity and peace.[100]

Touching on his relations with the British, the Dalai Lama stated that:

> The British, indeed, have a mind to draw me to their side. Nevertheless, I know the importance of guarding the national sovereignty and I have never surrendered a bit of it in spite of the necessity of having to deal with them, their character and customs being so different from ours.[101]

In regard to the situation in Sikang, the Dalai Lama wished to see the corrupt and adventurous civil and military officers removed and replaced by some honest and well-intentioned men who would work for the mutual interest of the two peoples. He was confident that the Tibet-Sikang question would be easily settled in a conference if the central government would consolidate its own position and make such a change of the personnel on the spot. He said he was ready to withdraw Tibetan troops at any moment. Finally, the Dalai Lama expressed his readiness to choose representatives to be sent to Nanking and his hope that the Chinese Government would provide Tibet with weaving and leather-manufacturing machines together with skilled workers.

It is significant that the Dalai Lama during this interview expressed his sympathy towards the Indian people, who, he emphasized, were suffering from British oppression, and his hope that China could render them some practical help. He mentioned his relations with Nepal, saying that he never recognized the latter's independence and that he still addressed her chief by the old title granted by the late Imperial Government.[102]

On July 27 Miss Liu returned to Nanking via India. No doubt she succeeded in eliminating some of the suspicion which the Dalai Lama had of the new Nationalist regime and helped pave the way for the resumption of formal relations between Lhasa and Nanking. But, after all, her mission was a semi-official one. Discussion of matters of a political character and concerning Tibet's status was entrusted to Kung-chüeh-chung-ni, who left Nanking on November 7, 1929, three months after Miss Liu, and arrived at Lhasa on January 16, 1930, by way of India three weeks before Miss Liu, who undertook a much harder journey by land and who encountered en route difficulties and delays which would have been nonexistent in the case of Kung-chüeh-chung-ni even if he had taken the same route.[103]

Kung-chüeh-chung-ni, who, as mentioned above, had been sent in 1922 to Peking to serve at the Yung-Ho-Kung temple, had remained there ever since. It was found out that he enjoyed the confidence of the Dalai Lama, and for this reason he, instead of a Chinese, was entrusted with this important mission. Sir Charles Bell made a mistake in saying that he was accompanied by Miss

Liu and in referring to them as members of one and the same mission when he described the way they were warmly welcomed and entertained.[104]

The Dalai Lama's Answer to the Eight Questions

Here are the eight questions the Chinese Government put to the Dalai Lama, and the latter's answer to them brought back by Kung-chüeh-chung-ni, who returned to Nanking on August 30, 1930:

1. *Q.* How might relations between Tibet and the Central Government be restored?
   A. If the Central Government would treat the patronage relationship between China and Tibet with sincerity and good faith as it previously did, Tibet on its part, having always shown sincerity in its dealings in the past, would from now on make an even greater effort to give full support to the Central Government.
2. *Q.* How shall the Central Government exercise administrative control over Tibet?
   A. It would be advisable to work out a written understanding on the measures to be taken for securing a fundamental stabilization both in the political and the religious affairs of Tibet.
3. *Q.* How shall the autonomy of Tibet and its scope be defined?
   A. As from now on, the patronage relationship between the Central Government and Tibet is going to be faithfully observed and the Central Government is to show sincerity to make Tibet feel safe and secure; the area over which autonomy is to be exercised should naturally be the same as before. It is expected that the Central Government will return to Tibet those districts which originally belonged to it but which are now not under its control so that a perpetual peace and harmony will surely be the result.
4. *Q.* Shall the Dalai and Panch'en Lamas join the Kuomintang?
   A. On account of his advanced age and the tremendous burden in managing temporal and religious affairs, and also considering the fact that he is not able to proceed to the capital until the consent of the three leading monasteries and of the members of the National Assembly is obtained, the Dalai Lama is not at the present time in a position to join the Kuomintang. As the Panch'en Lama is now residing in China Proper and his duty has always been confined to the religious affairs of

Tashi-lhunpo, for he has no political affairs to attend to, he should be available for membership of the Kuomintang. It must be understood, however, that he has never had any say in the settlement of Tibetan affairs.

5. *Q.* Shall the relative position of the Dalai and the Panch'en Lama and their respective jurisdiction in political as well as religious affairs be maintained as before or new provisions be made?

   A. Political and religious affairs have always been administered by the Tibetan Government at Lhasa. The Panch'en Lama has had only the Tashi-lhunpo monastery in his control. Actually the Tashi-lhunpo monastery was built by the first Dalai Lama. It was the second Dalai Lama who entrusted the administration to a fellow monk and conferred upon the latter the honorary title of Panch'en, when he moved his seat to Lhasa. Later, in view of the tutor-disciple relationship existing in turn through generations between the Dalai and the Panch'en, the fifth Dalai Lama awarded this monastery to the fourth Panch'en Lama. If this age-old practice were to be continuously observed, all Tibetans would be only too pleased.

6. *Q.* How shall the Dalai welcome the Panch'en back to Tibet and how shall the Central Government escort him? .

   A. Among the Panch'en's retinue, many employed the terms "Anterior" and "Ulterior" Tibet with intent to sow discord. They disobeyed orders of the Tibetan Government and acted frequently against their superiors. Both their thought and conduct are corrupt. In the year Chia Ch'en (1904), the Panch'en went to India and conspired with the British, but all his efforts were of no avail. In the year Hsin Hai (1911), he intrigued with the Resident Lien-yü and made an attempt to seize the reins of government and control of the church during the absence of the Dalai Lama. But his efforts were thwarted by the opposition of the people and especially of the clergymen of the three leading monasteries. According to established practice, the Panch'en should contribute one quarter of the provisions for the Army. Not only did he fail to make such contributions, but also committed acts in violation of law. Had the offenders been punished strictly in accordance with the letter of the law, there would have been no such state of affairs as now exists. It is only in consideration of the long-standing and close tutor-disciple relationship between the Dalai and the Panch'en through generations that a policy of tolerance and forgiveness has been followed. Yet these people not only remained unrepentant, but further advised and urged the Panch'en to flee away from Tashi-lhunpo. A dispatch inviting him back was soon sent to the Panch'en, but he refused to accept. He then fled to Urga and had secret dealings with the communists. Only upon the death of the Chief Lama of Mongolia, Cheputsuntanpa, was he obliged to come to China Proper. Consequently, the Tibetan Government dispatched officials to Tashi-lhunpo to take proper care of the monastery. Now, these offenders are still conspiring and making trouble. As the matter stands, Tibet would find it very difficult to welcome them unless they can give a satisfactory explanation as to their reason for taking to flight.

7. *Q.* Has the Dalai Lama the intention of setting up in the Capital an office for the convenience of keeping closer contact? As to its expenses, the Central Government is prepared to grant the necessary funds.

   A. At first, offices are to be set up in Nanking, Peiping, and Sikang. If and when such offices are required for other places, applications will be filed accordingly.

8. *Q.* Is there anything else that Tibet expects of the Central Government?

   A. For the purpose of protecting itself against aggression, Tibet's hope for the present is only that the Central Government will supply it with arms. In case any other help may be needed in the future for strengthening its security, it will make requests to the Central Government.[105]

The above-quoted document shows clearly what stood in the way of a better understanding and further rapprochement, to wit, the definition of Tibet's status in relation to the Central Government the demarcation of the boundary between Tibet and China Proper, and the readjustment of the relationship between the two Grand Lamas. Kung-chüeh-chung-ni, when he reported to the Chinese Government with this written reply from the Dalai Lama, acted in a dual capacity because he had been appointed by the Dalai Lama as his representative in Nanking to discharge "all the official affairs and handle all communications for the Tibetan government."[106] A few months later the Dalai Lama sent Chu-cheng Tantsun to Nanking as his deputy representative.[107]

A desire for reconciliation on the part of the Tibetan authorities can be found from the 1930 correspondence between the Dalai Lama, the bKa'-blon, and the Tibetan Commander-in-Chief, Lung-shar, on the one hand, and on the other, Lu Hsing-chi, the acting Chinese High Commissioner to Tibet,[108] who remained in India after his appointment in 1913.[109]

The Chinese Government, having contemplated for a time holding a conference in Nanking, finally decided to make use of Hsieh Kuo-liang's mediation mission [110] to open negotiation with the Dalai Lama in Lhasa. Unfortunately, Hsieh's death only one day's march from Lhasa deprived the mission of any chance of success. The written instructions which Hsieh had received from the Central Government were brought back by his private secretary, Tang Yün-san, and returned to the Commission for Mongolian and Tibetan Affairs.[111] Here are the proposed terms contained in Hsieh's instructions: [112]

1. Tibet should restore its close relationship with the Central Government.
2. Tibet should not foster any political relations with any foreign state.
3. All treaties and agreements still in force between Tibet and foreign states should be submitted to the National Government for reexamination.
4. The Dalai Lama should welcome the Panch'en Lama back to Tibet.
5. The Dalai Lama should restore to the National Government all the districts of Sikang which he had occupied.
6. Important diplomatic, military, and political affairs of Tibet should be the responsibility of, and administered by, the National Government.
7. The National Government should grant Tibet the right to complete autonomy.
8. The secular and religious authority of the Dalai and the Panch'en Lamas should be maintained as before.
9. The National Government should appoint a special commissioner to be stationed in Tibet "to conduct Tibetan affairs." [113]
10. Tibet might set up an office in Nanking and the National Government should make an appropriation for the expenses of that office.

Armed Conflict Initiated by the Ta-chieh Ssu Incident

The effort for rapprochement was frustrated by an incident in Sikang known as the Ta-chieh Ssu affair which involved not only the rivalry, if not hostility, between the Dalai and the Panch'en, but also the boundary dispute. It doomed all the previous attempts for an amicable settlement to failure.

The incident started from a dispute over a monastery named Yala Ssu in Pei-li village of the Kanze district.[114] The abbot of Yala Ssu, who had spent his novitiate in the powerful Ta-chieh Ssu monastery, wanted to have the one incorporated in the other. But the new chieftain of the village, who was on bad terms with the abbot, strongly opposed the latter's proposition. In June, 1930, the abbot called in the monks of Ta-chieh Ssu and occupied the village. The Chinese garrison troops intervened and clashed with the monks of Ta-chieh Ssu who had a record of pro-Tibetan activities during the armed conflict of 1918.[115]

According to the Dalai Lama's telegram received by the Central Government in October, 1930, it was the followers of the Panch'en Lama who instigated the Chinese garrison troops to side with Pei-li and deliberately oppress the Ta-chieh monks. According to General Liu Wen-hui, the Commander-in-Chief of Sikang Garrison Forces, it was the Lhasa authorities who sent reinforcements to back the Ta-chieh monks and renew the attack. Charges and countercharges went on till at last the Dalai Lama refused to deal with Liu Wen-hui any more and asked the Central Government "to dispatch someone fair-minded and friendly to both sides to mediate on the spot." [116] The Commission for Mongolian and Tibetan Affairs, therefore, sent one of its members, T'ang Ko-san, and a technical expert, Liu Tsan-ting,[117] to undertake the mediation work.

While T'ang and Liu were making preparations for the journey, three Tibetan high-ranking officers with four thousand horsemen were sent to the front, and upon their arrival in March they launched an offensive. As a result of this sudden attack, the Chinese force was thrown into great confusion. Resisting vainly for a few days, they began to retreat towards Kanze. As reinforcements failed to arrive in time, they made another retreat to Luho. The Central Government thereupon telegraphed to the Dalai Lama asking for an immediate explanation. The latter replied on March 24 saying that a cease-fire order was being issued but that it would take more than twenty days to reach the front. He shifted the responsibility of resuming hostilities to the Chinese side. But, contrary to the Dalai Lama's promise of cease-fire, the Tibetans continued their drive towards Nyarong.

Before T'ang and Liu could have reached the place of rendezvous with the Tibetan delegate, Nyarong had been captured by the Tibetans who took the Chinese magistrate of Nyarong, Chang Tz'u-pei, prisoner and sent him to Chamdo under custody. By now the Tibetan commander had changed his tune, and he told Liu Wen-hui[118] that his troops were restoring to the control of the Lhasa Government Nyarong, which the Manchu Emperor had once given to the Dalai Lama;[119] while the Tibetan delegate wrote to T'ang Ko-shan mentioning only the cease-fire arrangement and refusing to reply to the question of withdrawal to the original positions.[120] On the 28th of July the Commission for Mongolian and Tibetan Affairs received a telegram from the Dalai Lama asserting that Kanze and Nyarong were originally under Tibetan jurisdiction.[121] It is clear that the issue was no longer a dispute over one monastery, but an attempt on the part of the Lhasa authorities to fix a boundary line with China Proper by force.

This sudden change of attitude of the Dalai Lama puzzled the Chinese Government. The Chinese press attributed it to British string-pulling[122] and pointed out the various British aids, especially the sale of a large quantity of munitions to Tibet. In 1932 the Chinese Foreign Office lodged a protest with the British Government, charging that the sale of munitions to Tibet was an unfriendly action, and the British Minister at Nanking, while arguing that the Indian Government was acting in accordance with its treaty obligations, expressed his readiness to mediate and to help in finding a peaceful solution.[123] The Japanese Foreign Office Archives give evidence that according to Japanese Intelligence reports, it was the British who backed the Tibetan military adventure and helped the Tibetan army with officers and munitions,[124] while at the same time they reveal the fact that Japan was also a supplier of arms and munitions to the Tibetans from 1921, a fact hitherto unknown to the outside world.[125]

No doubt the higher honor shown to the Panch'en Lama by the National Government[126] and the activities of his followers in Sikang, Ch'inghai, Kansu, and Inner Mongolia must have made the Dalai Lama feel very uneasy. The jealousy and ill-feeling between the two Grand Lamas, the extent of which can be seen from the accusatory documents mentioned above,[127] was perhaps one of the factors bringing about this sudden change of attitude towards Nanking. Whether or not the British were at the back of it, one thing is certain: the so-called Young-Tibet party[128] consisted mainly of military leaders, some of whom perhaps were patriots, but most of whom had received military training either in Gyantze or in India, and tended therefore to be pro-British. In Tibet there was no such thing as a political party in our use of the word. They were just a pressure group; the most outstanding among them was Tsarong, whom Sir Charles Bell spoke of as "always very pro-British."[129] They wanted the substitution of some form of civil government for the lama hierarchy, the carrying out of national reform and economic development along Western lines, and close cooperation with the British authorities in India in order to establish a "Greater Tibet" independent of Chinese interference.[130] This group was probably as responsible as any for the military adventure intended to push their boundary eastward for the purpose of realizing a "Greater Tibet."

The Chinese National Government Not in a Position to Force the Issue

The reader might wonder why the National Government did not settle the outstanding Tibetan issue by force and then define the status of Tibet by an agreement, as the Communists did in 1950-51, at a time when its military success was almost as amazing and impressive, having knocked out one militarist after another during its Northern Expedition. An answer to this question would help us to understand the circumstances that made the vague status of Tibet remain unaffected in spite of a sweeping Chinese Nationalist Revolution.

Besides the hopes of further reconciliation and the actual progress towards rapprochement as described above, there were other factors that prevented the National Government from resorting to force. In the first place, from a theoretical point of view it would be self-defeating if the National Government, which stood for equality of all nations within the Republic and for harmony and peace,[131] should use force to subdue the Tibetan people and impose a certain status. In the second place, from a realistic consideration, the National Government could not employ force even if it had no theoretical scruples. The reasons may be summarized as follows:

Firstly, it was always the British who had to be taken into account if any solution of the Tibetan issue was to be effected. The National Government, in carrying out its Northern Expedition, had encountered repeated menaces from the foreign powers. In January of 1927 incidents at Hankow and Kiukiang brought a heavily reinforced British fleet to the Yangtze ports and created an explosive situation.[132] In March of the same year the Nanking incident, when Nationalist troops attacked foreigners, killing some, brought about the concerted action of five powers whose threatening note contained demands the National Government had to accept at last.[133] Two months later Japan landed her troops at Shantung and in May of the following year created a much greater incident, as a result of which her troops occupied Tsinan and attacked the Nationalist force which was advancing towards Peking. Again the National Government yielded to a foreign power and accepted its terms.[134] It therefore was not in a position to force the Tibetan issue, which would give offense to Great Britain, especially when it had severed relations with the U.S.S.R. in December, 1927.

Secondly, the internal situation would not allow the National Government to adopt such a risky measure as a military campaign in Tibet. The Nationalist force, indeed, succeeded in knocking out the leading militarists like Wu P'ei-fu and Sun Ch'uan-fang, and ousting Chang Tso-lin from Peking, but there soon developed dissension among its own ranks.[135]

Thirdly, the Nationalist Revolution which started with so much anti-militarist and anti-imperialistic fury, cooled down on going through the experiences just related. The National Government, since its removal from Canton to Nanking, had become more compromising than revolutionary in character. Many former militarists with their ill-disciplined troops joined the Nationalist forces with only their banners changed. Even if the National Government had decided to embark on a military expedition to

Tibet, it would have had to fight its way to the Tibetan border first, as all roads leading to Tibet, whether from Yünnan, Szechwan, Ch'inghai, or Sinkiang, were all in the hands of those military governors over whom the National Government had but a nominal control.

Fourthly, the complexity of the situation on the spot would make any government hesitate to start a military campaign against Tibet. The old Chinese garrison troops at the Tibetan frontier, as remarked by Teichman,[136] "degenerated into little better than brigands." Liu Wen-hui's troops, originally of Szechwan, were comparatively better equipped and better fed, but not much better disciplined. For example, they even ventured to kill summarily a local Kuomintang leader who said something in public against their oppression of the people. As a result of this outrageous act, Ke-sang-ts'e-jên, the Commissioner for Kuomintang Affairs of Sikang, with the support of the masses, easily disarmed the garrison force of Liu Wen-hui at Ba-t'ang, and in March, 1932, declared the establishment of an autonomous regime.[137] Another instance of the corruption of Liu's troops was clearly shown in the mutiny of the garrisons at Tach'ienlu on February 10, 1932, during which the commanding officer, Brigadier General Ma Su, paid with his life for his corruption.[138] These two incidents alone give a picture of how complex was the situation on the spot. Yet the local situation was further complicated by the presence of Moslem elements. In Chapter III mention was made of the serious Moslem revolt in the latter part of the Ch'ing dynasty. Moslems have always been a factor in northwest China politics which no responsible government could afford to neglect. Ch'inghai and Ninghsia were then governed by Moslems, while a greater part of Kansu was also garrisoned by Moslem troops. Even the leading figures responsible for dealing with the Tibetan issue were Moslems: Ma Fu-hsiang, the former Chairman of the Commission for Mongolian and Tibetan Affairs, and the above-mentioned Miss Liu Man-ch'ing, T'ang Ko-san, and Brigadier General Ma Su were all Moslems. There was talk of a Pan-Moslem movement against Buddhist Tibet. The National Government would certainly not do anything to create a fresh danger.

Finally, the location and composition of the National Government would preclude any possibility of a positive plan, military or otherwise, in regard to Tibet. The seat of the National Government was first set up in the extreme south, Canton, and then moved to Nanking, still toward the south. Had it been in Peking, more attention would have been paid to the Tibetan problem. Most of the Kuomintang leaders who occupied key positions in the government were born and brought up in the south and could hardly realize the importance of Tibet's position. Another factor often neglected by observers was the submission of the National Government to the pressure group in Shanghai who took advantage of the unique position of this "sinners' paradise" created by the Unequal Treaties to absorb all the idle money from the tumultuous inland and wield it as a powerful weapon for their own interest, thus leaving the rural economy on the verge of bankruptcy and making the standard of living of the people proceed from bad to worse. As their interest was so closely tied up with the maritime trade and local speculations, they would not finance any constructive plan for the northwest, to say nothing of a military campaign in Tibet.

The above explanation applies to the situation up to the middle of 1931. On September 18 of that year Japan created the Mukden Incident and easily occupied Manchuria after having inflicted undeclared war on China. Henceforth every move of the National Government was overshadowed by the Japanese menace. Any plan for Tibet, had there been one, would have had to give way to the more urgent measures for making preparations against further Japanese invasion.

In view of the far more serious crisis in Manchuria, the National Government turned down the petitions of General Liu Wen-hui and T'ang Ko-san asking for the issuing of an order to mobilize the troops of Szechwan, Yünnan, and Ch'inghai with the object of settling the Tibetan issue by force.[139] Instead, it urged T'ang to continue negotiations and make a peaceful settlement even at a sacrifice. Accordingly, T'ang and the Tibetan delegate Ch'un-jang came to an agreement of eight items[140] which the government approved in spite of local protests.[141] On the other hand, the Lhasa Government became more stubborn on hearing the news of the worsening situation in Manchuria caused by the Japanese invasion. The Dalai Lama refused to sanction the agreement as he insisted that the Chuwo (Driwo) and Ch'iung-hsia districts should not be turned back to the Chinese garrison as provided for in the agreement. Later in February, the Tibetan delegate Ch'un-jang informed T'ang that his government claimed even more territory and that the boundary should be fixed at least at Tai-ning if not at the Lu-ting Bridge. Facing such a complete deadlock, the hard-pressed National Government was obliged to reach a decision on February 19, 1932,[142] leaving the matter entirely in the hands of General Liu Wen-hui and recalling T'ang Ko-san, who returned to Nanking on May 20.

When the Dalai Lama was informed of this decision, he wired back by the end of March strongly protesting against the choice of General Liu, who, he charged, had always shown ill feelings toward the Tibetans. In the meantime, the Tibetan forces raided Ch'inghai and occupied a part of Yu-shu. An arrangement for concerted action was then made between Liu and General Ma Pu-fang, Division Commander of the Chinese garrisons at Jyekundo in the Ch'inghai province.[143]

No sooner had Liu's reinforcement advanced to the front than the Tibetans began their attack against the Chinese positions. They were, however, not only repulsed but also driven out of Kanze on May 2. A few days later, another column of Liu's retook Nyarong, thus restoring the original position prior to the incident with the exception of Ta-chien monastery, which they finally subdued on July 9.[144]

By the end of July the Chinese forces recovered Chiang-ch'ia (Markam Gartok)[145] and De-ge which had been lost to the Tibetans in the armed conflict of 1918. The National Government learned in the meantime that the Lhasa authorities were enlisting more men and negotiating a large quantity of munitions from India for which they were asked to give some concessions they had hitherto repeatedly rejected.[146] Considering the Manchurian crisis and fearing that Tibet might be driven more closely into the arms of the British, it decided not to carry its military success beyond the restoration of the status quo ante bellum.

On August 1, Kung-chüeh-chung-ni presented to the Commission for Mongolian and Tibetan Affairs a telegram from the

Dalai Lama which, though repeating his protest against Liu Wen-hui, expressed his desire for peace. In September he conveyed to Generalissimo Chiang Kai-shek a telegram from the three leading monasteries and the Tibetan National Assembly which reiterated their request for removing the title and honor of the Panch'en Lama,[147] and welcomed the decision of the Dalai Lama to invite a high-ranking representative from the Central Government to come to Lhasa for a peaceful settlement. The National Government thereupon issued orders to General Liu Wen-hui and General Ma Pu-fang to halt their military actions. By then Liu's troops were approaching Chamdo and Ma's troops had just recovered the lost part of Yu-shu.

On October 7, the British chargé d'affaires made a representation in person to the Chinese Foreign Office calling the latter's attention to the serious situation created by the expanding hostilities between Sikang and Tibet, and proposing an immediate cease-fire arrangement by both sides. A few days later, he was informed that orders to halt military action had already been issued and that the Dalai Lama had been told to leave the whole issue to the mediation of the Central Government.[148]

In the meantime civil strife broke out between Liu Wen-hui and his nephew Liu Hsiang, the Commander in Chungking, who for no other purpose than self-aggrandizement suddenly attacked his uncle's forces left in Szechwan. Liu Wen-hui was then compelled to withdraw a large part of his troops from Sikang and thus relieved the tension on the Sino-Tibetan front.

The Truce with Sikang Signed in 1932 and with Ch'inghai in 1933

On October 10, 1932, a truce was signed at Gonchen in De-ge whereby the Chinese forces kept the eastern bank of Chin-sha-chiang (Upper Yangtze River) as their frontier, with the Tibetans on the opposite bank. It provided for the free flow of mutual trade, the protection of monasteries and pilgrimages, while its sixth and last article made it clear that this instrument was subject to revision by the Dalai Lama and the Central Government.[149] A similar truce was signed on June 15, 1933, between General Ma Pu-fang and the Tibetan commander, drawing a demilitarized zone to avoid future conflict and providing for the repatriation of war prisoners taken by the Ch'inghai force. It is significant that in the preamble both expressed regret that "in view of the prevailing national crisis, a civil strife should have happened."[150]

Immediately after the conclusion of the truce, the Lhasa Government discovered that Liu's troops in Sikang had been largely withdrawn to Szechwan. A second drive was planned. But due to the strong opposition of the lamas,[151] the plan failed to materialize.

On December 17, 1933, the Dalai Lama died. According to a special article contributed to *The Times* by a "special correspondent lately at Lhasa,"[152] "Tibet is stunned by the sudden death of the Dalai Lama. Those who knew him thought that he would live for at least another 15 years. An integral part of the political machinery of Asia has unexpectedly given way." This well-informed British correspondent tells us that the Lonchen or prime minister, a nephew of the late Dalai Lama, a young man of about 26 years, was powerless and that Kumbela, the late Dalai Lama's chief official favorite and a British protégé, was not yet in a position to "do great work for his country." He pinned hopes on "another strong man," Tsarong, whom, as mentioned above, Sir Charles Bell spoke of as "always very pro-British,"[153] and ended the article with these words: "Should ambition stir him [Tsarong] to seize the reins of government, he would have strong support backed as he would be by the army and by the great monastery of Sera of which he has been a generous benefactor."

In fact, this ex-Commander-in-Chief did try to seize the reins of government but failed to get any backing from Sera or any other monastery. The lamas, being loath to lose the grants which they used to receive from the Chinese Government and realizing that their former influence was being curtailed by the new army which the late Dalai Lama and the Lhasa Government were fostering,[154] intensified their struggle with the pro-British Young-Tibet group for control of the Lhasa Government. At one time the Tibetan political situation was so tense that civil war seemed quite possible between the conservative priests and the ambitious military men.[155]

The main target of the struggle was the post of the regency, the occupant of which would be in control of political and religious affairs until the maturity of the new Dalai Lama. Through the cooperation of the lamaistic class and the strict adherence on the part of the general public to the old tradition that the regency should go to a priest and not to a layman, Ra-dreng Hutukhtu, the abbot of the Ra-dreng monastery at two days' march northeast of Lhasa, was elected as the regent of Tibet in January, 1934.[156]

Immediately after his election as the regent of Tibet, Ra-dreng sent a telegram to the National Government, not only reporting the fact of his being elected, but, still more significant, requesting confirmation of his appointment by the Chinese Government.[157] In reality, this was the first time since the Chinese Revolution of 1911 that an appointment in Tibet was ever referred to the Chinese authority. Without the least delay the Chinese Government granted its confirmation.[158]

As they had done four years before in trying to frustrate the rapprochement with China by resorting to military action on the frontier, the Young-Tibet group decided to make another drive in Sikang to recover their lost prestige at home and to forestall the pro-Chinese tendency inaugurated by the newly elected regent.

On February 8, 1934, the Tibetan command called a meeting at Ai-ta under the pretext of solving pending questions and suddenly handed to the delegate of Sikang the following demands:

1. that the truce agreement signed at Gonchen be canceled;
2. that De-ge (including Tengko—otherwise spelled as Dengko; Shihch'u—also known as Seshu; and Paigu—also known as Beyu, districts), Kanze, Nyarong, Chuwo, Yen-ching (in the south of Sikang), and all the villages west of the river in Ba-t'ang be surrendered to Tibet; and
3. that the monks of the Ta-chieh monastery be allowed to return without any molestation.[159]

When these demands met with a flat rejection and the conference broke up without reaching any agreement, the Tibetan force, making use of the Ta-chieh monks as vanguards, launched an attack on the Chinese position in Tengko on February 13. Tengko was lost to the Tibetans on the 15th, but recovered two days later. On March 4 fighting started around De-ge, which was captured by the Tibetan force after almost two weeks of siege.[160]

The Chinese Government wired the Lhasa authorities asking for an explanation of the breach of truce. The regent then issued an order to the Tibetan commander at Chamdo demanding a cease fire at once.[161] He wired back to the Chinese Government attributing the cause of resuming hostilities to the Ta-chieh monks, to whom he suggested the Chinese Government should give due care and protection.[162]

Agreement to Halt the Armed Conflict Resumed after the Dalai Lama's Death

Being denied the authority to continue fighting, the Tibetans reached a conciliatory agreement with the Chinese command on May 17, which provided for the withdrawal of troops of both sides to their original positions as laid down in the Gonchen Truce Agreement (Article II). Seven of the twelve articles were devoted to the disposition of the Ta-chieh monks and their weapons and the settlement of questions in connection with the management and the jurisdiction of this powerful monastery. Both parties reiterated their willingness to abide by the Gonchen Truce Agreement and leave the solution of other matters to the joint effort of their respective high authorities.[163] It is significant that this agreement was signed by a delegate on behalf of "the three leading monasteries and the Tibetan government," while his counterpart signed in the name of the local military command, that is, Liu Wen-hui's headquarters.

Following this incident, the Regent became fully aware of the insubordination of the army officers and decided to curtail their power.[164] In the first place, he ordered the disbandment of a large portion of the army. Then he restricted the purchase of arms and munitions from the government of India.[165] Finally, he took another drastic step by putting the above-mentioned Lung-shar in prison, and appointed Tsang Yang Lama his right-hand man, as the Commander-in-Chief of the Tibetan army.[166]

It is true that the intention of the Regent in taking such

measures was not so much to improve relations with China as for the purpose of diminishing the strength of his opposition. Nevertheless, the reduction of the power of the army group which had repeatedly resorted to military action to frustrate a rapprochement undoubtedly facilitated better understanding with the Chinese authorities. Taking advantage of this opportunity for promoting closer relations with Lhasa, the National Government decided to send a mission to Tibet.

General Huang's Mission to Tibet

General Huang Mu-sung, Deputy Chief of the General Staff, was chosen as "Special Commissioner to Tibet" for the purpose of paying posthumous tribute to the late Dalai Lama. A number of technical experts in various fields were assigned to his mission.[167] On April 25, 1934, he and his retinue reached Lhasa via Sikang. Immediately upon arrival, the mission set up a radio service in order to keep contact with Nanking.[168] Besides taking part in the memorial service for the late Dalai Lama, General Huang issued a proclamation emphatically urging the Tibetan people to place their trust and reliance in the National Government which alone, he claimed, could assure them everlasting prosperity and happiness.[169]

With a view to readjusting relations between the National Government and Tibet, General Huang conducted a number of discussions with the Regent and other high Tibetan officials on the basis of the following proposal: [170]

A. Two fundamental points that Tibet is asked to observe:
   1. Tibet must be an integral part of the territory of China.
   2. Tibet must obey the Central Government.
B. Declarations in regard to the political system of Tibet:
   1. Buddhism shall be respected by all and given protection and its propagation encouraged.
   2. In the preservation of the traditional political system, Tibet shall be granted autonomy. Any administrative measures within the authority of the autonomy of Tibet, the Central Government will not interfere with. On foreign affairs, there must be unitary action [with the Central Government]. All administrative matters which are nation-wide in character shall be administered by the Central Government, such as:
      a. Foreign affairs shall be directed by the Central Government.

b. National defense shall be planned by the Central Government.
c. Communications shall be managed by the Central Government.
d. The names of important officials of Tibet, after they have been elected by the autonomous government of Tibet, shall be submitted to the Central Government for their respective appointments.

C. The Central Government shall grant Tibet autonomy, but for the purpose of exercising full sovereignty in an integral part of its territory, the Central Government shall appoint a high commissioner to be stationed in Tibet as the representative of the Central Government, on the one hand to carry out national administrative measures, and on the other to guide the regional autonomy.

The above proposal, if agreed to and carried out, would have settled the status of Tibet in a constitutional sense. But the intensified internal struggle between the conservative lamas and the ambitious military men, the fear of the consequences that might result from offending the British power or from coming more directly under Chinese authority, as well as from the loss of the advantage of sitting on the fence as a buffer state, prevented the newly installed Lhasa authorities from taking such a bold step. Avoiding a categorical answer to the four points under B2, they submitted a counterproposal containing the following ten points:

1. In dealing with external affairs, Tibet shall remain an integral part of the territory of China. But the Chinese Government must promise that Tibet will not be reorganized into a province.
2. Tibetan authorities, big or small, external or internal, and Tibetan laws, regulations, etc., may be subjected to the orders of the Chinese Government provided such orders are not, either religiously or politically, harmful to Tibet.
3. Traditional laws and regulations dealing with the internal affairs of Tibet shall remain independent as at present, and the Chinese Government will not interfere with Tibetan civil and military authorities. On this matter it shall be in accordance with the oral promises made at different times in the past.
4. To maintain the present peaceful condition of Tibet, there shall be friendly relations with all its neighboring states and all the peoples believing in Buddhism. In the future, any important treaty making between Tibet and any foreign country shall be made by joint decisions with the Chinese Government.
5. One representative of the Chinese Government may be stationed

in Tibet, but his retinue shall not exceed twenty-five. There shall be no other representative either civil or military. This representative must be a true believer in Buddhism. When a new representative is appointed to replace the old, the route he and his retinue take to and fro must be by sea and not through Sikang.

6. Before the recognition of the reincarnation of the Dalai Lama and before his taking over reins of government, the inauguration of the regency and the appointments of officials from the bKa'-blon up shall be conducted or made by the Tibetan Government as at present. Of such inauguration and appointments, the representative of the Chinese Government in Tibet shall be notified soon after they have taken place.
7. Those Chinese people who have long resided in Tibet and have been under the jurisdiction and protection of the Agricultural Bureau since the Chinese-Tibetan War of the year jen-tzu (1912) shall remain under the control of the Tibetan Government and abide by the local laws and regulations. The representative of the Chinese Government shall exercise no control over them.
8. Military forces to be stationed on the borders of Tibet for defense purpose shall be dispatched by the Government of Tibet as at present. If and when there should be foreign invasion, the Chinese Government shall be consulted on military measures to be taken.
9. For permanent harmony and friendship, to avoid any possible disputes, and to maintain peace on the borders, the northeastern boundary between Kokonor and Tibet should be maintained as proposed during the negotiations of the year before last, with O-Lo which has long been under Tibet to be included on the Tibetan side. As for the boundary between Tibet and Szechwan, the territory and people, together with the administration of De-ge, Nyarong, Ta-chieh Ssu, should be turned over to the Tibetan Government at the earliest possible date.
10. The Chinese Government should not give asylum to or acknowledge as representative, any Tibetan, ecclesiastical or secular, who has rebelled against the Tibetan Government and escaped to China Proper.

The Tibetan counterproposal shows clearly that the Lhasa authorities were not yet ready to place their trust and reliance on the Chinese Government of the day. In particular, point five indicates a British shadow behind the scene, though point eight betokens the Tibetan fear of a possible British invasion. However, they went a considerable way to meet the Chinese wishes. First of all they accepted the Chinese proposition that full relations be resumed in principle, but insisted that the commissioner or representative's office in Lhasa should not be established until the over-all differences were settled. They nevertheless permitted the Chinese Government to have some liaison officers stay in Lhasa together with the radio service to take care of communications. In regard to the Panch'en Lama's return to Tibet they expressed great suspicion and scepticism, because this question not only involved Chinese-Tibetan relations but also the internal struggle for power between Lhasa and Shigatse. Yet as a result of Chinese insistence as well as for the sake of the Tibetan religious tradition, which established a practice that when either of the two Grand Lamas died, the education of the reincarnated successor would rest on the shoulders of the other, the Regent agreed to the return of the Panch'en Lama on condition that no large Chinese escort should come along, nor should the latter exercise any political influence over the Lhasa Government.[171]

Realizing the difficulties that the Lhasa authorities were facing from within[172] and without, and considering the inadvisability of forcing an issue with the friendly regent or with the British while the rich and industrialized part of the country—Manchuria—was under Japanese occupation, General Huang decided not to negotiate further and left Lhasa in October, 1934. Messrs. Liu P'u-chen and Chiang Chi-yu, councillors of the mission, were ordered to remain as liaison officers for the Central Government. In addition, the radio service was left behind to continue its operation in order to maintain quicker, easier, and cheaper communication between Lhasa and various parts of China.[173] General Huang's mission aroused some criticism among the British,[174] but it did undoubtedly succeed in bringing about a new phase in Sino-Tibetan relations by setting up a direct two-way contact between Nanking and Lhasa, though it failed to solve the fundamental issue of Tibet's status.[175]

Upon his return General Huang made several important recommendations to the Central Government. He found that in Tibet British influence was still prevalent, and suggested that the Panch'en Lama's wish to go back should be met, and a Chinese escort provided so that a solution to the fundamental political issue could be found. He also recommended the creation of the new province of Sikang out of the "Szechwan Border Territory" which was later carried out after four years of preparation.[176]

The creation of a new province of Sikang, marking the realization of a policy inaugurated by Chao Erh-feng, would have been distasteful to the Tibetans. But Kham, which forms the main part of the present-day Sikang Province, was not regarded as Tibet proper, and on one occasion the Lhasa Government[177] told the British Trade Agent at Gyantse in an official letter dated July 24, 1905, that they could not be responsible for the conduct of Khambas, "the people of Kham being evil persons."[178] If merely on ethnographic grounds, they actually have no better claim on Kham than on Kashmir's Ladakh which was a province of Tibet.[179] As the Nanking Government at that time in fact did not show much activity and enthusiasm toward its realization beyond the setting up of a preparatory commission, this matter, though distasteful, was tolerable to the Tibetans.

The Panch'en Lama's Plan to Return and His Death

In the eyes of the Lhasa authorities, therefore, it was the return of the Panch'en with a Chinese escort that constituted an immediate danger threatening their very existence. The Panch'en Lama for his part originally has not intended to force a way home. He had, prior to the Dalai Lama's death, sent An-ch'in Hutukhtu as his personal representative to Lhasa with a view to reaching an understanding on his plan for a peaceful return. The sudden death of the Dalai Lama frustrated An-ch'in's effort and brought about a new state of affairs.[180] While the Young-Tibet group strongly opposed the Panch'en's return, the march of events in China, as related below, made the Panch'en more suspected by and less acceptable to the Lhasa authorities, and finally made his return impossible without the aid of an armed Chinese escort.

In February, 1934, the Panch'en was sworn in as a member of the National Government. In other words, he was admitted to the Supreme Council—the highest Chinese honor he could have possibly received. On that occasion he emphatically declared that "the utmost efforts would be exerted for the purpose of promoting the national interest and unity, and the well-being of the whole people, with the blessings of Buddha."[181] This utterance shows clearly how far he was committed to the Nationalist cause. The Lhasa authorities, who had requested Nanking to deprive the Panch'en of his titles, would certainly be displeased, if not offended, to hear of his gaining a new distinction.[182]

On February 8, 1935, the Panch'en Lama was appointed "Special Cultural Commissioner for the Western Regions" with his headquarters at Sining in the province of Ch'inghai. Five hundred Chinese soldiers were assigned as his personal escort.[183] When General Huang succeeded Shih Ch'ing-yang as Chairman of the Commission for Mongolian and Tibetan Affairs in March of 1935, he naturally did all he could to carry out his own recommendations including the one to give early effect to the Panch'en's return. At that time the director of Tibetan Affairs in the Commission was a Tibetan named Lo-sang-chien-tsan who was a follower of the Panch'en and who would spare no effort to see that his master could go back home at the earliest possible date.

As mentioned above, General Huang while he was in Lhasa procured the reluctant consent of the Regent to the Panch'en Lama's return. Later, the Lhasa Government laid down another condition, i.e., that the Panch'en should make no attempt to enter Lhasa. This the Panch'en and his entourage agreed to, deciding to travel by Nachuka, north of the Tibetan capital. In May, 1936, the National Government sent a special envoy to accompany the Panch'en,[184] who reached Jyekundo in southern Ch'inghai in March, 1937, while Nong-yong, the Panch'en's Treasurer, with an enormous consignment of boxes and bundles, arrived at Tach'ienlu by a different route.[185]

The reluctance of the Lhasa authorities on this matter was clearly shown in an incident occurring even before General Huang's return from his mission to Tibet. In the late spring of 1934, An-ch'in Hutukhtu came back to Nanking from Lhasa and told the press that the government and people in Tibet had keenly felt the need of the Panch'en Lama's leadership, and that the delegates from Lhasa would soon come to urge him to return.[186] No sooner had this announcement been made known than a categorical denial was issued by the Tibetan representative at Nanking. It was stated that "no official deputation would be sent to welcome the Panch'en Lama to Tibet, nor was there any intention of doing so in the foreseeable future." To clear up this misunderstanding, An-ch'in Hutukhtu went back to Lhasa for the second time, but with no better result.[187]

When General Huang was made the Chairman of the Commission for Mongolian and Tibetan Affairs, the Lhasa authorities' reluctance became more pronounced, and gradually turned to open opposition. They attacked Lo-sang-chien-tsan and called him "the Panch'en's protégé who had nothing to do with the affairs of Tibet." They even refused to submit official communications through the Commission.[188]

Now when the news of the Panch'en's embarking on his journey with a Chinese escort reached them, their attitude became hostile, and they eventually decided to offer armed resistance should the Panch'en persist and force his way toward Nachuka. The Panch'en dispatched delegates to Chamdo to hold meetings with the Tibetan commander with a view to reaching an understanding, but their effort proved fruitless.[189]

As obviously the Panch'en's return could solve the fundamental issue of the status of Tibet and would tremendously affect the British position, it is conceivable that the British had a hand in its opposition.[190] In August, 1935, Frederick Williamson, British Political Officer in Sikkim, was sent to Lhasa and his visit was connected with the issue of the Panch'en Lama's return.[191] According to the reports of Chiang Chi-yu, the liaison officer in Lhasa, to the Mongolian and Tibetan Affairs Commission, the British were, in the meantime, exerting pressure on the Tibetan Government, demanding either the withdrawal of the liaison officers of the National Government and its radio service, or the equal right to such establishments themselves.[192] The British Government regarded Chinese sponsorship of the Panch'en's return as a "military penetration."[193] On November 9, 1935, the British Ambassador, Sir Alexander Cadogan, came to the Chinese Foreign Office and raised his government's objections to the armed escort provided for the Panch'en Lama by the National Government. He made a similar representation on November 27 and left a memorandum on December 23. Failing to secure a satisfactory answer, he took up the matter again with the Wai-chiao-pu on February 4 and 22, March 31, and October 24 of the next year.[194]

In August, 1936, J. B. Gould, the successor of Williamson as Political officer in Sikkim, was sent to Lhasa, heading a mission.[195] As reported by Chiang Chi-yu, he persuaded the Lhasa Government not to allow the Panch'en Lama to return and at the same time made every effort to bolster the morale of the Young-Tibet group who hovered between the Dalai Party and the Panch'en Party, and who stood for the substitution of some form of civil government for the lama hierarchy.[196] In the spring of 1937 when the Panch'en and his escort were about to enter Tibet, the British Embassy in Nanking made further representations to raise strong objections. Mr. Chou K'un-t'ien, then a Senior Secretary of the Commission for Mongolian and Tibetan Affairs, and later made Chairman of the Commission, told this writer that in April of that year both the Wai-chiao-pu and the Commission refused to receive a note from the British Embassy which raised strong objections to the escorted return of the Panch'en as its content was regarded as interfering with China's internal administration. This impasse demonstrated the determination of the Chinese Government to see that the Panch'en be escorted home.

An inspired article entitled "Lhasa Government Forbids Official's Entry" relates a story that the Panch'en was prepared to carry with him a ready-made reincarnation of the Dalai Lama, and actually found a boy for this purpose. The writer calls this an unfortunate *faux pas* made by the Panch'en, and believes this was a probable cause of the sudden withdrawal of permission to enter Tibet by the Lhasa authorities.[197] Nothing in Chinese sources can be found to tally with such a story. It is much more likely that the sudden withdrawal of their permission, and the decision to block the Panch'en's entry by force, was due to hostility to the Panch'en's return, which had been building up since 1934, reinforced by news received over the wireless concerning the Marco Polo Bridge Incident of July 7 created by the Japanese army, and the subsequent announcement of armed resistance to Japanese aggression made by the National Government.

On August 18, more than one month after the Japanese militarists had started their second phase of aggression in China,[198] the Panch'en and his entourage left Yu-shu (Jyekundo) and after three days' march arrived at the La-hsiu monastery on the border between Ch'inghai and Tibet where he planned to stay ten days to perform religious ceremonies before resuming his journey to enter Tibet.[199] A few days later he was told by Ma Ho-t'ien, councillor of the escort mission, that the Central Government had decided to halt his journey in consideration of the national emergency created by renewed Japanese aggression. The Panch'en expressed sympathetic understanding of the situation though the news must have been a blow to him.[200] He still hoped against hope that an agreement might be reached with the three leading monasteries of Lhasa, but nothing materialized. Without any definite prospect of his return, he withdrew to Yu-shu where he fell ill and died on December 1, 1937.[201]

The death of the Panch'en Lama removed a source of friction between the Chinese Government and the Lhasa authorities, and the latter soon showed signs of rapprochement toward the former. The Regent dispatched a special delegate to the wartime capital to pledge Tibet's sincere cooperation with the Central Government in the struggle for national existence. He also assembled the lamas of the three leading monasteries to pray for China's victory.[202] No Tibetan troops, however, were sent to the Chinese front. Among the reasons for this may be listed the lack of communications and transportation; the difficulties Tibetans would encounter in living away from their plateau;[203] and the presence of anti-war sentiments among the lamas. Nevertheless, the Tibetan Government offered 10,000 sheepskins worth $500,000 in Chinese national currency as a token of the support of lamas, officials, and poor peasants by whom these gifts were donated.[204]

Further rapprochement was shown in the search for and the subsequent installation of the new Dalai Lama. Even before the death of the late pontiff, rumors had been spreading far and wide that the line of reincarnation of the Dalai Lama was to be terminated with the 13th, after which would come a drastic change of government. As the 13th Dalai Lama failed to give the needed information as to the exact location of his next appearance on earth, which had usually been given by his predecessors, doubts were expressed even in lamaistic circles as to whether there ever would be another Dalai Lama.[205] The Young-Tibet group, whose ultimate object was to abolish priest rule, naturally viewed the search for the new Dalai Lama with unusual apprehension. They therefore exerted every effort to exploit these rumors and doubts to confuse the people and to weaken the administration so as to enable themselves to come back to power.

The Regent, whose primary duty was to find the Dalai Lama's successor in strict conformity with well-established traditions,[206] disregarded all these maneuvers of the opposition and went ahead to put in motion the traditional machinery for the discovery of the next pontiff. The delicate procedure leading to the discovery and the events connected with the installation were amply reported in the western press.[207] We shall later see an official version, from a communication sent by the Regent of Tibet to the Chairman of the Commission for Mongolian and Tibetan Affairs, of how they found and identified the new Dalai Lama. Sir Charles Bell, retired from active service yet still indispensable to British activities in Tibet, who had been in Lhasa "on a private visit" while General Huang and his party were there, came again "on a private visit" nine months after the Dalai Lama's death.[208] He tells us a colorful story about the search for, and the installation of, the new Incarnation, basing his information chiefly on the account of Sir Basil Gould who was the man officially responsible for carrying out British policy in Tibet and who was at the time in Lhasa and elsewhere in Central Tibet.[209]

A comparison of Sir Charles's story with the following account will show discrepancies. Since Sir Charles predicted that "the Chinese . . . can later refer to their press records and present an account of historical events that is wholly untrue," [210] this writer here purposely refrains from citing any Chinese press records, though other press records, such as those of the United States,[211] could be produced as supporting evidence, and bases the following account entirely on the official records in the Chinese Government archives, and Mr. Wu Chung-hsin's report on his mission to Tibet. Behind all the writings of Sir Charles Bell in connection with Tibet there seems to be an unspoken theme: to undermine Chinese authority in Tibet and to justify the British position there—a theme shared by most English writers on Tibet. He gives us to understand that Tibet is not only independent today, but was independent in the time of the Fifth Dalai Lama.[212] According to him, the Tibetans like the British so much and hate the Chinese to such an extent that they would not want to have anything to do with the Chinese Government. So in his eyes, "the Tibetan Government allowed a Chinese envoy, Mr. Wu Chung-hsin, to come to Lhasa for the ceremony, and the British representative was also admitted; . . . Mr. Wu was merely a passive spectator; he did no more than present a ceremonial scarf, as was done by others, including the British representative."[213]

Although it is not the purpose of this study to take issue with any single author, this writer feels obliged for the sake of truth to devote a few lines to clearing up this part of Sir Charles's story. Apparently basing his story on Sir Basil Gould's account, Sir Charles informs us that the Chinese governor, as a price for letting the little boy depart, demanded "a payment of a hundred thousand Chinese dollars (£7,500) which Kyi-tsang, the chief of the searching party, managed to raise." Later, "the governor also put in a demand for a further installment of blackmail, this time amounting to three hundred and thirty thousand dollars (£25,000)."[214] Kyi-tsang "was able to arrange for a further payment of three hundred thousand dollars through a party of rich Mohammedan merchants who were going to Lhasa and India, and would provide the escort." Therefore, "only twenty Chinese soldiers" were sent.

During all these years when the new Dalai Lama was sought, found, and later installed, the writer was staying in Lanchow not far from Ch'inghai and Tibet. Once he flew to Sining and had the opportunity of seeing the recently found fourteenth Dalai Lama at the Kum-bum monastery. He heard nothing of such a scandal. It is incredible that this governor, himself a Moslem, should dare to hold the claimant to the Pontiff Chair as a hostage and blackmail repeatedly—an act which would antagonize the numerous Buddhistic Mongolians and Tibetans in his province—while fighting was going on with the Japanese in the neighboring provinces of Ninghsia and Suiyuan, and a heavy concentration of half a million Central Government troops with watchful eyes were stationed in the neighboring provinces of Kansu and Shensi. It is true that the lamas of the Kum-bum monastery refused to let the boy depart unless he was immediately declared to be the Dalai Lama. The National Government ordered the governor of Ch'inghai Province, General Ma Pu-fang, to tell A-chia Hutukhtu, the abbot of the monastery, not to place any obstace in the way of the boy's departure. It took the initiative in making a special appropriation of a generous sum to cover all the expenses for the boy's journey. It also instructed General Ma to provide careful protection along the route and the latter reported that Major General Ma Yuan-hai was dispatched as a special commissioner to escort the boy with a battalion of bodyguards composed of 500 soldiers.[215]

As early as September 13, 1938, the Tibetan representative stationed at the wartime capital transmitted to the National Government a dispatch from the Lhasa authorities reporting that the choice of one of three boys, two found in Tibet and one in Sining near the Kum-bum monastery, was to be decided by the traditional practice of oracle revelation and lot-drawing, and requesting that a permit be issued for the boy found in Sining to proceed to Lhasa to take part in the pending ceremony. The Chinese Government, fully realizing that the choice and the installation would tremendously affect its position in regard to Tibet and might offer an opportunity to solve the fundamental issue of Tibet's status in relation to itself, decided that the Chairman of the Commission for Mongolian and Tibetan Affairs should be jointly responsible with the Regent in supervising the ceremony. This decision was conveyed to the Lhasa Government by Chang Wei-pei, who was in charge of the radio service set up since General Huang's last mission, and who, after the death of Liu Pu-ch'en at his post and the departure of Chiang Chih-yu in the summer of 1938, had been acting as the liaison officer for the Mongolian and Tibetan Affairs Commission. After long deliberation, the Lhasa Government finally expressed its concurrence, which was transmitted by its representative to the National Government in a communication dated December 18, 1938. The National Government therefore issued an order on December 28 appointing Wu Chung-hsin, Chairman of the Commission for Mongolian and Tibetan Affairs, and Ra-dreng Hutukhtu, the Regent of Tibet, jointly to supervise all matters in connection with the re-incarnation and installation of the new Dalai Lama. Of this order the Regent acknowledged the receipt and expressed his acceptance.[216]

Wu Chung-hsin's Mission to Officiate at the Installation of the Present Dalai Lama

The Chinese Government at first thought of designating some-one near or in Tibet to officiate on its behalf, but later decided that the Chairman of the Commission in charge of Tibetan Affairs should himself undertake the mission in order to carry more weight in the discussions regarding the readjustment of Sino-Tibetan relations. On March 29, 1939, this decision was com-municated to the Lhasa Government. On April 23 a reply was received expressing hearty welcome, but suggesting that Mr. Wu come by sea. The latter part of the message implied the Tibetan fear of offending the British power. In reality, it amounted to leaving the final decision to the British Government, which could have easily blocked Mr. Wu's entry by refusing to give him the necessary transit visa.[217]

In fact, the British transit visa was not given until October, and it was given only after repeated efforts had been made by the Chinese Embassy in London. The Chinese Ambassador was at first told by the British Foreign Office that application for a transit visa to enter Tibet should have been made by the Tibetan authorities through the Indian Government. Of course, the Chinese envoy would not accept such a procedure, which was contrary to diplomatic practice. He argued that no visa should require that an application be made by a local government in-stead of through the proper diplomatic channel. But he was kept waiting till October after the European war had broken out. It is likely that the granting finally of a transit visa was due more to change in the international situation than to the efforts of the Chinese Embassy. The British Foreign Office might have by then realized that they had to loosen their grip on Tibet a bit and that it was advisable not to hurt unnecessarily[218] the feelings of the

Chinese who had been fighting desperately against one of the Axis powers.

Mr. Wu and his staff left Chungking by plane on October 21, bound for Calcutta by way of Rangoon. After a short stay at Calcutta and Kalimpong, they took the Yatung-Gyantse route (the same route traveled by the Younghusband Mission in 1903-4) and reached Lhasa on December 15 amidst a colorful welcome. Mr. Wu, while awaiting the British transit visa, directed Kung Ch'ing-tsung, who succeeded Lo-sang-chien-tsan as director of Tibetan Affairs, and nine other members of the staff of the Mongolian and Tibetan Affairs Commission, to proceed to Lhasa by land via Tach'ienlu so that Kung would be able to officiate on his behalf at the installation ceremony in case he was prevented from attending in person. Kung and his party left Chungking on July 2 and reached the Tibetan capital on November 25, only three weeks before Wu's arrival.[219]

Wu was supposed to come to Lhasa to supervise the oracle revelation and lot-drawing procedures for the purpose of choosing the true incarnation out of the three candidates. But upon his arrival he found that the Regent had eliminated the two other candidates and the candidate from Kokonor was the only claimant to the Pontiff Chair. In fact, the Silon (equivalent to Prime Minister and sometimes misinterpreted as King of Tibet) sponsored one of the two other candidates and raised objections to what the Regent had done, but the latter succeeded in having the Silon's opposition overruled by the National Assembly.

The Chinese Mission of course supported the pro-Chinese Regent. As a matter of procedure, it demanded that a request should be made by the Regent to the National Government for the exemption of the lot-drawing process, and that the boy should be identified by Mr. Wu in a private interview. To this the Regent readily expressed his consent.

Thus on January 26, 1940, the Regent sent Mr. Wu a communication asking the Central Government to confirm La-mu-tan-chu as the reincarnation of Dalai Lama without the performance of drawing lots. The communication stated that after many investigations and according to all the indications, this boy has been proved without any doubt to be the reincarnation of the 13th Dalai Lama. It went on to say:

When he was born, an image of the house where his parents dwelt appeared in the Holy Lake of Ch'u-k'o-chi, and this was later again seen and confirmed by an investigating party headed by myself. Furthermore, various divine omens foretold that he was to be born in the eastern part of Tibet. Yet three parties were sent out in three different directions to make sure a true reincarnation would be located. The party sent to the east headed by Chi-ts'ang (Kyi-tsang) Hutukhtu at first had found fourteen male children who bore extraordinary omens and rare appearances. Among these was this boy by the name of La-mu-tan-chu, born on the sixth day of the sixth month of the I-hai year (1935) into the family bearing the surname of Ch'i in the vicinity of Kum-bum Monastery in Kokonor. At the time of his birth, all the people in the same village saw a felicitous rainbow pointing towards his house. Afterwards, when the investigating party arrived at his house, although both the father and the mother had no knowledge of the Tibetan language, the little boy was very happy to see the party and uttered words in the Tibetan dialect. Then he was tested by four articles which had been in daily use by the Dalai Lama, each of the four articles having a replica. The boy picked up the genuine one in each case. Therefore, all the people, ecclesiastical and secular, rich and poor, old and young, sincerely believed that he was the true incarnation of the 13th Dalai Lama. Since this had been agreed upon unanimously, the performance of lot-drawing from the golden vase would seem to be unnecessary, and he should have his hair shaved and be ready to take the vows. As Keng-ch'en year is astrologically appropriate, the 14th day of the 1st month (February 21, 1940) has been selected for the installation ceremony of ascending the Pontiff Chair. It is hoped that this will meet with the approval of the Central Government, and an early reply is requested.[220]

The National Government, upon receiving the above communication and the favorable recommendations of Mr. Wu, issued an order on February 5 for dispensing with the lot-drawing process and for proclaiming the boy as the 14th Dalai Lama. At the same time, it made a special appropriation of four hundred thousand dollars in Chinese National currency as a grant to cover the expenses of the installation ceremony. The Regent and the members of bKa'-blon sent a telegram on the 17th to express their thanks to the Central Government.[221]

As to the private interview between Mr. Wu and the boy for the purpose of identification, some objections were raised among the high dignitaries of the Church. The latter insisted that the boy could only receive Mr. Wu in audience, while Mr. Wu refused to recognize the boy as Dalai Lama designate unless he was so proclaimed by the Central Government, and the private interview was necessary before he could make a recommendation for dispensing with the lot-drawing process. Only after the personal intervention of the Regent did the opposition give in. The private interview took place on the morning of January 31 inside a small pavilion in the Jewel Park (Nor-pu-ling-ka), one and a half miles out of Lhasa. Mr. Wu conversed with the boy for about a quarter of an hour and presented him with four gifts, including a watch, which greatly pleased him. Mr. Wu was deeply impressed by the dignified and natural manner of the boy who was only four and a half years old. A photograph was taken on this occasion with Mr. Wu and the boy sitting side by side in front of the pavilion.[222]

The solemn installation ceremony was held at the Potala Palace at 5 A.M. on February 22, 1940. About five hundred persons were privileged to attend. As remarked by Sir Charles Bell, "in the Tibetan mind etiquette is of the first importance";[223] therefore the arrangement of seats presented special difficulty. The Pontiff Chair was facing south; the members of the Chinese Mission, the Chinese liaison officer, and other Chinese officials together with the representatives of Nepal and Bhutan were placed on the right facing west; while the Regent, the Silon, the Hutukhtus, and other high ecclesiastic dignitaries were on the opposite side facing east. Down in the hall facing the Pontiff Chair were seated the members of bKa'-blon, secular officials, and representatives of aristocratic families. The master of ceremonies at first intended to place Mr. Wu at the top of the right hand row vis-à-vis the Regent or Silon. No doubt he had it in mind to place Sir Basil Gould, who was sent there to attend the ceremony on behalf of the British Government, on the right also. But the Chinese Mission insisted that the precedent set by the Resident or Amban should be followed. At last the Tibetans agreed and Mr. Wu sat on the same side as the new Dalai Lama, his parents, and his tutor, all facing south. It was because of this seating arrangement that Sir Basil Gould refused to be present.

He tendered congratulations the next day when the new Dalai Lama received him in audience. From the seating of Mr. Wu alone we can see that the Chinese representative asserted the traditional position of China in Tibet and did much more than present a ceremonial scarf.[224]

There were several other things he did which have a bearing on the status of Tibet. A week before the installation ceremony on February 15, Mr. Wu, in the name of the President of the Republic of China, conferred on the Regent a title with golden patent and golden seal, and decorated him with the Grand Order of Auspicious Jade Second Class in a solemn ceremony at the Regent's own monastery. The title conferred was actually announced in November, 1935, and the intention at that time had been that it should be presented by the special Commissioner who was to have escorted the Panch'en's return. In the afternoon of the same day Mr. Wu sent his aides to decorate the members of bKa'-blon with the Third Class Plaque of the same order.[225]

Since Wu's mission was intended to readjust Sino-Tibetan relations, he brought up three problems, viz.:

1. the improvement of, and increase of facilities to, the communications between Tibet and the Central Government;
2. the return to Tibet of the Panch'en's remains;
3. the demands proposed by the Panch'en's followers as conditions of their return to Tibet;

and he dispatched Chou K'un-t'ien, Kung Ch'ing-tsung, and Chang Wei-pei to discuss them with the members of bKa'-blon at the Ko-hsia (Kashag, or the Cabinet Office) on March 10. The members of bKa'-blon promised to give a written reply after a careful deliberation. Mr. Wu was then told that the Regent was having great difficulty in solving them and that Sir Basil Gould has warned the Lhasa authorities against discussing any political problems with Wu or anybody designated by him, and asked to be informed should any such discussion take place.[226]

On April 2 a written reply was received. The Tibetan Government expressed therein their appreciation of the increasing patronage shown by the Central Government. They explained the difficulties they were facing, such as a shortage of food production, lack of sufficient funds to provide offerings to the Buddha and maintenance for the monks, and the drain on the treasury from military expenses necessitated by the stationing of troops on the border, whose presence prevented the pilgrims from coming and therefore reduced the income of the monasteries. They finally expressed the hope that De-ge, Huo-k'o, and Nyarong would be returned to their control so that peace might be assured and communications facilitated. In other words, they wanted first to settle the boundary issue and asked the Central Government to pay a territorial price before the problems of communication improvement and the return of the Panch'en's followers were discussed. However, they expressed welcome to the remains of the Panch'en, but asked also concerning the whereabouts of his valuables.[227]

Mr. Wu, realizing that there was no prospect of settling these problems even if he prolonged his stay for a few months, decided to send a letter to Ko-hsia (Kashag) on April 14, the day of his departure, in which he told the Tibetan Cabinet that these problems were to be taken up further by the Director of the Office of the Mongolian and Tibetan Affairs Commission in Tibet, and that he could not transmit to the Central Government their request for the return of De-ge, Huo-k'o, and Nyarong, as these districts since the reign of Emperor Shih-tsung (1723-35) had been placed under the jurisdiction of Ya-chow-fu of the province of Szechwan and had not originally belonged to Tibet.[228]

The Setting Up in Lhasa of a Permanent Office by the National Government

Before his departure, Mr. Wu managed to have a permanent office set up in Lhasa to act on behalf of the Commission for Mongolian and Tibetan Affairs. As mentioned before, of the two liaison officers left in Tibet by General Huang, one had died at his post and the other had left Tibet in the summer of 1938. Their work since then had been taken over by Chang Wei-pei who, though a very capable man, was handicapped by his relatively low rank and whose duty as master of the radio station prevented him from devoting adequate time to liaison work. Mr. Wu on March 13 sent his adviser, Hsi Lun, to see the Regent and inform him that the Central Government intended to establish a High Commissioner in Tibet. The Regent instantly explained his difficulties as follows: (1) The internal situation of Tibet was delicate and complicated. For the Central Government to set up a high post in Tibet at this time would easily give rise to misunderstanding. (2) Sir Basil Gould was still there. As he was paying such close attention to the development of Sino-Tibetan relations, especially their political aspect, the Tibetan Government had to be scrupulous and should not give him a pretext for intervention or for pressing a similar demand. (3) According to the practice established by the late Dalai Lama, matters of such importance ought to be referred to the National Assembly, where, as far as he could see, there was no chance of getting it passed. Should it be rejected, he would feel guilty of having damaged the prestige of the Central Government. As he was ever grateful to the Central Government, he would do whatever he could to realize its intentions at a more promising moment. For the time being he suggested, therefore, that Mr. Wu leave the matter in his hands without pressing for an immediate solution.[229]

Wu reported the Regent's answer to Chungking. On March 22, 1940, he received instructions to the effect that instead of a high commissionership, an "office of the Mongolian and Tibetan Affairs Commission in Tibet" should be set up. This time Mr. Wu chose to avoid any negotiation. He simply notified the Regent and the Cabinet in writing of its inauguration on April 1, and appointed on March 25 Kung Ch'ing-tsung as the director of the office, and Chang Wei-pei as deputy. To allay any possible misunderstanding, Mr. Wu sent his aides to explain the meaning of this establishment and its function to the Regent and the members of the bKa'-blon.

The dispute between the Regent and the Silon over the choice of the new Dalai Lama has already been mentioned. According to Wu's report,[230] the Silon collaborated with *taiji* Yu-to, Kusang-tzu (former director of the Bureau of Finance), and the above-mentioned An-ch'in Hutukhtu,[231] and tried in 1939 to overthrow the Ra-dreng regency. The plot was discovered and Kusang-tzu was condemned to exile. But the Silon, though his function had been suspended, was still a potential enemy of the Regent.

The struggle for power between the Regent and the predominantly pro-British Young-Tibet group has also been mentioned. Now this ambitious military clique became even more uneasy when they saw the honor done to their rival by the Chinese Mission and the setting up of the permanent office by the Commission for Mongolian and Tibetan Affairs. Moreover, the establishment in Tach'ienlu of a Preparatory Commission to Create the Province of Sikang, and the talk by some irresponsible elements of extending the Sikang boundary by force to Giamda which Chao Erh-feng's army had reached and Fu Sung-mu had claimed as the demarcation line in his proposal to the Throne,[232] provided these military men with means of persuasion. They therefore joined hands with the Silon's group and accused the Regent of dictating the choice of the Dalai Lama in order to satisfy his personal ambition. They also charged him with inducing the Chinese force to enter Tibet to suppress them and to consolidate his own rule.[233]

The Pro-British Young-Tibet Group Coming to Power

Facing this combined opposition and realizing the dissatisfaction of the British with the Tibetan situation and the increasing British support given to the Young-Tibet group,[234] the Regent Ra-dreng thought it advisable to withdraw for a time and appointed in 1941 Yün-tseng Ta-dsa,[235] an abbot of a small monastery, to be the acting Regent. For the first few months he managed to hold the reins behind the scene, but gradually the acting Regent was being won over by the opposition, and the appointees of the ex-Regent were ousted one after another until the Young-Tibet group gained full control of the government.

In the early part of 1947, when every indication pointed to a showdown, Ta-dza expressed on several occasions his readiness to resign on the pretext of old age. To eliminate any chance of Ra-dreng's regaining power, the Young-Tibet group decided to resort to force. On April 14 they surrounded Ra-dreng monastery and arrested Ra-dreng on the charge that he had plotted against the acting Regent to regain power through improper means. The three leading monasteries immediately took up arms and demanded Ra-dreng's release. The Young-Tibet group at first adopted delaying tactics until reinforcement came from Gyantse and then launched an attack on Sera monastery which was supposed to be the center in the anti-army movement. After a week's fighting the monks were defeated.

While the fighting was going on, the National Government sent a radiogram to the Lhasa authorities asking them to give due protection to Sera monastery, one of the most sacred centers of Buddhism, to settle the dispute by peaceful means, and not to do any harm to the ex-Regent. In reply they wired back the following message:

> Ra-dreng Hutukhtu, the ex-Regent, was arrested on the charge that he had plotted to overthrow the present Regent. Unfortunately the monks of the Sera Monastery, as well as some other monasteries, misunderstood this fact and opposed this government. To maintain law and order this government sent troops to quell all subversive activities. No damage was done to the monastery, and, more important, all Chinese officials and traders in Lhasa were well protected.

It was said that the radiogram from Chungking had the effect of hastening the end of Ra-dreng's life. He was first made blind and then poisoned in prison.[236]

The change in Lhasa in 1941 which brought the eventual downfall of the pro-Chinese Regent greatly affected Sino-Tibetan relations. The pro-British Young-Tibet group soon after they had established themselves in power, set up in the summer of 1943 a Bureau of Foreign Affairs under the Ko-hsia (Kashag) and informed the Office of the Mongolian and Tibetan Affairs Commission in Tibet that its business should henceforth be conducted with that Bureau and no longer with the Ko-hsia directly. This move amounted to treating Chungking as a foreign power and asserting that Tibet was an independent country. The Chinese officials in Lhasa would not, of course, recognize this new establishment and insisted on having direct contact with the Ko-hsia as usual. The Young-Tibet group employed every possible means to make the Chinese officials yield to their new creation. For example, they arrested the Chinese residents in Lhasa and subjected them to all kinds of ill-treatment. Then they gave the

Chinese officials to understand that if they would merely protest to the Bureau of Foreign Affairs, these Chinese residents would be released at once and even compensated for their damages. When that failed, they resorted to the stoppage of all provisions to the Chinese officials, which, however, proved unsuccessful. This deadlock dragged on for some time. At last Chungking warned them that should they continue to force the Chinese officials to conduct business through this so-called Foreign Office, the National Government would be compelled to use force in order to safeguard its traditional position. At the same time, a concentration of Ch'inghai and Sikang troops on the Tibetan border was ordered and carried out. Perhaps due to the realization of their military impotence, or perhaps due to the timely advice of some foreign power, they abandoned their attempt to force the issue. But their Bureau of Foreign Affairs remained in existence.[237]

After the Burma Road had been cut off by the Japanese in 1943, the Chinese Government planned to construct a Chinese-Indian Highway through Tibet. Being asked to sound out the opinion of the Lhasa authorities on the matter, the Director of the Office of the Mongolian and Tibetan Affairs Commission in Tibet reported that they would not favor such a project. He stressed the necessity of getting British consent in advance and suggested that military pressure should be brought to bear on the Tibetan Government to show Chinese determination to carry it through. In fact, neither the British Government nor the Lhasa authorities were willing to have such a highway, which would bring not only additional Chinese influence but also new American influence into Tibet. At first each made excuses that the matter should be referred to the other. When they were finally pressed for a definite answer, the Lhasa authorities replied, "It conflicts with the Buddhist belief of the country to permit any work of that magnitude." [238] The Chinese survey groups on the Sikang-Tibetan border were driven back by the Tibetan garrison force. In connection with the transport through Tibet, an American military mission was sent to Lhasa in 1942-43 and dealt with the so-called Tibetan Bureau of Foreign Affairs.[239] This American mission might have created good will among the Lhasa authorities, but its effort to get transport facilities from Tibet was made in vain.

In order to readjust the strained relations with the unfriendly Lhasa authorities, the Chinese Government thought of sending new men and strengthening its office in Tibet. In August, 1944, Shen Tsung-lien was appointed to replace Kung Ch'ing-tsung, and Chen Hsi-chang was appointed as the deputy. As soon as Shen reached Lhasa and assumed the office, he started a series of talks with the Tibetan Government which dragged on for many months. As no common ground could be found, the talks met with no success.[240]

The Chinese National Government made further efforts to try to win over the estranged Lhasa authorities. In 1945, as a result of the secret Yalta agreements later recorded in the Soviet-Chinese Treaty of Friendship and Alliance of August 14, 1945, it recognized the independence of Outer Mongolia.[241] As repeatedly shown in this study, there was a long-standing close tie between Mongolia and Tibet. Such a recognition would have an impact on Sino-Tibetan relations. As an expression of good will, the Chinese Government immediately made it clear to the Tibetans that they would receive without any restriction a high degree of autonomy. Moreover, to further the advancement of Tibet, the Chinese Government decided to assist it in political and economic development.[242] In fact, on August 25, 1945, Generalissimo Chiang Kai-shek made a statement in the following words:

> If and when the Tibetans attain the stage of complete self-reliance in political and economic conditions, the Chinese Government would like to take the same attitude as it did toward Outer Mongolia, by supporting their independence. However, Tibet should be able to maintain and promote its own independent position in order that the historical tragedy of Korea might not be repeated.[243]

Tibetan Participation in the Chinese National Assembly

When World War II came to an end and China began to play her role as one of the Big Five Powers, the attitude of the Lhasa authorities, or rather that of the Young-Tibet group, toward the Chinese National Government became less hostile, but still far from friendly.[244] In 1946,[245] at the time when the National Assembly was about to be convened to adopt a constitution, an invitation was issued to the Tibetan Government to send delegates to take part in the deliberation which was to determine the legal status of Tibet. As mentioned above, seats had always been allotted to Tibet since the first National Assembly convened soon after the establishment of the Republic. In 1941 Tibetan delegates had participated in the National Assembly to draft an organic law for the National Government. If chronological order may be disregarded for a moment, mention might as well be made here of the participation of the Tibetan delegates in the National Assembly convened in 1948 to elect the President and the Vice-President of China according to the new constitution, and of the fact that there were Tibetan members in the Legislative Yüan and the Control Yüan even on the eve of the evacuation of the National Government from Nanking in 1948.[246]

In 1946 the Kuomintang and the Chinese Communists, together with some smaller parties, were still negotiating for a compromise plan for national unification, and the international situation was highly favorable to the National Government. Though some foreign pressure was exerted on it with respect to this unification issue, none was then exerted on it for China's dismemberment. Faced with such an international situation, the Lhasa authorities found themselves even less in a position to depart from established precedent. In response to the invitation, they dispatched delegates to Nanking.[247] Upon their arrival, however, these Tibetan delegates took the position that they had received no power to discuss the draft constitution. Yet, when the assembly came to discuss the proposal "Tibet's local autonomy shall be decided by law," they demanded that this article be deleted. Finally, a compromise solution was reached whereby the wording was changed to: "Tibet's autonomy shall be duly guaranteed." [248]

The Installation of the Tenth Panch'en Lama

In the meantime another difference arose between Nanking and Lhasa, concerning the incarnation of the Panch'en Lama, whose death, as we have already seen, had facilitated better Sino-Tibetan relations. In 1941 the followers of the late Panch'en Lama, Lo-sang-chien-tsan and others, found in Ch'inghai a boy named Kung-pao-tz'u-tan who seemed to answer to their traditional requisites, and identified him as the real incarnation. The Lhasa authorities immediately raised objections to their choice and refused to recognize the boy even as a legitimate candidate. It looked as if history were going to repeat itself—that China would back a Panch'en to oppose a Dalai who was being alienated by a foreign power and influenced by the Young-Tibet group. But the Chinese National Government acted very cautiously and tried to avoid creating such a situation. It did not recognize the incarnation until August, 1949, when the Lhasa Government had driven out all the Chinese officials from Tibet, and when most provinces had been lost to the Chinese Red Army and the seat of the National Government had been moved to Canton. On August 10 it deputed the Chairman of the Commission for Mongolian and Tibetan Affairs, Mr. Kuan Chi-yü, to preside at the installation ceremony of the Tenth Panch'en which took place at the famous Kum-bum monastery, the birthplace of the founder of the Yellow Sect, Tsong-k'a-pa.[249] Three weeks later, on September 5, Sining, the capital of Ch'inghai, together with the newly installed Panch'en, fell into the hands of the Chinese Communists, and the Chinese National Government retreated to Taiwan when Canton and Chungking were lost on October 15 and December 1, respectively.

So far we have seen that though many attempts and some progress had been made, the Chinese National Government did not reestablish China's original position in Tibet, and the legal status of the latter in its relation to China remained undefined. On the part of the Lhasa authorities, they demonstrated more than once signs of reconciliation toward the Chinese Central Government, but each time the rapprochement effort was frustrated by the Young-Tibet group who eventually gained control of the Tibetan Government. In 1930, the late Dalai Lama told the semi-official delegate, Miss Liu, that what he expected most of China was real unity and peace.[250] Indeed, only a united and peaceful China can give Tibet needed assistance and protection. If Tibet had entirely turned away from the powerful Great Britain and leaned toward a divided China fully engaged in international war or civil strife, it would have stood the risk of endangering its own existence. Unfortunately, China, since the establishment of the Republic, had hardly enjoyed any peace. Eight years of continuous hard struggle with Japan were followed by a bloody strife between the Kuomintang and the Chinese Communists. Even if the Tibetans were anxious to return to the fraternity of the Chinese family, a realistic consideration of the situation would make them hesitate.

Let us not forget that behind the internal contest for power between the lamas and the ambitious military clique in Tibet, behind the repeated border incidents and sporadic fighting between the Chinese and Tibetan forces, and behind the sudden decision of the Chinese National Government to stop the ninth Panch'en from proceeding to Tashi-lhunpo when he had already got as far as the Ch'inghai-Tibetan border, there was always the international picture and the manipulation of invisible foreign hands. Needless to say, the protracted Sino-Japanese war and the no less bitterly fought Kuomintang-Communist strife were precipitated by the international situation, and they themselves were (and in the case of the latter still is) only a link in world politics.

As we have already seen, the status of Tibet as a buffer state created by international politics was greatly affected by the changes (such as the Russian Revolution) brought about by World War I. Now let us see what effect World War II had on that status.

The Status of Tibet Affected by World War II

World War II, more true to its name as a world war than World War I, would have affected the status of Tibet one way or the other even if its outcome had been in favor of the Axis Powers. As shown above, the Japanese Imperial Government, long prior to the raid on Pearl Harbor, had exchanged so-called Buddhistic missions with Tibet, sent an agent to Tibet to perform "a special duty," and provided the Lhasa Government with arms and munitions.[251] According to the archives of the Japanese Foreign Office, a plan to invite Lama Tan-pa-ta-cha to Japan as a Tibetan Government delegate was carried out by the Japanese Foreign Office with the support of the Japanese General Staff. The Lama, accompanied by several others, left Peiping, where he had been staying, on June 12, 1942, and arrived in Tokyo on

June 20. He also visited Nagoya, Yamada, Kyoto, Nara, Osaka, and Buddhistic Shingon-shu headquarters at Koyasan.

At the Japanese Foreign Office he was received by the vice minister on behalf of the foreign minister and he conferred also with the directors of the Asiatic Affairs Department and the Department of Information and Intelligence. He was requested to obtain Tibet's cooperation as a nation in the "co-prosperity sphere" in Asia and its help in the building of a new order in the world. At the Japanese Army General Staff Headquarters he was interviewed by General Okamoto and other high officers who told him that the purpose of the war was to establish perpetual peace in Asia and to build a new order free from any vestige of unlawful British and American influence. He was also received by the education minister at his office and the director of the Culture Department at the Board of Asia Development, and was welcomed by Buddhistic organizations and learned societies, and wherever he went he was told that Tibet was in the co-prosperity sphere of Asia and was destined to be cooperative.[252] This gives a fairly clear idea of what the status of Tibet would have been had Japan been victorious.

The fact that China was victorious did not help to solve the fundamental issue of the status of Tibet in her favor, though World War II did bring changes to that status. As mentioned above, Outer Mongolia was disposed of at the Yalta Conference without China's participation and without even her knowledge until some time afterwards. This deeply hurt Chinese prestige and inspired the Tibetans to follow the example of their kindred Mongolians. Therefore the declaration made and the provision in the Constitution adopted by the Chinese National Government to guarantee Tibet's autonomy, with a promise of support for its eventual independence, failed to make the Young-Tibet group rest assured. While the civil strife between Kuomintang and Chinese Communists made the Tibetans hesitate to come to terms with Nanking even if they had had the intention of doing so, the same international development alienated them and encouraged them to assert immediate independence.

In 1947 Great Britain recognized the independence of India. This development must have greatly affected the status of Tibet. The Chinese Government and people expected that this move would at least facilitate the improvement of Sino-Tibetan relations, while the Tibetans might have regarded it as an incentive to a greater degree of self-government in a truer sense of the term. The Chinese are always proud of their historical relations and cultural ties with India,[253] and they took a keen interest in seeing her freed from British rule. They believed that once India got rid of British influence, Tibet would gladly return to the Chinese family as they took it for granted that India would not inherit the same old British policy in Tibet—a policy under which the Indians themselves must have had enough bitter experience. For a time they were very disappointed[254] because the new Indian Government, perhaps from strategic considerations, showed no departure from its predecessor's policy, not only in Tibet, but also in Bhutan, Nepal, and Sikkim.

In March-April of 1947 the Asiatic Conference, which was intended as a maneuver to force the British out of India, took place in New Delhi under the presidency of Mrs. Naidu.[255] Besides the Chinese delegation, a Tibetan delegation was invited. At the opening ceremony there was displayed in the Conference Hall a huge map of Asia on which Tibet was drawn outside the boundary of China.[256] The correction was reluctantly undertaken only after representation had been made to Mr. Nehru by Mr. George Yeh who was then the Director of the European Affairs Department in the Ministry of Foreign Affairs and who attended the Conference as an observer attached to the Chinese delegation.[257]

It seems strange that such an incident happened again in the autumn of 1948 when the members of the diplomatic corps in New Delhi were invited to see a film entitled "Kashmir" while the Kashmir dispute between India and Pakistan was being taken up by the Security Council of the United Nations. The Chinese Ambassador, Professor Lo Chia-lun, saw on the film a map of Kashmir with its neighbor Tibet drawn outside the Chinese boundary line. He lodged a written protest on his return to the Embassy. The Indian Government did not reply for some time. After having been urged several times, it replied to say that the film was not made by the Indian Government, which would, however, pay attention to this matter henceforth. Yet the map in the film remained uncorrected.[258]

Two more cases which show more clearly the continuity of

British policy were the retaining in service of Mr. H. E. Richardson, the former British Trade Agent in Tibet, and the appointing of Captain Sathe as Consul at Kashgar in Sinkiang without previous consultation with the Chinese Government. Mr. Richardson, whose office, in practice, became a permanent British Mission as a counterpart of the Office of the Mongolian and Tibetan Affairs Commission in Tibet, was much involved in Tibetan politics.[259] The Chinese Ambassador, Mr. Lo, suggested to Mr. Nehru that he should get rid of this British official and, according to Lo, the latter promised to do so as soon as he took over the government; but Mr. Richardson's service was still retained though he was due to retire and an Indian named G. K. Gokhale, who had been sent as his deputy, could have taken his place.[260]

As to the consular post at Kashgar, it was formerly under the External Affairs Department of the British Indian Government, which is different from the regular British consular service. When the British handed over power in India to the new Indian Government, they evacuated their consul-general at Kashgar, and India and Pakistan contested the right to succeed to this strategic post. According to established practice, arrangements should first have been made with China, but India chose to present China with a *fait accompli* by appointing Captain Sathe, a former Secretary of the Indian Embassy, to the post. The Chinese National Government refused to grant the necessary visa and asked for the reciprocal right of setting up a consulate at Srinagar or Kalimpong. After three months' deadlock and, finally, at the suggestion of the Chinese Foreign Office, India recognized the principle of reciprocity and promised to consider Kalimpong or some other suitable place for a Chinese consulate to be set up in the future. On this understanding the Chinese visa was granted and India succeeded in taking over a disputed post as heir to the legacy of the British Empire.[261]

The Indian asusmption of the role previously played by the British can also be seen from the Indian measures adopted in connection with the three close neighbors of Tibet. In June of 1949, under the pretext that there was a local dispute and confusion, whereas the prime minister of the local transitional government told the Indian press afterwards that there was none, the Indian

Government dispatched troops to Sikkim and appointed a commissioner to take over the administration. This former British protectorate thus became incorporated into the Indian dominion. Less than two months later India signed a new treaty with Bhutan, increasing the former British annual subsidy from one hundred thousand to five hundred thousand rupees; and declared the latter to be her protectorate on August 8. On August 15, the second anniversary of India's regained independence, the map of India printed in the souvenir publication for that occasion included Bhutan within the boundary line.[262]

Also in the summer of 1949, there were intensive activities on the part of the members of the Nepalese Congress Party, which was in reality a branch of the Indian National Congress Party. They were then living in exile in India and kept asking for Indian help to overthrow the existing regime and to "liberate" their fatherland. A large-scale demonstration led by Dr. Rouhah, the Secretary-General of the Indian Socialist Party, was held in front of the Nepalese Embassy in New Delhi. It elicited much criticism among the diplomatic corps, and the Indian Government then took Dr. Rouhah into custody and arraigned him under the Security Act. In court he insisted upon calling Mr. Nehru to the witness stand, but the latter did not appear. According to what Ambassador Lo heard, the leaders of this demonstration had previously come to an understanding with the Indian Prime Minister.[263]

Now let us see what reaction this dramatic international development brought about in Tibet. In February of 1948, a Tibetan trade mission headed by Hsia-ku-pa (Shakabpa) arrived at New Delhi and held several talks with the Indian Government. As the mission included a military man named Sui K'ang (Suikhang),[264] one might presume that their talks were not confined to commercial matters such as the relaxation of Indian control on Tibetan exports of wool and musk, and the Tibetan request to be allowed to receive payments in American dollars instead of rupees. After repeated persuasions by the Chinese Embassy in New Delhi, the mission then went to Nanking, where they managed somehow or other to get special facilities to visit Great Britain and the United States without obtaining a passport from the Chinese Government.[265] The mission returned to New Delhi toward the end of 1948. They then changed their tune and talked about immediate independence.[266] On New Year's eve, Mr. Lo, the Chinese Ambassador, wrote a letter to Mr. Nehru expressing his hope that Indian dealings with the Tibetan mission would not be in any way detrimental to the sovereignty and territorial integrity of China. As the Indian Prime Minister (currently the Foreign Minister) was leaving for Alahabad the next day, he directed the Vice Minister of Foreign Affairs, Mr. K. P. S. Menon, who was formerly Ambassador to China, to reply on his behalf. Mr. Menon assured the Chinese Ambassador that there was no such intention on the part of the Indian Government. In February of 1949 this Tibetan mission came again to the Indian capital and got in touch with the Indian Government.[267]

Chinese Nationalist Officials Ousted by the Lhasa Authorities

On July 8, 1949, the Tibetan Cabinet (Ko-hsia or Kashag) decided to get rid of all the persons connected with the Chinese National Government, including those working in the radio station and hospital, and the teachers of the Chinese primary schools in Lhasa and at Gyantse.[268] The Lhasa authorities took over the Chinese Government radio station and sealed all its equipment. They forbade any Chinese to send telegraphic messages even through the Indian wireless service. A part of the Chinese personnel, including medical doctors and school teachers, together with their families, left Lhasa on the 13th. Mr. Chen Hsi-chang, the acting director of the Mongolian and Tibetan Affairs Commission's office in Tibet,[269] and the rest left a week later. The Chinese Embassy in New Delhi had been kept in the dark until the 21st when the news finally reached them. On the 23rd Lo went to see Mr. K. P. S. Menon, who informed him that the Indian Government had received telegrams from Lhasa saying that there were communists among the Chinese government personnel in Lhasa and the Tibetan Government had found it necessary to get rid of all of them.[270] General Yen-Hsi-shan, the President of the Executive Yüan of the Chinese National Government, issued a statement on August 6 in Canton, the temporary capital, repudiating the Tibetan anti-communistic pretext. He said that all the officials stationed in Tibet had undergone careful screening before appointment and their loyalty was beyond question. "Even if the local authorities of Tibet had had a real complaint about any one of them," he added, "the proper procedure would have been to report to the Central Government." In this statement he further implied that the drastic measure was probably not taken by the Lhasa authorities of their own volition, and he expressed the hope that they would make amends for their fault and not become the dupe of others.[271] Ambassador Lo also told the Indian press that the personnel of the Mongolian and Tibetan Affairs Commission's office in Tibet were not communists. He compared the move of the Lhasa Government to fishing for red herring on such a high plateau."[272] He talked with Chen Hsi-chang and questioned his staff separately when the latter arrived at Calcutta. He was told that at the time when the Tibetan authorities were about to take action, and right after the action had been taken on July 8, Richardson was extremely active and his office in Lhasa was unusually frequented by visitors.[273]

The Tibetan Government easily got rid of all persons connected with the Chinese National Government, but there remained the problem of how to stop the Chinese Communists from entering Tibet. To the Chinese Communists, the question of whether they should enter Tibet did not turn on whether there was a single Chinese Nationalist in Lhasa or whether there still remained an office representative of the Chinese National Government. They were claiming to "liberate" the whole of China; and Tibet, as Ambassador Liu Chieh, the representative of the Chinese National Government, told the United Nations General Committee during the Fifth Session of the General Assembly, was regarded as a part of China by "all Chinese whatever their party or religion."[274]

Those Tibetans who were responsible for the ousting of the Chinese officials from Tibet must have realized that their military strength was not in any way sufficient to back up such a drastic political decision. They therefore looked for foreign help. It was during this juncture that Mr. Lowell Thomas and his son got unusual permission from the Tibetan Government to visit

Lhasa.[275] His dramatic visit and the broadcasting records he made during his stay in Tibet, and the statement he issued on his return, aroused great interest in the Tibetan situation and produced divergent comment throughout the world.[276]

In the meantime, the Chinese Communists were intensifying their efforts in making preparations for "liberating" Tibet. On October 1, 1949, the Panch'en Lama sent a telegram from Ch'inghai to the Chairman of the People's Central Government, Mao Tse-tung, and the Commander-in-Chief of the People's Army, Chu Teh, to express his support of the "liberation" of Tibet, and a reply was given on November 23 to assure him of the impending liberation. On January 18, 1950, Chu Teh made a statement in the presence of some Tibetans in Peking which reiterated the determination to rid Tibet of imperialistic influence. Two days later a spokesman repudiated Tibet's right to dispatch a so-called good-will mission intended to declare its "independence."[277]

Facing such a menacing situation and realizing at the eleventh hour that no foreign power would back their assertion of independence with force while the Korean War overshadowed their problem on the international horizon, the Lhasa authorities decided to dispatch a delegation with a view to coming to terms with the Peking Government. But this delegation was delayed in India for a long time. According to the explanation given in their appeal to the United Nations, dated November 7, 1950,[278] as well as in the Indian note to the Peking Government, dated October 28, 1950,[279] the Tibetan delegation was "unable to leave India through no fault of their own, but for want of British visas which were required for transit through Hongkong."

The Peking authorities notified the Indian Government on August 31 that the Tibetan delegation should reach Peking not later than the middle of September, and then twice in September the Peking representative in New Delhi told the Tibetan delegation that they should at all costs reach Peking before the end of September and that they would be held fully responsible for any further delay and would take the consequences.[280] But the Tibetan delegation did not leave New Delhi until October 25.[281]

The Chinese Red Army had mobilized its forces by three routes: (1) from Hotien in Sinkiang, aiming at Gartok; (2) from

Szechwan and Sikang by the traditional military route to act as a decoy; and (3) from Jyekundo in Ch'inghai, over mountain trails, as a flanking movement, which proved most effective.[282] On October 7 it crossed the Dre-chu River at a number of places. Demar, Kamo, Tunga, Tshame, Rimochegotyu, Yakalo, and Markham fell to the Chinese after a few engagements. After having wiped out the Tibetan frontier garrisons in Kham, the Chinese Red Army converged from five directions on Chamdo, a very important strategic point containing a heavy concentration of Tibetan forces, and also the seat of the governor who was concurrently one of the four members of bKa'-blon. Chamdo fell soon after, and a Tibetan field commander surrendered to the Chinese with his troops.[283]

In the above, a detailed explanation has been given to the question why the Chinese National Government did not settle the outstanding Tibetan issue by force and then define the status of Tibet by an agreement as the Chinese Communists did in 1950-51. Here the writer wants to point out particularly (1) the changes made in the international situation as a result of World War II, and (2) the much-talked-of Western projects of opening air bases and setting up a radar network on the roof of the world. The former, especially the removal of the British power from India, helped the Chinese Communists to settle the Tibetan issue, while the latter gave the Chinese Communists an additional excuse to carry out a military campaign in Tibet even at a time when their participation in the Korean War must have already made heavy demands on their treasury and manpower.

As to their military success in the Tibetan campaign, two factors are particularly worth mentioning. (1) The Chinese Red Army had already wiped out all the local Moslem forces in Ch'inghai and the feudalistic forces in Szechwan and Sikang, and thus cleared the way for their military campaign into Tibet. (2) In 1935, when the Chinese Red Army retreated from Kiangsi to Shensi, they passed through Kanze, De-ge, and some other districts in Sikang and gained valuable knowledge of the topography of the northwest and the lives of the Tibetan people. Besides making friends with local leaders like Ke-ta Hutukhtu,[284] they set up cells and absorbed many youths into their party, among whom the most outstanding one today is named T'ien Pao in Chinese or Sang-chi-yueh-hsi in Tibetan, the chairman of the autonomous government for those of Tibetan nationality in the province of Sikang.[285] Later they were joined by many followers of the late Regent Ra-dreng, who were anxious to take their revenge on the existing Lhasa regime. Equipped with knowledge of the terrain and possessing the assistance of the indigenous people, the seasoned Chinese Red Army found little difficulty in subduing the poorly equipped and ill-disciplined Tibetan forces.

A Diplomatic Duel between Peking and New Delhi

When the news of Peking's resort to force in order to settle its relations with Tibet reached India, the Indian Government handed the Peking authorities a memorandum on October 21, through its ambassador, in which it expressed its concern and called the latter's attention to the serious effect this would have on their chances of entering the United Nations.[286] Again on October 28 the Indian Government sent to the Peking authorities a note in which it explained the reason for the delay of the Tibetan delegation and expressed its profound regret concerning the invasion of Tibet by Chinese troops, which it could not but regard as lamentable under the current international circumstances.[287] To these communications the Peking Government replied on October 30:

> Tibet is an integral part of Chinese territory, and the Tibetan problem is entirely the domestic problem of China. . . . Regardless of whether the Tibetan local authorities wish to proceed with peace negotiations and whatever the results of such negotiations, no interference whatsoever from a foreign country shall be tolerated.

The Peking reply also pointed out that the Tibetan problem was irrelevant to the question of admitting its representatives to the United Nations; expressed deep regret that the Indian Government should regard Chinese action in Tibet as lamentable; and retorted that the Indian point of view had been affected by anti-Chinese foreign influence in Tibet.[288]

The Indian Government categorically denied the charge of being under anti-Chinese foreign influence in its note to Peking dated November 1, in which it also made it clear that it had no intention of securing any interests or of interfering with the adjustment of Tibet's legitimate demand for autonomy within the scope of Chinese suzerainty. In this note the Indian Government stressed the fact of Tibetan autonomy and expressed the wish that some Indian rights in Tibet derived from practice or agreement should be maintained. It went on to enumerate these rights as: a representative at Lhasa; a trade agent at Yatung and another one at Gyantse; postal and telegraphic establishments along the trade route to Gyantse; and the stationing of a company of guards at Gyantse for the protection of the trade route. It ended with the reiterated plea for a peaceful settlement of the Tibetan issue without affecting Sino-Indian friendship.[289] Thus the Indian Government, like its predecessor, recognized only Chinese suzerainty in Tibet and tried to restrain Chinese action there by stressing Tibetan autonomy while at the same time claiming for itself in the name of established practice the rights that the British had enjoyed.

On November 16 Peking replied to this more seriously tuned Indian note with a clear-cut answer. It reiterated its statement that "Tibet is an integral part of China and the Tibetan issue is an entirely domestic problem," and declared that its army must enter Tibet "to liberate the Tibetan people and to defend the national frontier." It expressed its extreme surprise that the Indian Government should try to prevent the Chinese Government from exercising national sovereignty in Tibet. It recognized the regional autonomy of minorities within Chinese territory and also within the scope of national sovereignty, and blamed once again foreign force for having delayed the departure of the Tibetan delegation. It considered it most regrettable that the Indian Government should disregard the fact of Peking's peaceful efforts and take the internal problem of exercising sovereignty on its own territory as an action calculated to increase international dispute in an already deplorable and tense world situation.[290]

Tibet's Appeal to the United Nations

When the diplomatic duel between Peking and New Delhi led to an impasse, the Lhasa authorities turned to the United Nations for help. On November 7 they sent a cablegram through their delegation at Kalimpong[291] to the President of the United Nations Assembly, Fifth Session, citing "the armed invasion of Tibet for the incorporation of Tibet within the fold of Chinese communism through sheer physical force" as "a clear case of aggression" and asking the United Nations to intercede on their behalf and "restrain Chinese aggression." [292]

It was rather surprising that a small country in South America, El Salvador, and not any big power, made the request to have the Tibetan appeal put on the agenda.[293] The El Salvador delegate, Mr. Castro, told the general committee which was to decide whether his country's request should be acceded to, that his delegation had been questioned whether it had not been acting under the influence of another government. He stressed the fullest independence of his government's action and said that in so doing his government was performing a duty under the Charter of the United Nations.[294]

During the discussion in the general committee, every shade of opinion and each big power's stand on the Tibetan issue was clearly demonstrated. From the point of view of our study, suffice it to cite those which have a bearing on the status of Tibet.[295]

The British delegate, Mr. Young, said that the committee did not know exactly what was happening in Tibet, nor was the legal position of the country very clear. So he proposed to defer decision on the El Salvador delegate's request. We note here that the British delegate did not, and the writer believes that he could not, say that Tibet was an independent country and that he had to admit at least that Tibet's legal position was not very clear.

The Jam Saheb of Nawanager, delegate of India, told the committee that he had no desire to express an opinion on the difficulties which had arisen between China and Tibet. He believed that the Tibetan question could still be settled by peaceful means and that such a settlement could safeguard the autonomy which Tibet had enjoyed for several decades while maintaining its historical association with China. He proposed, therefore, that the idea of including that question on the agenda of the General Assembly be abandoned for the time being. We note here that the Indian delegate was very cautious and used the words "historical association" to avoid passing a judgment on the status of Tibet.

Mr. J. Malik, the delegate of the U.S.S.R., seconded the British proposal and added that "Tibet was an inalienable part of China and its affairs were the exclusive concern of the Chinese government." He pointed out that the El Salvador delegate referred to newspaper articles and encyclopedias, but had not cited any international instrument in support of his argument. He went on to say that Chinese sovereignty over Tibet had been recognized for a long time by the United Kingdom, the United States, and the U.S.S.R., and that as Tibet was under the national jurisdiction of China, the United Nations could not consider the Tibetan problem, and if it did so, it would be guilty of unwarranted intervention in the internal affairs of the Chinese people. He, therefore, agreed to the deferment of decision and would even vote for its outright rejection.

Mr. Liu, the delegate of Nationalist China, opposed putting the Tibetan appeal on the agenda as a separate item. He pointed out that Tibet had been a part of China for seven hundred years and had participated in the National Assembly of 1946 to draft the new constitution, as well as in that of 1948 [296] to elect the President and the Vice-President. He stressed the fact that Tibet had been and still was a part of China and added that "all Chinese whatever their party or religion regard it as such." He attacked the Chinese Communist military campaign into Tibet and thought that the Tibetan appeal should be included in Item 25 of the agenda, that is, to discuss it under the heading of Chinese complaint of Soviet aggression in China.

Mr. Gross, the United States delegate, voted for adjournment in view of the fact that India, an interested party, had told the General Committee that it hoped that the Tibetan question would be peacefully and honorably settled. Otherwise he would have voted for the inclusion of the item on the General Assembly agenda.

As there was not a single voice in the general committee to support the El Salvador delegate's request and his three-item draft resolution,[297] the Tibetan appeal was set aside. But the Tibetan delegation at Kalimpong was still hoping against hope. It sent a cablegram to the United Nations on November 28 to urge the immediate discussion of its appeal.[298] Again on December 8 it sent another cablegram to the United Nations voicing "great surprise and regret," "agony and despair," and expressing the wish to send a delegation to Lake Success to present its case while the Chinese Communist delegate was there in connection with a different matter. It also expressed its willingness to receive an Enquiry Commission or investigation party to be dispatched by the United Nations.[299] However, these two cablegrams met with no better fate and have been pigeon-holed ever since.

In the meantime, the Regent in Lhasa and the Young-Tibet group found the situation untenable in the face of military defeat and the lack of foreign support. They let the young Dalai Lama assume full power for the administration of Tibet on November 17 and later moved him to Yatung together with his treasures as if to prepare him for living in exile in India as his predecessor had done forty years before.

It was indeed a critical moment for the Tibetans who had to make a decision that would have a far-reaching effect. A Tibetan once predicted that if and when "British soldiers leave India, Tibet would throw her lot with any strong power that would treat her well, or would perforce gravitate back to a closer relationship with China."[300] Failing the former alternative, they acquiesced in the latter course in spite of Sir Charles Bell's belief that "to the people of Tibet, as to those of Mongolia, Bolshevism is abhorrent."[301]

The Peking Agreement on Measures for the Peaceful Liberation of Tibet

In February, 1951, the Tibetan Government under the new leadership of the young Dalai Lama[302] dispatched bKa'-blon Ngabou Ngawang Jigme to head a delegation composed of Dzasak Khemey Sonam Wangdi, Khentrung Thupten Tenthar, Khenchung Thupten Lekmuun, and Rimshi Samposey Tenzin Thundup to negotiate for a peaceful settlement. Ngabou Ngawang Jigme, accompanied by Thupten Lekmuun and Samposey Tenzin Thundup, arrived in Peking on April 22 by way of Chamdo, Tach'ienlu, Ya-an, Chungking, and Sian. Khemey Sonam Wangdi and Thupten Tenthar arrived four days later via India and Hong Kong.

On April 29 negotiations started with Li Wei-han as chief delegate on behalf of the Central People's Government and Chang Ching-wu, Chang Kuo-hua, and Sun Chih-yuan as delegates. As a result of the negotiations which were concluded on May 21, an agreement was signed on the 23rd containing seventeen articles.[303] A state banquet was given on May 24 to celebrate the event and attended by the Panch'en Lama and his followers, the Tibetan delegation, and all the high-ranking officials of the Peking regime.[304]

By this agreement the status of Tibet is clearly defined. The first article declares that "the Tibetan people shall unite and drive out imperial aggressive forces from Tibet, and shall return to the big family of the Motherland—the People's Republic of China." The agreement promises the maintenance of the status quo in the Tibetan regional government structure as well as in the inherent position and authority of the Dalai Lama, but calls on Lhasa actively to assist the People's Liberation Army to enter Tibet, and consolidate the national defenses (Articles II and IV), while permitting "autonomy under the unified leadership of the Central People's Government" (Article III). The Tibetan troops shall be gradually reorganized into the People's Liberation Army and shall become a part of the national defense forces of the People's Republic of China (Article VIII). The agreement further stipulates that all foreign affairs shall be handled only by Peking (Article XIV). In order to ensure the implementation of this agreement, the Central People's Government will establish in Tibet a military and administrative committee and a military area headquarters in which as many Tibetans as possible will be absorbed to work together with those officials sent by the Central People's Government. These may include patriotic elements from the local government of Tibet, various districts, and leading monasteries. They are to be chosen by the representative of the Central People's Government after consultation with all parties concerned and to be appointed by Peking (Article XV).[305]

In accordance with the provisions of the agreement, Chang Ching-wu was sent to Lhasa as the representative of Peking who was also to take up the post of Director General of the Military Headquarters in Tibet.[306] He left Peking on June 23 and arrived at Yatung on July 4 via Hong Kong and India. Following a conference with him on July 16, the Dalai Lama left Yatung on

July 21 and returned to Lhasa whence he sent a telegram on October 24 to Peking to announce his, the lamas', and the people's support of the agreement.[307]

In the meantime Chinese Communist troops were redoubling their efforts to construct a highway and make other preparations for entering Tibet.[308] On September 9, under the command of Wang Chi-mei, they entered Lhasa amidst a colorful welcome and were reinforced a month later by 20,000 regulars under the command of Generals Chang Kuo-hua and Tan Kuan-san.[309] By the end of December they had been deployed to set up check posts along Bhutan's northern frontier, the *Statesman's* special correspondent in Kalimpong reported. On March 13, 1952, they entered Yatung, fifty miles from Darjeeling, after having set up guards and check posts along the trade route from Gyantse to the Indian border covering a distance of 295 miles.[310]

Throughout this chapter we have repeatedly found the same three problems, to wit: (1) the demarcation of a boundary line between Tibet and China Proper, (2) the relationship between the Dalai and the Panch'en Lamas, and (3) the fundamental issue of defining the status of Tibet, which includes the problem of satisfying Tibetan aspirations. We have found also that behind these problems there was always British influence which made them more complicated and indeed insoluble for the past forty years. Now, as a result of World War II, British influence had been withdrawn and the independent Indian Government, which for a time appeared to have resumed the British role in Tibet, has at last found it advisable not to inherit the British policy that would lead to a clash with the Chinese Communists beyond the Himalaya Mountains. By virtue of the agreement explained above, Peking settled the issue of the status of Tibet. Its army entered Tibet with the assistance of the Tibetan Government, as the agreement stipulated, and took up positions along the western frontiers of Tibet for national defense. In fact, Tibet has been made a military district of China.[311] There can be no more question of boundary dispute between Tibet and its neighboring Chinese provinces. There remains to be settled, however, the question of the relationship between the two Grand Lamas.

According to Article V of the agreement, the inherent position and authority of the Panch'en shall be maintained. And Article I stipulates that the people of Tibet must be united. So, there should be no objection to the Panch'en's return. Backed by Chinese power he easily crossed the Tibetan frontier, guards of which had prevented his predecessor from so doing till the latter's death, and arrived at Lhasa on April 28, 1952. In the afternoon of the day of arrival he met the Dalai Lama at the Potala Palace. After a solemn ceremonial meeting, the Dalai Lama invited him to his private apartment for a talk. The Chinese Communist press made much of the occasion. It reported that they "held a friendly exchange of opinions on implementing the 'Agreement on the Peaceful Liberation of Tibet,'" and the Tibetan people rejoiced at the happy union of the two Grand Lamas.[312]

After forty-three days' stay in the Tibetan capital, he left on June 9 for Shigatse. He sent a telegraphic message to Peking declaring his determination to "unite with the Dalai Lama and fully carry out the agreement on measures for the Peaceful Liberation of Tibet and build a new, free, and happy Tibet."[313] He was warmly welcomed on the way, especially at Gyantse where he left on the 19th. When he returned to Tashi-lhunpo, he received a most jubilant ovation from the populace.[314]

In Chinese historical records, the Tibetans are known as an unruly people. There must be some truth in the words of their appeal to the United Nations that "there can be no kinship or sympathy between such divergent creeds (one highly materialistic, the other highly spiritual) as those espoused by China and Tibet."[315] And to adjust a feudal society and a theocratic and aristocratic government to the Peking pattern would unavoidably cause serious friction. There are reports of unrest in Tibet.[316] A *New York Times* editorial rightly remarked, "It is sad, but a case of simple common sense, to accept the fact that so long as Mao and his Communist regime are in control of China, they will also be in control of Tibet."[317] The Chinese Communists seem to have acted very carefully in Tibet. This writer has heard many severe criticisms on other measures of the Peking regime, but he has, so far, not heard any adverse comment from a nonpartisan compatriot of his on the agreed measures for the peaceful liberation of Tibet.

The Sino-Indian Pact on Tibet

Indeed, the status of Tibet was clearly defined in the Peking Agreement on Measures for the Peaceful Liberation of Tibet; but the external aspect of the issue remained to be settled. India might have given a tacit consent to the situation created by this agreement; yet she still maintained her claim of rights derived from practice or agreement as enumerated in her note to Peking.[318] From December, 1953, the two governments entered into negotiations on this issue. On April 29, 1954, a pact was signed in Peking laying down five broad principles in addition to the liquidation of the Indian claims.

According to the pact, the text of which was released in New Delhi by the Ministry of External Affairs, India accepted the principle that Tibet constitutes an integral part of China. She agreed to withdraw completely within six months the Indian contingent that had been stationed for decades at Yatung and Gyantse. Peking, it was stated, would render all assistance and facilities in aiding the withdrawal of the Indian troops.

India agreed also to hand over all her property in Tibet to the Chinese authorities, leaving questions of detail regarding cost and the manner of payment to be worked out later. These properties included all the telegraph, public telephone, and postal establishments, together with their equipment, and twelve rest houses situated in various parts of Tibet.[319]

The pact, containing six articles, related only to two issues concerning trade and pilgrim traffic. China would be permitted to open three trade agencies, in New Delhi, Calcutta, and Kalimpong, while India would be allowed to establish similar offices at Yatung, Gyantse, and Gartok. The two countries further agreed that trade and pilgrim traffic should henceforth be confined to six specific routes along the 2,000-mile common border.

In its preamble, the two contracting parties resolved to enter into the present pact based on the following principles: mutual respect for each other's territorial integrity and sovereignty, mutual nonaggression, mutual noninterference in each other's internal affairs, equality and mutual benefit, and peaceful coexistence.[320]

CONCLUSION

TIBET has never been, and is not, a forbidden or hidden land; nor is there anything mysterious about it so far as its status and its relations with the outside world are concerned. As early as 634 A.D. political relations between China and Tibet were established when Ch'i-tsung-lung-tsan (Sron Tsan Gampo), King of Tibet, sent the first embassy to the Chinese Emperor T'ai-tsung of the T'ang dynasty. Tibet was then a military power, actively engaging itself in military conquest and diplomatic intercourse as big powers are doing in the twentieth century. It was by virtue of its military strength that it secured a footing of equality and reciprocity with its two giant neighbors, China and India, and absorbed civilization mainly from the former, and only in a lesser degree from the latter. Its status, however we may regard it, was maintained till the death of Landarma in 842, when the country became divided.

Partly due to the *laissez-faire,* or, as someone puts it, isolationist, policy of the Sung dynasty (960-1279), and partly due to the natural barrier between Tibet and India, divided Tibet was left alone in its secluded position until the Mongolian Khan, Kublai, brought a fundamental change to its status. In 1253, Kublai, in command of the forces that took Ta-li in Yünnan by three routes, overran eastern T'ufan and frightened the Tibetans into submission. As soon as he was made Khan in 1260, he appointed Phags-pa as national mentor and later raised him to the rank of priest-king. From that time Tibet was ruled by the Sakyapa Lamas as a theocracy. The change from the Sakya dynasty to the Sitya dynasty in Tibet and from the Yüan (Mongolian) dynasty (1280-1368) to the Ming dynasty (1368-1644) in China did not affect the relations between China and Tibet. As the study shows, during the Yüan and Ming dynasties Tibet was in a status resembling or suggesting that of a vassal in the full sense of the word.

Sino-Tibetan relations entered upon a new phase in the Ch'ing (Manchu) dynasty (1644-1912). It was the march of events rather than the design of some individuals that brought about another change in the status of Tibet. Several successful military expeditions enabled the Imperial Government to strengthen its hold on Tibet, and eventually it went so far as to depose the Dalai Lama. For a time the Government not only exercised sovereignty over Tibet but also ruled it through the Lhasa Government which had been brought under its control.

As a result of mercantilism, the British authorities in India had been looking for trade possibilities beyond the Himalayas since the latter part of the eighteenth century. The Tibetans were soon to feel the impact of the West, and the Sikkim Convention of 1890 marked a real beginning of international complication in the Tibetan problem. After having made futile attempts to open Tibet not only from India but also from the other end through Peking, the British finally forced it open by sending an armed mission which fought its way to reach Lhasa on August 3, 1904. The convention then imposed, which was to make Tibet a British protectorate, was amended in deference to London authority and in consideration of the relations of Great Britain to other powers. In its amended form, the Lhasa Convention was intended to make Tibet a buffer state.

In spite of the impasse on the issue of Peking's claim of sovereignty over Tibet and British recognition of no more than its suzerainty, China and Great Britain managed to conclude a convention in Peking on April 27, 1906, which legitimized the Lhasa Convention and defined more clearly the new status of Tibet as a buffer state. The delicate question of Tibet's status in her relation to China remained undefined in the Trade Regulations signed by Anglo-Chinese plenipotentiaries and the Tibetan delegate on April 20, 1908. But Tibet's external status as a buffer state was confirmed by the Anglo-Russian Convention of 1907 which bound Russia to the recognition of such a status and which showed clearly that Tibet played the part of a pawn in world politics.

The Chinese Revolution of 1911 brought the downfall of the Manchu dynasty and consequently loss of control over Tibet, though on the eve of its outbreak the Imperial Government was still arguing with the British Government over the rights that it had exercised and claimed still to exercise, not only in Tibet, but also in Nepal and Bhutan. When China was proclaimed a Republic, efforts were soon made to regain control of Tibet. But owing to its internal difficulties and a gloomy international prospect, the Peking Government yielded to British pressure and agreed to participate in the Simla Tripartite Conference which, however, " broke up in the summer of 1914 without an agreement having been reached."[1] Diplomatic and military pressure was again brought to bear on China, and the Chinese Government actually made repeated efforts to come to terms with the Tibetan authorities as well as with the British Government. During the negotiations the British freely drew boundaries for Tibet and switched back and forth its plan for dividing Tibet into Inner and Outer Zones. But for reasons which can be attributed to international factors, the Sino-Tibetan issue long remained unsettled, Tibet having a status politically vague and legally undefined.

Two World Wars and four revolutions, however, did affect the status of Tibet. The Soviet Revolution during World War I minimized the prewar function of Tibet as a buffer state. Great Britain after World War I began to feel the overburden of her international obligations, and the situation in India started to give her cause for worry. As chaotic conditions in China precluded any possibility of China's regaining her position in Tibet, the British authorities in India were content with a so-called autonomous Tibet "under Chinese suzerainty . . . without Chinese interference,"[2] while they consolidated their own position and succeeded in establishing a predominant influence in Tibet.

The Chinese Nationalist Revolution should have afforded an opportunity to settle the status of Tibet, as "by 1925 the Dalai Lama was turning strongly away from Britain towards China."[3]

But as a result of the flight of the Panch'en Lama to China Proper and the creation of frontier incidents by the pro-British Young-Tibet group, the progress toward rapprochement between Nanking and Lhasa did not and could not go far enough to touch this fundamental issue of status. At the same time, for various reasons fully explained above, the National Government in Nanking was not in a position to force the issue by resorting to military action. From 1931, the Tibetan issue was overshadowed by the Japanese menace. After the death of the Dalai Lama in 1933 and that of the Panch'en Lama in 1937, further rapprochement was made by the pro-Chinese Regent, Ra-dreng. But before any step could be taken toward the settlement of the status issue, the pro-British Young-Tibet group seized power and did everything possible to undermine Chinese authority in Tibet.

World War II affected Tibet much more than World War I. As revealed by the Japanese Foreign Office's Archives, Tibet's status would have been fundamentally changed had Japan turned out to be a victor. Yet there was no less of a change when the Allies emerged victorious. The fact that the British power withdrew from India, though it affected the fate of the Young-Tibet group, did not help settle the political status of Tibet. It was another outcome of World War II—the Chinese Communist Revolution—that brought a "solution" to the long-pending issue as embodied in the Agreement on Measures for the Peaceful Liberation of Tibet, and affirmed by the Sino-Indian Pact signed on April 29, 1954, in Peking.

Throughout this study we find the status of Tibet was defined at certain times, while left in a vague state at others. This can be explained only in terms of world politics. Tibet was always considered as a military backwater, for its road led nowhere.[4] It was no less due to its lack of strategic value than to respect for its religious influence that it was often left alone in its secluded position. Even the Manchu expeditions and Dzungar and Gurkha invasions into Tibet were motivated not so much by strategic as by religio-political considerations. But today the operation of air power has made warfare truly three-dimensional. In a shrinking world divided into two hostile camps, such an extended area as Tibet, situated on the roof of the world, with its increasingly important strategical position, cannot escape the impact of world politics, and its status, should there be any change, would be determined more by world politics than by the Tibetans themselves.

The writer, in collecting data for the present study, has been struck by the prevalence of misinformation in regard to Tibet, especially in its relations with China. It was perhaps for the purpose of alleviating a guilty conscience or for winning support for a doubtful cause that some one painted a picture of Tibet as *res nullius* abandoned by its owner but acquirable by appropriation, or alleged that the Government of Tibet "have repeatedly declared that . . . Tibet had always been independent and was determined to remain independent"; "it did not at any time confer on the government of China the right to control the external relations of Tibet"; "at no time in the history of this relationship was there a definite *de jure* surrender of any powers of sovereignty"; "the claim now advanced by the Chinese Government . . . has no foundation whatsoever either in law or in fact."[5] The writer believes that there are enough historical facts cited in this study to repudiate these allegations.

In this connection, the writer wishes to point out that he has cited documentary evidence to show that the English recognized Tibet as a dependency of China as early as 1792 and that (1) Lord Hamilton, the British Secretary of State for India, said in a reply to Lord Curzon that His Majesty's Government still regarded Tibet as a province of China; (2) Lord Reay also said in the House of Lords that "the home government looked upon Tibet as a province of China"; and (3) as late as June 14, 1904, the British Foreign Minister in his official dispatch to the British Ambassador to Russia mentioned Tibet as "that province of the Chinese Empire."[6]

The writer is by no means a follower of Kipling's "East is East, West is West," but he does believe that relations between Eastern nations should not necessarily be judged by Western standards. The development of some Eastern systems has been independent of political development in the Western world. For example, the patronage relationship between China and Tibet in a Buddhistic sense is not comparable to any Western system and no exact equivalent can be found in Western terminology. At least, the Chinese part as a patron, who is supposed to give and not to take, should not be construed as a sign of weakness or as a sort of bribery.

The writer finds it most regrettable that sometimes the West uses two standards in treating of a state of affairs in the East. For example, it is still generally admitted today that "a state violates no legal duty by declining to enter into treaties with other states. If it prefers to live in isolation from the rest of the world, international law recognizes no lawful means of compelling it to abandon this policy."[7] Yet Lord Curzon could call it "the most extraordinary anachronism of the 20th century that there should exist within less than 300 miles of the borders of British India a state and a government with whom political relations do not so much as exist, and with whom it is impossible even to exchange a written communication,"[8] and he finally forced the door open and imposed a treaty on Tibet. And after that had been done, the British Secretary of State for India then recognized that "Tibet should remain in that state of isolation," but on condition that "British influence should be recognized at Lhasa in such a manner as to exclude that of any other power."[9] No wonder the Tibetans failed to understand why the British armed mission refused to stop its advance and return to the border, when it was clearly provided in the treaty that Yatung was the only place where foreigners could come and stay.

The development of the Tibetan situation since 1949 has rendered nugatory the predictions and judgments of many Western writers on Tibet and has pointed up a lack of understanding of the Tibetan issue among the general public of the West. Those books written by apologists for British policy toward Tibet should only be regarded as time-honored. This factual account of the changes in Tibet's status, written *sine ira et studio,* may, it is hoped, contribute a bit to a better understanding of this, not hidden or forbidden, but forgotten, land.

Bon gré mal gré, the status of Tibet has been defined by the Peking agreement, but the world situation is still fluid. Hans Kohn speaks of Oriental fellowship vis-à-vis the Anglo-Saxon and the European fellowships with two circles—the eastern one embracing India and Ceylon, Tibet, China, and Japan, and the western one stretching from the western coast of Africa eastward as far as India, China, Java, and the Malaya peninsula—intersecting in India.[10] N. L. Spykman speaks of the threat to what he calls the Asiatic Mediterranean by a modern, vitalized, and militarized China, and thinks it quite possible to envisage the day when this body of water will be controlled by Chinese air power.[11] Whatever the world situation proves to be, the writer believes that an understanding between China and India such as exists between the United States and Canada, with an agreement to demilitarize the Himalayas, which are the controlling fact of both Indian and Chinese geography, would be not only a guarantee of the autonomous status of Tibet[12] but also a stabilizing factor in the peace of the world.

NOTES

Introduction

1. See the topic on "The Simla Conference and Its Failure" in Chapter V. A fuller discussion about the so-called validity of the Simla Convention and even its existence is given by the writer in an article, "The Legal Position of Tibet," in the April, 1956, issue of the *American Journal of International Law*.

2. See p. 172. The Lhasa Government in a letter to the British Trade Agent at Gyantse, declined to assume responsibility for the counduct of Khambas. According to the Indian Prime Minister Mr. Nehru (as reported in the New York Times, March 31, 1959), the Lhasa revolt is a new development, not related to Khamba activities.

3. Shen Tsung-lien and Liu Shen-chi, *Tibet and the Tibetan,* p. 10. R. N. Rahul, an Indian expert on Tibet doing research at Columbia University, told the writer that the pass, Dzo-ji La as he rendered it in English, is seventy-five miles from Srinagar.

4. *The New York Times,* May 1, 1959 (A dispatch of the *Times,* London) and June 15, 1959.

5. *The New York Times,* April 25, 1959.

6. Sir Charles Bell, *The Religion of Tibet,* p. 190.

7. Shen Tsung-lien and Liu Shen-chi, *Tibet and the Tibetans,* p. 62.

8. The writer derived this information from the *Survey of China Mainland Press* issued by the American Consulate-General in Hong Kong.

9. Parliamentary Debate Vol. 130, p. 1140.

10. U.S. Bureau of Foreign and Domestic Commerce, *Special Consular Reports,* No. 72 (1915), pp. 562 and 572.

11. Alan Winnington, *Tibet, the Record of a Journey* (London, 1957), p. 122.

12. His book entitled *Hsi-tsang T'ung-lan* ("Chibetto tsuran") was revised by a Chinese named Wu Chi-po (1910 ed.). See especially sertion 3 of the 12th chapter in Pt. I.

13. W. W. Rockhill, *Diary of a Journey Through Mongolia and*

Tibet in 1891 and 1892 (Washington, 1894), pp. 187, 193, 303, and 330.

14. Sir Charles Bell, *The People of Tibet,* pp. 4 and 111.

15. *A Collection of Treaties, Engagements and Sanads Relating to India and Neighboring Countries,* Vol. XIV, p. 21.

16. Luciano Petech, *China and Tibet in the Early 18th Century,* pp. 9-10 and 25.

17. *Imperial Records of the Ch'ing Dynasty: Kao-tsung Shih-lu,* chap. 358, p. 9a.

18. Amaury de Reincourt, *Roof of the World: Tibet, Key to Asia* (1950), p. 207.

19. *Accounts and Papers* printed by Order of the House of Commons, Cd. 2370, No. 193, p. 86.

20. Documents des archives des gouvernements impérial et provisoire 1878-1917 (in Russian, Series II, Vol. 20, Part I; No. 228 pp. 220-21.

21. Bell, *Portrait of the Dalai Lama* (1946), p. 205; *Tibet: Past and Present* (Henceforth cited as Bell, *Tibet*), p. 152.

22. The *New York Times,* April 17, 1959.

23. *Journal of the Asiatic Society of Bengal* (1838), VII, Part 1, 147. Henceforth cited as JASB.

24. Bell, *Tibet,* p. 23.

25. W. W. Rockhill, *The Life of Buddha,* p. 210, n.l. Henceforth cited as Rockhill, *Buddha.*

26. S. W. Bushell, "The Early History of Tibet from Chinese Sources," *Journal of the Royal Asiatic Society, New Series,* XII (1880), Part IV, 438. Henceforth cited as JRAS.

27. *Cambridge History of India,* Vol. I, ed. by E. J. Rapson, p. 58.

28. J. Allan, Sir T. Wolseley Haig, and H. H. Dodwell, *The Cambridge Shorter History of India,* p. 117.

Chapter I: Foreign Relations up to the Thirteenth Century

1. Grenard, *Le Tibet, le Pays et les Habitants,* p. 224; *The Chinese Classics,* Vol. III, Part 1, *The Shoo King,* trans. by James Legge, Book 1, p. 40; "Biography of Emperor Shun" in the *Book of History.* J. Huston Edgar, in his article "The Tibetan and His Environment: An Interpretation," *JRAS,* Shanghai, LVII (1926), 30, mistook San-wei for a tribe. Edgar wrote, "Tradition, indeed, claims that the Emperor Shuen drove the San-wei into Tibetan country about 2225 B.C."

According to the *Chu shu chi nien,* the date would be 2221 B.C. The writer in the present study bases his date (2220 B.C.) on the Chinese *Tz'ŭ hai,* and Japanese *Mohan saishin sekai nempyô.*

2. *Tung-hua lu,* K'ang-hsi period, Vol. IV, Chüan 106, p. 14; or *Shêng-tsu shih-lu,* Chüan 290, p. 8a.

3. The earliest reference to the Ch'iang is probably its tribute-mission in 1765 B.C. See H. G. Creel, *Birth of China,* pp. 213-16, and also Grenard, *Le Tibet,* p. 236; Rockhill, *Buddha,* p. 204.

4. Sarat Chandra Das's translation of this Tibetan work, *JASB* (1881), L, Part 1, Nos. 3, 4.

5. *Ibid.,* p. 196.

6. According to Chinese records, *T'ung tien* by Tu Yu (735-812), ch. 190, he was the founder of the Tibetan Kingdom during the K'ai-huang period, 581-600 A.D., of the Sui dynasty. His name was rendered as Luntsan solungtsan in Chinese. J. Bacot, F. W. Thomas, and C. H. Toussaint (trans.), *Documents de Touen-Houang, relatifs à l'histoire du Tibet,* pp. 88 and 95, records him as the father of the celebrated Tsanpu Sroṅ-bcan sgan-po (Sron-tsan Gampo) or, as rendered in Chinese, Ch'i-tsung-lung-tsan. According to J. Bacot ("Le Marriage Chinois du roi tibétain Sroṅ-bcan sgan-po," *Mél Chin. et boud.* [1935], III, 4), a mission which had been sent by the father to India returned with an alphabet, a grammar, and some Buddhist texts in the reign of the son.

7. See Rockhill, *Buddha,* p. 211; Das, "Contributions on the Religion, History . . . of Tibet," Part 1, "Early History of Tibet," *JASB,* L, Nos. 3, 4, 217. Henceforth cited as Das, "Contributions."

8. The writer of this study bases his statements upon the *T'ang shu,* i.e., History of T'ang. The chapters dealing with Tibet were translated by S. W. Bushell, *JRAS,* New Series (1880), XII, Part IV. Henceforth cited as Bushell.

9. The first embassy was sent by Ch'i-tsung-lung-tsan to the Chinese Emperor T'ai-tsung in 634.

10. See *Documents de Touen-Houang, relatifs à l'histoire du Tibet,* pp. 48-52.

11. Bell, *Tibet,* p. 28; Das, "Contributions," p. 222. Rockhill suspects this event was interpolated on the ground that *T'ang shu* does not allude to it (*Buddha,* p. 217). The *Documents de Touen-Houang,* p. 32, records an armed conflict with the Chinese under Su Ting-fang in 659. (For details see biography of Su Ting-fang in *T'ang shu,* Lieh-chuan 33, *Hsin T'ang shu,* Lieh-chuan 36.) The writer wonders if it was not to this armed conflict that the Tibetan record refers.

12. Rockhill mistakenly declared that the Chinese chronicles do not mention any sovereign between the time of Mukhri's death in 804 and the commencement of the reign of Ralpachan (also known as Khri-ral, the Chinese Kolikotsu) in 816 (815, according to Tschen Yin-koh). Cf. Bushell, p. 512, and Rockhill, *Buddha,* p. 223.

13. According to the *Documents de Touen-Houang,* pp. 10, 34, 40, Chilipapu (Khri-man-slon) died in 676; Ch'inuhsilung (Khri-'dus-sroṅ) died in 704. Doubtless news of a death took time to reach Ch'ang-an in those days. We find also that the remains of the former

were kept unburied until 679 (*ibid.*, p. 35), while that of the latter until 706 (*ibid.*, p. 41), and that there was in each case a revolt after the death of the king. Perhaps the Chinese Imperial Court was only informed of the funeral service. Perhaps it was the revolt that prevented news of a death from reaching the Chinese capital at an earlier date. The Tunhuang *Documents* did not register the death of Ch'ilisulungliehtsan, but recorded that in 756 "the Btsanpo [Tsanpu or king's] name was published as Khri sroṅ lde brtsan" (*ibid.*, p. 63). We may assume that a king (Ch'ilisulungliehtsan or Khri-lde) died in the previous year or sometime earlier. Had there not been a hiatus of seven years (749-54) in the text, the death might have been registered therein.

14. The Tsanpu Ch'i-tsung-lung-tsan offered 15 presents of gold, silver, pearls, and other precious objects to be deposited before the ancestral tablet of the late Emperor T'ai-tsung (reigned 627-49) and had his statue, carved in stone, erected below the gateway of the Imperial Mausoleum.

15. This treaty was mentioned in *Hsin T'ang shu* (New T'ang History) Lieh-chuan 141, but not in *T'ang shu.* See Bushell's translation, p. 460.

16. Rockhill, *Buddha,* p. 222, n. 1, expresses some doubt about the treaty of 783. This doubt would have been at least partly allayed if he had not mistaken the year in which Tê-tsung became emperor. Rockhill assumed the date to be 799, whereas it was 780.

17. The facsimile and the translation can be easily identified with each other by comparing the subject matter of each. Sir Charles Bell supposed it to have been concluded during the first half of the eighth century. He evidently assumed it was the covenant made in 730 at Ch'ih-ling. Lee Wei-kuo in his doctoral thesis, *Tibet in Modern World Politics,* also identified it as concluded in the eighth century. But judging by the title of the Chinese Emperor given in the facsimile and the names of the officials alluded to (*infra,* n. 18, and *Wei-tsang tung chih, Chüan* VI, p. 123, which mentions the name of Niu Sêng-ju on the pillar), and comparing the facsimile and the translation with the record in *T'ang shu,* one can safely identify it as the treaty concluded in 821. For further supporting evidence, see Das, "Contributions," p. 226, and *Bodhimur* in Sanang Setsen, pp. 360-61. Both record a treaty inscription written on a high stone obelisk erected at Lhasa in the reign of Ralpachan, or Khri-ral, the Chinese Kolikotsu, in which it was agreed that the armies of neither kingdom should ever cross the boundary mark or on any pretext encroach upon the other's territories and that the uncle and nephew were to become friends. Emil Schlagintweit's *Die Könige von Tibet* (Abh. d. Philos.—philol. Cl. d. Kön. bayerischen Akad. d. Wiss., 1866, 10), p. 809, also records a treaty written on a monument in the reign of Ralpachan. (See also

"Notes on Sanang Setsen's 'Geschichte der Ost-Mongolem' by Tschen Yin-koh," *Bulletin of the Institute of History and Philology,* Academia Sinica [1930], II, Part 1, 1-5.)

M. E. Willoughby in his lecture delivered before the Central Asian Society on the subject "Relation of Tibet to China," *Journal of Central Asian Society,* henceforth cited as *CASJ* (London, 1924), II, 189, mentioned the treaty recorded on bilingual tablets as the one signed in 821 and ratified at Lhasa in 822. In translating part of Sir Charles Bell's book under the title *Hsi-tsang wai chiao wên chien* (1930), p. 34, Dr. Wang Kuang-chi pointed out Sir Charles's mistake, but he himself made an error in describing it as the treaty concluded in 783. Wang Ch'in-yü, in his book on *Hsi-tsang wên t'i* (p. 2), published one year earlier, made the same mistake. Presumably both Wangs based their judgment upon Ma Chueh and Shêng Shêng-tsu, *Wei-tsang t'u shih* (1792), which records: "Before Ta-chao-ssu, two stone pillars were erected—one recording the treaty of 783, the other the treaty of 821. At present there remains only the Tê-tsung pillar with the inscription of the treaty of 783 and it is in an impaired condition." Probably it is this wrong identification that gives rise to their mistake which is shared by some other Chinese scholars.

For a French translation of *Wei-tsang t'u shih,* see J. H. Klaproth, *Description du Tibet,* extrait du nouveau *Journal Asiatique* (1831), pp. 127, 168. For a comparative study of the text of the treaty of 783 with that of 821 as a means of establishing further the identity, see L. A. Waddell, "Ancient Historical Edicts at Lhasa," *JRAS* (1909) and (1911), in which the author took the Tibetan text on the verso as the "treaty edict of 783" and further advanced 9 points to claim the recto as an integral portion of the treaty edict of 783; and also Gijo Suwa, in *Asiatic Studies in Honor of Tôru Haneda* (Kyoto, 1950), pp. 561-83. The latter made a careful study of this issue and dealt with the former's error in a detailed analysis. H. E. Richardson's book on *Ancient Historical Edicts at Lhasa and the Mu Tsung/Khri Gtsug Lde Brtsan Treaty of A.D. 821-822 from the Inscription at Lhasa* (1952) should allay the last possible doubt on this point. See pp. 35-47.

18. Berthold Laufer regarded the reproduction and Lo's article as of first importance and dealt with the material in "Bird Divination among the Tibetans . . . with a Study of Tibetan Phonology of the Ninth Century," *T'oung Pao* (1914), pp. 70-72. The reproduction and Lo's article are mentioned also in *Bulletin de l'école française de l'extrême Orient,* IX (1909), 578. Meng-pao, Resident in Tibet from 1839 to 1842, copied only the Chinese text of the treaty from the pillar in his book, *Hsi-tsang pei wên* (Inscriptions in Tibet), published in 1852, pp. 26-27.

19. *The Cambridge Shorter History of India,* p. 107; Vincent A.

Smith, *Early History of India* (ed. 1914), pp. 352-53. For further particulars, see Sylvain Levi, "Les missions de Wang Hiuen-tzê dans l' Inde," *Journal Asiatique* (Paris), neuvième series, XV (mars-avril, 1900), and Fêng Ch'êng-chün's editing notes in Chinese (*Shih ti ts'ung k'ao,* pp. 40-56), and Paul Pelliot, "Notes sur quelques artistes des six dynasties et des T'ang," *T'oung Pao* (1923), pp. 274-82 and 291, in which the author made some corrections to Levi's article.

20. See text of treaty concluded at Ch'ing-hsui-hsien in 783. Bushell, p. 489.

21. Das, "Contributions," pp. 220, 223.

22. Rockhill, *Buddha,* p. 211.

23. *Ibid.,* p. 217.

24. Pages 338, 348.

25. Csoma, *Tibetan Grammar,* p. 196. Wang I-nuan, *Hsi-tsang wang t'ung chi* (1949) (trans. from a Tibetan chronicle compiled by Bsod-rgyal, tutor of Tsong-k'a-pa, in 1388), pp. 41-44 and 47, gives an account of the Nepalese princess's jealousy of the Chinese princess.

26. Rockhill, *Buddha,* p. 213, n. 1, and p. 218, n. 1.

27. Das, "Contributions," pp. 221, 224; Rockhill, *Buddha,* pp. 213, 218.

28. French translation of his *Le Bouddhisme* (Paris, 1865), p. 320, n. 4. "Nous nous souvenons ici à propos du recit de Bou-Done dans l'histoire de la religion: au commencement les Rhechanna Chinois furent les guides des Tibétains dans le Bouddhisme."

29. Das, "Contributions," p. 221. *Shêng wu chi,* Book V, pp. 33b-34a, throws some light on this statement, and repudiates the widely circulated tales about the builder of, and the image in, this monastery.

30. Bushell, p. 445; see also Grenard, *Le Tibet,* pp. 242-43.

31. Bushell, p. 446.

32. Ed. by Wang Fu (completed in 961), Chüan 97 (1935 ed.), pp. 1730-31, quoted in Berthold Laufer, "Loan-Words in Tibetan," *T'oung Pao* (1916), p. 509.

33. Bushell, pp. 466-67.

34. Sanang Setsen, *Bodhimur,* pp. 340-41.

35. Schlagintweit, *Könige von Tibet,* pp. 840-41; Rockhill, *Buddha,* p. 215, n. 1; Bell, *Tibet,* p. 25.

36. "Loan-Words in Tibetan," *T'oung Pao* (1916), p. 511.

37. Das, "Contributions," p. 218.

38. *Ibid.,* p. 221. Except for *Wei-tsang t'ung chih,* I, 133, which gives the site of the 108 chapels as Ch'ang-chu, Hsiao-lo, Lun-ta, and Tui-yang, the writer fails to find any confirmation of these 108 chapels. Most likely they were only caves like those found at Tunhuang (Touen-Houang). For the origin of Tibetan writing see Berthold Laufer's article, *Journ. Amer. Orient. Soc.* (1918), pp. 34-46.

39. "The Tibetan Tripitaka," *Harvard Journal of Asiatic Studies,* IX (1945), 53. Hereafter referred to as *HJAS.*

40. Lü Chêng, *Hsi-tsang fo hsüeh yüan lun* (Shanghai, 1933), p. 21.

41. Harvard-Yenching Institute Sinological Index, series no. 11, *Buddhistic Literature,* p. III/02793.

42. *Yin Tsang fo chiao shih,* published by the West China Frontier Research Institute (1946), p. 44.

43. Rockhill, *Buddha,* p. 217; Bell, *People of Tibet,* p. 12, and also his *Tibet,* p. 25. (But Dgung-srong was the great-grandson, not the grandson, of Sron-tsan who was succeeded by his grandson Khri-man-slon.) Laufer, in his article on "Loan-Words in Tibetan," p. 505, takes the Tibetan word for tea, which is an exact reproduction of the ancient Chinese "Dza" and which is the only one among many Asiatic languages adopting this Chinese designation that has preserved the ancient sonant, to justify the conclusion that the acquaintance of the Tibetans with tea goes as far back as the T'ang period. In fact, tea was then exported to the Tibetans from Chiung-chou in Szechwan, being made up into cakes or bricks. (*T'ai p'ing huan yü chi,* ch. 75, p. 3.)

44. Kun-shi sounds like "west of Lung Mountain" in Chinese. There was Lung-hsi Chün in Ch'in dynasty (B.C. 246-207) and Lung-yu Tao in T'ang dynasty—both composing part of the present-day Kansu Province. The *Documents de Touen-Houang,* p. 66 (cf. p. 153, n. 3), records the place Ken-si, which is also mentioned in the Lhasa inscriptions and is discussed by L. A. Waddell, who identifies it as Kingchow (*JRAS,* [1910], p. 1265), an administrative unit first set up in Wei dynasty (A.D. 220-264) and adopted by T'ang, with its headquarters at the present-day T'ien-shui of Kansu Province. H. E. Richardson in his book on *Ancient Historical Edicts at Lhasa,* pp. 26 and 66, identifies it as Ch'ang-an.

45. Das, "Contributions," p. 223.

46. Rockhill, *Buddha,* pp. 218-19.

47. *Ibid.,* p. 219, identifies him as the Chinese Ch'i-li-tsan. But *T'ang shu* records that Ch'ilisutsan was succeeded by Ch'ilisulung-liehtsan, whose death was announced in 755 (Bushell, p. 438, compares Ch'ilisulungliehstan with Khri-srong-lde-btsan of Csomo de Körös' list), and mentions Ch'i-li-tsan as Tsanpu in connection with Wei Lun's mission in 780. According to Padma Than-yig, *Ms. de Lithasi,* Chant LIV, he was the son of the Chinese Princess Chin-ch'eng. This has been often quoted by writers on Tibet. But as recorded by the *Documents de Touen-Houang,* p. 51, Ms. 103, he was born in 742, three years after the princess's death (739). Moreover, Ms. 249 (*ibid.,* p. 89)—an older record than the Ms. de Lithasi—gives the name of his mother as the lady from Sna-nam, Masi-mo-rjĕ bži-stesi.

48. Das, "Contributions," p. 226; both Lü Chêng and Liu Li-ch'ien in their works give the Chinese name of Maháyána as Ta-shêng Hoshang, this being merely a literary translation of his Sanskrit name.

49. See Rockhill, *Buddha,* p. 220, and Sanang Setsen, *Bodhimur,* pp. 356-57.

50. Journey made in 399-413 A.D. See J. Legge's trans., *A Record of Buddhistic Kingdoms* (1886), also Ts'ên Chung-mien, *Fo yu t'ien chu chi k'ao shih* (in Chinese; 1934), and Adachi Kisoku, *Kôshô Hokken-den* (in Japanese; 1936).

51. Journey made in 518-22. See Ed. Chavannes, *Voyage de Song-Yun dans l'Udyana et le Gandhāra* (1903).

52. Journey made in 629-45, mentioned in Markham, *Tibet,* p. xliv, and H. G. Rawlinson, *Indian Historical Studies,* chapter on Chinese Pilgrims in India (1913 ed.), pp. 55-92. For more particulars see S. Beal's trans. from Chinese of Hsüan-tsang, *Buddhist Records of the Western World* (1906); T. Watters, *On Yuan Chwang's Travels in India, 629-645* A.D., 2 vols., (1904-5); and S. Beal, *The Life of Hiuen Tsang,* new ed. with a preface by L. Cranmer-Byng (1911).

53. Journey made in 751-90. Francke, *History of Western Tibet* (hereafter cited as Francke), p. 44, states that he reached Kashmir in 759. See S. Levi and Ed. Chavannes, "L'itenèraire d'Ou-kong," *Journal Asiatique,* VI (1895), also Abbot Yūan Chao, "Wu-k'ung ju chu chi." For his life see preface to the Chinese translation of *Dasābhūm Kasūtra Sātra,* and Abbot Tsan-ning, *Sung kao sêng chuan,* published 982-88.

54. For the routes traveled, see "Trade Routes of China from Ancient Times to the Age of European Expansion," by Prof. L. Carrington Goodrich, in Labatut and Lane (eds.), *Highways* (1950), pp. 23-27.

55. Das, "Contributions," p. 227.

56. *Ibid.,* p. 228; Rockhill, *Buddha,* p. 224.

57. Bell, *Tibet,* p. 25.

58. Laufer, "Loan-Words in Tibetan," *T'oung Pao* (1916), p. 502.

59. *Ibid.,* p. 215.

60. Ch'ih-ling, the Red Hills, are 320 *li* from the modern Sining, the capital of Ch'inghai Province. Kansungling is in Szechwan, 30 miles north of Sung-pan, the T'ang Sungchou. Lungchou had its district government at the present-day Lung-hsien in Shensi Province. The Lungchou barrier here indicated must be somewhere north of Ch'ing-shui in the present Kansu Province.

61. *Le Tibet,* p. 242.

62. *T'ang shu,* Bushell's translation, pp. 486-87.

63. Francke, p. 60; Bell, *Tibet,* pp. 30-31; Das, "Contributions," p. 230.

64. See *Sung shih,* Book 492.

65. See also Bushell, pp. 523-26.

66. Francke, in his *History of Western Tibet,* Chap. VI, gives the line of direct descendants of Derigpa-gon up to Khri-btsug-lde (ca. 1375-1400). Cf. L. Petech, *A Study of the Chronicle of Ladakh* (1939), Part I, Chap. IX.; Part II, Chaps. I and II.

67. The Emperor's talk with his Prime Minister on the subject, recorded in the history of the Sung dynasty, shows clearly his peaceful policy toward Tibet. See *Sung shih,* Book 492, Chüan 25, pp. 3b-6a.

68. Das, "Contributions," pp. 235-39; cf. Sanang Setsen. For a comprehensive and detailed account, see Books I-II, of *The Blue Annals,* a translation of *Deb-ther sṅon-po* by George N. Roerich, published by the Royal Asiatic Society of Bengal, Calcutta (1949-53).

69. *Cambridge History of India,* III, 49-50.

70. *T'ang shu* records his death in 842; Csoma, *Tibetan Grammar,* p. 183, places it at 900; Sanang Setsen (pp. 49 and 51) says he was killed in 925. The year 842 is generally recognized as the correct date. See also Shimonaku Yasaburô and others, *Tôyô rekishi daijiten* (Encyclopedia of Oriental History) (Tokyo, Heibon-sha, 1937-39), IX, 46 c.

71. L. Carrington Goodrich, *A Short History of the Chinese People* (rev. ed., 1951), p. 148.

Chapter II: Tibet as a Vassal State

1. C. P. Fitzgerald, *China, A Short Cultural History* (rev. ed., 1950), p. 1.

2. According to Tibetan chronology, Jenghis Khan was born in 1182, ascended the throne as Khan in 1220, and died in 1243. (Das, "Contributions," pp. 239-40.) Chinese books usually give his period of life as 1162-1227; but after investigation some writers have placed it at 1154 or 1155-1227 (see Fêng Ch'êng-chün, *Ch'eng-chi-sŭ-han chuan*). Paul Pelliot gave a Chinese source and advanced a thesis to show that he was born in 1167 (*Journal Asiatique,* CCXXXI [1939], 133-34; mentioned and commented on by William Hung, "The Secret History of the Mongols" *HJAS,* XIV [Dec., 1951], 476-78, n. 104). His succession to Khanship is generally recognized among Chinese writers as occurring in 1206; but some give another coronation in 1179 or 1189 (see *ibid.,* pp. 468 d and 482, nn. 118 and 119). The Mongolian record *Tobchiyan* (for whose identity and connection with *Ch'in-chêng lu, Altan Debter,* and Rašīd al-Dīn's relevant portions of the *Jāmi'al-Tawārīkh,* see *ibid.,* pp. 469-71 and also Pelliot and Hambis, *Histoire des campagnes de Gengis Khan* [1951], p. xv) gives a mysterious origin to his family and birth.

3. See H. Desmond Martin, *The Rise of Chingis Khan and His Conquest of North China* (1950), pp. 102, n. 32, and 116.

4. *Tôyô rekishi dai-jiten,* VIII, 227 B.

5. In spite of the assertion of Rockhill, who says that "the forces of Yüan Emperors never advanced nearer Tibet than the western borders of Kansu, Szechwan and Yünnan" (*T'oung Pao* [1910], p. 2), and the doubt concerning Colonel Yule's observation that Tibet was always reckoned as a part of the Mongol-Chinese Empire, expressed by E. Bretschneider who wonders how Tibet came into subjection to the Mongols (*Medieval Researches from Eastern Asiatic Sources* [1888], II, 25), the writer considers that there are sufficient evidences to show that Kublai's forces did cross the Tibetan frontier. Shao Yüan-p'ing, *Yüan shih lei pien* (1699), which relates the Ta-li campaign in more detail than other compilations of Yüan-shih (History of the Yüan Dynasty), records the switch of a branch of the army to enter Tibet (Chüan II, p. 1b). Wei Yüan (1794-1856), *Yüan shih hsin pien,* Chüan V, p. 1-b, Chüan XVIII, pp. 8-b and 10-a, and Tsêng Lien, *Yüan shu* (1911), Chüan IV, p. 3a, also mentions their passing through, or entering into, Tibet. On referring to the biographies of Wu-liang-ho-t'ai (Uriangkadai), the Field Commander-in-Chief of the western route army (Sung Lien [1310-81], and others, *Yüan shih,* Chüan 121, pp. 5a-8b; K'o Shao-min [1850-1933], *Hsin Yüan shih,* Chüan 122, pp. 5b-8b; *Yüan shih lei pien,* Chüan XIX, pp. 1a-2b; *Yüan shih hsin pien,* Chüan XXXVII, pp. 1a-4a), one will find some supporting evidence. Above all, the record of the campaign inscribed on a stone erected at Ta-li in memory of the victory and written by Ch'êng Chü-fu (1249-1318) (*Kuo ch'ao wên lei,* Chüan XXIII, pp. 1a-3b) has the words "passing through T'u-fan," which cannot but mean the overrunning of at least a part of the eastern territory then under Tibet's control. Wu Chin-ao, basing his remarks on knowledge of the area gained through traveling, gives the itinerary of this campaign in his book, *Hsi ch'ui shih ti yen chiu,* pp. 30-40, which shows clearly the part of the Tibetan territory overrun by the Mongolian force. *Yüan shih lei pien* (Chüan II, p. 1b) and *Yüan shih hsin pien* (Chüan V, p. 1b) record the submission of the chief of T'u-fan (Tibet), So-huo-t'o. *Hsin Yüan shih* (Chüan VI, p. 7b; Chüan VII, p. 2b) and *Yüan shu* (Chüan IV, p. 3a) also mention So-huo-t'o's surrender.

6. *See Ta Ch'ing i tung chih,* Chia-ch'ing Ed., Chüan 547, p. 1b. But in fact he did not carry this out very far. As he had such a vast empire to administer, he may have found it not worth-while to put the whole scheme into force or unnecessary to consolidate any further the secular power of the Sakya hierarchy.

7. See *Yüan shih* by Sung Lien and others, Chüan VII, pp. 15a-b, and also *Yüan shih hsin pien* by Wei Yüan, Chüan V, p. 21b. Note that three years later (1275), Prince Auluchi was dispatched as Commander-in-Chief of a combined Mongolian force to subjugate the Tibetans. (*Ibid.,* p. 27b, and *Yüan shih,* Chüan VIII, p. 20b.) Be-

sides mentioning Auluchi's expedition in 1275 and Kublai's entering T'u-fan in 1254 (?), E. Bretschneider cited also from *Yüan shih* that sub anno 1251 Möngä Khan entrusted Ho-li-dan with the command of the troops against T'u-fan and that sub anno 1268 Kublai Khan ordered Meng-gu-dai to invade Si-fan with 6,000 men. And Bretschneider remarked that with the exception of these passages from the Chinese annals, nothing more is said of the warlike enterprises of the Mongols against Tibet. (*Mediaeval Researches,* II, 23-25.)

8. L. Austine Waddell, *Lhasa and Its Mysteries* (henceforth cited as Waddell), p. 26, tells a story of how Buddhism was chosen in the presence of Christian missionaries. They were unable to comply with Kublai's demand to perform a miracle, while the Lamas caused his wine-cup to rise miraculously to his lips. (Waddell mistook Kublai for the son of Jenghis Khan. He was the fourth son of Tului, brother of Möngä, grandson of Jenghis Khan.) Huang Ch'an-hua, *Chung kuo fo chiao shih* (1940), p. 340, mentions the debate between Phagspa, who took part in the debate by the Emperor's command, and the Taoists, who failed at last to answer the questions put to them. There were two debates, one in 1258, one in 1281. Cf. translations of Chavannes in *T'oung Pao,* 1904, pp. 385, 395.

9. This might have been the reason for Kublai Khan's embracing Buddhism. As he had Marco Polo in his service and as the Nestorian church and Islam were much more powerful in his Empire, he might just as well have gone over to either one. But it must not be assumed that he adopted Buddhism merely as a matter of expediency. He may have done so from religious convictions. He had as tutor the Abbot Yin-chien (a Chinese monk from Shansi Province, who died in 1257). This monk was held in high respect by Kublai's two grandmothers and had been appointed to have charge of all monastic affairs by Kublai's predecessors, Kwei-yu and Möngä.

Kublai had also in his service as a high ranking member of his staff Liu Ping-chung, who had been a Buddhist hermit and who was presented to him by Yin-chien.

10. Bell, *Tibet,* p. 31; Das, "Contributions," p. 240.

11. Das says that he was 19 years of age; but Chinese records place him at 15. According to Liu Li-chien's translation of *Tibetan History after Landarma* (p. 14), Phagspa, at the age of 11, accompanied his uncle, Sakya Pandita, to visit Godan (son of Gagan, grandson of Jenghis Khan) at Hsi-Liang. Here the uncle remained for 7 years, dying in 1251. Phagspa was 19 when Kublai sent for him. According to Kenneth K. S. Chen, "Buddhist-Taoist Mixtures in Pa-shih-i-hua-t'u," *HJAS,* IX (1945), 3, he was born ca. 1239 and died in 1280.

12. The Mongols under Jenghis Khan borrowed the Uigur alphabet and script. In 1269, Kublai ordered Phagspa to compose a system of

writing for official use. According to Pelliot there is nothing original in Phagspa's adaptation. *Journal Asiatique,* (1927), CCX, 372.

13. Das's article states that after a residence of twelve years in China with the Emperor, he returned to Sakya. Sanang Setsen (p. 115) gives his birth as 1235 and (p. 119) records his return in 1280 at the age of 46.

14. Clements R. Markham, *Narratives of the Mission of George Boyle to Tibet and of the Journey of Thomas Manning to Lhasa* (henceforth cited as Markham), xxviii.

15. Both Tibetan sources quoted by Das and Liu Li-chien relate a suppression of Buddhism in Tibet, for seventy years. Liu places its revival from 918. (See his translation of the *History after Landarma* [henceforth cited as *Liu's Translation*], p. 2, and *Yin Tsang fo chiao shih,* compiled by him, p. 49, together with the chronological table in the appendix); but Das, "Contributions," p. 236, states that the revival dates from 1013 A.D.

16. Tibetan monks studied at the monasteries of Nālandā and Vikramasila, and many Indian Buddhist monks visited Tibet, among whom the best known was Atisá.

17. M. G. Rawlinson, *A Concise History of the Indian People* (rev. 2nd ed., 1950), p. 84. See also V. A. Smith, *The Oxford History of India* (rev., 1928), p. 221, which places the conquest of Bengal at about the close of the year 1199, while the *Cambridge History of India* says it took place in 1202. The discrepancy has been pointed out by Schuyler Cammann, *Trade through Himalayas* (1951), p. 9, hereafter cited as Cammann.

18. 1277-1367. Kublai became virtually emperor of the whole of China in 1277, though he ascended to Khanship in 1260 and entered Peking in 1264. The *Yüan shih* gives a list of the names of the national mentors, dates of their appointment, and the dates of their deaths. On the control exercised by the national mentor and on the national mentor as an institution, see Shunjô Nogami, *Asiatic Studies in Honor of Tôru Haneda* (1950), pp. 779-95.

19. The writer of this study has drawn some of the material from the *Yüan shih,* especially Chüan 202.

20. A genealogical table of the Sakya regents is given by Das, "Contributions," p. 240.

21. *Liu's Translation,* p. 25.

22. Das, "Contributions," p. 241; *Liu's Translation,* pp. 20-21.

23. *Liu's Translation,* p. 16.

24. *Ibid.,* p. 20.

25. *Ibid.,* pp. 16-18.

26. *Ibid.,* p. 21, places the Sakya dynasty at 1253-1349; according to Das, "Contributions," p. 240, Sakya hierarchy lasted from 1270 to

1340. The *Yüan shih* records that Phagspa, though made national mentor in 1260, was not appointed the first priest-king until after his composition of a system of Mongol writing, which was adopted in 1269, but which is not now in use as some Chinese writers have asserted. Pelliot says in his article, "Les Mots à H Initiale, Aujourd'hui Amuie dans Le Mongol des XIIIe et XIV Siècles," *Journal Asiatique,* CCVI (1925), 198, that Phagspa's system of writing was hardly in real use for more than a period of some fifty years. But he said at the meeting of the Société Asiatique on March 11, 1927 (*Journal Asiatique,* CCX [1927], 372) that it had been used in central Asia at least till the sixteenth century. *Liu's Translation* (p. 14) also records that Phagspa's political power was given as a reward for his composition of the Mongolian script. So 1270 is about the right year to mark the beginning of the Sakaya rule.

27. *Supra,* pp. 16-17.

28. *Cambridge History of India,* III, 155.

29. R. C. Majumdar, H. C. Raychaudhurt, and K. D. Datta, p. 324, henceforth cited as Majumdar and others, *An Advanced History of India.*

30. For details of this sect see *Yin Tsang fo chiao shih,* pp. 67-68.

31. *Liu's Translation,* pp. 36-38.

32. *Ibid.,* p. 39; Das, "Contributions," p. 243.

33. *Liu's Translation* placed his appointment as hereditary chief of U in 1349 and his assumption of the control of the whole of Tibet in 1354 (pp. 21, 41).

34. Das, "Contributions," p. 243. For origin of Phagmo-du governorship and details concerning Chyañ-chhub Gyal-tshan himself, for further evidence of the Mongol Emperor's influence on Tibetan politics (in this case, to effect the change of a governor and to install one with the Emperor's sanction), and also for Chyañ-chhub's successors, see "A Short History of the House of Phagdu, which ruled over Tibet on the decline of Sakya till 1432 A.D.," by Rai Sarat Chandra Das, *JASB,* New Series, I (August, 1905), 202-7, henceforth cited as Das, "History of Phagdu."

35. Das, "Contributions," p. 244, and Das, "History of Phagdu," p. 206.

36. The distorted accounts of Das and Sanang Setsen (pp. 125-35) in regard to the establishment of the Ming dynasty must be wholly rejected.

37. See *Ming T'ai-tsu shih-lu,* Chüan 41, p. 1a, for the text of the decree.

38. According to Chinese records, among them one who called himself head of lamas was given the title of national mentor in 1372; the brother of his successor was made Shan-hua-wang in 1406. *Liu's Translation,* pp. 43, n. 1., and 44, n. 1., identifies the former as the

second priest-king of the Sitya régime, and the latter as his nephew, Dbañ-grags-pa-rgyal-mtshan who, succeeding his cousin, became the fifth ruler in the Sitya hierarchy. Das, "History of Phagdu," p. 205, identifies the latter as Tagpa Gyal-tshan (son of Çakya Rinchen and nephew of Chyañ-chhub), who succeeded his younger uncle Tagrin to the throne in the year Tree-bird.

39. Chang T'ing-yü (1672-1755), *Ming shih* (*History of the Ming Dynasty*). For details see Chüan 330 and 331.

40. *Ibid.*, Chüan 2, pp. 10a and 14a.

41. Liu Chün-jên, *Dictionary of Chinese Geographical Names,* p. 446, identifies To-kan-sze as the region southeast of the present-day Ho-yüan in Ch'inghai to the borderland of Szechwan Province. *Ta ch'ing i tung chih* gives a name of To-car-mo instead of To-kan-sze.

42. *Wei-tsang t'u shih* (Chüan I, p. 16b) gives the name Kermapa and identifies it with Halima. The author of *Wei-tsang t'ung chih,* in his note on p. 16 of Chüan I, also mentions Kermapa as Halima and identifies him as of Black Sect. Rockhill, "Tibet—a Geographical, Ethnographical and Historical Sketch Derived from Chinese Sources," henceforth cited as Rockhill, "Tibet," *JRAS,* New Series (1891), p. 199, gives the name as Karmaka (Ha-li-ma).

43. See Yü Tao-ch'üan's article on "I chu Ming Ch'êng-tsu ch'ien shih chao Tsong-k'a-pa chi shih chi Tsong-k'a-pa fu Ch'êng-tsu shu" in Academia Sinica's *Tsai Yüan-p'ei Anniversary,* II, 939-62.

44. *Ibid.,* pp. 963-66. Das, "The Monasteries of Tibet," *JASB,* New Series, I (April, 1905), 112, states that "Emperor Yunglo of the Ta'-ming dynasty had sent an invitation to Tsong-k'a-pa to visit Peking, but the great reformer . . . sent Çkaya Yeces as his representative." Emperor Yunglo can doubtless be identified as Ch'êng-tsu whose reigning years (1403-24) were titled Yunglo. *Wei-tsang t'ung chih,* I, Chap. 6, p. 135, attributing the building of Sera Monastery to Yeces after his return from the Ming Court, tallies with Das's account. But Ta-tz'u-fa-wang (*Ming shih,* Chüan 331, pp. 7a-9b) was identified by the noted historian Wei Yüan (*Shêng wu chi,* Book V, pp. 2 a-b) as a lama of the Red Sect. The writer has wondered why no mention was made of Yeces in the *Ming shih* since he first (in 1935) came across the above cited passages in Das's article and in the *Wei-tsang t'ung chih.* Thanks to Yü Tao-ch'üan's re-identification of Ta-tz'u-fa-wang and his discovery of Tsong-k'a-pa's reply to Ch'êng-tsu, we can safely affirm the early contact of the Yellow Sect with the Ming Court.

45. *Ming shih,* Chüan 331, pp. 7a-8a.

46. For details about the capture and the release of Ying-tsung, see D. Pokotilov, *History of the Eastern Mongols during the Ming Dynasty from 1368 to 1634,* trans. from the Russian by Rudolf Loewenthal, pp. 48-56 (henceforth cited as *History of the Eastern Mongols*), and also E. H. Parker, "Mongolia after the Genghizides and before

the Manchus," *JRAS,* North China Branch, XLIV (1913), 83-86 (henceforth cited as Parker, "Mongolia").

47. Refer to *History of the Eastern Mongols,* pp. 99-100.

48. Tsang was then under the control of Rinpûng, only nominally acknowledging the supremacy of the Phagmo-du chief; the latter had to contend with internal dissensions both in the north and south of U. Das, "Tibet under Her Last Kings (1434-1642 A.D.)," *JASB,* New Series, I (June, 1905), 165-67.

49. *Ming shih,* Chüan 330, p. 5a. See also J. K. Fairbank and S. Y. Têng, "On the Ch'ing Tributary System," *HJAS,* 1941, pp. 139-40, 148-49, 154-57.

50. *Ming shih,* Chüan 330, pp. 8b, 9a, and 10a; Chüan 331, p. 12b, records that profit-making tribute-missions came more frequently and with increasing number of members; in 1569 the court found it necessary to restrict these missions to once every three years and their members to not more than one thousand each.

51. Yü Tao-ch'üan, "I chu Ming Ch'êng-tsu ch'ien shih chao Tsong-k'a-pa chi shih chi Tsong-k'a-pa fu Chêng-tsu shu," in Academia Sinica's *Tsai Yüan-p'ei Anniversary,* II, 950, n. 1.

52. Csoma, *Tibetan Grammar,* pp. 186-87; *Liu's Translation,* Appendix, pp. 4-5; *Mélanges Chinois et Buddhiques* (Jullet, 1935) "Tson-kha-pa le Pandit," par Eugène Obermiller, pp. 321 and 337, basing mainly on a biography written by Tsong-k'a-pa's disciple Khai-dub; Huc, *Souvenirs d'un Voyage,* tome II, pp. 105 and 109; Rockhill, "Tibet," pp. 289-90; Francke, p. 74; Bell, *Tibet,* p. 33; Hackin, *Asiatic Mythology* (London, 1932), p. 175; Pelliot, *Journal Asiatique* (mai-juin, 1913), p. 639 (Hackin and Pelliot were quoted by Baron A. von Staël-Holstein in his article, "On the Sexagenary Cycle of the Tibetans," *Monumenta Serica,* I, 312 and 314, n. 7); Georgi, *Alphabetum Tibetanum,* p. 319.

53. Wei Yüan, *Shêng wu chi,* Book V, p. 2b, gives 1417-78; Ho-ning, *Hsi-tsang fu* (1797), p. 4b, n., also places the year of his birth at 1417. Yü Tao-ch'üan, "Ming Ch'êng-tsu's Invitation and Tsong-k'a-pa's reply," p. 950, n. 1, states that to his knowledge Wei Yüan, *Shêng wu chi* (1842) is the earliest Chinese record of Tsong-k'a-pa: apparently it is not. This writer thinks that Wei Yüan must have based his information on the imperial edict of 1792 which is engraved on a stone erected in the Young-Ho-Kung lamasery of Peking. A facsimile of the edict has been edited by Franke and Laufer in *Lamaistische Klosterinschriften aus Peking, Johol und Si-ngan* (Berlin, 1914).

54. E. H. Parker, "Manchu Relations with Tibet or Sitsang," *JRAS,* China Branch, New Series, XXI (1886). Henceforth cited as Parker, "Manchu Relations," 290.

55. Das, "The Monasteries of Tibet," pp. 108-9, states that Tsong-k'a-pa started the building of this monastery in 1408; *Liu's Transla-*

tion, p. 44, and Appendix, p. 5, records his building of Gah-Dan in 1409 with the aid of Dbaĥ-grags-pa-rgyal-mtshan; Rockhill, "Tibet," p. 290, states that in 1410 he founded the Gah-Dan monastery which was finished in 1422. On p. 109, Das states that in the 64th year of his age, Tsong-k'a-pa erected the principal chapel in the monastery. But among the sources quoted above, no one except Georgi (whose date has been discredited) gives his period of life as long as 64 years. In his account of the monastery of Sera, p. 112, Das mentions 1418 as the year of Tsong-k'a-pa's death. It is amazing to note that in an earlier article ("Contributions," *JASB,* VI (1882), 53-56), Das relates that Tsong-k'a-pa was born in 1378, was 53 in 1429, and died in the 63rd year of his age.

56. *Supra* n. 44.

57. *Supra* n. 45.

58. Yü Tao-ch'üan, "I chu Ming Ch'êng-tsu ch'ien shih chao Tsong-k'a-pa chi shih chi Tsong-k'a-pa fu Ch'êng-tsu shu," p. 940.

59. An account of the introduction of the Yellow Sect into western Tibet and the way King Lde received it is given by Francke, pp. 77-80; see also Petech, *A Study on the Chronicles of Ladakh,* p. 114.

60. Grenard, *Le Tibet,* p. 245.

61. *Supra* p. 27; *Ming shih,* Chüan 331, p. 4b-5a.

62. Little wonder that Altan Khan should have made such a suggestion, as he himself paid allegiance to the Chinese Emperor and was made Shun-i-wang (equivalent to the rank of a prince) in 1571. For details of the peace which Altan Khan concluded with the Chinese Emperor, see *History of the Eastern Mongols,* pp. 115-16 and 126-33, and also Parker, "Mongolia," pp. 93-94. As to the influence of the Tibetan lamas on Altan Khan, see *History of the Eastern Mongols,* pp. 112, 135-36, and 139.

63. *Ming shih,* Chüan 331, p. 5b. Parker, "Manchu Relations," p. 295, says that during the reign of Wan-li (1573-1619) he was made great national instructor. Parker's statement is apparently based on *Shêng wu chi,* Book V; "K'ang yü chi hsing," p. 13b.

64. *Shêng wu chi,* Book V; Appendix, "abridged Mêng-ku yüan liu," p. 29b.

65. *Supra,* p. 27.

66. Das, "Tibet under Her Last Kings," *JASB,* New Series, I (June, 1905), 166-67.

67. Das, "Contributions," p. 244, only mentions the fact that Tagpa Gyal-tshan was succeeded by his son Vaĥ-juĥ-ne who was recognized by the Chinese Emperor, and his grandson Kin-Dorje (the eighth in the table of the genealogical succession of the Sitya dynasty on p. 242) also obtained the title of *wang* from China. *Liu's Translation,* pp. 44-47, mentions the granting of the title *wang* to Dbaĥ-grags-pa-rgyal-mtshan's descendants up to his successor and also brother's great-

grandson Nag-dbaṅ-bkra-çis-grags-pa (a contemporary and a patron of the third Dalai Lama). Liu identifies the latter with the one who, according to *Ming shih,* sent a tribute-mission to the Emperor in 1579 to ask for permission to inherit his father's title. But *Ming shih* records that at the death of this one, his son's request for succession was again granted. From then on the vestige of the authority of the Sitya dynasty was dying out and the Ming government was no longer in a position to exercise any measurable influence.

68. Both Das ("Contributions," p. 242) and Bell (*Tibet,* pp. 32 and 86) say that the Sitya dynasty ruled till 1635. But according to *Liu's Translation,* pp. 74-75, the new dynasty was founded in 1618 and overthrown in 1642.

69. For details see Das, "Tibet, a Dependency of Mongolia (1643-1716)," *JASB,* New Series, I (May, 1905), 152-54.

70. Bell, *Tibet,* p. 34, says that he received from Altan Khan the title of Dalai Lama Vajradhara, "The All-Embracing Lama, the holder of the thunderbolt." Actually, they both exchanged titles, and Altan Khan got in return the title of "Defender of Faith."

71. Dalai is considered as the reincarnation of the first disciple, Panchen of Tashi-lhunpo as that of the second disciple. This new creation later became the Grand Lama of Urga. Bell (*Tibet,* p. 225) said of him in 1924: "The Grand Lama of Urga, the immediate head of the Mongolian Church, has invariably been a Tibetan; the present incumbent was born under the walls of the Potala."

72. Rockhill, *The Dalai Lamas of Lhasa and Their Relations with the Manchu Emperors of China, 1644-1908,* p. 3 (henceforth cited as Rockhill, *Dalai Lamas*), *T'oung pao,* XL (1910).

73. Das, "Contributions," p. 187, n. 2.

Chapter III: The Establishment of Chinese Sovereignty in Tibet

1. *Supra,* Chap. II, n. 69. Das, "Tibet a Dependency of Mongolia," *JASB,* New Series, I (May, 1905), gives the period as 1643-1716.

2. Parker, "Mongolia," p. 99.

3. *History of the Eastern Mongols,* p. 148.

4. Cammann (p. 12, n. 35) points out that the *Ch'ing-shih kao* and the *Shêng wu chi* disagree as to who made the first overtures. Actually not only *Ch'ing-shih kao* (Chap. 525, fan 8, p. 2b), but *Shêng wu chi* (Book 5, p. 4a), also records the message sent by T'ai-tsung in 1639. The latter's wording clearly indicates that the Tibetan mission was sent upon the receipt of this message. Cf. Rockhill, *Dalai Lamas,* p. 9. Cammann also remarks that the message was sent to ". . . the temporal king of Tibet (Gushi Khan's son) in 1639." But in that year

Gushi Khan's son was not yet established in Tibet; he was made only a garrison commander three years later. *Infra.*, n. 19.

5. Lee Wei-kuo, *Tibet in Modern World Politics,* p. 83, citing incorrectly Ch'i Yün-shih, (1751-1815), *Huang ch'ao fan pu yao lüeh* (The Dependencies of the Imperial Dynasty), Book 17, p. 3b, says, ". . . the Dalai and the Panch'en Lamas came to Mukden and tendered allegiance to the Manchu Emperor. That was in the year 1642." Ch'i makes no mention of this, and in fact, neither ever came to Mukden in person.

6. *Ch'ing-shih kao* does not mention the Tibetan mission of 1646; it is recorded in *Shih-tsu shih-lu,* Chap. 27, p. 23b.

7. *Ibid.,* Chap. 55, p. 7a. According to *Ch'ing-shih kao,* another message was sent in 1648 to invite the Dalai Lama who, in reply, promised to come in the year of 1652. *Ch'ing-shih kao* does not mention the mission sent in 1651.

8. *Shih-tsu shih-lu,* Chap. 68, pp. 2a-3a, 31b-32b.

9. *Ibid.,* Chap. 72, pp. 10b and 12a-b; Chap. 74, p. 18a; *Ch'ing-shih kao,* Chap. 525, fan 8, p. 3a; *Shêng wu chi,* Book 5, p. 46.

10. In an edict by Shih-tsu issued to the princes of various ranks and the officials of the Imperial Court (*Tung-hua lu,* Shun-chih period, xlx, p. 6a; *Shih-tsu shih-lu,* Chap. 68, p. 1b, trans. by Rockhill, *Dalai Lamas,* p. 14), it is written: ". . . considering the fact that all the Tibetans and Mongols obeyed the words of the Lamas, the Dalai Lama was sent for."

11. *Ch'ing-shih kao,* Chap. 525, fan 8, pp. 2b-3a. *T'ai-tsung shih-lu,* Chap. 64, pp. 21b-22a, records a message sent from Tai-tsung to Lama Karma of the Red Sect. Among those who received patents, we find Shan-hua-wang; *supra,* Chap. II, n. 38, and also Rockhill, "Tibet," p. 204.

12. Parker, "Manchu Relations," p. 295; *Ch'ing-shih kao,* Chap. 525, fan 8, p. 4a.

13. Sir Charles Bell, *Portrait of the Dalai Lama* (1946), p. 352. But Rockhill, *Dalai Lamas,* p. 18, says only that the Dalai Lama "had been treated with all the ceremony which could have been accorded to any independent sovereign, and nothing can be found in Chinese works to indicate that he was looked upon in any other light."

14. *Ch'ing-shih kao,* Chap. 525, fan 8, p. 2a; *T'ai-tsung shih-lu,* Chap. 49, pp. 3a-4a.

15. Parker, "Manchu Relations," p. 292; Rockhill, *Dalai Lamas,* p. 8.

16. Waddell (p. 32) describes Sang-kieh as son of the Dalai Lama V; see also Rockhill, *Dalai Lamas,* p. 19, Markham, xlviii, and Bell, *Tibet,* p. 37.

17. According to Bell, *Tibet,* p. 35, Gushi Khan came to the as-

sistance of the Yellow Sect in 1641; Rockhill, *Dalai Lamas,* p. 8, n. 2, places the conquest between 1641 and 1643. The official document, *T'ai-tsung shih-lu,* Chap. 64, pp. 22b-23a, records that the Manchu Emperor T'ai-tsung, as shown in his messages sent to Tsangpa Khan and Gushi Khan in 1643, on the occasion of their representatives' return to Tibet, knew of the defeat of the former and the role played in Tibet by the latter. The conquest must have therefore taken place before that year. *Shêng wu chi,* Book 5, p. 5a, places the event in the 10th year Chung-teh. Since there is no such year, Chung-teh having only eight years, the 10th year must be a mistake for the 7th year (1642), as the Chinese characters 10 and 7 are liable to be misread because of their resemblance. Das, "Contributions," p. 245, did not place this conquest in 1645 as Rockhill remarked. Das, *JASB,* LI (1882), p. 73, clearly states that "afterwards, he made a present of the whole of Tibet proper to the fifth Dalai Lama in the year 1645." *Supra,* Chap. II, n. 68.

18. For a fairly clear account of Gushi Khan's unification of Tibet see Arthur W. Hummel (ed.), *Eminent Chinese of the Ch'ing Period,* p. 265 (henceforth cited as *ECCP*) (article on Galdan). The terms of Gushi Khan's donation were not clear. Apparently he made the donation as a gesture to show his devotion to the Yellow Sect. *Ch'ing-shih kao,* Chap. 525, fan 8, p. 2a, records that it was Gushi Khan who gave Panch'en the province of Tsang. See also Cammann, p. 11; but Bell, *Tibet,* p. 84, states that the Panch'en Lama had only temporal power over three districts, of which Shigatse was not one.

19. Waddell, p. 27; Das, "Contributions" (1882), p. 73; Rockhill, *Dalai Lamas,* p. 8.

20. L. Petech, *China and Tibet in the Early 18th Century* (1950), p. 8 (hereafter cited as Petech); Tucci, *Tibetan Printed Scrolls,* p. 67.

21. *Shih-tsu shih-lu,* Chap. 68, p. 5a; *ibid.,* Chap. 69, pp. 8b-9a.

22. Cammann, p. 13. Fang Chao-ying in *ECCP,* p. 256, says the Lama came in person to recognize the suzerainty of the new empire. M. E. Willoughby wrote these words in a paper read before the Royal Central Asian Society in 1924: "In 1642 the Dalai and Panch'en Lama were induced by the Mongol chief Gushi Khan to send an embassy tendering allegiance to the Manchu sovereign on the eve of ejecting the Ming Dynasty from the throne of China. The Manchu throne thereupon assumed sovereignty over Tibet." *CASJ,* XI, Part III, 189.

23. *T'ai-tsung shih-lu,* Chap. 64, pp. 21b-22a; *Shih-tsu shih-lu,* Chap. 74, pp. 18a-19a; *ibid.,* Chap. 71, pp. 20a-b.

24. Parker, "Manchu Relations," p. 299.

25. Rockhill, *Dalai Lamas,* p. 18; Bell, *Portrait of the Dalai Lama,* pp. 72-73; Cammann, p. 13.

26. Parker, "Manchu Relations," pp. 292-93; Rockhill, *Dalai Lamas,* pp. 19-20, 23-24. Both Parker and Rockhill mistook Wu Shih-p'an for Wu San-kuei's son.

27. *Shêng wu chi,* Book 5, pp. 6a-b.

28. *Shêng-tsu shih-lu,* Chap. 174, p. 14b.

29. Markham, p. xlviii.

30. *Shêng-tsu shih-lu,* Chap. 181, p. 15b, and Chap. 182, p. 2a.

31. *Ibid.,* Chap. 181, p. 15a, and Chap. 182, p. 1b.

32. Waddell, p. 32; Parker, "Manchu Relations," p. 293; Howorth, *History of Mongols,* I, 518; and *ECCP,* p. 265, all mention Latsang as Gushi Khan's great-grandson. Chinese official records, *Ta Ch'ing hui tien,* Chap. 66, p. 5a, and *Ta Ch'ing hui tien shih-li,* Chap. 972, p. 46, register Latsang as Gushi Khan's great-grandson. It is likewise mentioned in *K'uo-êrh-k'a chi lüeh* (Intro. III, p. 166, n.) and *Wei-tsang t'u shih,* II, T'u-k'ao b, pp. 2b-3a. *Wei-tsang t'ung chih,* II, Chap. 13a, p. 217, relates that Latsang's father and predecessor, Dalai Khan, was Gushi Khan's grandson. But Dalai Khan was recorded in *Ch'ing-shih kao,* Chap. 525, fan 8, p. 2b, and *Shêng wu chi,* Book 5, p. 8b, as Gushi Khan's son. Presumably for this reason Chinese writers on Tibet like Wang Ch'in-yü (*Hsi-tsang wên t'i,* p. 7), Hsieh Pin (*Hsi-tsang wên t'i* [2nd ed., 1935], p. 89), and Hung Ti-ch'ên (*Hsi-tsang shih ti ta kang* [Shanghai ed., 1947], p. 150) mistake Latsang as Gushi Khan's grandson. Hua Ch'i-yün (*Hsi-tsang wên t'i* [2nd ed., 1933], p. 97), basing his account apparently on *Shêng wu chi,* made a similar mistake.

33. *P'ing ting Chün-ko-êrh fang lüeh,* Intro. Chap. 1, p. 7. For a Tibetan account of the end of Sang-kieh, see Petech, p. 10.

34. *Shêng-tsu shih-lu,* Chap. 227, p. 24b. Sang-kieh was made king by the Emperor in 1693 on his own application in the name of the dead Dalai Lama. *Shêng-tsu shih-lu,* Chap. 161, pp. 9b-10b.

35. After Galdan's defeat, his people at home made his nephew Chewanlaputan (*Shêng-tsu shih-lu,* Chap. 189, p. 13a, mentions Galdan as Chewanlaputan's uncle) ruler of the Dzungar tribes. Galdan then committed suicide. (*Shêng-tsu shih-lu,* Chap. 183, p. 7b.) *Shêng-tsu shih-lu,* Chap. 227, p. 9a, records the words of the Emperor showing the reason why he needed to get hold of Tsang-yang and the serious consequences if the latter fell into the hands of Chewanlaputan. See also *P'ing ting Chün-ko-êrh fang lüeh,* Intro. Chap. 1, p. 8.

36. *Shêng-tsu shih-lu,* Chap. 227, p. 28b; but Rockhill, *Dalai Lamas,* p. 34 and Waddell, p. 32, believe that he was murdered. Fang Chao-ying in *ECCP,* p. 760 also says he was murdered; he gives the date as 1706. Petech, p. 13, says: "The official account both Chinese and Tibetan maintains that he died of illness, and I think there is no sufficient reason for doubting that this is true."

37. The Emperor's envoy asked the Panch'en Lama for his opinion about the succession dispute. The Panch'en supported the view of Latsang. (*Shêng-tsu shih-lu,* Chap. 236, p. 17b, and also Rockhill, *Dalai Lamas,* p. 34.) Bell, *Tibet,* p. 40, asserts that Yeshes was the selection of the Chinese. This statement is without foundation. Al-

though the Emperor started in 1700 to consolidate his hold at Tach'-ienlu (Rockhill, "Tibet," pp. 34-35), he was still not in a position to make a choice of Dalai Lama at Lhasa, Tibet proper being garrisoned by Mongolian forces under Latsang and more influence from Kokonor being felt in Tibet proper than from Peking. It is interesting to note Rockhill's words (*Dalai Lamas,* p. 35): ". . . another long minority of the Dalai Lama . . . would be seriously prejudicial to the maintenance and the hoped for extension of Chinese influence in Tibet. The memory of the regent [Sang-kieh] was fresh in their minds. Chinese policy required not only an adult in the pontifical chair, but one who owed his position to China and whose chief support was Chinese," as Western writers often accuse the Imperial Government of having murdered the Dalai Lamas and kept the pontifical chair from being occupied by an adult.

38. *Shêng-tsu shih-lu,* Chap. 241, pp. 14b-15a.

39. The Mongol chiefs of Kokonor at a meeting decided to apply to the Emperor at Peking for recognition of the new claimant. See Petech, pp. 17-18. This shows the position of the Emperor in this succession dispute and his influence being extended over that region.

40. Wei Yüan, author of *Shêng wu chi,* Book 5, p. 8b, and Parker, "Manchu Relations," p. 293, both seriously erred in saying that the claimant from Li-t'ang, Blo-bzang Rgyamts'o, was then 20 years old, born in 1683. In fact, he was born in 1708, as recorded in *Ch'ing-shih kao,* Chap. 525, fan 8, p. 5a. They apparently confused him with Tsang-yang who was born in 1683. *Ch'ing-shih kao* mentions him as the sixth Dalai Lama because Tsang-yang did not receive any formal recognition from the Emperor and was therefore omitted from the official list of Dalai Lamas. Cf. Petech, pp. 59-60, who wrote that Tsang-yang had been recognized by the Emperor; and also Rockhill, *Dalai Lamas,* p. 27, relates a Tibetan story that the Emperor was represented by the Changchia Hutukhtu of Peking when Tsang-yang was installed. No official records can be found to this effect. *Ch'ing-shih kao* is not consistent in eliminating Tsang-yang; it jumps from the tenth Dalai Lama to the twelfth and addresses the same pontiff as the tenth and eleventh (pp. 13a and 14a), as if it suddenly takes Tsang-yang into account without any explanation.

41. A high official named Ho-shou was sent to Lhasa for this purpose. *Shêng-tsu shih-lu,* Chap. 236, p. 18a; Rockhill, *Dalai Lamas,* p. 37, calls this step the beginning of direct intervention in Tibetan affairs. Actually, this step rather marks the beginning of the decline in power of the Mongols in Tibet as a result of their own dissensions. He was sent to "assist Latsang" who, according to the official record, was on bad terms with the Kokonor chiefs and it was therefore thought not advisable to leave the reins of the Tibetan Government in his hands alone. Rockhill, *Dalai Lamas,* p. 42, assumes that the

agency established at Lhasa in 1709 was kept open since that time, but Ho-shou was definitely recalled in the next year and transferred to a post in charge of the inland water transport. *Shêng-tsu shih-lu,* Chap. 244, p. 21a. *Man-chou ming ch'ên chuan,* Chap. 23, p. 52b. Biography of Ho-shou records that he was ordered to proceed to Tibet in the first moon of 1709 and transferred to the above-mentioned new post in the twelfth moon of the next year.

42. For details see Petech, pp. 18-19.

43. *Shêng-tsu shih-lu,* Chap. 278, pp. 19b-20a. The Emperor ordered Ho-shou to write a letter to Latsang, warning him of a possible Dzungar invasion. (*P'ing ting Chün-ko-êrh fang lüeh,* Intro. Chap. 4, pp. 18a-19a). The Emperor was then not sure of Latsang's stand and suspected a collaboration between Latsang and the Dzungar chief. For an account of the sack of Lhasa see Waddell, Appendix V, who mistakenly believed that the sack had taken place in 1710. For details about the Dzungar invasion and occupation, see Petech, pp. 25-54.

44. *Shêng-tsu shih-lu,* Chap. 277, pp. 23a-b; *P'ing ting Chün-ko-êrh fang lüeh,* Intro. Chap. 4, pp. 45a-b.

45. *Shêng-tsu shih-lu,* Chap. 281, pp. 13b-14a. The defeat was sustained in 1718. Rockhill, *Dalai Lamas,* p. 40, erred in placing it in 1719.

46. *Shêng-tsu shih-lu,* Chap. 287, p. 5b, and Chap. 289, p. 17b, and *Ch'ing-shih kao,* Chap. 525, fan 8, p. 6a. *P'ing ting Chün-ko-êrh fang lüeh,* Intro. Chap. 7, p. 16b; Chap. 8, pp. 4b-5a.

47. *Shêng-tsu shih-lu,* Chap. 286, pp. 24b-25a; Chap. 287, pp. 18a-b. And 3,000 Yünnan troops were dispatched to take part in the campaign. See *P'ing ting Chün-ko-êrh fang lüeh,* Intro. Chap. 7, pp. 21b and 24b.

48. *Shêng-tsu shih-lu,* Chap. 285, pp. 16a-18a; Chap. 286, pp. 23a-b; Chap. 287, p. 12a.

49. The installation took place on October 16, 1720, according to *ECCP,* p. 908; cf. Petech, p. 65.

50. *Shêng-tsu shih-lu,* Chap. 289, p. 17a.

51. *Ch'ing-shih kao,* Chap. 525, fan 8, p. 7a.

52. Petech, p. 63.

53. *Shêng-tsu shih-lu,* Chap. 291, p. 11b. It was intended to reinforce with another thousand, but the plan did not materialize. *Ibid.,* Chap. 291, pp. 30a-31b.

54. The text inscribed on the stone, written by the Emperor, is given on pp. 3-4 of Vol. I of *Wei-tsang t'ung chih,* which also records the text inscribed on another stone erected and written by General Ko-le-pi, who led the army from Tach'ienlu to conquer Lhasa, and his report to the throne on the successful conclusion of the campaign. *Ibid.,* Vol. II, XIIIa, pp. 218-21; see also *Shêng-tsu shih-lu,* Chap. 289,

pp. 13b-15a, for the report of General Ko-le-pi. For other details see the notes of Father Desideri, who was a witness of these events and who tells us that on the whole the Chinese behaved with great moderation (quoted in Rockhill, *Dalai Lamas,* p. 41).

55. Rockhill, *Dalai Lamas,* p. 41, and cf. *Desideri, An Account of Tibet,* ed. by F. de Filippi (1932), p. 170.

56. *Shêng-tsu shih-lu,* Chap. 283, pp. 17a-18a; Chap. 284, pp. 22a-b.

57. *Ibid.,* Chap. 287, p. 14a.

58. Parker, "Manchu Relations," p. 292.

59. The three councillors of state were Na-p'od-pa, Lum-pa-nas, sByar-ra-ba, with K'an-c'en-nas as Chairman. P'o-lha-nas and the father of the Dalai Lama were not members of the cabinet but they gradually became a kind of unofficial members, according to the Tibetan source quoted by Petech, p. 81. P'o-lha-nas was admitted at the suggestion of the Emperor to the cabinet as a full member in 1723. (Petech, p. 67.)

60. Petech, p. 69, remarks that the young Dalai Lama's "position under the new form of government was that of an honored figurehead, with no power whatsoever. But his spiritual power gave him a real importance, and he was therefore always treated with punctilious deference by the Chinese."

61. For Mongolian divisions and alliances, see René Grousset, *Histoire d'extreme-Orient* (1929), II, 531-32.

62. Waddell, p. 34, and Markham, p. xlviii, say that the Emperor in 1720 placed two Chinese mandarins at Lhasa as political residents or Ambans with large powers or with an adequate force. This is an error. See also *supra,* n. 41.

63. See Petech, p. 80, which furnishes us with this information from Tibetan sources.

64. *Shih-tsung shih-lu,* Chap. 5, pp. 2b-3b.

65. *Ibid.,* Chap. 5, p. 18b.

66. *Ibid.,* Chap. 38, pp. 2a-3b.

67. Petech, pp. 94-95.

68. *Shih-tsung shih-lu,* Chap. 52, pp. 29b-30a.

69. *Ibid.,* p. 30b.

70. Petech (p. 101) gives "18 VI = August 6, 1727"; but according to both Le Rév. père P. Hoang, *Concordance des Chronologies néoméniques Chinoise et Européenne,* and Chên Yüan, *A Comparative Daily Calendar for Chinese, European and Mohammedan History,* 18 VI should be August 5. For comment on Petech's treating Tibetan dates as identical with the Chinese see R. A. Stein, "Récentes études tibétaines," *Journal Asiatique,* CCXL (1952), p. 96.

71. *Shih-tsung shih-lu,* Chap. 59, pp. 22a-b.

72. *Ibid.,* Chap. 61, pp. 6a-b.

73. *Ibid.,* Chap. 63, pp. 1a-3a.

74. Petech, p. 102.

75. *Ibid.*, p. 127.
76. *Ibid.*, p. 128.
77. *Shih-tsung shih-lu*, Chap. 62, pp. 21b-22b.
78. *Ibid.*, Chap. 73, pp. 26a-27a.
79. Petech, pp. 136-37.
80. *Shih-tsung shih-lu*, Chap. 145, p. 8b.
81. Petech, p. 139; *supra*, n. 18.
82. The Chinese garrison strength was first determined as 3,000 men, and was reduced to 2,000 because of the expected difficulties of supply as a result of bad harvests. See *Shih-tsung shih-lu*, Chap. 72, pp. 18a-b.
83. Petech, p. 236, considers Ho-shou a permanent representative, but he is mistaken. (See *supra*, n. 41.) The office of Resident in Tibet (Chu-tsang ta ch'ên) was not established until 1728, at which time Seng-ko and Mailu became its first occupants. *Huang ch'ao fan pu yao lüeh*, Book 17, p. 21b, relates that the Residency was first set up in 1726, when the Emperor sent Seng-ko and Mala to Tibet. But the writer is of the opinion that the state of affairs in 1726 did not warrant an establishment of the Residency. It was only after the outbreak of 1727 and its subsequent civil war that the Emperor found it necessary to have permanent representatives stationed on the spot. See *Shêng wu chi*, Book V, pp. 17a-18a, which supports this view.
84. The office of Deputy Resident was then abolished, and two counselors were established instead, one to be posted at Lhasa and the other at Shigatse. See *Hsüan t'ung chêng chi* of *Ta Ch'ing shih-lu*, Chap. 47, p. 44.
85. *Shih-tsung shih-lu*, Chap. 75, pp. 18a-19a.
86. *Ch'ing-shih kao*, Chap. 525, fan 8, p. 7b.
87. *Shih-tsung shih-lu*, Chap. 103, p. 4b.
88. *Ibid.*, Chap. 103, pp. 8b-9b.
89. *Ibid.*, Chap. 109, pp. 15b-17a, 24a-b; Chap. 111, pp. 11b-12a.
90. Petech, p. 151, based upon a Tibetan account.
91. *Shih-tsung shih-lu*, Chap. 112, pp. 26b-27a.
92. Petech, pp. 155, 158.
93. Petech (p. 157) mistook Yün-li for a son of the reigning Emperor. See *Ch'ing-shih kao*, Lieh-chuan, 7, pp. 15a-b, for the identity and the biography. Prince Kuo's diary covering this mission, entitled *Hsi tsang jih chi*, was published by Yü-kung-hsüeh-hui in 1937.
94. Petech, pp. 157-58; *Shih-tsung shih-lu*, Chap. 155, pp. 1a-2a; *Wei-tsang t'ung chih*, II, Chap. XIIIa, pp. 224-25.
95. Quoted in Rockhill, *Dalai Lamas*, p. 44.
96. *Wei-tsang t'ung chih*, II, Chap. XIIIa, p.224.
97. *Kao-tsung shih-lu*, Chap. 208, pp. 11b-13b; Chap. 210, pp. 2a-4a.
98. *Ibid.*, Chap. 158, pp. 4b-5b. Fairbank and Têng, "On the Ch'ing Tributary System," pp. 161, 177, and 198.
99. Petech, pp. 177-78.

100. *Ch'ing-shih kao,* Chap. 525, fan 8, p. 8a.

101. *Kao-tsung shih-lu,* Chap. 286, pp. 25a-26a.

102. *Ibid.,* Chap. 286, pp. 26a-28a.

103. *Ibid.,* Chap. 377, p. 2a; *Ch'ing-shih kao,* Chap. 525, fan 8, p. 8b; *Shêng wu chi,* Book V, p. 13a.

104. *Kao-tsung shih-lu,* Chap. 351, pp. 6b-7a.

105. *Ibid.,* Chap. 343, pp. 19a-20b.

106. *Ibid.,* Chap. 351, pp. 10b-13a.

107. *Ibid.,* Chap. 351, pp. 7b-8a.

108. *Kao-tsung shih-lu,* Chap. 354, pp. 17b-20a.

109. *Ibid.,* Chap. 383, pp. 7a-8b; Chap. 386, pp. 23a-b; *Ch'ing-shih kao,* Chap. 525, fan 8, p. 9a.

110. *Kao-tsung shih-lu,* Chap. 364, pp. 6a-8b. The Emperor thought Gyurmed-namgyal could gain no benefit should he rebel. Nor could the Emperor see any immediate danger that would drive him to resort to open rebellion. "The existence of the Residents," according to the Emperor, "does not constitute any restraint or inconvenience on his part. The Residents neither supervise his conduct, nor share or minimize his influence or prestige." (*Ibid.,* Chap. 364, p. 7a.) We can see from his own words the reluctance of the Emperor to employ force in Tibet. He told his court ministers that "to use the useful in a non-beneficial place is not necessary. Even though we know pretty well that we are being fooled, we would rather leave the matter to take its own course and pay no attention to it." (*Ibid.,* Chap. 358, p. 9a.) Later he said to them, "Unless we are absolutely forced by that eventuality [Dzungar invasion of Tibet], we should not lightheartedly take any military step in that remote region." (*Ibid.,* Chap. 366, p. 13a.)

111. *Ibid.,* Chap. 359, pp. 13a-b.

112. *Ibid.,* Chap. 366, pp. 11b-13b.

113. *Ibid.,* Chap. 374, pp. 10a-11a; Chap. 375, pp. 10a-b.

114. Petech, pp. 200-201.

115. *Kao-tsung shih-lu,* Chap. 379, pp. 22b-24a.

116. *Ibid.,* Chap. 376, p. 35a; Chap. 377, p. 4b.

117. *Ibid.,* Chap. 385, pp. 15b-19b.

118. Petech, p. 213.

119. *Ibid.,* pp. 218-19.

120. *Ibid.,* pp. 127-28.

121. *Ibid.,* pp. 219 and 240. Gushi Khan himself received the seal and patent of investiture from Emperor Shih-tsu in 1653. *Shih-tsu shih-lu,* Chap. 74, pp. 19a-20a; see also Petech, p. 15.

122. Petech, p. 219.

123. *Kao-tsung shih-lu,* Chap. 386, pp. 17b-18a.

124. Petech, p. 212.

125. *Kao-tsung shih-lu,* Chap. 386, pp. 18b-19a.

126. Petech, pp. 199, 201.

127. *Kao-tsung shih-lu,* Chap. 377, p. 9b.

128. *Ibid.,* Chap. 377, pp. 4a-b, 16b-17a. Rockhill errs in saying that Pandita had been "King of Tibet . . . . He was put at the head of the Tibetan government by the Dalai Lama and confirmed in the office by the Chinese government." (*Dalai Lamas,* p. 56, n. 1.) The very document he quotes (*Tung-hua ch'üan-lu,* Ch'ien-lung period, xxxii, p. 13) addresses Pandita as duke, and Pandita was told by the Emperor in a decree (*ibid.,* p. 21a) to serve in the new bKa'blon in the capacity of his original rank of duke, denying his promotion.

129. *Kao-tsung shih-lu,* Chap. 377, pp. 19a-20a.

130. *Ibid.,* Chap. 383, pp. 23b-24b.

131. *Ibid.,* Chap. 387, pp. 4b-5a.

132. *Ibid.,* Chap. 377, p. 17b.

133. *Shêng wu chi,* Book V, p. 19b, quoted but not literally translated by Rockhill, *Dalai Lamas,* p. 46.

134. *Bogle's Embassy to Tibet* (Daskalkar, 1933), p. 424; Markham, p. 195.

135. *Kao-tsung shih-lu,* Chap. 1417, p. 13a; *infra,* n. 157.

136. For details, see E. Ludwig, *Visit of the Tashoo Lama to Peking. Ch'ien-lung's Inscriptions; Turner's Embassy,* pp. 449-73; and Cammann, "The Panch'en Lama's Visit to China in 1780: An Episode in Anglo-Tibetan Relations," *The Far Eastern Quarterly,* IX (1949), 3-19.

137. Most Chinese books on Tibet place the event in 1790. The year 1788 is given, based upon the imperial edict (*Kao-tsung shih-lu,* Chap. 1411, p. 8b). Further evidence supporting the year as 1788 is contained in *K'uo-êrh-k'a chi lüeh,* VI, 1a; XV, 5a; XXXVIII, 9b.

138. Cf. Markham, p. lxxvi.

139. *Kao-tsung shih-lu,* Chap. 1391, pp. 8b-9a.

140. Pao-t'ai did not, however, carry off the Dalai Lama to a place of safety, as Cammann (p. 121) alleges.

141. *Kao-tsung shih-lu,* Chap. 1388, pp. 16a-b. *K'uo-êrh-k'a chi lüeh,* IV, 8a-9b, 20a-b; V, 25a-b; XIV, 1a-2b.

142. *Kao-tsung shih-lu,* Chap. 1390, pp. 31a, 20a.

143. Rockhill, *Dalai Lamas,* p. 60, n. 1, points out that the text of Lord Cornwallis's letter to the Raja of Nepal, written on September 15, 1792, referring to Tibet as the dependency of China, to the Company's trade interests in Canton, and offering mediation but declining help, agrees with the statements in the Chinese version (*K'uo-êrh-k'a chi lüeh,* LI, 3a-9b). For the text of the letter, see Col. William Kirkpatrick, *Account of the Kingdom of Nepaul,* being the substance of observations made during a mission to that country in the year 1793, pp. 349 *et seq.*

144. *Kao-tsung shih-lu,* Chap. 1411, p. 14b.

145. Rockhill, *Dalai Lamas,* p. 52, n. 2. But Ko Sui-ch'êng, *Chung kuo chin tai pien chiang yen ko k'ao,* p. 208, says they sent another mission with presents to Peking in 1924.

146. *Kao-tsung shih-lu,* Chap. 1411, pp. 15a, 24b; *Li-fan-pu tsê li,* Chap. 61.

147. Rockhill, *Dalai Lamas,* p. 53. From the source cited by Rockhill, the writer can find no reference to this effect. According to Emperor Kao-tsung (*Kao-tsung shih-lu,* Chap. 1393, p. 13a), "originally the Dalai Lama was authorized to memorialize the throne." The only reference which may be quoted to support Rockhill's view is a later edict by Emperor Kao-tsung, issued in the autumn of 1794 (*ibid.,* Chap. 1458, pp. 34b-35a), in which the Emperor expressed satisfaction over the report that "the Resident Ho-lin did not kneel before the Dalai Lama and the latter took the Resident's order faithfully," and the Emperor ordered the newly appointed successor to Ho-lin, named Sung-yün, a Mongol of the Khorcin clan, who had the highest respect for the Yellow Sect, not to kneel to the Dalai Lama as long as he was there as the Imperial Resident.

148. *Kao-tsung shih-lu,* Chap. 1393, pp. 12a-b; Chap. 1411, pp. 24a-b; Chap. 1414, p. 22b.

149. *Ibid.,* Chap. 1393, p. 13a; Chap. 1417, p. 3b. For details see *Ta Ch'ing hui tien,* Chap. 67, p. 3.

150. *Shêng wu chi,* Book V, pp. 22a, 46a.

151. Sir J. F. Davis, *China during the War and Since the Peace* (1852), I, 149.

152. *Kao-tsung shih-lu,* Chap. 1417, p. 16a.

153. *Ibid.,* Chap. 1418, pp. 8b-9a. Cammann, p. 131, asserts that Dza-marpa took poison to avoid falling into the hands of the Chinese alive. To determine whether he committed suicide or died of illness, refer to *K'uo-êrh-k'a chi lüeh,* XXXV, 22b-23a; XXXVII, 1b-2b, 16a-b; XXXIX, 30a; XL, 10b. Cammann apparently overlooked the Chinese word for "even if" in the reference he cited. As to Chumba, he was later taken to Peking and also spared from capital punishment. (*Ibid.,* V, 26b-27a; XIV, 4a-b.)

154. *Kao-tsung shih-lu,* Chap. 1415, pp. 15a-b. From the Chinese official record, it was the old Tibetan silver coins that were debased and mixed with copper; the Gurkhas had therefore asked for a better rate of exchange of their own coins. Cf. Rockhill, *Dalai Lamas,* p. 50, which says that the Gurkhas made highhanded attempts to force their debased silver coins upon Tibet. A fuller explanation on this point is given by Cammann, pp. 108-11, based mainly upon Colonel Kirkpatrick's *Account of the Kingdom of Nepaul.*

155. For details and subsequent modifications, see reports to the Emperor in *Wei-tsang t'ung chih,* I, Chap. 10, 191-95.

156. *Ibid.,* Chap. 11, pp. 197-200.

157. To quote Emperor Kao-tsung's words, "Heretofore the Resi-

dents had nothing to do with these two treasuries. Their accumulated funds were subject to misappropriation and usurpation by the members of the bKa'-blon and high officials in charge." (*Kao-tsung shih-lu,* Chap. 1411, p. 24a.) For new measures and financial data memorialized to the throne by Fu-k'ang-an and others, see *Wei-tsang t'ung chih,* I, Chap. 9, 179-82.

158. *Kao-tsung shih-lu,* Chap. 1387, pp. 10b-11a; Chap. 1411, p. 24b. For details of the new administrative system, see *Li-fan-pu tsê li,* Chap. 62.

159. *Kao-tsung shih-lu,* Chap. 1414, p. 23b.

160. *Wei-tsang t'ung chih,* I, Chap. 9, 182-83.

161. *Ibid.,* I, Chap. 2, 19-31.

162. *Kao-tsung shih-lu,* Chap. 1416, p. 18a; *supra,* n. 135 and n. 157. The brother of the Dalai Lama was summoned to Peking because of his part in the corruption. *Ibid.,* Chap. 1387, p. 13a.

163. *Ibid.,* Chap. 1417, pp. 14a-15a.

164. *Kao-tsung shih-lu,* Chap. 1472, pp. 19a-20b; Chap. 1478, p. 9b; Chap. 1481, pp. 18a-19b; for more details, see *Wei-tsang t'ung chih,* II, Chap. 14, 329-78.

165. Rockhill, *Dalai Lamas,* p. 90.

166. Bell, *Tibet,* p. 214.

167. *Ch'ing-shih kao,* Chap. 525, fan 8, p. 10b.

168. Turner, *An Account of an Embassy,* pp. 230, 249, relates that their fathers were brothers.

169. *Ch'ing-shih kao,* Chap. 525, fan 8, p. 11a.

170. *Kao-tsung shih-lu,* Chap. 1411, pp. 22b-23b; Chap. 1412, pp. 28a-b; and Chap. 1417, pp. 4a-5b.

171. *Jên-tsung shih-lu,* Chap. 192, pp. 11a-12a. The orders of the Emperor were embodied in a long inscription in Tibetan, the translation of which was made by L. A. Waddell, "Chinese Imperial Edict of 1808, on the Origin and Transmigrations of Grand Lamas of Tibet," *JRAS* (1910), pp. 75-86. The present Dalai Lama was also exempted from the lots-drawing process; see *infra,* Chap. V, pp. 181-82.

172. *Ch'ing-shih kao,* Vol. 70, table 11, p. 40b, gives the tenure of Ch'i-shan as 1843-46; but he was ordered to stay on and he remained in office till the autumn of 1847. His successor, Pin-liang, did not arrive at the post until August of 1847. See *Hsüan-tsung shih-lu,* Chap. 445, p. 8b, and Chap. 446, p. 16b.

173. *Ch'ing-shih kao,* Chap. 525, fan 8, p. 14a.

174. Ts'e-pa-k'e and his deputy accused each other of misconduct and both were cashiered. Bills written in Tibetan were found posted on the walls in Lhasa accusing Ts'e-pa-k'e of taking bribes in choosing bKa-blons and other high officials. This accusation, though made anonymously, was brought to the attention of the Emperor who, realizing that the Tibetans had become less docile, ordered a thor-

ough investigation of the matter. See *Jên-tsung shih-lu,* Chap. 150, pp. 9a-10b; Chap. 151, pp. 9a-12; Chap. 159, pp. 27b-29b; and also *Ch'ing-shih kao,* Chap. 525, fan 8, p. 11b.

175. *Ch'ing-shih kao* (p. 12b), blames Wên-kan for having sided with the Lhasa authorities in their quarrel with the Tashi-lhunpo administration, and points out his irresponsible way of handling the Sikkimese request which had the effect of alienating the Sikkim vassal state from its suzerain power, and thus facilitating the later British penetration. See *Hsüan-tsung shih-lu,* Chap. 26, pp. 34b-35b.

176. *Hsüan-tsung shih-lu,* Chap. 341, pp. 36b-37a.

177. *Ibid.,* Chap. 359, pp. 26b-27a.

178. *Ibid.,* Chap. 363, pp. 20a-b.

179. *Ibid.,* Chap. 345, pp. 20a-b; Chap. 348, pp. 15a-16a.

180. Bell, *Tibet,* p. 46. Cf. *A Collection of Treaties, Engagements and Sanads Relating India and Neighboring Countries,* compiled by C. U. Aitchison, XLV, 15. A later imperial edict (*Hsüan-tsung shih-lu,* Chap. 439, p. 9b) identified "sen-pa" as "what the Germans call 'si-k'e' [singh or sikh]."

181. *Hsüan-tsung shih-lu,* Chap. 356, pp. 26a-b.

182. *Ibid.,* Chap. 357, pp. 44a-45b.

183. *Ibid.,* Chap. 372, p. 23b.

184. *Ibid.,* Chap. 361, pp. 1b-2a; Chap. 366, pp. 10b-11b; Chap. 370, pp. 29a-30a; Chap. 371, pp. 20a-21b. The fighting lasted till the early summer of 1842. For some details about the origin and the development of the armed conflict see *Shêng wu chi,* Book V, "K'ang yü chi hsing," pp. 50b-51b.

185. *Hsüan-tsung shih-lu,* Chap. 407, pp. 1b-2b.

186. *Ibid.,* Chap. 407, p. 26b-28b, and also Chap. 411, pp. 3a-b, 5a-6b; Chap. 414, pp. 2b, 11a; Chap. 419, pp. 4b-5a.

187. *Ibid.,* Chap. 406, pp. 5a-b. Note that it was the Panch'en Lama who accused the No-men-han. For details of the case see *ibid.,* Chap. 410, pp. 5a-7a; Chap. 414, pp. 2a-b; Chap. 415, pp. 11b-12b, 14a-15a; Chap. 416, pp. 9a-b; Chap. 421, pp. 9b-10a.

188. *Ibid.,* Chap. 412, pp. 13a-b.

189. *Ibid.,* Chap. 402, pp. 10a, 29a-b; Chap. 403, p. 12a; Chap. 440, p. 17a.

190. *Ibid.,* Chap. 437, pp. 24b-25b, 32a-34b; Chap. 438, pp. 9b-10a, 10b-11b; Chap. 440, pp. 15a-16a; Chap. 442, pp. 17b-18b; Chap. 444, p. 19a.

191. *Ibid.,* Chap. 445, p. 8a.

192. *Ibid.,* Chap. 441, pp. 8b-9b.

193. Article II of the Treaty, the translation of the text of which is given by Sir Charles Bell, *Tibet, Past and Present.*

194. *Wên-tsung shih-lu,* Chap. 168, p. 3b.

195. *Ibid.,* Chap. 186, pp. 8b-9a; Chap. 189, p. 22b.

196. *Mu-tsung shih-lu,* Chap. 123, pp. 33-34; Chap. 134, pp. 25a-26b.

197. *Ibid.,* Chap. 147, pp. 30a-31a.

198. *Ibid.,* Chap. 151, pp. 5b-6a.

199. *Ibid.,* Chap. 152, pp. 18a-b, 45b-46a.

200. *Ibid.,* Chap. 163, pp. 8b-10b. See also Sir Eric Teichman, *Travels in Eastern Tibet,* p. 5, and Bell, *Tibet,* p. 47.

201. See H. B. Morse, *The International Relations of the Chinese Empire,* II, 307-13.

202. In the case of Tibet, the British statesman Disraeli would have used the word "dismemberment" instead of "partition" as he did in the case of Egypt. But as pointed out by W. L. Langer, it makes little practical difference to the victims.

203. *Infra.,* n. 207, and Chap. IV, n. 61.

204. *Ch'ing chi ch'ou Tsang tsou tu* (Dispatches and Memorials to the Throne concerning Tibet in the Ch'ing Period), edited by Wu Fêng-p'ei, Vol. I, *Ting Pao-cheng tsou-tu,* p. 9.

205. Wên-shih was very popular among the Tibetans. He was cashiered because of his backing of the Tibetan arguments in the dispute with the British and declining to carry out the imperial order to force the Tibetans to withdraw from Lingtu. His merit and his keen sense of responsibility can be seen from his official papers and memorials to the throne collected in *ibid.,* Vol. I, "Wên-shih tsou tu," Chüan I-VIII.

206. Shêng-t'ai was appointed deputy Resident in 1887. He succeeded Wên-shih in 1888 and died at his post in 1892. He performed his duty to the best of his ability and knowledge and did a commendable job under most difficult circumstances. For his record, see *ibid.,* Vol. II, "Shêng-t'ai tsou tu." Chüan I-V.

207. As an illustration, one Resident was not able even to guard an important document from being stolen. In Lu Chuan-ling's memorial to the throne, it was stated that during the armed conflict with the British over the Sikkim frontier issue, some Russian travelers gave Tibetans three confidential letters and promised the latter military assistance. Resident Shêng-t'ai heard of the existence of these letters and took them over. After he had left the post, these letters disappeared from the secret files. It was said that the Tibetans got them back through bribing the keeper of the archives. (*Ibid.,* Vol. II, "Lu Chuan-ling tsou tu," Chüan III, p. 1. Lu Chuan-ling was governor-general of Szechwan from 1895-97.)

208. Residency in Tibet was a post reserved mainly for Manchus, but sometimes for Mongols. Chang Ying-tang was sent to investigate affairs in Tibet (*infra,* p. 114). He carried out some most needed reforms and made valuable suggestions. While in Tibet he was appointed Deputy Resident, the first Chinese ever admitted to the high office of Residency in Tibet. He declined the honor and his resigna-

tion was accepted. See *ibid.*, III, Chüan II, pp. 15-16. For his suggestions see *ibid.*, Chüan II, pp. 31-33; Chüan V, pp. 1-10.

209. *Ibid.*, Chüan II, pp. 17-20, 22, 25, 35-37, 38.

210. *Ch'ing-shih kao* (p. 16a) erroneously gives the date as 1884; we find the dispute recorded in the previous year of *Tê-tsung shih-lu,* Chap. 170, p. 4a, and Chap. 172, pp. 11a-b. See also Chao Han-chung, *Shih K'uo chi lüeh* (A Brief Account of My Mission to Nepal), p. 1a.

211. *Tê-tsung shih-lu,* Chap. 179, pp. 3a-b, and Chap. 183, pp. 5a-b.

212. *Ibid.*, Chap. 186, pp. 13b-14a; Chap. 187, pp. 9a-b. See also *Ch'ing chi ch'ou Tsang tsou tu,* Vol. I, "Ting Pao-cheng tsou tu," pp. 36-39.

213. *Ibid.*, pp. 20-26.

214. *Ibid.,* Vol. II, "Lu Chuan-ling tsou tu," Chüan I, p. 6. The Resident at that time was K'uei-huan, another grasping one, despised by the Tibetans (*ibid.*, p. 5).

215. For Lu Chuan-ling's arguments, see *ibid.*, pp. 13-15, 28; Chüan II, pp. 1-4, 12-15, 28-30; Chüan III, pp. 1-29. For Kung-shou's memorial, see *Ch'ing chi wai chiao shih liao* (The Sources of Diplomatic History toward the End of the Ch'ing Dynasty), ed. by Wang Liang and Wang Yen-wei, Vol. 127, pp. 28a-31b (hereafter cited as *WCSL*).

216. *Ch'ing chi ch'ou Tsang tsou tu,* Vol. II, "An-ch'eng tsou tu," p. 28. An-ch'eng was Deputy Resident from 1900 to 1903.

217. *Ibid.*, "Lu Chuan-ling tsou tu," Chüan I, pp. 5-6.

218. *Ibid.*, "An-ch'eng tsou tu," pp. 17-19; *Tê-tsung shih-lu,* Chap. 505, pp. 10a-b; their resignation was not accepted. They faced more difficulties, which were fully described in Yü-kang's dispatches to Wai-wu-pu (the Chinese Foreign Office), *WCSL,* Vol. 179, pp. 1a-b; Vol. 180, pp. 16a-b; Vol. 182, pp. 6a-7a. Yü-kang was finally replaced by Yu-t'ai and left Tibet in the spring of 1904. The helpless situation in which Yu-t'ai found himself is to be inferred from the following chapter.

219. *Ch'ing-shih kao,* Chap. 525, fan 8, p. 20a. The Dalai Lama apparently realized the formidable opposition to what he had done to Demo Hutukhtu and his followers and the danger of possible revenge. Among the conditions put to Lo Chang-chi when the latter came to India to urge the Dalai Lama's return, one was "not to raise the Demo case and never reverse the verdict." (*Infra,* n. 229.) Bell, *Tibet,* p. 140, mentions the widely held criticism of the Dalai Lama because of "his treatment of Ten-gye-ling Regent, which resulted in the latter's death."

220. For example, the treaty of 1890 and the Regulations of 1893, signed between China and Great Britain, were denounced by the Tibetans.

221. *Three Years in Tibet,* p. 297.

222. For an account of the mission, see Francis Younghusband, *India and Tibet,* and *infra,* Chap. IV.

223. For details refer to *Hsi-k'ang chien shêng chi* (Province Building of Sikang). The author, Fu Sung-mu, was the successor to Chao Erh-feng as frontier high commissioner.

224. Bell, *Tibet,* p. 93.

225. *CASJ,* XI (1924), Part III, 196, 203.

226. Teichman, *Travels in Eastern Tibet,* p. 37.

227. The imperial decree issued in November, 1908, conferring this title on the Dalai Lama—ostensibly as an additional honor—contained in reality, as Sir John Jordan put it, "the first unequivocal declaration on the part of China that she regarded Tibet as within her sovereignity"—sovereignity, be it noted, not suzerainty. Younghusband, *India and Tibet,* pp. 364, 384; Accounts and Papers printed by Order of The House of Commons (henceforth cited as *A and P*), Cd. 5240 (1910), No. 264, p. 170.

228. *Hsüan-t'ung chêng chi* of *Ta Ch'ing shih-lu,* Chap. 30, pp. 1a-3a.

229. The Imperial Court at first felt that it would have been awkward to ask the deposed Dalai Lama to return (*Hsüan-t'ung chêng chi,* Chap. 30, pp. 22b-23a), but its representative on the spot, the same Lien-yü who had made the suggestion of the Lama's deposition, found it necessary to persuade the Lama to come back. The counsellor Lo Chang-chi was sent to India for this purpose. His report of the interview with the Dalai Lama and the latter's demands for the evacuation of Szechwan troops and other conditions to be laid down in a written agreement, with the British as witness, was published by his son, Ch'un-yü, after the tragic death of his father, under the title *Ch'i hsüeh ch'i ts'un.* After the mutiny, another counsellor, Chien Hsi-pao, left his post when he found the situation untenable, under the pretext of going to India to urge the Dalai Lama to return.

230. Teichman, *Travels in Eastern Tibet,* p. 39, says that the new republican government cashiered the Manchu Amban Lien-yü and appointed Chung-yin, a Chinese, as Amban in his place.

231. Grover Clark, *Tibet, China and Great Britain,* p. 29, says that he was imprisoned by Chung-yin partly as a means to protect him from the wrath of the troops.

232. Clark says Chung-yin was to remain as Resident with his 200 soldiers. The writer bases his account on Lu Shing-chi's manuscript, which was mimeographed by the Mongolian and Tibetan Affairs Commission for official reference. Lu was considered an expert on Indian and Tibetan affairs and was appointed (on April 2, 1913, according to Yin Fu-i, *Hsi-tsang chi yao,* published by the Mongolian and Tibetan Affairs Commission, p. 194) acting high commissioner to succeed Chung-yin but never had the chance to set up his office in Tibet. Lu was in a position to know what had happened in Lhasa in those days.

233. Refer to Bell, *Tibet,* pp. 120-21.

234. David Macdonald, *Twenty Years in Tibet,* pp. 110-12. But the author goes on to relate the deposition of Lien-yü and the election of Chien Hsi-pao which took place in the previous year. Chien had long left when fighting was resumed in September, 1912.

235. *The Times* (London) last reported on November 21, 1912 (p. 5F), that fighting at Lhasa continued up to November 9 but that General Chung-yin, however, was short of supplies and ammunition and would probably seek permission to leave for India with the last remnant of his troops. *The North China Herald* last recorded on December 28, 1912 (p. 877), a dispatch from its own correspondent at Tach'ien-lu, dated November 28, that the trouble on the north road to Lhasa broke all communication with the interior of Tibet, and information about the Dalai Lama and what remained of the small Chinese garrison could not reach the border. See also Clark, *Tibet, China and Great Britain,* p. 31. Two years later Chung-yin was put to death. His sentence appeared in the Gazette of March 22, 1915, wherein he was charged with failure to maintain discipline, leaving Tibet against orders, and murdering Lo Chang-chi.

Chapter IV: Tibet as a Buffer State

1. Gratham Sandberg, *The Exploration of Tibet* (1914), pp. 21, 23.
2. Markham, p. xlvi.
3. See his article, "Was Odoric of Pordonone Ever in Tibet?" *T'oung Pao* (1914), pp. 405-18.
4. C. Wessels, *Early Jesuit Travellers in Central Asia 1603-1721* (The Hague, 1924), pp. 43-68. On Easter day, April 12, 1626, was laid the foundation-stone of the first Roman Catholic Church in Tibet, which was completed on August 15 of the same year. (*Ibid.*, pp. 63, 71.) Cf. Jean Deauvillier, in *Mélanges Cavallera* (Toulouse, 1948), pp. 261-316.
5. Wessels, *Early Jesuit Travellers,* pp. 164-202.
6. Parker Thomas Moon, *Imperialism and World Politics,* p. 64.
7. S. C. Sarcar, "Some Notes on the Intercourse of Bengal with the Northern Countries in the Second Half of the 18th Century," *Bengal Past and Present,* XLI (Calcutta, 1931), 121.
8. Cammann, p. 26.
9. Turner, *An Account of an Embassy,* p. xiv, quoted by Cammann, p. 31.
10. *Supra,* Chap. III, n. 87, and pp. 44-45.
11. Cammann, pp. 155-56.
12. Cf. Younghusband, *India and Tibet,* p. 5.

13. Markham, p. 203.

14. *Ibid.*, p. 148. See also p. 151 for the words of the Panch'en Lama, who told Bogle that the Regent's apprehensions of the English arose, not only from himself, but also from his dread of giving offense to the Chinese, to whose empire Tibet was subject.

15. Cammann, p. 96.

16. *Ibid.*, p. 87; Turner, p. 245.

17. A. Aspinal, *Cornwallis in Bengal* (Manchester, 1931), p. 178, quoted in Cammann, p. 118.

18. The text of the treaty is given in Aitchison, XIV (1929 ed.), 56-57.

19. Cammann, p. 127.

20. *Ibid.*, pp. 126-27.

21. *Ibid.*, p. 129, based upon Diskalkar, "Tibeto-Nepalese War", No. 13, pp. 383-85, and Kirkpatrick, pp. 349-50; *supra*, Chap. III, n. 143.

22. *Kao-tsung shih-lu*, Chap. 1398, pp. 11b-13b.

23. Cammann, p. 128.

24. *Ibid.*, p. 129.

25. Diskalkar, "Tibeto-Nepalese War," No. 18, pp. 395-98.

26. Cammann, pp. 135, n. 57; 138; 139, n. 70.

27. John Barrow, *Some Account of the Public Life and a Selection from the Unpublished Writings of the Earl of Macartney* (1807), II, 203-4; Cammann, p. 138, n. 65.

28. Earl H. Pritchard, "Anglo-Chinese Relations during the 17th and 18th Centuries," *University of Illinois Studies in the Social Sciences* (1929), XVII, Nos. 1-2, 152.

29. *Ibid.*, pp. 142-43. The Emperor's reply is recorded in *Kao-tsung shih-lu*, Chap. 1493, pp. 16b-18a.

30. *Shêng wu chi*, Book V, p. 46b; the author did not verify the English story. Cf. Cammann, p. 143.

31. Earl H. Pritchard, "The Crucial Years of Early Anglo-Chinese Relations 1750-1800," *Research Studies of the State College of Washington* (1936), IV, Nos. 3-4, 239.

32. H. B. Morse, *The Chronicles of the East India Company Trading to China 1635-1834*, II, 156; Pritchard, "Anglo-Chinese Relations during the 17th and 18th Centuries," *University of Illinois Studies in the Social Sciences* (1929), XVII, Nos. 1-2, 177.

33. Sandberg, *The Exploration of Tibet*, p. 116.

34. Besides a formal audience, he paid two visits to the Dalai Lama, then a boy of seven, and treated, with his limited medical knowledge, one of the Lama's physicians. (Markham, pp. 265-67, 288, and 292.)

35. Taraknath Das, *British Expansion in Tibet* (Calcutta, 1927), p. 6.

36. Markham, p. clviii.

37. Cammann, p. 84, n. 7.

38. Sir John Francis Davis, *Chinese Miscellanies: A Collection of Essays and Notes* (1865), p. 48.

39. At that time the frontier was between Kashmir and the Ladakh territory. *Ibid.,* p. 47 (Ladakh, formerly a province of Tibet; see *Cambridge History of India,* I, 33).*

40. For the criticisms, see H. B. Morse, *The International Relations of the Chinese Empire,* II, 303-5.

41. S. T. Wang, *The Margary Affair and the Chefoo Agreement,* p. 115.

42. Markham, p. 131.

43. Majumdar and others, *An Advanced History of India,* p. 722.

44. *Ibid.,* p. 723.

45. Taraknath Das, *British Expansion in Tibet,* p. 10.

46. John Claude White, *Sikkim and Bhutan, Twenty-one Years on the North-East Frontier 1887-1908* (1909), pp. 267 *et seq.*

47. *Ibid.,* pp. 280-81.

48. Majumdar and others, *An Advanced History of India,* p. 768.

49. White, *Sikkim and Bhutan,* p. 17.

50. Quoted in Taraknath Das, *British Expansion in Tibet,* p. 12.

51. Bell, *Tibet,* p. 106.

52. *Supra,* Chap. III, n. 87, and p. 44.

53. Bell, *Tibet,* pp. 8, 46.

54. Sandberg, *The Exploration of Tibet,* pp. 163-72; see also Bell, *Tibet,* p. 59, which says that the secret exploration of Das, carried out under the auspices of the Indian Government, filled the Tibetans with distrust of the power that ruled India. In this connection, see also L. Austine Waddell, *Lhasa and Its Mysteries,* pp. 8-9.

55. *Supra,* Chap. III, n. 211, and p. 64.

56. *Supra,* Chap. III, n. 160, and p. 55.

57. Hertslets, *China Treaties,* I, 89. The way by which the Chinese Government got out of the dilemma was by no means an easy one. The Earl of Rosebery once told the British House of Lords: "I shall never forget the anguish . . . with which the Chinese Government pressed on us the abandonment of that expedition, and the abandonment of that expedition was one of the main factors in securing that Convention [on Burma]." *Parliamentary Debates,* Vol. 130, p. 1140.

58. Majumdar and others, *An Advanced History of India,* p. 908.

59. Shêng Kung Ch'in Kung, *Tsang Yin pien wu lu* (The Resident Shêng-t'ai's Records and Official Papers Concerning Tibetan and Indian Frontiers), I, 7b-8b. The British troops withdrew from the valley after representation had been made by a Chinese colonel sent there by the Resident.

60. *A and P,* Cd. 1920 (1904), No. 1, p. 1; Younghusband, *India and Tibet,* p. 50; Bell, *Tibet,* p. 61.

*According to Jagdish Chandra Kundra, "Both Ladakh and Western Turkistan came under the Chinese Empire about 800 A.D. About 950 A.D. Ladakh was completely 'Tibetanized.' It remained under Central Tibetan rule from 1000 A.D. to 1400 A.D." See his book, *Indian Foreign Policy 1947-1954,* p. 8, and an article, "Ladakh," by D. N. Kachru in *India Quarterly,* Vol. 6, No. 1, 1950, p. 62.

61. See the Resident Shêng-t'ai's memorial to the throne, which explains the situation and his fears; *Tsang Yin pien wu lu,* I, 29b-31a; and also *Ch'ing-shih kao,* Chap. 525, fan 8, p. 19a.

62. *A and P,* C. 6208 (1890-91), Commercial 102; Hertslets, *China Treaties,* I, 92-93; *A and P,* Cd. 1920, No. 5, enclosure, pp. 6-7; Bell, *Tibet,* pp. 280-81; for details see *Tsang Yin pien wu lu,* I, 33b-34b.

63. Hertslets, *China Treaties,* I, 97; *A and P,* C. 7312 (1894), Treaty Series No. 11; Cd. 1920, No. 12, enclosure 1, annexure, pp. 22-23; Bell, *Tibet,* pp. 282-84. For details see *Tsang Yin pien wu lu,* I, 54a, 57b, 61a-62a, 64b-67a; II, 24b-36a.

64. *Ch'ing-shih kao,* Chap. 525, fan 8, p. 20a.

65. *Ch'ing tai Hsi-tsang shih liao ts'ung k'an (*1937), ed. by Wu Fêng-p'ei, pp. 9, 15; *A and P,* Cd. 1920, No. 29, enclosure 1, annexure 3, pp. 105-6; Shêng Kung Ch'in Kung, *Tsang Yin pien wu lu,* I, 1a-21, 5b-7a, 21a, 25a, and 36a.

66. *A and P,* Cd. 1920, No. 16, p. 52. The Government of India admitted that, "In respect to territory near Giaogong, the Tibetans probably possess claims which it would not only be impolitic but inequitable to ignore." See *ibid.,* No. 18, enclosure 3, pp. 58-59, and A. Maccallum Scott, *The Truth about Tibet* (1905), p. 17. It also admitted that "there is . . . no evidence that the mischief [demolition of the pillars] is to be directly attributed to Tibetan officials" and that "demarcation was not . . . provided for in the Treaty of 1890; no serious practical inconvenience had apparently arisen through the frontier being undemarcated." *A and P,* Cd. 1920, No. 13, p. 25.

67. *A and P,* Cd. 1920 (1904), No. 26, enclosure 8, annexure 1, pp. 93-95; *Ch'ing tai Hsi-tsang shih liao ts'ung k'an,* pp. 13-14.

68. *A and P,* Cd. 1920, enclosure in No. 18, p. 58.

69. *Ch'ing tai Hsi-tsang shih liao ts'ung k'an,* pp. 16-17.

70. *Ibid.,* pp. 14-16.

71. *A and P,* Cd. 1920, No. 18, enclosure 1, annexure, p. 55. The British Foreign Minister, the Marquess of Lansdowne, once told Parliament: "As a matter of fact I believe that a Tibetan official accompanied the Chinese Ambam who negotiated the treaty of 1890." *Parliamentary Debates,* Vol. 130, pp. 1147. *A and P,* Cd. 2540, No. 293, p. 182, mentioned the newly appointed Tibetan Regent, Shata Shapé, as "the same who had been to Darjeeling in connection with the Sikkim-Tibet Convention of 1890." The Ambam, in his memorial to the throne commending the merits of his staff on that mission, mentioned Tibetan officials. Sheng Kung Ch'in Kung, *Tsang Yin pien wu lu,* I, 47b-48b. The British would not, of course, use this fact to argue with the Tibetans on this point as they themselves were seeking direct relations with them.

72. *A and P,* Cd. 1920, No. 26, enclosure 8, annexure 1, p. 94.

73. *A and P,* Cd. 1920 (1904), No. 29, enclosure 1, annexure 1, p. 104.

74. *Ibid.,* No. 18, enclosure 1, annexure, p. 56.

75. *Ibid.,* No. 26, pp. 74-75; No. 27, p. 99; No. 29, pp. 102-3; No. 30, p. 111.

76. *Ibid.,* No. 66, pp. 151, 153, and 155.

77. *Ibid.,* No. 29, p. 103; No. 37, pp. 118-19.

78. *Ibid.,* No. 44, p. 125.

79. *Ibid.,* No. 44, p. 127.

80. *Ibid.,* No. 66, p. 154.

81. Department of State Archives, Great Britain Instructions, Vol. 34, pp. 636-39, No. 1455, Hay to Choate, June 3, 1904. In this dispatch we learn that the Secretary of State had an exchange of views with the British Ambassador, Sir Mortimer Durand, who told him that there was no intention on the part of the British Government of the permanent occupation of Tibet, nor of any action in violation of the integrity of China. But when Mr. Choate made his formal representation to the Marquess of Lansdowne on June 29, 1904, asking for assurance that no steps would be taken by the British Government which might tend to disturb the present government of Tibet or lessen Chinese control over it, and assuming that the British "still regarded Tibet as a part of the Chinese Dominions" and that the British "did not desire to alter the status of the country in that respect," he received a most evasive reply (A. Whitney Griswold, *The Far Eastern Policy of the United States,* p. 101).

82. *A and P,* Cd. 1920, No. 78, p. 185.

83. According to Ho's report, the British delegates had the memorandum read by an interpreter first and then handed it over to the Tibetan official who refused to accept it. It was Ho who instructed his own interpreter, Shen Chin-hsi, to take it so as to break the deadlock. *Ch'ing tai Hsi-tsang shih liao tsung k'an,* p. 29.

84. *Ibid.,* p. 30; *A and P,* Cd. 1920, annexure to enclosure 21 in No. 129, p. 232.

85. Pio-carlo Terenzio, *La rivalité Anglo-Russe en Perse et en Afghanistan jusqu-aux Accords de 1907* (1947), Chaps. IV and V, pp. 38-92.

86. Hsû Erh-hao, *Ch'ing K'ang Tsang Hsin hsi jên k'ao ch'a shih lüeh,* pp. 3-7, 9-10. After the death of Prijvalsky in 1888, the Russian "Tibetan expedition" was led by Pievtsov.

87. *Ibid.,* pp. 2-7, 18-19.

88. Bell, *Tibet,* pp. 222-23.

89. *A and P,* Cd. 1920 (1904), No. 66, p. 153.

90. Bell, *Portrait of the Dalai Lama,* p. 62.

91. *A and P,* Cd. 1920, No. 66, p. 153.

92. *Ibid.,* Nos. 49, 52, pp. 140-41; No. 55, p. 143; No. 57, p. 145.

93. Perceval Landon, *The Opening of Tibet,* p. 21.

94. *A and P,* Cd. 1920, No. 66, p. 151.

95. *Ibid.,* enclosure in No. 53, p. 142; annexure 4 to enclosure 7 in No. 66, p. 161.

96. *Ibid.,* No. 61, p. 148.

97. *Ibid.,* No. 66, p. 153; No. 74, p. 182; No. 76, p. 183.

98. *Ibid.,* No. 83, p. 187; *infra,* p. 120.

99. *Ibid.,* No. 78, p. 185.

100. *Ibid.,* Nos. 86 and 87, p. 189; annexure to enclosure 7 in No. 99, p. 201.

101. *Ibid.,* annexure to enclosure 5 in No. 66, p. 159; annexure 4, enclosure 7, in No. 66, p. 161.

102. *Ibid.,* No. 85, p. 188.

103. *Ibid.,* Nos. 95 and 96, p. 193.

104. *Ibid.,* annexure to enclosure 2 in No. 99, p. 196.

105. *Ibid.,* No. 66, p. 151; Nos. 78 and 79, p. 185.

106. *Ibid.,* No. 116, p. 212.

107. *Ibid.,* annexure to enclosure 7 in No. 99, pp. 200-201.

108. *Ibid.,* enclosure 6 in No. 99, pp. 198-200.

109. *Ibid.,* enclosure 5 in No. 99, p. 197; for details of Colonel Younghusband's preparations, see his letter written on June 1.

110. Scott, *The Truth about Tibet,* pp. 29-30.

111. *A and P,* Cd. 1920, annexure 2, enclosure 1, and annexure to enclosure 2 in No. 99, p. 196.

112. *Ibid.,* No. 86, p. 189.

113. *Ibid.,* annexure 1, enclosure 5 in No. 129, p. 223. Later, on July 23, the Chinese Resident wired to Lord Curzon reiterating that Khamba was in Tibetan territory and unsuitable for discussion, and requesting that the British Commissioners be removed to the boundary. Enclosure 20 in No. 129, p. 230. See also Nos. 108, 109, pp. 205-6.

114. *Ibid.,* enclosures 9, 12, and 17, pp. 224-25 and 229.

115. *Ibid.,* enclosure 22, in No. 129, p. 231.

116. *Ibid.,* No. 97 and enclosure, pp. 194-95.

117. *Ibid.,* enclosure 25 in No. 129, p. 243.

118. *Ibid.,* enclosure 24 in No. 129, pp. 241-42.

119. *Ibid.,* enclosure 54 in No. 129, p. 267.

120. *Ibid.,* enclosure 30 in No. 129, p. 245, Captain W. F. O'Connor's Diary.

121. *Ibid.,* Nos. 112, 113, 123, and 128, pp. 209, 210, 215, and 219. The British Foreign Minister told the Russian Ambassador: "The Tibetans have seized, and as we believe barbarously put to death two British subjects." *Ibid.,* No. 141, p. 299.

122. Scott, *The Truth about Tibet,* p. 35; *A and P,* Cd. 2370 (1905), No. 130, p. 52; Part II, enclosure No. 265, pp. 224-25, and No.

293, pp. 236-37. When "the two dubious and anonymous British subjects" (to use the Earl of Rosebery's words) were handed over, Younghusband held a full durbar and made a great fuss, saying that the arrest of these two men formed one of the main reasons why the mission had been moved forward from Khamba to Gyantse and that he was satisfied that "the ill-treatment had not been severe."

123. *A and P,* Cd. 1920 (1904), No. 113, p. 210; No. 120, p. 213; Nos. 125 and 126, p. 216; No. 132, p. 294. To strengthen his appeal, Lord Curzon reported, "An overt act of hostility has taken place, Tibetan troops having attacked Nepalese yaks on the frontier and carried off many of them." *Ibid.,* No. 127, p. 218.

124. For details of the slaughter at Geru, see E. Candler, *The Unveiling of Lhasa,* p. 102-9. The author was an eyewitness, serving as the correspondent of the *Daily Mail.* For the official report, see *A and P,* Cd. 2054, No. 10, p. 5; No. 11, p. 6; No. 23, pp. 9-10. Among the Tibetans killed were two commanding officers, one from Lhasa, the other from Shigatse; another officer in command of the Phari Regiment was taken prisoner while seriously wounded. *Ibid.,* No. 29. p. 11. The writer is inclined to believe that it was due to the English sense of fair play, rather than the official explanation, that the Geru incident was not included in calculating the indemnity of 75 Lakhs. Cf. *A and P,* Cd. 2370, No. 317, p. 246.

125. *A and P,* Cd. 1920, No. 153, p. 304.

126. Scott, *The Truth about Tibet,* p. 44; *A and P,* Cd. 2054, Nos. 22 and 25, pp. 9 and 10.

127. *A and P,* Cd. 2370 (1905), No. 2, pp. 1-2. Colonel Younghusband was then expecting the Chinese Resident, who would have found that had he come, he was not to negotiate at Gyantse but to be instrumental for a further advance of the British Mission.

128. *Ibid.,* No. 7, pp. 3-4, in which the Viceroy mentioned the attack on the British camp at Gyantse as evidence that the Lhasa Government was irreconcilable. This attack was made by 700 Tibetans from Shigatse; as a result, 250 were killed or wounded, while the British casualties were only 2 wounded.

129. In reply to the British ultimatum, the Tibetan General said that it was not their custom to receive communications from the British and that it should be received by a Chinese official.

130. *A and P,* Cd. 2370 (1905), No. 72, p. 24; No. 83, p. 28; see also No. 95, pp. 32-33, for Tongsa Penlop's repeated solicitation. The Dalai Lama wrote to ask him to assist in peaceful settlement, "fighting being bad for both animals and men." Younghusband calls Tongsa Penlop "so staunch a friend of the British Government" in enclosure No. 328, p. 256.

131. *Ibid.,* Part II, No. 237, enclosure, pp. 201-3.

132. The national assembly of Tibet (*Tsong-du* in Tibetan, Wad-

dell, *Lhasa and Its Mysteries,* p. 396) was a creation of the thirteenth Dalai Lama. It was not a representative body; it was composed of all ecclesiastical and secular officials below the rank of the Cabinet, or rather such of them as happened to be stationed in or near Lhasa. (Bell, *Portrait of the Dalai Lama,* p. 144.) Nor was it a responsible organ. It could only make recommendations on questions referred to it by the government, and the Dalai Lama often ignored its recommendations and made autocratic decisions. (*Ibid.,* p. 147, and Bell, *Tibet,* p. 152.)

133. *A and P,* Cd. 2370 (1905), No. 111, p. 44. The date was not the 26th as given on p. 48, Lee Wei-kuo, *Tibet in Modern World Politics.* See enclosure No. 245, annexure 1, p. 207; enclosure No. 246, p. 209.

134. *A and P,* Cd. 2370 (1905), No. 118, p. 48; Part II, enclosure No. 252, p. 211.

135. *Ibid.,* enclosure No. 256, p. 217.

136. *Parliamentary Debates,* Vol. 138, p. 1334.

137. *A and P,* Cd. 2370 (1905), No. 2, p. 2.

138. *Ibid.,* No. 85, p. 29; No. 95, p. 33.

139. For a complete list of the officers, civil and military, of the mission who actually reached Lhasa, and the force which moved to Lhasa from Gyantse, see Landon, *The Opening of Tibet,* Appendix E.

140. Quoted by Das, *British Expansion in Tibet,* p. 65; for reference to the contrary, see *A and P,* Cd. 2370, Nos. 122 and 125, pp. 150-51; enclosure No. 274, p. 228. On the question raised in the Parliament as to the reported loot, see *Parliamentary Debates,* Vol. 140, pp. 11-12.

141. *A and P,* Cd. 2054 (1904), No. 14, p. 7; Cd. 2370 (1905), Part II, enclosure No. 23, pp. 104-5.

142. *Ibid.,* Cd. 2370 (1905), No. 119, p. 49.

143. *Ibid.,* No. 121. Younghusband, *India and Tibet,* p. 266.

144. *Ch'ing-shih kao,* Chap. 525, fan 8, p. 19; *Ch'ing chi ch'ou Tsang tsou tu,* Vol. III, "Yu-t'al tsou tu," Chüan I, pp. 9-10.

145. *Ibid.,* "Chang Ying-tang tsou tu," Chüan II, p. 18; cf. *A and P,* Cd. 2370 (1905), Part II, enclosure No. 264, p. 223.

146. *A and P,* Cd. 1920 (1904), No. 135, p. 296.

147. *Ibid.,* Nos. 133, 136, 141, pp. 294, 296, 298, 299.

148. *A and P,* Cd. 2370 (1905), Nos. 37, 43, pp. 13, 15.

149. Scott, *The Truth about Tibet,* p. 49.

150. *A and P,* Cd. 1920, No. 132, p. 294.

151. See Art. IX of the Convention.

152. *A and P,* Cd. 2370 (1905), No. 79, p. 26.

153. See the subsidiary agreement; Younghusband, *India and Tibet,* pp. 299-300.

154. Scott, *The Truth about Tibet,* p. 50.

155. *A and P,* Cd. 2370 (1905), No. 106, pp. 42-43.

156. "Shappé," also known as bKa'-blon, is a member of the Kashag or Cabinet which is usually composed of one priest and three laymen.

157. There was, in addition, a single-clause subsidiary agreement, the content of which is referred to on p. 98.

158. Younghusband, *India and Tibet,* pp. 291-92.

159. *Ibid.,* pp. 300-302. By insisting on the potala, Younghusband had in mind to strike the imagination of the Nepalese, Bhutanese, Sikkimese, and men of Kashmir and Turkestan, and to leave unmistakable evidence that the Tibetans had been compelled to come to terms.

160. For the text of the instructions, see *Ching chi ch'ou Tsang tsou tu,* Vol. III, "Yu-t'ai tsou tu," Chüan I, pp. 21-23, 24, and 26.

161. Articles VI and VII of the Convention.

162. Younghusband, *India and Tibet,* p. 305.

163. *A and P,* Cd. 2370 (1905), enclosure 1 in No. 194, p. 87.

164. Das, *British Expansion in Tibet,* p. 66; Clark, *Tibet, China and Great Britain,* p. 9.

165. *A and P,* Cd. 2370, No. 165, p. 67.

166. Younghusband, *India and Tibet,* p. 297.

167. *A and P,* Cd. 2370, (1905), No. 139, p. 57; in a telegram to the Viceroy, Younghusband said: "Amount of indemnity which I am demanding is excessive and I would not press it seriously," but he pressed it by even asking for more (i.e., an additional Rs 50,000 for each day's delay in accepting his terms); cf. Nos. 148, 155, pp. 60 and 63. For details in connection with indemnity, see also *ibid.,* Part II, Nos. 300, 305, 316, 317, 328, 340, and 342, pp. 239, 241, 245, 246, 254-56, 260, and 262. Younghusband reported that the Tibetans had only asked that "the term of payment of the indemnity might be extended and that it might be paid in 75 annual installments of one lakh of rupees each." *(Ibid.,* No. 343, p. 263.) They asked for nothing but that, because all their requests for exemption, reduction, and other considerations had been of no avail. In fact, Ti-Rimpoche had told him repeatedly that the Tibetans disliked the idea of prolonging the time during which they would be under obligation to the British, as "the row would be kept up and friendship would be difficult," and they wanted to settle the business at once and have done with it. *(Ibid.,* No. 317, p. 246; No. 340, p. 260.)

168. *Ibid.,* No. 131, p. 53; enclosure 1 in No. 194, p. 88.

169. *Ibid.,* Nos. 153 and 156, pp. 62, 63.

170. *Ibid.,* No. 154, pp. 62-63; No. 169, p. 68.

171. *Ibid.,* No. 114, p. 45; Nos. 170 and 184, pp. 69, 77.

172. *Parliamentary Debates,* Vol. 125, pp. 401-2.

173. *Supra,* n. 76.

174. *Parliamentary Debates,* Vol. 130, pp. 1112, 1116-17.

175. *Ibid.*, pp. 1132, 1133-34, 1137.

176. *Ibid.*, p. 1141; Lord Reay also brought up this point on tea, p. 1113.

177. *Ibid.*, pp. 1140, 1142.

178. *Ibid.*, Vol. 140, p. 464.

179. *Ibid.*, Vol. 141, p. 23. Lee Wei-kuo mentioned this passage in his book, *Tibet in Modern World Politics,* p. 55. He mistakenly gave the name of the Marquess of Winchester instead of Earl Spencer.

180. *Parliamentary Debates,* Vol. 141, pp. 134-35.

181. *Ibid.*, p. 149.

182. *A and P,* Cd. 2370, No. 115, dated August 5, 1904, p. 46.

183. H. B. Morse, and H. F. MacNair, *Far Eastern International Relations,* pp. 512-13, 515.

184. *A and P,* Cd. 2370, No. 193, pp. 84-86.

185. *Parliamentary Debates,* Vol. 141, Feb. 14, 1905, p. 14.

186. *Ibid.*, Vol. 137, July 11, 1904, pp. 1203, 1204.

187. *A and P,* Cd. 2370, enclosure No. 264, p. 224; No. 127, p. 51. The Resident found the Tibetan reply so impertinent that he told Younghusband that he could not even mention it to him officially. See enclosure 289, p. 233.

188. *Ibid.*, Nos. 276, 278, pp. 228-29; enclosure No. 318, p. 247; enclosure Nos. 300, 305, pp. 239, 241.

189. Even the Chinese Resident seemed not to have his way in the least. He told Younghusband that he would have to discuss the clause regarding trade marts with him. The latter said he was prepared to talk the matter over. But nothing happened. (*Ibid.*, enclosure No. 318, p. 247.)

190. *Ibid.*, enclosure No. 339, p. 259.

191. *Ibid.*, enclosure No. 318, p. 247; enclosure No. 243, p. 206.

192. *Ibid.*, enclosure No. 367, p. 225; No. 318, p. 247.

193. *Ibid.*, enclosure No. 316, p. 245.

194. *Ibid.*, enclosure No. 360, p. 271.

195. *Ibid.*, enclosure No. 344, pp. 263-64.

196. Younghusband, *India and Tibet,* pp. 421-22.

197. *A and P,* Cd. 2370, Part II, enclosure No. 360, p. 270, annexure 1, p. 271. *Supra,* n. 162. On leaving Lhasa, Younghusband presented the Resident with 8 or 10 repeating rifles he had among his articles for presentation, and he gave no rifles to the Tibetans. (*India and Tibet,* p. 422.)

198. *A and P,* Cd. 2370, Part II, enclosure No. 339, p. 259; *Ch'ing tai Hsi-tsang shih liao tsung k'an,* p. 63.

199. *A and P,* Cd. 2370, Part II, enclosure No. 340, p. 260.

200. *Ibid.*, Part I, No. 127, p. 51 (the date was mistakenly given as August 16); see enclosure No. 259, p. 219, and enclosure No. 312, p. 243.

201. *Ch'ing tai Hsi-tsang shih liao ts'ung k'an,* p. 64.

202. *Supra,* n. 127, and p. 90.

203. *A and P,* Cd. 2370 (1905), No. 97, p. 39.

204. *Ibid.,* enclosure No. 341, p. 262.

205. *A and P,* Cd. 1920 (1904), No. 66, p. 155. *Supra,* p. 82.

206. *A and P,* Cd. 2370, Part II, enclosure No. 291, pp. 235-36.

207. *Ibid.,* enclosure No. 280, p. 229; No. 325, p. 253.

208. Arnold D. McNair, *Law of Treaties,* p. 135; see also L. Oppenheim, *International Law* (7th ed. by H. Lauterpacht), I, 795-96, and Georg Schwarzenberger, *A Manual of International Law* (1951), pp. 58 and 62.

209. *A and P,* Cd. 2370, Part II, enclosures No. 291, p. 235; No. 266, p. 225.

210. *Ibid.,* enclosures No. 267, p. 225; No. 280, p. 229.

211. *Ibid.,* enclosure No. 325, p. 253.

212. *Ibid.,* No. 130, p. 52; enclosures No. 266, p. 225; Nos. 273 and 319, p. 249.

213. Quoted from a letter from the Government of India to the Secretary of State for India, dated June 30, 1904. *Ibid.,* No. 97, p. 36.

214. For the text of the telegraphic recommendation, see *Ch'ing chi ch'ou Tsang tsou tu,* Vol. III, "Yu-t'ai tsou tu," Chüan I, pp. 14 and 21; his memorial to the throne on the same subject is given in *ibid.,* p. 19.

215. *A and P,* Cd. 2370, Part II, enclosure No. 307, p. 241.

216. Scott, *The Truth about Tibet,* p. 59. Vincent A. Smith remarked in his *The Oxford History of India* (rev. ed., 1928), p. 771: "So far as I can judge the expedition was unnecessary and all but fruitless."

217. *A and P,* Cd. 2370, Part II, annexure to enclosure No. 363, p. 276.

218. *Ibid.,* annexure to enclosure No. 362, pp. 274-75. The translation here used is the version sent by Younghusband to his government.

219. *Political Diary of the Mission,* in *ibid.,* enclosure No. 320, p. 250.

220. *Ibid.,* enclosure No. 339, p. 259.

221. *Ibid.,* enclosure No. 334, p. 258.

222. *Ibid.,* No. 167, p. 67.

223. *Ibid.,* No. 171, p. 69; Nos. 186, 187, 188, pp. 77-78.

224. *WCSL,* Vol. 188, p. 46.

225. Lu Hsing-chi's manuscript on *Hsi-tsang chiao shê chi yao* (important Diplomatic Dealings concerning Tibet) (*supra,* Chap. III, n. 232), Ch. VI, pp. 25a-27a; *WCSL,* Vol. 196, pp. 8b-9b; Ho Tsao-hsiang, *Tsang yü,* pp. 18a-24b (the author was a secretary to the Chinese

delegation); *Ch'ing-shih kao,* Chap. 525, fan 8, p. 22b; *A and P,* Cd. 5240 (1910), No. 59, p. 35. Here the reader is reminded of a parallel case. In the Convention of 1890 relating to Sikkim and Tibet, the British had provided in Art. II that ". . . neither the ruler of the Sikkim State nor any of its officers shall have official relations of any kind, formal or informal, with any other country."

226. *A and P,* Cd. 5240 (1910), Nos. 46, 47, pp. 30-31; enclosure in No. 63, p. 39; and also Cd. 2370 (1905), No. 144, p. 58.

227. *Ibid.,* Cd. 5240, No. 31, p. 23. T'ang did not go to London to take up his post and was appointed junior vice-president of the Board of Foreign Affairs in December, 1905.

228. *Ibid.,* No. 42, p. 29; No. 59 and also its enclosure, p. 35.

229. *Ibid.,* No. 43, pp. 29-30; No. 46, pp. 30-31; enclosure in No. 63, p. 39. Besides strategical considerations, both the Chinese and the Tibetans had reason to fear a long occupation of the Chumbi Valley, as the latter were told that the British Government would act according to their own will and pleasure in Chumbi, and Bell, then assistant Political Officer there, who called himself the master of the Valley, was creating a number of new precedents. (See enclosure 1 in No. 39, enclosure 3 in No. 40, pp. 25-26, 27-28.)

230. *WCSL,* Vol. 196, pp. 1a-2b and 9a.

231. *A and P,* Cd. 5240, No. 50, p. 32; No. 54, p. 33; and No. 56, p. 34.

232. *Ibid.,* No. 61, p. 38; No. 68, p. 42.

233. *Ibid.,* No. 61, p. 38; No. 77, p. 45.

234. *Ibid.,* No. 76, p. 44; No. 79, p. 45.

235. *Ibid.,* Nos. 83-87 and 89-91, pp. 46-48.

236. *Ibid.,* Nos. 210-13, pp. 135-38; No. 217, p. 139; No. 226, p. 143.

237. *Ibid.,* Nos. 218-21, pp. 139-40.

238. Given by the Under-Secretary of State for Foreign Affairs, Lord Fitzmaurice, in answer to the Marquess of Lansdowne; by the Local Government Board, Mr. Runciman Dewsberry for Sir Edward Grey in answer to Sir H. Cotton; the two are identical except for the phrase "on their part." (*Parliamentary Debates,* Vol. 156, pp. 372, 553.) For the text of the Agreement see *British and Foreign State Papers,* Vol. 99, pp. 171 *et seq.*; MacMurray, *Treaties and Agreements with and concerning China,* I, 576-77; Bell, *Tibet,* pp. 287-89; *A and P,* Cd. 5240, pp. 51-52; Cd. 3088 (1906), Treaty Series No. 9.

239. It is noteworthy that as late as June 14, 1904, the British Foreign Minister, in his official dispatch to the British ambassador to Russia, wrote: "Count Lamsdorff had added that it had given him great satisfaction to note that the British Government, for their part, recognize, in terms of the memorandum, which I had recently handed to Count Benckendorff [June 2, No. 43, p. 14], the utility and neces-

sity of maintaining the political status quo in that province of the Chinese Empire." (*A and P,* Cd. 2370, No. 55, p. 18.) See also *supra,* nn. 82 and 174, and pp. 83 and 99.

240. *Ibid.,* Cd. 5240, No. 57, p. 34. According to Chang Ying-tang's reports to Wai-wu-pu the British had designs to bar the return of the Dalai Lama and to make use of the Panch'en Lama to turn Tibet into a British protectorate. See *Ch'ing chi ch'ou Tsang tsou tu,* Vol. III, "Chang Ying-tang tsou tu," Chüan I, pp. 10-11, 11-12, and 13-15.

241. *Ch'ing tai Hsi-tsang shih liao ts'ung k'an,* Part II, pp. 6, 11, 17, 25, 27, and 28-29.

242. *A and P,* Cd. 5240, No. 51, p. 33.

243. *Ibid.,* No. 141, p. 86.

244. *Ibid.,* No. 143, p. 87. *Infra,* n. 285.

245. *Ibid.,* No. 103, p. 56; No. 105 and enclosure, pp. 57-61; No. 113, p. 63; Nos. 122 and 124, p. 66; Nos. 128, 129, p. 67; Nos. 133 and 134, p. 75; annexures and enclosures in No. 135, pp. 75-84; No. 148, p. 93; No. 150, pp. 94-95; No. 160, p. 100; No. 162, p. 101; No. 177, p. 107; No. 192, p. 116; No. 196, p. 119.

246. *Ibid.,* enclosure 2 in No. 190, p. 116.

247. *Ibid.,* enclosure 1 in No. 193, p. 117.

248. *Ibid.,* enclosure 1 in No. 239, p. 151; and also Nos. 194 and 195, p. 118.

249. *Ibid.,* No. 213, p. 138.

250. *Ibid.,* No. 251, p. 160. For the text of the Regulations see *British and Foreign State Papers,* Vol. 101, pp. 170-75; *A and P,* Cd. 4450 (1908), Treaty Series No. 35; Cd. 5240, Enclosure I in No. 239, pp. 151-54; MacMurray, I, 582-85; Bell, *Tibet,* pp. 291-97. For the criticisms of Chao Erh-feng on the Adhesion Agreement and the Regulations, see his letter to Wai-wu-pu (*WCSL,* Vol. 216, pp. 2b-5b) and also Wai-wu-pu's comment on Chao's letter (*ibid.,* pp. 6a-10b). For details of preparatory works and arguments advanced and concessions made by both parties as well as the answers to Chao's charge, see the memorial of Wai-wu-pu and four other competent ministers (*ibid.,* pp. 12b-17b). For a time, the British Government expected in return for the withdrawal of troops from the Chumbi Valley, that the Trade Regulations would be speedily concluded in a satisfactory manner, i.e., to meet the British wishes. (*A and P,* Cd. 5240, No. 216, p. 139.)

251. Bell, *Tibet,* p. 19. The writer adds "at Kalimpong," which was not given in the Blue Book; he drew this information from the minutes of negotiations kept in the Chinese Foreign Office Archives.

252. *A and P,* Cd. 5240, No. 239, p. 151, and also No. 227, p. 143; No. 269, p. 173.

253. *Supra,* nn. 82, 174, and 239.

254. Lu Hsing-chi, *Hsi-t'ang chiao shê chi yao,* pp. 33a-b and 38a.

255. *A and P,* Cd. 5240, No. 141, p. 86.

256. Lee Wei-kuo, *Tibet in Modern World Politics,* n. 2, p. 65; see also *A and P,* Cd. 5240, enclosure in No. 208, pp. 133-34; No. 227, p. 143; No. 269, pp. 172-73; No. 257, p. 162; No. 272, p. 174; No. 353, pp. 217-18.

257. *Parliamentary Debates,* Vol. 142, p. 407.

258. *A and P,* Cd. 1920 (1904), No. 66, p. 153.

259. *Supra,* n. 175, and p. 99.

260. Dorjieff, known by his Tibetan name Ghomang Lobzang and called by Kawaguchi as Dorje, the Tsan-ni Kenbo, was born a Russian Buriat and Buddhist by religion. He settled in Tibet in 1881 at the age of 35. (*A and P,* Cd. 1920, enclosure No. 34, p. 157.) He became one of the four tutors of the Dalai Lama and virtually monopolized the confidence of the pontiff. (Kawaguchi, "Russia's Policy in Tibet," *Open Court,* XXX [1916], 370-80.)

261. *Supra,* p. 85; *A and P,* Cd. 1920 (1904), No. 35, p. 116; Nos. 39 and 40, p. 124. Dorjieff went to Russia and was received by the Tzar in the palace of Livadia at Yalta on Sept. 30, 1900 (*ibid.,* No. 31 and enclosure, p. 113). He went there again in 1901 and was given an audience with the Tzar at Peterhof on July 6. For related details, see *ibid.,* Nos. 32-36 and enclosures, pp. 113-18. In March, 1906, he arrived at St. Petersburg with a message from the Dalai Lama to the effect that he looked to the Tzar for protection, and as before, was granted an audience. This time the Russian Foreign Ministry, apparently in view of the forthcoming rapprochement with Great Britain, informed the British Ambassador of exactly what had occurred, as they were afraid the press would probably make out that the audience had a political character. (*A and P,* Cd. 5240 (1910), No. 74, p. 43.) Percival Landon, *The Opening of Tibet* (p. 21), mentions Dorjieff's earlier journey to Russia in 1898. For Dorjieff's activities in Lhasa, see Bell, *Tibet,* p. 63, and *A and P,* Cd. 2370 (1905), enclosure No. 244, p. 207.

262. *A and P,* Cd. 1920 (1904), No. 83, p. 187, and Cd. 2370 (1905), No. 61, p. 20; No. 115, p. 46. As to the Chinese side, earlier in September, 1902, when Sir E. Satow saw Prince Ch'ing and the Ministers of the Foreign Board to transmit a warning from his government against the conclusions of an alleged agreement between Russia and China in regard to Tibet, the latter strongly denied that there was any such agreement. Both Prince Ch'ing and Chu, a member of the Grand Council, declared that no such agreement had ever formed a subject of discussion between the Chinese and Russian Governments (Cd. 1920, No. 55, p. 143).

263. *Parliamentary Debates,* Vol. 133, p. 119.

264. *A and P,* Cd. 2370 (1905), No. 55, p. 18.

265. *Parliamentary Debates,* Vol. 133, pp. 130-31.

266. Oscar T. Crosby, *Tibet and Turkestan* (1905), p. 229.

267. Krasnyi Arkhiv, II, 21 (1923), quoted in S. B. Fay, *The Origins of the World War,* I, 366-67.

268. *A and P,* Cd. 1920, Nos. 83, 84, pp. 187-88. *Supra,* p. 86.

269. Griswold, *The Far Eastern Policy of the United States,* p. 99.

270. Ramsay Muir, *The Expansion of Europe* (6th ed., 1939), p. 199.

271. R. B. Mowat, *A History of European Diplomacy, 1815-1914,* p. 272.

272. *British Documents on the Origins of the War 1898-1914,* ed. by G. P. Gooch and Harold Temperley (1926-38), III, No. 422, p. 364; the German representative in St. Petersburg commented on the Anglo-Russian convention in a dispatch: "These plans need not necessarily be ascribed to any anti-German tendency, yet Germany is the country most affected by the agreement." The Emperor William minuted this dispatch as follows: "Yes, when taken all round, it is aimed at us."

273. Harold Nicolson, *Portrait of a Diplomatist* (1930), pp. 150, 152, 158, 159.

274. *Ibid.,* pp. 160 and 175. For the full text of the Draft Instructions to Nicolson, see *British Documents on the Origins of War,* Vol. IV, No. 310, p. 331.

275. Nicolson, *Portrait of a Diplomatist,* p. 175.

276. For the full text, see *A and P,* Cd. 5240 (1910), No. 203, pp. 128-31; Cd. 3753 (1907), Treaty Series No. 34; Bell, *Tibet,* pp. 289-91.

277. Viscount Grey of Fallodon, *Twenty-five Years 1892-1916* (1925), I, 160. Morley was then Secretary of State for India.

278. Refer to *A and P,* Cd. 5240, Nos. 206, 207, pp. 132-35. The British and Russian ministers to China agreed to drop the matter after having received a memorandum in reply to their draft note. This episode afforded the Chinese Government an opportunity to reassert its authority in Tibet.

279. *The Times* (London), Sept. 27 (p. 7b), 28 (p. 5c), 30 (p. 9b), 1907.

280. *Parliamentary Debates,* Vol. 183, pp. 999-1024.

281. *Ibid.,* Vol. 184, pp. 460-64.

282. In this connection, mention could be made of Louis Fischer's remark on the Tibetan Convention: ". . . London recognized Russia's right to trade with Tibet and thus by implication, her special position in Chinese Turkestan on the borders of the Indian province of Kashmir." (*The Soviets in World Affairs* 1930, I, 424.) But the writer fails to see such an undertaking and such an implication.

283. Viscount Grey, *Twenty-Five Years,* I, 154.

284. Speaking of the whole Convention, Harold Nicolson remarked that it was faithfully observed by Great Britain but not by Russia. (*Portrait of a Diplomatist,* p. 187.)

285. For representations made by the British to the Chinese Government in this connection, see *A and P,* Cd. 5240 (1910), Nos. 287,

288, pp. 180-81; Nos. 298-301 and 303, pp. 188-90; No. 315, p. 195; No. 336, pp. 205-6; No. 347, p. 215; No. 350, p. 216. For Chinese replies see No. 319, p. 196; No. 325, p. 199; No. 329, p. 201; No. 334, pp. 203-4; No. 340, pp. 207-10.

286. *A and P,* Cd. 5240 (1910), No. 222, p. 141.

287. Rockhill, "The Dalai Lamas," *T'oung Pao,* XL (1910), 91; *CASJ,* XI, Part I, 48.

288. Tancred Borenius, *Field Marshal Mannerheim,* pp. 38, 51-55; C. G. Mannerheim, *Across Asia,* I, 692-95.

289. Reel S 656, *Chibetto mondai oyobi jijô kankei zassan,* S 1. 6-1. 3-4. A report on Tibetan affairs submitted by Bunkyo Aoki, in September, 1944. Bunkyo Aoki is the author of *Chibetto bunka no shin-kenkyû* (A New Study of the Tibetan Culture).

290. *A and P,* Cd. 5240, No. 260, p. 165; also No. 80, p. 46; No. 253, p. 161. Note: The British Blue-book did not mention any Japanese contact with the Dalai Lama either prior to his arrival, or during his stay, at Peking.

291. *Ibid.,* No. 279, p. 176; also No. 74, pp. 43-44.

292. *Ibid.,* No. 324, p. 198.

293. Russian claims to North Manchuria had the approval of Japan in the secret portion of the Treaty of July 30, 1907, and in the Convention of 1910.

294. *Supra,* n. 278. Ernest B. Price, *The Russo-Japanese Treaties of 1907-1916 concerning Manchuria and Mongolia* (1933), pp. 61-64; Edward H. Zabriskie, *American Russian Rivalry in the Far East* (1946), pp. 173-74. Note: Mongolia was then intriguing with Russia for a separation move. *Infra* Ch. V, n. 10.

295. *A and P,* Cd. 5240, No. 302, p. 189; see No. 312, p. 194, for the Dalai Lama's communication with the British Representative in Peking.

296. *Ibid.,* No. 311, p. 193. The Dalai Lama told the British political officer when he arrived in Sikkim that he came to India for the purpose of asking the help of the British Government against the Chinese. (No. 328, p. 200.)

297. *Ibid.,* No. 337, pp. 206-7.

298. *Ibid.,* Nos. 349 and 352, pp. 215-17.

299. *Documents des archives des gouvernements impérial et provisoire 1878-1917* (in Russian), Series II, 1900-1913, Vol. 18, No. 140, p. 152; *supra,* Chap. III, n. 219.

300. *A and P,* Cd. 5240 (1910), No. 302, p. 190; No. 354, p. 218; and *supra,* p. 114.

301. *Documents des archives des gouvernements impérial et provisoire,* Series II, Vol. 18, No. 106, pp. 114-15. The letter reached its destination in March, 1911.

302. *Ibid.,* No. 122, p. 132; No. 140, pp. 151-53. The Russian Gov-

ernment once had the intention of informing the British of the Dalai Lama's letter in a modified form.

303. *Ibid.,* No. 147, pp. 160-61.

304. *Ibid.,* Series II, Vol. 19, No. 544, pp. 193-97. The Russian Consul-General, in making the report to the Russian Foreign Office, remarked that the Dalai Lama was not really pro-British and that the British design to put Tibet sooner or later within their own orbit was but an open secret. Cf. Bell, *Portrait of the Dalai Lama,* pp. 117-18. The Japanese Foreign Office Archives, 3 1. 6. 1. 3-4, made a revelation of similar nature. It records that in 1910 the Japanese Government sent Bunkyo Aoki (*supra,* n. 289) to see the Dalai Lama in India. He succeeded in escaping the notice of the British authorities and reached an understanding with the Lama on exchange of scholars and "peace envoys." In 1911, in accordance with this understanding, a Tibetan priest was sent to Japan as a peace envoy, and concurrently Bunkyo Aoki was sent to Tibet on a similar mission "to study Buddhism."

305. *Documents des archives des gouvernements impérial et provisoire,* Series II, Vol. 20, Part 1; No. 228, pp. 220-21.

Chapter V: Tibet under the Republican Regime

1. *A and P,* Cd. 5240 (1910), No. 347, p. 125; No. 350, p. 216; Lu Hsing-chi's manuscript, *Hsi-tsang chiao shê chi yao,* I, 46a-b; *WCSL* (Hsüan-t'ung period), Vol. 17, pp. 41a-b; Vol. 20, p. 31.

2. *A and P,* Cd. 5240, No. 345, p. 213; No. 347, p. 215. Note that in both the Adhesion Convention of 1906 and the Trade Regulations of 1908 there is no provision that China should exercise only suzerain, not sovereign, rights in Tibet; China was not a party to the Anglo-Russian Convention of 1907 which recognizes the suzerain rights of China in Tibet.

3. British Foreign Office, *Peace Handbooks,* No. 70, "Tibet," pp. 40-41.

4. Teichman, *Travels in Eastern Tibet,* pp. 41-42.

5. *Supra,* Chap. IV, n. 285, and also pp. 114, 127, 129.

6. Lu Hsing-chi, *Hsi-tsang chiao shê chi yao,* II, 1b-2a.

7. *Ibid.,* pp. 4b-5a; *Tsang an chi lüeh* (a document on Tibet in the Wai-chiao-pu [Chinese Foreign Office] archives), Part II, p. 1; Bell, *Tibet,* p. 149; *North China Herald,* Sept. 7, 1912, p. 686; *Tung fan tsa chih,* Vol. IX, No. 4, p. 16.

8. *The Japan Weekly Chronicle,* Sept. 12, 1912, p. 473, reported that the Peking correspondent of the Asahi had inquired concerning the views of the United States Legation and learned that the United States had no interests in Tibet. According to the Anglo-Chinese Treaty, however, it was thought there was no reason why the Chinese troops could not enter Tibet.

9. *North China Herald,* Nov. 30, 1912, pp. 569-70; Dec. 21, 1912, pp. 821-22. Wu Chao-chu was a noted lawyer and diplomat. At the time of writing his pamphlet on the Tibetan issue he was not in government service.

10. *A and P,* Cd. 6604 (1913), No. 1, pp. 2-3; No. 2, pp. 3-6. For documental evidence of the Russian activities in Mongolia see "Tsarist Russia and Mongolia in 1913-14," trans. from Krasnyi Arkhiv, XXXVII, 15-68, *The Chinese Social and Political Science Review,* XVI, 652-88; XVII, 170-205.

11. *The Japan Weekly Chronicle,* May 16, 1912, pp. 872-73; Sept. 12, 1912, p. 473.

12. At the outbreak of the revolution, the Imperial Government was facing bankruptcy (facing an annual deficit variously estimated at from twenty to seventy million taels); the new Republican Government found itself in even greater financial difficulties. For details about the advances and loans, see T. W. Overlach, *Foreign Financial Control in China* (1919), pp. 236-66.

13. *The Times,* Sept. 18, 1912, p. 3c; *North China Herald,* Nov. 23, 1912, p. 526. The correspondence of Yuan Shih-kai, I, 11-12; Teichman, *Travels in Eastern Tibet,* p. 39; Bell, *The Religion of Tibet,* pp. 191-92. Yuan did not apologize but acknowledged the wrong done to the Dalai Lama by the Resident Lien-yü who, he added, had been dismissed from his post pending a trial.

14. Lu Hsing-chi, *Hsi-tsang chiao shê chi yao,* II, 5b-6a.

15. *Tsang an chi lüeh,* Part II, p. 2; *Tung fan tsa chih,* Vol. IX, No. 8, p. 6.

16. Bell, *Portrait of the Dalai Lama,* p. 345; Bell, *Tibet,* pp. 151-52. The Dalai Lama and the Tibetan Government later denied that Dorjieff's credentials justified anything in the nature of a treaty.

17. *Tung fan tsa chih,* Vol. IX, No. 9, p. 1; *China Year Book,* 1921-22, p. 62.

18. Bell, *Tibet,* p. 229.

19. Lu Hsing-chi, *Hsi-tsang chiao shê chi yao,* II, 6a.

20. *Hsi-tsang wên t'i chih chin hsi* (another document on Tibet in the Wai-chiao-pu archives), p. 3; see the *Far Eastern Review,* Jan. 13, 1913, p. 350.

21. Teichman, *Travels in Eastern Tibet,* p. 44.

22. *The Times,* March 29, 1913, p. 7c; *North China Herald,* July 20, 1912, p. 117.

23. *Supra,* p. 115, and Chap. IV, nn. 247 and 248.

24. Some Chinese books on Tibet, e.g., Hsieh Pin, *Hsi-tsang chiao shê lüeh shih* (A Short Diplomatic History concerning Tibet) (4th ed., 1933), p. 46; Hua Ch'i yün, *Hsi-tsang wên t'i,* p. 219; and also Lu Hsing-chi, *Hsi-tsang chiao shê chi yao,* II, 7a, give the date as November 13. Shih Ch'ing-yang's manuscript, *Tsang shih chi yao,* Chap. IV, p. 13b (written in 1933 when the author was the Chairman of the

Commission for Mongolian and Tibetan Affairs), relates that the preliminary meeting opened in November. Teichman (p. 44) mentions that the tripartite conference met towards the close of 1913. The date given by the writer as well as some of the accounts below are based upon the notes he took from the archives of the Chinese Foreign Office in 1941. Bell, then adviser to the British delegate at the Conference, writes of the meeting as opened in October, 1913 (*Tibet,* p. 154), in the autumn of 1913 (*Portrait of the Dalai Lama,* p. 204); *The Times* reported on Oct. 14, 1913, p. 7c, that the meeting had opened on the previous day.

25. What the Dalai Lama asked for was not necessarily the criterion of independence as known to students of political science (e.g., Walter Holmes Ritscher, *Criteria of Capacity for Independence* [Jerusalem, 1934]). He wanted "Tibet to manage her own internal affairs." See Bell, *Tibet,* p. 152; *Portrait of the Dalai Lama,* p. 205.

26. *CASJ,* IX (1924), Part III, 201-2.

27. *Ibid.,* p. 188. Even Sir Charles Bell conceded that some of the districts claimed by the Tibetan delegate had been brought under Chinese control during the last two hundred years. (*Tibet,* p. 152.)

28. *Tsang an chi lüeh,* pp. 3-4; Lu Hsing-chi, *Hsi-tsang chiao shê chi yao,* II, 7a-8a.

29. *Supra,* Chap. III, n. 223. For details about the boundary issue, see Hu Chi-lu, *Hsi-k'ang chiang yü shou ku lu* ("A Historical Study of the Boundary of Sikang") (Shanghai, 1928).

30. Bell, *Tibet,* pp. 305-6, gives the text of the agreement. The Chinese text is given in the *Chung Ying Chung-O kuan yü Hsi-tsang Meng-ku yo chang ho pien* (Treaties between China, Great Britain and Russia concerning Mongolia and Tibet), published by the Mongolian and Tibetan Affairs Commission.

31. For details see Hsieh Pin, *Hsi-tsang chiao shê lüeh shih,* pp. 49-51.

32. According to Lu Hsing-chi (*Hsi-tsang chiao shê chi yao,* II, 13b), besides the loss of a part of Szechwan and Ch'inghai, a small slice of the territory in the Yünnan, Kansu, and Sinkiang (Chinese Turkestan) provinces were also enclosed within the line drawn as the boundary of Tibet.

33. *Tsang an chi lüeh,* p. 20.

34. Refer to *supra,* Chap. IV, n. 239.

35. *Supra,* p. 98, and Chap. IV, n. 171.

36. *Tsang an chi lüeh,* pp. 5-16.

37. Chen's telegraphic report to the Chinese Foreign Office, *Tsang an chi lüeh,* p. 21; Hsieh Pin, *Hsi-tsang chiao shê lüeh shih,* p. 51.

38. *Tsang an chi lüeh,* p. 22.

39. The British notes, dated June 2 and 25, warned China of the consequences of denying herself the rights accorded by this conven-

tion, and nullifying all the previous treaties entered into between China and Great Britain, and between Great Britain and Tibet, and went so far as to say that the British Government would be obliged to render substantial help to the Tibetan Government against any aggression from whatsoever source. The further Chinese concessions were made on June 13 and 29. *Tsang an chi lüeh,* pp. 23-26. For some details see Hung Ti-chên, *Hsi-tsang shih ti ta kang* (An Outline of the History and Geography of Tibet.) (henceforth cited as Hung Ti-chên), pp. 220-22.

40. Bell, *Portrait of the Dalai Lama,* p. 206. We may assume from Bell's account that the Dalai Lama did not ratify these Simla documents, as Bell wrote that he was dissatisfied with his delegate's conduct of negotiations and not fully satisfied with the Simla Treaty. For details of the new trade treaty see British Foreign Office, *Peace Handbooks,* No. 70, pp. 72-73. It is significant too that neither the so-called Simla Treaty nor the new trade treaty is to be found among the comprehensive collection entitled *Treaties, Engagements and Sanads Relating to India and Neighboring Countries,* compiled by C. U. Aitchison, 5th ed., revised, and continued to 1929 by the authority of the Foreign and Political Department. Cf. Oppenheim (7th ed. by H. Lauterpacht), p. 233, n. 8. MacMurray's *Treaties and Agreements with and concerning China,* p. 582, quotes *Statesman's Year Book, 1916,* p. 805, saying, "the convention and exchanges of notes signed by the British and Tibetan representatives on July 3rd, 1914, have not yet been officially made public". *Infra,* nn. 53 and 55.

41. *Supra,* pp. 112-13, 124, and Chap. IV, nn. 238 and 283, and also *Parliamentary Debates,* Vol. 184, pp. 492-93.

42. *Parliamentary Debates,* 1914, LXIV, 1447-48.

43. Griswold, *The Far Eastern Policy of the United States,* p. 99.

44. Hsieh Pin, *Hsi-tsang chiao shê lüeh shih,* p. 52; Bell, *Portrait of the Dalai Lama,* p. 205.

45. Sir Ernest Satow, *A Guide to Diplomatic Practice* (3rd ed., rev. by H. Richie, 1932), § 570, 571, 573, 719, and 720.

46. Charles Cheney Hyde, *International Law Chiefly as Interpreted and Applied by the United States* (1945), II, 1430.

47. John Westlake, *International Law* (1910), I, 291.

48. Oppenheim, *International Law* (7th ed. by H. Lauterpacht), p. 797. It is further stated that although a treaty is concluded as soon as the mutual consent is manifest from acts of the duly authorized representatives, its binding force is, as a rule, suspended till ratification is given (p. 813). See also William Edward Hall, *A Treatise on International Law* (8th ed., 1924), p. 385, which says: ". . . tacit or express ratification by the supreme treaty-making power of the state is necessary to its validity."

49. Hyde, *International Law,* II, 1431.

50. Bell, *Tibet,* p. 156.

51. Arnold D. McNair, *The Law of Treaties, British Practice and Opinions,* pp. 83 and 146. *The Harvard Research* (1935), Part III, "Law of Treaties," pp. 799-812, also takes the view that treaties shall become effective from the date of ratification. See also *ibid.,* pp. 769-87, 796-98.

52. Charles Fenwick, *International Law* (3rd ed., 1948), p. 435.

53. Teichman, *Travels in Eastern Tibet,* p. 46. The document, even if duly signed by the British and Tibetan delegates at Simla, would have been void because of Tibet's incapacity arising from status. See McNair, *The Law of Treaties,* p. 135.

54. Lo Chia-lun, for years a professor of history, was appointed as first Chinese ambassador to India when the latter regained her independence. He had remained in that post until India recognized the Peking regime. The revelation was made in his article, "Chieh kai Chung Yin chien yu kuan Hsi-tsang ti Mu" (Raise up the Curtain on the Tibetan Issue in Sino-Indian Relations), *Tzŭ yu chung kuo,* III (Oct., 1950), No. 7, 229-31 and 235.

55. Identical notes were sent to the British Government in London and the Pakistan Government. The first British reply, dated October 29, 1948, states that the matter was being consulted with the Indian and Pakistan Governments. The second British reply, dated May 24, 1949, told the Chinese Government that the matter no longer concerned London and referred the latter to the two Dominions. Note that both replies did not, however, deny the continued validity of the Trade Regulations of 1908. Had there been a valid instrument like the alleged Anglo-Tibetan Treaty or Anglo-Tibetan Trade Regulations which were supposed to have replaced the previous trade regulations, the British Government would have denied their continued validity. *Supra,* n. 40. The Pakistan reply, dated January 6, 1949, expressed its willingness to take up the matter with a view to concluding a new treaty in regard to Tibet.

56. In his article cited *supra,* n. 54, Ambassador Lo, in relating the last phase of his mission, especially acclaimed the fact of having delivered this note.

57. *Documents des archives des gouvernements impérial et provisoire 1878-1917,* Series III, 1914-17, Vol. 1, p. 500, No. 384.

58. *Ibid.,* p. 515, No. 396.

59. *Ibid.,* p. 565, No. 430.

60. Hsieh Pin, *Hsi-tsang chiao shê lüeh shih,* pp. 59-61.

61. Bell, *Tibet,* p. 164. The Tibetan army band played "God Save the King" (not intended as a national anthem) at the reception given in honor of the Chairman of the Commission for Mongolian and Tibetan Affairs, Wu Chung-hsin (Chu Shao-i, *La-sa chien wên chi,* p. 44), and also played the same tune in the presence of Lowell Thomas

in 1949. ("Out of This World: A Journey to Lhasa," *Collier's*, Feb. 25, 1950, p. 36.) See also Hsieh Pin, *Hsi-tsang chiao shê lüeh shih*, p. 78.

62. For details see Teichman, *Travels in Eastern Tibet*, pp. 51-58 *et seq*.

63. For the full text of the two documents see Hsieh Pin, *Hsi-tsang chiao shê lüeh shih*, pp. 64-67.

64. *Ibid.*, p. 69; *Tsang an chi lüeh*, p. 38. Note that Lord Curzon was then the Foreign Secretary.

65. *Tsang an chi lüeh*, p. 40; Lu Hsing-chi, *Hsi-tsang chiao shê chi yao*, II, 27a-b.

66. *Hsi-tsang chiao shê chi yao*, pp. 28a-30a.

67. He saw the Prime Minister on August 27 and had an audience with the President, Hsü Shih-chang, on September 4; in London, the British Foreign Minister, Lord Curzon, protested orally to the Chinese Minister, Alfred Sze. *Ibid.*, p. 27b; *Tsang an chi lüeh*, pp. 42-43.

68. *Tsang an chi lüeh*, p. 43; *Hung Ti-chên*, pp. 237-38.

69. *Hsi-tsang wên t'i chih chin hsi*, p. 4, records that the British Minister expressed his willingness to persuade the Tibetans to accept the Chinese proposal of May 30, 1919 (it was to this proposal that the British presented the above-mentioned counterproposal, *supra*, p. 145), but apparently the Chinese Government had adopted by then a stronger stand and declined to reopen negotiations on a once-rejected proposal.

70. Hung Ti-chên, pp. 238-40; Bell, *Tibet*, p. 202.

71. Hung Ti-chên, p. 241.

72. Bell was sent "to explain the present political position" which he found "tangled and unpromising" and to counteract the Chinese mission which stayed in Lhasa from January to April in 1920, and which "considerably augmented" Chinese influence in the Tibetan capital. (All words in quotations are Sir Charles's; see *Tibet*, pp. 176-77 and *supra*, n. 90.) He reached Lhasa on November 17, 1920. His arrival was, as he called it, "opportune" in that it frustrated the further progress of a mission headed by the Commissioner of Ili of Chinese Turkestan who came "to negotiate on behalf of China with the Tibetan Government in order to bring Tibet back to the Chinese fold and to oust British influence from the country." (*Tibet*, p. 183.) During his stay he had frequent private conversations with the Dalai Lama which "ranged over a wide variety of subjects" and discussed plans for increasing the Tibetan army. (*Portrait of the Dalai Lama*, pp. 249-53.) It was these plans of his that aroused strong opposition among the priesthood and led to unsuccessful outbreaks while he was there. (*Tibet*, pp. 187-89.) Upon his return to New Delhi (he left Lhasa on October 19, 1921) he worked out with the Indian Foreign Department the details of a new policy to be adopted toward Tibet

which consisted of seven main items. (*Portrait of the Dalai Lama,* pp. 241-43; *Tibet,* pp. 193-95.) Every one of his proposals was accepted by the British Government. (*Tibet,* p. 197.) His only disagreement with the Foreign Secretary was in the selection of the expert who would prospect for minerals in Tibet. (*Portrait of the Dalai Lama,* p. 342; *Parliamentary Debates,* 1922, Vol. 156, p. 1461.) It is noteworthy that since Bell's mission, five hundred to a thousand more men were recruited yearly to be trained by British officers at Gyantse and the British Government allowed an import of munitions from India. (*Portrait of the Dalai Lama,* p. 252.) In July, 1922, construction of telegraphic communications between Lhasa and India was completed. (*The Times,* August 10, 1922, p. 7.) An English school was established at Gyantse in 1923 with a view to facilitating British activities in Tibet through educational means. (Spencer F. Chapman, *Lhasa the Holy City,* 1939, p. 109.) This school, like the telegraphic line between Gyantse and Lhasa, was suggested by Sir Charles in his seven-item new policy.

73. *Supra,* pp. 106-8, and Chap. IV, nn. 212, 214, 215, 216.

74. *Supra,* p. 113, and Chap. IV, nn. 240, 241.

75. Ho Tsao-hsiang, *Tsang yü,* pp. 26-27.

76. Bell, *Tibet,* pp. 83-84.

77. A David-Neel, "Tibetan Border Intrigue," *Asia,* XLI (May, 1941), 219.

78. The Panch'en Lama committed the mistake of letting his retinue beat their drums on passing the Potala and was thereby fined 990 taels by the Dalai Lama. This was cited by some Chinese books as the origin of their ill-feeling.

79. Ma Ho-t'ien, *Kan Ch'ing Tsang pien ch'ü k'ao ch'a chi* (A Study of the Frontier Districts of Kansu, Ch'inghai, and Tibet) (Shanghai, 1947), Part III, pp. 548-55, compares the position of the Dalai and the Panch'en and gives a detailed account of the causes and the development of their rift.

80. David Macdonald, *Twenty Years in Tibet,* pp. 100-101, states that two dismissed officials of the Panch'en Lama who went over to Lhasa and wielded considerable influence in the Potala were responsible for a great deal of trouble between the Grand Lamas. Cf. Clark, *Tibet, China and Great Britain,* p. 46.

81. *The China Year Book,* 1933, p. 215.

82. Bell, *Portrait of the Dalai Lama,* p. 127, says that the Dalai Lama was pro-British and pro-Russian, but anti-Chinese; the Panch'en Lama was pro-British, but anti-Lhasa. See also Bell, *Tibet,* p. 225.

83. *Supra,* Chap. IV, n. 304.

84. When Lung-shar was imprisoned and made blind in May, 1934, the Chinese press reported that his punishment was due to his pro-British activities. The writer then had a hunch that it was not the

case. When Wu Chung-hsin, the Chairman of the Commission for Mongolian and Tibetan Affairs, was in Lhasa in 1939 to preside at the coronation of the 14th Dalai Lama, Lung-shar presented a bronze Buddha as a token of his respects. Wu sent his secretary, Chu Shao-i, to thank him. The latter had a lengthy talk with the blind man, who had only been released from prison in the previous year. From the talk (Chu Shao-i, *La-sa chien wên chi* [1947], pp. 91-95), we can see that he was a patriot with pro-Chinese leanings. No wonder Sir Charles called him markedly anti-British. Lung-shar is still labeled as pro-British by some Chinese writers. The pamphlet entitled *Shih shih shou ts'ê* (Handbook on Current Events), No. 16, p. 33, published by the Chinese Communist organ, made the same mistake.

85. *The Times,* Oct. 9, 1924, p. 13, gives an unconfirmed report that he and Macdonald were besieged in Lhasa.

86. All the quotations in this paragraph are taken from Bell, *Portrait of the Dalai Lama,* p. 366; the rest is based upon Pai Mei-chu, *Hsi-tsang shih mu chih yao* (Peiping, 1930), Chap. 4, pp. 52-53.

87. For the full texts of the petitions submitted by both sides, see Hung Ti-chên, pp. 258-66; the author copied them from the archives of the Mongolian and Tibetan Affairs Commission.

88. Shih Ch'ing-yang's manuscript, *Tsang shih chi yao,* Chap. 1, p. 9b.

89. Cf. Bell. *Portrait of the Dalai Lama,* pp. 135, 360.

90. *Supra* n. 72. Sir Charles Bell does not believe that the mission was purely from the government of Kansu (*Portrait of the Dalai Lama,* p. 217). From the Chinese Government archives the writer finds no evidence to justify his doubt. The mission was merely a provincial move, though it had to be, and in fact was, reported to the central government.

91. Shih Ch'ing-yang's manuscript, pp. 9b-10a.

92. Tun-chu-wang-chieh's arrival in 1924 is mentioned in Shih Ch'ing-yang's manuscript. His mission in 1922 is mentioned in *Hsi-tsang wên t'i chih chin hsi,* p. 4.

93. *CASJ,* XI (1924), Part III, 188. But in concluding his speech, he gave "a final croak" in these words: "Let us not to be too confident that Chinese control in Tibet has passed away for ever. . . . I cannot think that a great and populous nation will quietly for ever be shut out entirely from a region which they have controlled for centuries."

94. *Supra,* n. 86.

95. Bell, *Tibet,* p. 208.

96. *The Times,* April 22, 1929, p. 14.

97. C. Y. W. Meng, "Miss Liu's Mission to Tibet," *China Weekly Review,* LIV (Sept. 6, 1930), 22. Official documents in connection with Miss Liu's mission are given in her book, *K'ang Tsang yao chêng* (My Mission to Tibet and Sikang).

98. Bell, "Tibet's Position in Asia Today," *Foreign Affairs,* X (October, 1931), 143.

99. Liu Man-ch'ing, *K'ang Tsang yao chêng* (Shanghai, 1933), pp. 95-97.

100. *Ibid.,* pp. 118-19.

101. *Ibid.,* pp. 119-20.

102. *Ibid.,* pp. 120 and 121. Nepal was then threatening Tibet with the use of force as the result of some commercial dispute. According to a telegraphic report of Kung-chüeh-chung-ni sent from Gyantse and received on February 16, "Nepalese government ordered on Jan. 26th mobilization of 9,000 troops. Tibet preparing for armed resistance." In this report Kung-chüeh-chung-ni explained that the Nepalese move was perhaps motivated by jealousy of Sino-Tibetan rapprochement (while some Chinese writers ascribed it to British manipulation behind the scenes, e.g., Hung Ti-chên, pp. 246-49) and appealed to the Chinese Government for immediate counter-measures. The Commission for Mongolian and Tibetan Affairs thereupon, with the approval of the supreme authorities, dispatched Hsieh Kuo-liang to Tibet and Pa Wen-chun to Nepal for the purpose of mediation. The former started his journey in May and died in November only a short distance from Lhasa. (Bell, *Portrait of the Dalai Lama,* p. 368, mentions the death of a Chinese representative in 1931 and adds, "His body was brought to Lhasa and the Dalai Lama himself is said to have performed the funeral ceremony." The year should be 1930.) The latter reached the Nepalese capital and was warmly received. He brought back presents intended for the Chinese Government. For details, see Shih Ch'ing-yang's manuscript, pp. 12b-13a, and the archives of the said Commission.

103. Shih Ch'ing-yang's manuscript, Chap. I, p. 10b.

104. Bell, *Portrait of the Dalai Lama,* p. 368.

105. Shih Ch'ing-yang's manuscript, Chap. I, pp. 11a-12b. The Chinese official translation of the Tibetan text of this document is taken word for word from the archives of the Mongolian and Tibetan Affairs Commission, to which Shih, as Chairman of the Commission, naturally had full access. As to the tutor-disciple relationship between the two Grand Lamas, Fa-tsun, a Chinese monk who spent nine years studying Buddhism in Sikang and Tibet, relates as follows: The fourth Panch'en (1567-1662) was the tutor to the fifth Dalai (1617-82), while the fifth Panch'en (1663-1737) was the fifth Dalai's disciple, and the tutor to the sixth (1683-1707) and the seventh (1708-57) Dalais. The sixth Panch'en (1738-78) was the seventh Dalai's disciple, and from there on the two Grand Lamas have always been either tutor or disciple to each other. (Fa-tsun, *Hsien tai Hsi-tsang* [1943], p. 110.) According to Shih Ch'ing-yang's manuscript (Chap. II, p. 3b), the second Dalai (1476-1543) was a disciple of the second Panch'en (1439-

1504). The dates cited here for the Dalai and Panch'en Lamas are based upon *ibid.*, pp. 3b-6b, 9a-b, 10b-11b.

106. *Ibid.*, pp. 10b-11a; *Mêng Tsang chou pao* (The Mongolian and Tibetan Weekly), LXI (Feb. 23, 1931), 9.

107. *North China Herald,* August 12, 1930, p. 230. The Dalai Lama sent an additional representative with a view to participating in a conference which had been suggested but never took place.

108. *Supra,* Chap. III, n. 232.

109. For the text of the correspondence, see Lu Hsing-chi's manuscript, II, 78a-81a.

110. *Supra,* nn. 102 and 107.

111. Shih Ch'ing-yang's manuscript, Chap. I, p. 13a.

112. *Ibid.*, pp. 17a-18a.

113. Here the drafter deliberately used the same term as stipulated in the *Li fan pu tsê li* of the Ch'ing dynasty.

114. The following account is based mainly on the report of T'ang Ko-san who was sent to the spot for mediation. The report is kept on file in the Mongolian and Tibetan Affairs Commission.

115. Liu Wen-hui, *Chung kuo tui Tsang chih hsin chêng ts'ê* (1946), pp. 65-66. Liu's story is a bit different. He described the extremely strained relations between the Ta-chieh monastery and the Chinese garrisons existing since 1918. According to Liu, it was a dispute between the monastery and the chieftain of Pei-li over the "Ula" or transport service that led to the sudden attack on, and immediate occupation of, Pei-li.

116. See the telegrams of the Dalai Lama dated November 14 and December 28, quoted in Shih Ch'ing-yang's manuscript, Chap. V, pp. 1b-2a. In the meantime, the National Government, accepting the request of the Dalai Lama for cessation of hostilities, issued orders to Liu to stop fighting. Liu reported (telegrams dated the 4th and 19th of December) that despite his compliance with the orders, the Ta-chieh monks, backed by the reinforced Tibetan troops, had renewed the attack. The Dalai Lama, however, categorically denied this.

117. The ex-commander at Ba-t'ang who signed the truce in August, 1918, with Teichman acting as middleman. *Supra,* n. 62, and p. 144.

118. According to Liu's telegraphic report, dated June 1, 1931, received by the Commission for Mongolian and Tibetan Affairs on June 6.

119. *Supra,* p. 62, and Chap. III, n. 200. Nyarong was later taken by Chao Erh-feng in the summer of 1911. See Teichman, *Travels in Eastern Tibet,* pp. 32-33.

120. According to T'ang's telegraphic reports dated June 23 and 24.

121. Liu Wen-hui, *Chung kao tui Tsang chih hsin chêng ts'ê,* p. 66, mentions the Dalai Lama's telegram claiming Kanze and Nyarong, but mistakenly gives the date as in August.

122. *New York Times*, Sept. 12, 1932, p. 1, col. 2, reports a wide Tibetan drive eastward with British aid; *China Weekly Review*, LXI (July 23, 1932), 282, mentions an alleged Anglo-Tibetan secret agreement.

123. *China Weekly Review*, LXVII (Dec. 30, 1933), 204; see also Hung Ti-chên, p. 251.

124. (Reel S 656) S 1.6.1.3-4. On January 10, 1927, K. Yoshizawa, Japanese Minister to China, reported to the Japanese Foreign Office that the British Government was trying to assist the newly organized Tibetan army, and was ready to concede to the Tibetan request to levy taxes on the border trade between Tibet and India. On August 30, 1929, Major Usuda, Military Attaché to the Japanese Embassy in Nanking, reported to the Vice Chief of General Staff that the Tibetan army, under the leadership of British officers, advanced across the western border of Szechwan Province. On a date not given, the military officer at Shanghai, attached to the Japanese Embassy, reported to the Vice Minister of War that the British Government was supporting the Dalai Lama in establishing a Great Tibet Kingdom and in trying to occupy Ch'inghai, Scechwan border territory, and Yünnan; on September 24, 1932, the Military Attaché to the Japanese Embassy in Nanking reported to his Vice Minister of War saying that "judging from all news available, Tibet is at present attempting to expand her sphere of influence with British support" and that "no doubt there is a great deal of support of British imperialism behind the Tibetans' . . . dream of building a 'Great Tibet Kingdom' by regaining their lost lands"; on May 31, 1933, A. Ariyoshi, Japanese Minister to China, reported to K. Uchida, the Japanese Foreign Minister, that according to the information furnished by Tokan Tada, a professor of the Tohoku Imperial University, Sendai, who had been sent to Tibet to study Buddhism by the late Sonyu Otani, ex-Colonial Minister, and stayed there for twelve years, "the Tibetan government was trying to organize new troops to oppose the Chinese army who had recaptured Nyarong, Kanze, and De-ge; and though the British government was now prepared for the conflict, the Tibetan government expressed the wish that Japan, a brotherly Buddhistic nation, should check the Chinese power and prevent Chinese troops from being stationed in Tibet."

125. It is known to the outside world that some Japanese were there to help train the Tibetan army when the latter was formed after the Chinese garrison had been forced out as a result of the Chinese Revolution. (See report of J. Nobuo, Japanese Consul-General at Calcutta, to K. Kato, Foreign Minister, in the Japanese Foreign Office's archives [Reel 126, T 1.6.1.4-7 Kakkoku naisei kankei zassan. Shina: Chibetto, Shinkyô], which says that "the Tibetan army are building fortresses here and there, and training soldiers under the leadership of Japanese,

Mongolian, and Tibetan officers." See also Bell, *Tibet,* pp. 220-21, and Lai Tze-sheng, *Le Probleme thibetain,* pp. 173-74.) It is also known to the outside world that the Tibetans got arms and munitions from British India and the British Armed Mission of 1903-4 captured some Russian-made rifles from the Tibetans. (See *A and P,* Cd. 2370 (1905), No. 17, p. 8, and enclosure No. 85, p. 135, and also Younghusband, *India and Tibet,* p. 320, for rifles of American manufacture found to be in Tibetan possession.) But the outside world was kept in the dark about the Japanese secret dealings with the Tibetans in regard to the selling of arms and munitions. Here is the telegraphic report of Sakai, the Japanese Consul-General at Shanghai, to K. Uchida, the Japanese Foreign Minister, dated September 28, 1932. "In 1921, in India, our General Headquarters had contracts with the Tibetan Government to sell arms and munitions for the purpose of their defense, a part of which was recently traded with the following items:

Field artillery	4
Machine guns	8
Rifles	1,500
Shells	1,000
Bullets	1,000,000
Grenades	1,000

It seems to me that the above quantity was less than expected."

126. In May, 1931, the Panch'en Lama came to Nanking. He participated in the National Assembly and discussed Tibetan problems with the government authorities. He was given a new title and a jade seal. For the memorandum he submitted to the Commission for Mongolian and Tibetan Affairs, see Shih Ch'ing-yang's manuscript, Chap. I, pp. 13a-14a; for the proposal he submitted to the Western Defense Conference summoned by the General Staff, see Hung Tichên, p. 268.

127. *Supra,* n. 87.

128. *The Times,* April 30, 1923, p. 11c; *China Critic,* Vol. 7, No. 24, p. 558.

129. *Supra,* p. 148.

130. *North China Herald,* July 4, 1934. See also Lêng Liang, "Hsitsang wên t'i chih chên hsiang chi ch'i chieh chüeh fang fa" (Tibetan Problem, Its Facts and Solution), *Tung fang tsa chih,* Vol. 31, No. 9, pp. 22-23.

131. Manifesto issued by the First Plenary Session of Kuomintang held at Canton in 1924; *San Min Chu I,* translated into English by Frank W. Price, pp. 132-33, 146-47.

132. Hung Chün-p'ei, *Kuo min chêng fu wai chiao shih* (Diplomatic Records of the National Government) (1930), I, 86-104 (ed.).

133. *Ibid.,* pp. 139-64. They demanded apologies, indemnity, and

punishment of those responsible for the incident, while refusing to compensate the losses sustained by the Chinese army and civilians as a result of the shelling of the city by their gunboats.

134. *Ibid.,* pp. 165-94.

135. Besides fighting with the Communist insurgents and engaging in a local war with the U.S.S.R. (July-Dec., 1929, in Manchuria), the following is a list of armed conflicts which broke out among the Nationalist Forces' own ranks. Oct.-Nov., 1927, vs. Gen, T'ang Sheng-chih in Hankow, Chia I-chün, *Chung hua min kuo shih* (Political History of the Chinese Republic) (1930), pp. 198-99; Nov.-Dec., 1927, vs. Gen. Chang Fa-k'uei in Canton, *ibid.,* pp. 202-6; February, 1929, Gen. Li Tsung-jên vs. Gen. Lu Ti-p'ing in Hunan, *ibid.,* pp. 231-32; March-April, 1929, vs. Kwangsi generals in Hupel, *ibid.,* pp. 233-38; May, 1929, latter generals to force Gen. Fèng Yü-hsiang to resign, *ibid.,* pp. 248-51; Sept., 1929, Gen. Chang Fa-k'uei's second anti-Chiang move joined by Gen. Yu Tso-pei in Kwangsi and caused uprising of Gen. Fang Chên-wu's troops in Anhui, *ibid.,* pp. 262-66; Oct.-Nov., 1929, vs. Gen. Fêng Yü-hsiang's followers in Honan and Hupeh, *ibid.,* pp. 269-70; Nov.-Dec., 1929, vs. combined force of Gens. Chang Fa-k'uei and Li Tsung-jên in Kwangtung, *ibid.,* 266-67; Dec., 1929, rebellion of Gen. Shih Yu-san at Pukow, *ibid.,* pp. 271-72; Dec., 1929-Jan., 1930, Gen. T'ang Shêng-chih's second anti-Chiang move in Honan, *ibid.,* pp. 272-75. Note: the above list does not include the local incidents which occurred in Yünnan, Sinkiang, Manchuria, Inner Mongolia, Szechwan, Kueichow, and Fukien. (For details see *ibid.,* pp. 277-83.)

136. *Travels in Eastern Tibet,* p. 51.

137. Hung Ti-chên, pp. 255-57. The autonomous regime set up without authority from the Central Government was later dissolved when Ke-sang-ts'e-jên was recalled to Nanking.

138. Liu Man-ch'ing, *K'ang Tsang yao chêng,* pp. 162-63. The author was sent in the summer of 1932 to Sikang to make an investigation of the local conditions. She gives here a vivid description of the corruption of Liu's garrisons.

139. Liu's telegram dated September 21, received the same day; T'ang's telegram dated September 6, received on September 25.

140. T'ang's telegraphic report dated November 7, received on November 21, 1931. See Shih Ch'ing-yang's manuscript, Chap. V, p. 6b.

141. Order of approval issued by the Executive Yüan received by the Mongolian and Tibetan Affairs Commission on December 11. For Liu Wên-hui's protest, see *Chung kuo tui Tsang chih hsin chêng ts'ê,* p. 67.

142. Resolution passed at meeting No. 8 of the Executive Yüan held on February 19.

143. Liu's telegraphic report dated April 30; *China Weekly Review,* LXVII (Dec. 30, 1933), 148. The armed conflict between Tibet and Ch'inghai was also caused by a dispute over a monastery. See Ma Ho-t'ien, *Kan Ch'ing Tsang pien ch'ü k'ao ch'a chi,* pp. 297-99. R. A. Stein points out in *Journal Asiatique,* CCXL (1952), 97, that the Tibetan orthography for Jyekundo, the Chinese Yu-shu, is sKye-dgu-mdo, not rGyal-kun-mdo.

144. The report of Liu's representative at Nanking, Leng Yung, to the Mongolian and Tibetan Affairs Commission.

145. Chiang-ch'ia was recovered on May 29 by the militia of Ke-sang-ts'e-jên who, in the face of the Tibetan attack, composed their differences and fought shoulder to shoulder with Liu's troops.

146. The report of the Chinese Consulate-General at Calcutta to Wai-chiao-pu mentioned in the latter's dispatch dated July 22 to the Mongolian and Tibetan Affairs Commission, and also the report of the correspondent K. F. A. of the Mongolian and Tibetan Affairs Commission in India and its investigator at Sikang, kept in the archives of the Commission.

147. *Supra,* n. 87.

148. Shih Ch'ing-yang's manuscript, Chap. V, p. 11b.

149. For the full text see Hung Ti-chên, pp. 270-71.

150. For the full text, *ibid.,* pp. 271-72.

151. It was reported that the lamas' opposition to being drafted into the army became so strong that the Dalai Lama was compelled to leave Lhasa for a while. (*Ibid.,* p. 269.)

152. *The Times,* January 29, 1934, pp. 13f.

153. *Supra,* n. 86, and p. 148.

154. Bell, *Tibet,* p. 214. In this connection, these words of Sir Charles are noteworthy: "There is undoubtedly a pro-Chinese party in Tibet among the officials, the priests, and the people. . . . The pro-Chinese element in Tibet should not be underestimated, but if money can be found to pay for an increased army, the Dalai Lama and the Tibetan Government should be able to control the priests. And the gradual improvement in the Tibetan officers will probably remove the occasional discontent among the peasantry." (*Ibid.,* pp. 214-15.)

155. For more information see Harry Paxton Howard, "Dalai Lama's Death Brings Crisis to Tibet," *China Weekly Review,* LXVII (Jan. 27, 1934), 341-42; and also *ibid.,* pp. 368-70; *New York Times,* April 22, 1934, Sec. 4, p. 8, col. 3.

156. *The Times,* March 3, 1934, p. 12b.

157. *Mêng Tsang hsün k'an,* Nos. 78-79, March 20, 1937, p. 7; *Chung yang jih pao* (Central Daily News), Feb. 7, 1934, p. 1. This sudden pro-Chinese move finds an explanation not only in the natural affinity and the long connection between China and Tibet, as

Sir Charles remarked (*Tibet,* p. 214), but also in the current situation when the priests needed Chinese backing to counterbalance the British-backed army group. The Dalai Lama's manifesto to his people, issued in May, 1932, in which, among other things, he emphasized that "Tibet is Chinese territory having close relations with the Chinese people," greatly helped in cultivating the subsequent pro-Chinese tendencies. For details about this manifesto, see *China Weekly Review,* LXVII (Dec. 30, 1933), 204.

158. *The Times,* Feb. 9, 1934, p. 13a; Chên Chien-fu, *Hsi-tsang wên ti* (1937), p. 40.

159. *Shen pao nien chien,* 1935, Sec. D, p. 59; *China Weekly Review,* LXVII (Feb. 3, 1934), 369; Hung Ti-chên, p. 272.

160. *Ibid.,* p. 273.

161. *Mêng Tsang hsün k'an,* No. 181, April 20, 1934, p. 5.

162. Shih Yin, "Da-lai shih shih hou chih K'ang Tsang chiu fên" (Sikang-Tibetan Conflicts after the Dalai Lama's Death), *Tung fang tsa chih* (April 16, 1934), XXXI, No. 8, 129-30.

163. Hung Ti-chên, pp. 273-74.

164. *K'ang Tsang ch'ien fêng,* No. 8, April 5, 1934, p. 99.

165. *China Weekly Review,* LXVIII (April 21, 1934), 297; *North China Herald,* April 18, 1934, p. 54.

166. Chung Chün, "Hsi-tsang chün shih chuang k'uang" (The Military Situation in Tibet), *K'ang tao* (semi-official publication of the Sikang Provincial Government) (Dec., 1934), V, No. 9, 62.

167. *Mêng Tsang hsün k'an,* Nos. 78-79, March 20, 1934, p. 7; "Death of Dalai Lama of Tibet Spurs China to Regain Control," *Trans-Pacific,* XXII (Aug. 30, 1934), 54.

168. *The Times,* Sept. 6, 1934, p. 11g; *Hsi-ch'ui-hsüan-hua-shih kung shu yüeh k'an* (Panch'en Lama Headquarters Monthly), Feb., 1935, pp. 35-38.

169. *North China Herald,* Sept. 26, 1934, p. 450; *The Times,* Sept. 13, 1934, p. 10b.

170. The proposal and the Tibetan counterproposal are cited from General Huang's Report to the Central Committee of the National Government in the archives of the Mongolian and Tibetan Affairs Commission.

171. *Kuo min chêng fu nien chien,* ed. by the Executive Yüan (1934), p. 319. General Huang's report states that the Lhasa authorities at first made it a condition that the Panch'en Lama should return by sea, i.e., by way of India.

172. In May, 1934, while General Huang was there, a plot to overthrow the Regent was discovered. General Lung-shar, formerly the Commander-in-Chief, was arrested and sentenced to have his eyes put out and to be confined to prison. In this connection, see *The Times,* May 31, 1934, p. 13d; "Tibet as It Stands Today," *China Critic,* VII, No. 24, 558; *North China Herald,* April 25, 1934, p. 94.

173. *Chinese Year Book,* prepared under the auspices of the Council of International Affairs (Shanghai, 1940), p. 319; *The Times,* Dec. 13, 1934, p. 15b; Lin Tung-hai, "Three Months in Lhasa," *China Critic* (Feb. 21, 1935), VIII, No. 8, 173-74; Bell, *Portrait of the Dalai Lama,* p. 394. Sir Charles Bell was on a private visit to Tibet while Huang was still there. (*The Times,* July 5, 1934, p. 14b.)

174. *The Times,* Aug. 16, 1934, pp. 10c, 11d; Nov. 22, 1934, p. 13; Bell, "Tibet and Its Neighbors," *Pacific Affairs,* X, No. 4 (December, 1937), 438.

175. *New York Times,* Feb. 10, 1935, p. 24, col. 2.

176. For an explanation of the Chinese decision to create this new province, see *New York Times,* April 14, 1935, Sec. 4, p. 12, cols. 3-4; in February, 1935, the Commission for the creation of Sikang Province was set up; but its work was not much in progress until the removal of the capital to Chungking. In July, 1938, it was decided, in spite of Szechwan's bitter opposition, that 14 districts of Szechwan together with its two special districts should be transferred to the new province to make the latter self-supporting. On January 1, 1939, the provincial government was formally instituted at Tach'ienlu.

177. Note that the Government was formed after the flight of the Dalai Lama, during the presence of the British Armed Mission.

178. *A and P,* Cd. 5240, enclosure 3 in No. 40, p. 28.

179. *Cambridge History of India,* I, 33.

180. An-chin Hutukhtu went to Lhasa in 1933 with a secretary of the Panch'en Lama named Tang-chin-pa (*Hsi-tsang wên t'i chih chin hsi,* p. 9).

181. Huang Fêng-shêng, *Mêng Tsang hsin chih,* I, 457.

182. *Supra,* nn. 87 and 147, and pp. 149 and 164.

183. *The Times,* Oct. 28, 1937, p. 15c.

184. The National Government first appointed Ch'eng Yün, and upon the latter's resignation in August, 1936, appointed Chao Shou-yü to take his place.

185. *The Times,* July 22, 1937, p. 13f. Chao Shou-yü and his party joined the Panch'en at Jyekundo on July 18, 1937 (Ma Ho t'ien, *Kan Ch'ing Tsang pien ch'ü k'ao ch'a chi,* pp. 361, 372).

186. *K'ang Tsang ch'ien feng,* No. 8, April 5, 1934, p. 99; *North China Herald,* April 11, 1934, p. 2; *New York Times,* April 20, 1934, p. 10, col. 4.

187. *Mêng Tsang hsün k'an,* No. 86, June 30, 1934, p. 12.

188. Ex-Chairman of the Commission for Mongolian and Tibetan Affairs, Wu Chung-hsin's report on his mission to Tibet, *Ju Tsang pao kao,* p. 100.

189. Liu Wen-hui, *Chung kao tui Tsang chih hsin chêng ts'ê,* p. 54.

190. The Panch'en Lama realized the necessity of clearing the way with the British. In 1934, he sent friendly messages of greetings to the British King-Emperor and the Viceroy and solicited the help of

the Government of India to facilitate his return. (*The Times,* July 5, 1934, p. 14b; June 13, 1935, p. 12e; cf. April 6, 1934, p. 11b.)

191. *Ibid.,* June 13, 1935, p. 12e; *North China Herald,* June 19, 1935, p. 464. Williamson succeeded Lt. Col. Weir as British Political Officer in 1933, and died in Lhasa in 1935 (Bell, *Portrait of the Dalai Lama,* pp. 369-70).

192. *Hsi-tsang wên t'i chih chin hsi,* pp. 11-12.

193. Chapman, *Lhasa, The Holy City,* p. 4.

194. *Hsi-tsang wên t'i chih chin hsi,* p. 12.

195. *The Times,* Feb. 19, 1937, p. 13f.

196. *Hsi-tsang wên t'i chih chin hsi,* p. 13; *The Times,* Oct. 28, 1937, p. 15c.

197. A special article from Tach'ienlu, dated September 23, signed "by Tibetan," but must have been written by an Englishman, appeared on October 27, 1937, in the *North China Daily News.*

198. Their creation of the Mukden Incident on September 18, 1931, and subsequent occupation of the whole of Manchuria and part of Inner Mongolia, and their establishment of a puppet regime in the eastern part of Hopei Province, are considered as the first phase.

199. Ma Ho-t'ien, *Kan Ch'ing Tsang pien ch'ü k'ao ch'a chi,* p. 449.

200. *Ibid.,* p. 457. The executive Yüan's telegraphic order to halt the Panch'en's journey reached Chao Shou-yü on August 24; Chao sent Ma to transmit the message on the next day and came himself to explain this order on August 31. (*Ibid.,* p. 463.)

201. For other relevant information about the Panch'en's death see Ma Ho-t'ien, pp. 651-53, 654-56, 657-59, 665-66, and 671.

202. C. Y. W. Meng, "Tibetans Are Praying for China's Victory," *China Weekly Review,* LXXXVIII (April 15, 1939), 205.

203. According to Theodore Bernard, "The Peril of Tibet," *Asia,* XXXIX (Sept., 1939), 503, a large delegation of Tibetans brought along with them ten thousand sheepskins and five hundred thousand Chinese dollars to be given to the soldiers.

204. *New York Times,* Nov. 28, 1938, p. 6, col. 4.

205. *Ibid.,* Jan. 21, 1934, Sec. 4, p. 4; Bell, "While Europe Prepares for War, Pious Tibet Searches for Child Ruler," *China Weekly Review,* LXXXI (July 10, 1937), 217.

206. Gordon B. Enders, "A New Role for the Panch'en Lama," *Asia,* XXXIV (August, 1934), 466-67.

207. A. T. Steele, "Boy Ruler of Shangri-la," *Saturday Evening Post,* April 13, 1946, pp. 14-15; *The Times,* March 11, 1939, p. 14a; Oct. 28, 1939, p. 9f; Feb. 9, 1940, p. 8d; *Time,* Feb. 26, 1940, p. 54; *New York Times,* Sept. 29, 1939, p. 12, col. 5; Jan. 31, 1940, p. 8, cols. 3-4; Jan. 27, 1940, p. 5, col. 2; Feb. 22, 1940, p. 11, cols. 2-3; James Shen, "New Dalai Lama Is Found," *Asia,* XL (Jan., 1940), 25-27; "Three Nations Hunt a Lama," *Living Age,* No. 357 (Jan. 1940), pp. 430-33.

208. Bell, *Portrait of the Dalai Lama,* p. 396, and *supra,* n. 173.
209. *Ibid.,* pp. 397-99.
210. *Ibid.,* p. 400.
211. For example, the *New York Times* reported the request made by the Regent to the Chinese Government to be allowed to dispense with the lot-drawing procedure, and the latter's affirmative reply (Jan. 31, 1940, p. 8); the appointment of the Regent by the Chinese Government to supervise the reincarnation and installation of the new Dalai Lama, and the Regent's acceptance; (Jan. 27, 1940, p. 5); and the message of thanks sent from the Regent to the Chinese Government particularly for the abandonment of the lot-drawing procedure (Feb. 22, 1940, p. 11).
212. *Supra,* p. 49.
213. Bell, *Portrait of the Dalai Lama,* pp. 399-400.
214. In giving the equivalent amount in pounds sterling, Sir Charles apparently forgot the effect on the rate of exchange of the much inflated Chinese currency during wartime.
215. The boy was sent as one of the claimants, not as the Dalai Lama elect. He was thus spared all the ceremonial performances en route. He and the escorts left the Kum-bum monastery on July 1 and reached their destination on October 7. See Wu Chung-hsin's report, pp. 5 and 7. Sir Charles Bell mentions that the Chinese Government contributed fifty-five thousand dollars for the search and the journey back. *Portrait of the Dalai Lama,* p. 399.
216. Wu Chung-hsin's official report on his mission to Tibet, *Ju Tsang pao kao,* pp. 3-4.
217. *Ibid.,* p. 9.
218. In using the word "unnecessarily" here, the writer has in mind the closing of the Burma Road for three months in the next year (1940) which the British authorities explained as a necessary measure in the circumstances. But the Chinese people failed to understand the necessity for such an appeasement, especially when the end did not justify the means.
219. Wu Chung-hsin, *Ju Tsang pao kao,* p. 7. For the organization and the personnel of the mission see Chu Shao-i, *La-sa chien wên chi,* pp. 46-47. Chu was a chief of section of the Mongolian and Tibetan Affairs Commission who went to Lhasa with Kung, served as secretary to Wu, and visited Tashi-lhunpo with another member of the mission, Hsi Lun, on Wu's behalf
220. *Ju Tsang pao kao,* pp. 18-20. The original text is much longer and contains many Buddhistic terms, a literal translation of which would hardly be worth-while. Only a synopsis is given here.
221. *Ibid.,* p. 22.
222. *Ibid.,* p. 22. For details see Chu Shao-i, *La-sa chien wên chi,* pp. 60-63.
223. Bell, *Portrait of the Dalai Lama,* p. 246.

224. *Ju Tsang pao kao,* pp. 23-25; Chu Shao-i, *La-sa chien wên chi,* pp. 77-82.

225. Chu Shao'i, *La-sa chien wên chi,* pp. 73-74. According to the Chinese Regulations Governing Conferment of Decorations, the First Class Auspicious Jade is confined to the Chief of State. So this second class is the highest that could be conferred on the Regent. See also Wu's report, pp. 15-16.

226. Wu's report, pp. 17 and 26.

227. *Ibid.,* pp. 27-28.

228. *Ibid.,* pp. 28-29.

229. *Ibid.,* p. 30.

230. *Ibid.,* p. 58.

231. *Supra,* pp. 172, 174. An-ch'in was an outstanding follower of the late Panch'en Lama. In the spring of 1937, after a quarrel with other members of the Panch'en's entourage, he went to Peiping. Following the outbreak of the war with Japan, he did not make contact with the National Government. It was reported that he had been appointed by the puppet regime in Peiping as the Chairman of its Commission for Mongolian and Tibetan Affairs and that he had returned to Tibet in April, 1939, to engage in subversive activities. Mr. Wu asked him to send a telegram to Chungking to declare his allegiance, which he did. (See Wu's report, *Ju Tsang pao kao,* pp. 16 and 31.) This writer found in the Japanese Foreign Office Archives (Reel S 656, S 1.6.1.3-4, Bunkyo Aoki's report) that it was An-ch'in who helped to get a Japanese named Jinzo Nomoto into Tibet to perform "a special duty." Had his anti-Regent activities in Tibet been connected with the Japanese, and had they been successful, the status of Tibet might have changed radically.

232. Some Chinese writers assert that in 1912 Yin Chang-heng's army also reached Giamda. *Hsi-tsang chi yao* (pp. 197, 199) states clearly that it did not go that far. For the full text of Fu's proposal dispatched on the eve of the outbreak of revolution in 1911, see Hung Ti-chên, *Hsi-tsang shih ti ta kang,* pp. 189-92.

233. The following account of Ra-dreng's downfall and the defeat of the monks is based chiefly upon Jên Nai-ch'iang, "Hsi-tsang chêng pien," *K'ang Tsang yen chiu,* No. 9, Sept. 30, 1947, pp. 16-22.

234. *New York Times,* Feb. 4, 1940, Sec. 4, p. 4, col. 8, reported that J. B. Gould was watching over British and Indian interests in the new reign.

235. Ilia Tolstoy, "Across Tibet from India to China," *National Geographic Magazine,* XC (Aug., 1946), 178 and 198, gives the name as Nywang Sungrab Thutoh Galtsen.

236. Li Fang-ch'en, *Shên pi ti Hsi-tsang* (Taipeh, 1951), p. 54.

237. Li Yu-i, "Ti-kuo-chu-i ch'in lüeh Hsi-tsang ti shih shih" (Historical Facts of Imperialistic Invasions of Tibet), an article embodied in a booklet entitled *Tai chieh fang ti Hsi-tsang* (Tibet Pending Lib-

eration) (1950), p. 33. The author was one of the eleven officials sent to Lhasa by the National Government in the spring of 1944; he was a member of staff in the Ministry of Education. (Actually, more than thirty were appointed at the time, but only eleven got the British transit visa, the rest being rejected.)

238. Yen Tê-i, "Chung Yin kung lu chih ching chi chia chih," *Pien ch'iang shih ch'ing,* (Sept., 1947), VI, No. 3, 54.

239. Ilia Tolstoy, "Across Tibet from India to China," *National Geographic Magazine,* XC (Aug., 1946), 201, 206; Amaury de Reincourt, *Roof of the World: Tibet, Key to Asia,* pp. 206-7.

240. *Kuo min chêng fu nien chien* (1945), Chap. 17, p. 3.

241. *Current History,* New Series, IX (Oct., 1945), 329-38.

242. *Ta Kung Pao,* Aug. 25, 1945, p. 1, mentions that the Sixth Plenary Session of Kuomintang decided to grant Tibet a high degree of autonomy.

243. This statement was made in addressing the National Supreme Defense Council and the Central Executive Committee of Kuomintang. *Ta Kung Pao,* Aug. 25, 1945, p. 1; *New York Times,* Aug. 25, 1945, p. 1, cols. 6-7; p. 3, col. 2. Here by "the historical tragedy of Korea" he meant the declaration of independence in 1895, only to be annexed by the instigator fifteen years later.

244. There is another point which has a bearing on the Tibetan attitude toward the Chinese National Government. In 1943, the Chinese Central Government's troops entered Sinkiang (Chinese Turkestan) and brought this big province, the next-door neighbor of Tibet, under the actual (as heretofore only nominal) control of the National Government. For details see Aichen K. Wu, *China and the Soviet Union* (1950), pp. 261-62.

245. In treating of events since 1946 the writer realizes that apart from the usual risk attached to the treatment of current events, he is prevented from collecting data which would have been available but for the existing world situation. Though he has tried to acquire as much information as possible, he has not been able, for a variety of reasons, to get as much concerning India's view of the problem as he would have liked, and certainly he has not had access to the latest publications of the Chinese mainland, except those available in the Library of Congress and in Columbia University. Also, owing to the removal of the National Government to Taiwan, official data relating to recent years has been difficult, if not impossible, to obtain.

246. In the Legislative Yüan ten seats were allotted for the Tibetan members, among whom five were to be sent from Tibet, while the other five were to be elected by Tibetans living in China Proper. (*Mêng Tsang yüeh pao,* the official publication of Mongolian and Tibetan Affairs Commission, Vol. 19, No. 6, p. 9.) The last occupants of these seats were T'u-tan-sang-pu, Chiang-pa-a-wong, Tan-tseng-tang-ch'üeh, Chi-chin-mei, Ts'ai-jen-t'uan-chu, T'u-tan-ni-ma, Lo-sang-chien-

tsan, and Na-wang-chin-pa. The last six Tibetan members of the Control Yüan were: Chiang-pa-cha-hsi, Tan-pa-p'eng-ts'o, La-min-yi-hsi-ch'u-ch'en, Chi-yü-chieh, Ho-pa-tun, and T'u-tan-ts'ê-tan.

247. Namely, So-lang-wang-tui, Ts'ê-wang-tun-chu, T'u-teng-sheng-ke, T'u-tan-ts'ê-tan,Chiang-pa-a-wang, To-chi-oǔ-chu, and Yi-hsi-ta-chi. For the full list of the names of the Tibetan delegates, including those chosen by the Tibetans living in China Proper, see *ibid.*, Vol. 18, Nos. 11-12, p. 13.

248. *Pien Shêng Pao,* Oct. 18, 1946, p. 1. Constitution art. 120.

249. Ma Fu-hsiang, *Mêng Tsang chuang k'uang,* pp. 185-86.

250. *Supra,* n. 100, and p. 151.

251. *Supra,* nn. 124, 125, and 231. The Japanese Foreign Office's Archives also record the visits to Tibet of Ekai Kawaguchi, Yasujiso Yajima, Bunkyo Aoki, Tokan Tada, and Jinzo Nomoto.

252. Photographic record of the Japanese Foreign Office's Archives kept in the Library of Congress (Reel S 656, S 1.6.1.3-4), under the *Report of Tibetan Affairs* submitted by Bunkyo Aoki in September, 1944.

253. P. C. Bagchi, *India and China, A Thousand Years of Cultural Relations* (1950), pp. 197-202; Hsü Kung-wu, *Chung Yin li tai kuan hsi shih lüeh* (1942), pp. 1-35; Hu Shih, "The Indianization of China: A Case Study in Cultural Borrowing," *Independence, Convergence, and Borrowing,* Harvard Tercentenary Publications (1936), pp. 219-47.

254. Expressions of disappointment and severe criticism are found not only in the press of Nationalist China and the nonpartisan Chinese press, but also among Chinese Communist publications. For example, the editorial of the Hsin Hua Agency, articles written by Tien Pao, Ho Szu-ching, Tu Po, and Li Yu-i embodied in the booklet, *Tai chieh fang ti Hsi-tsang,* pp. 2-4, 8-19, and 35-36.

255. At the time when the Conference opened, Great Britain had already expressed her willingness to evacuate India and Mr. Nehru had been made deputy prime minister. He found it unnecessary and inconvenient for him to preside at the Conference which was supposed to be a nongovernmental organization.

256. Most of the maps printed in the United Kingdom and some printed in other countries made this mistake. No wonder the chairman of the El Salvador delegation to the United Nations, in his letter to the President of the General Assembly, requested the inclusion of the Tibetan appeal on the agenda of the Fifth Session, saying: "Anyone who takes the trouble to look at a map of Asia will realize that Tibet is separate and entirely different from the territory of China" (U. N. Document A/1534, Nov. 18, 1950). Here the writer is reminded of an incident that occurred in 1935 when he was studying at the London School of Economics and Political Science. In that year a Chinese Exhibition under Royal patronage was held in Lon-

don. The Chinese Government sent a part of the Palace Treasure to be displayed, and dispatched Dr. Cheng Tien-hsi as a special envoy on this cultural mission. Dr. Cheng had a map of China printed on the cover of the catalogue by a London printing house. On the opening day some Chinese students discovered that Tibet was not included within the boundary line on the map. A censure of the matter was called for by the Chinese Student Association and the error was immediately corrected. The writer wonders why the same mistake was persistently made in spite of the repeated efforts of the Chinese official representatives and private individuals to call the publisher's attention to this obvious error.

257. Lo Chia-lun, "Chieh k'ai Chung Yin chien yu kuan Hsi-tsang ti mu," *Tzŭ yu chung kuo,* III, No. 7, 230.

258. *Ibid.,* p. 231.

259. *Ibid.,* p. 234; *supra,* pp. 187-88.

260. *Ibid.,* pp. 230 and 234. "The retaining of Mr. Richardson's service demonstrated the collaboration of Nehru's reactionary government with British Imperialism," Tu Po pointed out in an article published in the Chinese Communist organ, *Jên Min Jih Pao,* on Sept. 7, 1949.

261. Lo Chia-lun, "Chieh k'ai Chung Yin chien yu kuan Hsi-tsang ti mus," *Tzŭ yu chüng kuo,* III, No. 7, 232-33.

262. *Ibid.,* p. 232.

263. *Ibid.*

264. Tu Po's article in *Jên Min Jih Pao.*

265. Li Yu-i, in his article, "Ti-kuo-chu-i ch'in lüeh Hsi-tsang ti shih shih," pp. 36-37, blamed his old professor, Ambassador Leighton Stuart, for his alleged part in bringing the mission over to the United States.

266. According to Li Yu-i (*ibid.,* p. 36), after the return of the Tibetan delegation from the Asiatic Conference, the Lhasa Government received a lot of letters and documents from abroad urging them to secure independence and advising them how to apply for admission to the United Nations. As the Tibetan Bureau for Foreign Affairs had only one member who could do the translation from English, Li Yu-i was often asked privately to lend a hand.

267. Lo Chia-lun, "Chieh k'ai Chung Yin chien yu kuan Hsi-tsang ti mu," *Tzŭ yu chung kao,* III, No. 7, 234.

268. A Chinese Primary School was first established in Lhasa by the liaison officer, Chiang Chi-yu, in 1937 and later taken over by the Commission for Mongolian and Tibetan Affairs, which also set up one at Gyantse afterwards. See Chu Shao-i, *La-sa chien wên chi,* pp. 11-12, 116, 120-21.

269. Director Shen Tsung-lien left Lhasa for consultation with Nanking in 1946. Since then Chen had been in charge of the office. Hsiung Yao-wên was afterwards appointed to succeed Shen when the

latter's resignation was accepted, but Hsiung did not proceed to the post.

270. Lo again saw Menon on July 26 and 30 to talk on the same subject. For details see Lo Chia-lun, "Chung Yin chien kuan yü Hsi-tsang wên t'i ti mu nei chêng chien," (Documentary Evidence on Tibetan Issue in Sino-Indian Relations), *Tzŭ yu chung kuo* (January, 1951), IV, No. 2, 56-58.

271. See the text of his statement in *Yen yüan ch'ang chêng lun chi yao* (A Collection of Statements on Political Matters Made by Yen Hsi-shan While in Office as President of Executive Yüan), pp. 274-75.

272. Lo Chia-lun, "Chieh k'ai Chung Yin chien yu kuan Hsi-tsang ti mu," p. 234.

273. *Ibid.,* p. 235. For Chen's report on what actually happened from the middle of June to July 20 see Lo Chia-lun, "Chung Yin chien kuan yü Hsi-tsang wên t'i ti mu nei chêng chien," pp. 53-56. When Chen and his secretary went to see the Dalai Lama in the presence of the Regent to say good-by, they were duly received, but neither the Dalai Lama nor the Regent said a word. Chen, on the eve of his departure, got a message informing him that "the mother of the Dalai Lama wishes to let the director Mr. Chen know that His Holiness did not know he was leaving for good when he came to take his leave. The Dalai Lama was under the impression that he was going to India to spend a vacation."

274. U. N. Documents, Summary Records of Meeting of the General Committee, September 21 to December 5, 1950, p. 19.

275. See Lowell Thomas, Jr., *Out of This World; Across the Himalayas to Forbidden Tibet* (1950).

276. *Tai chieh fang ti Hsi-tsang* includes a Chinese translation of a Russian article, "Ti-kuo-chu-i-che tsai Hsi-tsang ti yin mou" (The Intrigues of the Imperialists in Tibet), by T. Yelsoff, in which sharp criticism is passed on Mr. Thomas's visit (pp. 24-25).

277. *Ibid.,* pp. 1, 5, and 6.

278. U. N. Document A/1549, November 24, 1950.

279. The Indian note was transmitted by the Indian Ambassador in Peking. Its text in Chinese is given in a booklet entitled *Chin chün Hsi-tsang* (Military Campaign into Tibet), published by the Chinese Communist official organ, Jên Min Press (1951), pp. 10-11.

280. Peking reply, dated November 1, given in *Chin chün Hsi-tsang,* p. 8.

281. The date of the Tibetan delegation's departure from New Delhi is mentioned in an Indian note dated October 28, 1950. *Ibid.,* p. 11.

282. Li Fang-ch'ên, *Shên pi ti Hsi-tsang,* pp. 56-57.

283. U. N. Document A/1549, cablegram received from the Tibetan delegation, Shakabpa (House Kalimpong).

284. Ke-ta Hutekhtu, the abbot of Pai-li monastery, was made chairman of the government set up by the Red Army at Kanze in 1935 with Hsia-ke-tao-teng and Pong-ta-to-chi as members. (*Chin chün Hsi-tsang,* p. 74.) He was made Vice Chairman of Sikang in 1950, and is said to have been poisoned by a British agent named Ford at Chamdo on August 22 of that year. (*Ibid.,* pp. 26-27.)

285. *Hsin chung kuo jên wu chih* (Who's Who in New China) (Hongkong, 1950), pp. 163-66.

286. The full text of the memorandum is given in *Chin Chün Hsi-tsang,* pp. 9-10.

287. For the full text in Chinese, see *ibid.,* pp. 10-11.

288. For the full text in Chinese see *ibid.,* pp. 11-12.

289. For the full text in Chinese, see *ibid.,* pp. 13-14.

290. For the full text in Chinese, see *ibid.,* pp. 7-9.

291. The cablegram was signed in the name of Kashag and the National Assembly, dated Nov. 7, 1950, and sent from Kalimpong in the name of the Tibetan delegation, dated Nov. 11, 1950.

292. U. N. Document A/1549, November 24, 1950.

293. U. N. Document A/1534, November 18, 1950.

294. U. N. Document, Summary Record of Meeting (September 21-December 5, 1950) of the General Committee, p. 17.

295. *Ibid.,* pp. 19-20.

296. The Chinese delegate mistakenly gave the date here as 1947.

297. For the text of the El Salvador delegate's draft resolution and other communications, see U. N. Document A/1534.

298. U. N. Document A/1565, November 30, 1950.

299. U. N. Document A/1658, December 11, 1950.

300. Bell, *Tibet,* p. 244.

301. *Ibid.,* p. 214.

302. The Peking *People's Daily,* in an editorial on May 28, 1951, praised the Dalai Lama for altering the past "erroneous policy" of the Tibetan Government.

303. A booklet, *Kuan yü ho p'ing chieh fang Hsi-tsang pan fa ti hsieh i* (Agreement on Measures for the Peaceful Liberation of Tibet) (Jên Min Press, Peking, 1951), pp. 26-27.

304. *Ibid.,* pp. 21-23.

305. *Ibid.,* pp. 1-5.

306. Paris, June 14 (AFP), and Calcutta, July 4 (AFP).

307. *Hong Kong Standard,* Aug. 15 and Oct. 27, 1951.

308. San Francisco, May 29 and July 17 (AP). Chamdo is in Kham and outside of Tibet proper. The Chinese Communist army, though it had captured Chamdo, which was considered a part of Sikang, could not be said to have entered Tibet proper.

309. Tokyo, Sept. 14 (Pan Asia); *Hong Kong Standard,* Oct. 31, 1951.

310. Kalimpong, March 14 (Reuter).

311. *Hong Kong Standard,* Feb. 22, 1952.
312. *The Shanghai Daily News,* May 10, 1952.
313. Lhasa, May 8, 1952 (Hsinhua).
314. *The Shanghai Daily News,* June 18 and 24.
315. U. N. Document A/1549.
316. *South China Morning Post* (Hong Kong), May 5, 1952; *New York Times,* Aug. 26, 1952, pp. 1 and 2.
317. *Ibid.,* p. 24.
318. *Supra,* p. 203.
319. It was reported in the *New York Times* (April 2, 1955, p. 4) and in one of the Chinese newspapers in New York, *China Daily News* (April 4 and 14, 1955, both p. 1), that India handed over to Communist China on April 1, 1955, Indian postal, telegraph, and telephone facilities in Tibet without charge, and received 316,828 rupees as the payment for the twelve rest houses and their equipment.
320. *New York Times,* April 30, 1954.

Conclusion

1. Teichman, *Travels in Eastern Tibet,* p. 46.
2. *Documents des archives des gouvernements impérial et provisoire 1878-1917* (1900-13), Series II, Vol. 20, Part 1, No. 228, pp. 220-21.
3. Bell, *Portrait of the Dalai Lama,* p. 336.
4. Petech, *China and Tibet in the Early 18th Century,* pp. 9-10 and 25.
5. Cited here only as a recent example from a non-Western source. D. K. Sen (author of *Indian Studies in International Law and Diplomacy* and minister of Bhopal state), "China, Tibet and India," *India Quarterly* (April-June, 1951), VII, No. 2, 113, 123, 128.
6. *Supra,* Chapter IV, nn. 21, 82, 174, 239, and pp. 73, 83, 99, 262.
7. McNair, *Law of Treaties,* p. 129. Cf. Oppenheim, *International Law* (7th ed.), p. 288.
8. *A and P,* Cd. 1920, No. 44, p. 127.
9. *A and P,* Cd. 2370, No. 193, p. 86.
10. Kohn, *History of Nationalism in the East,* pp. 6, 8, and 9.
11. Spykman, *America's Strategy in World Politics,* pp. 468-69.
12. *China Daily News* in New York reports (March 23, 1955, p. 1) that on the eve of the departure of the Dalai Lama and the Panch'en Lama from Peking, it was decided to set up a preparatory committee of fifty-one members for the implementation of regional autonomy in Tibet with the Dalai Lama as Chairman, the Panch'en Lama and Chang Kuo-hua as Deputy Chairmen.

BIBLIOGRAPHY

I. *Unpublished Works*

Lu Hsing-chi. Hsi-tsang chiao shê chi yao. (The author, a Chinese expert on Indian and Tibetan affairs, was appointed Acting High Commissioner in 1913, but never had the chance to set up his office in Tibet.)

Shih Ch'ing-yang's manuscript. Tsang shih chi yao. (Written while the author was the Chairman of the Mongolian and Tibetan Affairs Commission.)

II. *Documentary Sources*

A. CHINESE SOURCES

Ch'ing-chi ch'ou Tsang tsou tu (Dispatches and Memorials to the Throne concerning Tibet in the Ch'ing Period), ed. by Wu Fêng-p'ei.

Ch'ing chi wai chiao shih liao (The Sources of Diplomatic History toward the End of the Ch'ing Dynasty), ed. by Wang Liang and Wang Yen-wei.

Ch'ing shih-lu (Imperial Records of the Ch'ing Dynasty).
T'ai-tsung shih-lu
Shih-tsu shih-lu
Shêng-tsu shih-lu
Shih-tsung shih-lu
Kao-tsung shih-lu
Jên-tsung shih-lu
Hsüan-tsung shih-lu
Wên-tsung shih-lu
Mu-tsung shih-lu
Tê-tsung shih-lu
Hsüan-t'ung chêng-chi

Ch'ing tai Hsi-tsang shih liao ts'ung k'an (Source Material concerning Tibet from the Ch'ing Dynasty), ed. by Wu Fêng-p'ei.

Hsi-tsang wên t'i chih chin hsi (The Tibetan Question: Past and Present). A document in the Chinese Foreign Office Archives.

Li fan pu tsê li (Regulations Enforced and Precedents Established by the Ministry of Dependencies).

Ming shih-lu (Imperial Records of the Ming Dynasty).

Shêng Kung Ch'in Kung. Tsang Yin pien wu lu (The Resident Shêng-t'ai's Records and Official Papers concerning Tibetan and Indian Frontiers).

Special Commissioner to Tibet, General Huang Mu-sung's Report to the Chinese National Government.

Ta Ch'ing hui tien (Collected Statutes of the Ch'ing Dynasty).

Ta Ch'ing hui tien shih-li (Cases and Precedents under the Statutes of the Ch'ing Dynasty).

Tsang an chi lüeh (An Essence of the Records on Tibet), ed. by the Chinese Foreign Office.

Wu Chung-hsin. Ju Tsang pao kao (Report on his mission to Tibet).

B. BRITISH AND AMERICAN SOURCES

Accounts and Papers. Printed by Order of the House of Commons.
C 6208
C 7312
Cd. 1920
Cd. 2054
Cd. 2370
Cd. 3088
Cd. 3753
Cd. 4450
Cd. 5240
Cd. 6604

British and Foreign State Papers.

British Documents on the Origin of the War, 1898-1914, ed. by G. P. Gooch and Harold Temperley. London, 1926-38.

Parliamentary Debates. Vols. 125, 130, 133, 137, 138, 140, 141, 142, 156, 183, 184, and LXIV (1914).

U. S. Department of State Archives. Great Britain Instructions. Vol. 34, No. 1455.

C. JAPANESE SOURCES

Reel 126 MT 1.6.1.4-7. Kakkoku naisei kankei zassan. Shina: Chibetto, Shinkyô (Miscellaneous Documents Relating to the Internal Political Conditions in Foreign Countries. China: Tibet and Sinkiang).

Reel S 656 S 1.6.1.3-4. Chibetto mondai oyobi jijô kankei zassan (Miscellaneous Documents Relating to Problems and General Conditions in Tibet).

D. RUSSIAN SOURCES

Documents des archives des gouvernements impérial et provisoire 1878-1917 (in Russian).

Krasnyi Arkhiv, II, 21 (1923); XXXVII, 15-68.

E. UNITED NATIONS SOURCES

UN Documents.
A/1534, Nov. 18, 1950.
A/1549, Nov. 24, 1950.
A/1565, Nov. 30, 1950.
A/1658, Dec. 11, 1950.

UN Document, Summary Record of the Meeting of the General Committee, September 21 to December 5, 1950.

III. *Secondary Sources*

A. IN ORIENTAL LANGUAGES

Adachi, Kiroku. Kôshô Hokken-den (A Study of Fa-hsien's Travels in Central Asia, India, and the South Seas). Tokyo, 1936.

Altan Debter (A History of the Early Mongolian Regime, derived from the revised *Tobičyan* and written in gold).

Aoki, Bunkyo. Chibetto bunka no shin-kenyû (A New Study of the Tibetan Culture). Tokyo, 1940.

Chang T'ing-yü (1672-1755) and others. Ming shih (A History of the Ming Dynasty).

Chao Han-chung. Shih Kao chi lüeh (A Brief Account of My Mission to Nepal in 1884). 1888.

Ch'ên Chien-fu. Hsi-tsang wên t'i (The Tibetan Question). Shanghai, 1937.

Ch'ên Yüan. Chung hsi hui shih jih li (A Comparative Daily Calendar for Chinese, European, and Mohammedan History). Peking, 1926.

Ch'êng Chü-fu. The article in memory of Kublai's Yünnan campaign, Kuo-ch'ao-wên-lei, Chüan XXIII.

Ch'i Yün-shih (1751-1851). Huang ch'ao fan pu yao lüeh (Concerning the Dependencies of the Imperial Dynasty). 1884 ed.

Chia I-chün. Chung hua min kuo shih (Political History of the Chinese Republic). Shanghai, 1930.

Chin chün Hsi-tsang (Military Campaign into Tibet). Peking, 1951.

Ch'ing-shih kao (Draft History of the Ch'ing Dynasty), compiled by Chao Erh-sun and others. 1928.

Chu Shao-i. La-sa chien wên chi (What I Saw and Heard in Lhasa). Shanghai, 1947.

Chu shu chi nien (Bamboo Books on the Ancient History of China).

Chung Chün. "Hsi-tsang chün shih chuang k'uang" (The Military Situation in Tibet), *Kang tao* (semi-official publication of the Sikang Provincial Government), V, No. 9 (Dec., 1934).

Chung Ying, Chung O kuan yü Hsi-tsang Mêng-ku yo chang ho pien (Treaties between China, Great Britain, and Russia concerning Mongolia and Tibet). Published by Mongolian and Tibetan Affairs Commission, Nanking, 1930.

Daśabhūmikasūtra śāstra (A Buddhist Canon in Sanskrit). Trans. into Chinese circa 514.

Fa-tsun. Hsien tai Hsi-tsang (Modern Tibet). Chungking, 1943.

Fêng Ch'êng-chün. Ch'êng-chi-sŭ-han chuan (A Biography of Genghis Khan). Shanghai, 1934.

——— Li tai ch'iu fa fan ching lu (Chinese and Foreign Monks Who Have Contributed to the Formation of the Chinese Tripitaka. Shanghai, 1931.

——— Shih ti ts'ung k'ao (A Collection of Papers on History and Geography). Shanghai, 1935.

Fu Sung-mu. Hsi-kang chien shêng chih (Province Building of Sikang). The author was successor to Chao Erh-fêng as Frontier High Commissioner at Tach'ienlu.

Harvard-Yenching Institute, Sinological Index, Series No. 11. Buddhistic Literature. Peiping, 1933.

Ho-ning. Hsi-tsang fu (A Narrative of Tibet in Verse). 1797. The author was a Resident of Tibet from 1800-1801.

Ho Tsao-hsiang. Tsang yü. A record of what he saw and did during 1906-8 while the author was a secretary to Chang Ying-tang.

Hsieh Pin. Hsi-tsang chiao shê lüeh shih (A Short Diplomatic History concerning Tibet). 4th ed. Shanghai, 1933.

——— Hsi-tsang wên t'i (The Tibetan Question). 2d ed. Shanghai, 1935.

Hsin chung kuo jên wu chih (Who's Who in New China). Hong Kong, 1950.

Hsin T'ang shu (History of the T'ang Dynasty). A new edition by Ou-yang Hsiu, Tsêng Kung-liang, and others.

Hsü Erh-hao. Ch'ing K'ang Tsang Hsin hsi jên k'an ch'a shih lüeh (A Brief Account of the Exploratory and Route Surveys by Westeners in Ch'inghai, Sikang, Tibet, and Sinkiang). Chungking, 1945.

Hsü Kung-wu. Chung Yin li tai kuan hsi shih lüeh (A Short History of Sino-Indian Relations). Chungking, 1942.

Hu Chi-lu. Hsi-k'ang chiang yü shou ku lu (A Historical Study of the Boundary of Sikang). Shanghai, 1934.

Hua Ch'i-yün. Hsi-tsang wên t'i (The Tibetan Question). Shanghai, 1930.

Huang Ch'an-hua. Chung kuo fo chiao shih (Buddhism in China). Shanghai, 1940.

Huang Fêng-shêng. Mêng Tsang hsin chih (New Records on Mongolia and Tibet). Canton, 1938.

Hung Chün-p'ei. Kuo min chêng fu wai chiao shih (Diplomatic Records of the National Government). Shanghai, 1930.

Hung Ti-chên. Hsi-tsang shih ti ta kang (An Outline of the History and Geography of Tibet). Shanghai, 1947.

I-tsing (635-713). Ta t'ang hsi yü chiu fa kao sêng chuan (Biographies of the High Priests Who Went to the Western Regions to Study Buddhism during the T'ang Period).

Jên Nai-ch'iang. "Hsi-tsang chêng-pien" (The Recent Coup d'État in Tibet), *K'ang Tsang yen chiu,* No. 9, Sept. 30, 1947.

K'o Shao-min. Hsin yüan shih (A History of the Yuan Dynasty). A new edition. Tientsin, 1922.

Ko Sui-ch'êng. Chung-kuo chin tai pien chiang yen ko k'ao (A Study of the Vicissitudes of the Chinese Frontiers in Modern Times). Shanghai, 1934.

Kuan yü ho p'ing chieh fang Hsi-tsang pan fa ti hsieh i (Concerning the Agreement on Measures for the Peaceful Liberation of Tibet). Jên Min Press, Peking, 1951.

Kuo min chêng fu nien chien (Year Book), ed. by the Executive Yüan.

K'uo-êrh-k'a chi lüeh (The Official Digest of the Records of the Gurkha Campaign).

Lêng Liang. "Hsi tsang wên t'i chih chên hsiang chi ch'i chieh chüeh fang fa" (Tibetan Problem, Its Facts and Solution), *Tung fang tsa chih,* Vol. 31, No. 9.

Li Fang-ch'ên. Shên pi ti Hsi-tsang (Mysterious Tibet). Taipeh, 1951.

Li Yu-i. "Ti-kuo-chu-i ch'in lüeh Hsi-tsang ti shih shih" (Historical Facts of Imperialistic Invasions of Tibet), in Tai chieh fang ti Hsi tsang (Tibet Pending Liberation).

Liu Chün-jên. Chung kuo ti ming ta tz'ŭ tien (Dictionary of Chinese Geographical Names).

Liu Li-chien. Hsü Tsang shih chien (Tibetan History after Landarma). Translated from Tibetan works. Chengtu, 1945.

——— Yin Tsang fo chiao shih (A History of Hindu-Tibetan Buddhism). Published by the West China Research Institute, 1946.

Liu Man-ch'ing. K'ang Tsang yao chêng (My Mission to Tibet and Sikang). Shanghai, 1933.

Liu Wen-hui. Chung kuo tui Tsang chih hsin chêng ts'ê (Chinese New Policy toward Tibet). Sikang, 1946.

Lo Chia-lun. "Chieh k'ai Chung Yin chien yu kuan Hsi-tsang ti mu" (Raise up the Curtain on the Tibetan Issue in Sino-Indian Relations), *Tzŭ yu chung kuo,* III, No. 7 (Oct., 1950).

——— "Chung Yin chien kuan yü Hsi tsang wên t'i ti mu nei chêng chien" (Documentary Evidence on the Tibetan Issue in Sino-Indian Relations), *Tzŭ yu chung kuo,* IV, No. 2 (Jan., 1951).

Lo Ch'un-yü (ed.). Ch'i hsüeh ch'i ts'un (A collection of the official papers of the editor's father Lo Chang-chi). 1914.

Lü Chêng. Hsi-tsang fo hsüeh yüan lun (A Treatise on Tibetan Buddhism). Shanghai, 1933.

Ma Chieh and Shêng Shêng-tsu. Wei-tsang t'u shih (Maps and Information concerning Eastern and Western Tibet). Peking, 1792.

Ma Fu-hsiang. Mêng Tsang chuang k'uang (The Situation in Mongolia and Tibet). Nanking, 1931. The author was Chairman of the Mongolian and Tibetan Affairs Commission.

Ma Ho-t'ien. Kan Ch'ing Tsang pien ch'ü k'ao ch'a chi kao (A Study of the Frontier Districts of Kansu, Ch'inghai, and Tibet). Shanghai, 1947.

Man-han ming-ch'ên chuan (Biographies of the Prominent Officials of the Manchu Court). Peking, 183-.

Mêng-pao. Hsi-tsang pei wên (Tibetan Tablet Inscriptions—copied and compiled while he was a Resident in Tibet). 1851.

Mohan saishin sekai nempyô (Latest Chronological Tables of World History). Tokyo, 1943.

Nogami, Shunjô. "Gen no Sensei-in ni tsuite" (The Hsüan-chêng-yüan of the Yüan Dynasty), in Asiatic Studies in Honor of Tôru Haneda (1950), pp. 779-95.

Pai Mei-ch'u. Hsi-tsang shih mo chih yao (The Tibetan Story in a Nutshell). Peiping, 1930.

Pai pai ch'an hui ching (A Buddhist Canon).

Pao ch'ieh ching (A Buddhist Scripture).

Pao yün ching (Ratnamegha-sūtra) (A Buddhist Scripture).

P'ing ting Chün-ko-êrh fang lüeh (Records of the Military Campaigns against the Dzungars).

Prince Kuo. Hsi-tsang jih chi (Diary on My Mission to Tibet). Published by Yü-kung-hsüeh-hui, Peiping, 1937.

Rašīd al-Dīn. Jāmi' al-Tawārīkh (A Complete Collection of Histories) (in Persian).

Shao Yüan-p'ing. Yüan shih lei pien (History of the Yüan Dynasty Classified). Shanghai, circa 1800.

Shên chou kuo kuang chi (Facsimiles of the National Treasure in Arts, Literature, and History). Shanghai, 1909.

Shên pao nien chien (Year Book). Published by Shên Pao Corp., Shanghai.

Shêng wu ch'in chêng lu. Author unknown, written during the early part of the Yüan dynasty about the Imperial military exploits. Rev. ed. by Ho Ch'iu-t'ao, 1897.

Shih shih shou ts'ê (Handbook on Current Events), No. 16. Peking, 1951.

Shih Yin. "Da-lai shih shih hou k'ang tsang chiu fên" (Sikang Tibetan Conflicts after the Dalai Lama's Death), *Tung fang tsa chih,* XXXI, No. 8.

Su Ting-fang Lieh-chuan, in T'ang shu and Hsin T'ang shu.

Sung Lien and others. Yüan shih (History of the Yüan Dynasty). Completed in 1369.

Sung shih (History of the Sung Dynasty), compiled by T'o-t'o, Ou-yang Hsüan, and others, and completed in 1345.

Suwa, Gijô. "Rasa Tô-ban Kaimei-hi no Kensetsu nenji" (The Date of the Establishment of the Lhasa Treaty Inscription), in Asiatic Studies in Honor of Tôru Haneda. Kyoto, 1950. Pp. 561-83.

Ta Ch'ing i tung chih (Gazetteer of the Whole Ch'ing Realm). Rev. ed., 1849.

Tai chieh fang ti Hsi-tsang (Tibet Pending Liberation). Shanghai, 1950.

T'ang shu (History of the T'ang Dynasty), compiled by Liu Hsün and others.

Tao-shih. Fa yüan chu lin (A comprehensive collection of Buddhist teachings and events). Completed in 668.

Tobičyan, also written as Tobchiyan (Secret compilations of the Mongolian Court relating to the life of Genghis Khan and the deeds of his successors).

Tsan-ning. Sung kao seng chuan (Biographies of the Buddhist High Priests of the Sung Dynasty). Published 982-88.

Tschen Yin-koh. "Mêng-ku yüan liu kao" (Notes on Sanang Setsen's *Geschichte der Ost-Mongolen*), *Bulletin of the Institute of History and Philology,* Academia Sinica, II (1930), Part 1.

Ts'ên Chung-mien. Fo yu t'ien chu chi k'ao shih (A Study of Fa-hsien's Pilgrimage to India). Shanghai, 1934.

Tsêng Lien. Yüan shu (Another compilation of the History of the Yüan Dynasty, published in 1911).

Tu Yu (735-812). T'ung tien (Encyclopedia of Chinese Political and Economic Institutions, Administration, and Defense System).

Tz'ŭ hai (A Comprehensive Dictionary of Chinese Language and Usage). Shanghai, 1937.

Wang ch'in yü. Hsi-tsang wên t'i (The Tibetan Question). Shanghai, 1929.

Wang Fu. T'ang hui yao (Digest of the Records of the T'ang Period). Edition completed in 961. Nanking, 1884.

Wang Hsien-ch'ien and others (eds.). Tung-hua lu (Records of China). Changsha, 1884-90.

Wang I-nuan. Hsi-tsang wang t'ung chi. Shanghai, 1949. Translated from a Tibetan chronicle.

Wang Kuang-ch'i (trans.). Hsi-tsang wai chiao wên chien (Diplomatic Documents concerning Tibet). Shanghai, 1930.

Wei-tsang tung chih (Records in connection with Tibet and its administration). Author unknown. 1896. Outstanding secondary source.

Wei Yüan. Shêng wu chi (A compilation from Imperial Edicts and Official Records relating to the military exploits of the Manchu Emperors). Peking, 1842.

——— Yüan shih hsin pien (A History of the Yüan Dynasty Newly Compiled). 1905.

Wu Ching-ao. Hsi ch'ui shih ti yen chiu (A Study of the History and Geography of the Western Regions). Shanghai, 1948.

Wu-liang-ho-t'ai chuan, in Yüan shih, Hsin yüan shih, Yüan shih lei pien, and Yüan shih hsin pien (Biography of Uriang Kadai).

Yasaburô, Shimonaku, and others. Tôyô rekishi dai-jiten (Encyclopedia of Oriental History). Tokyo, 1937-39.

Yen Hsi-shan. Yen yüan ch'ang chêng lun chi yao (A Collection of Statements on Political Matters Made by Yen Hsi-shan while in Office as President of the Executive Yüan). Taipeh, 1950.

Yen Tê-i. "Chung Yin kung lu chih ching chi chia chih" (Economic value of the Proposed Sino-Indian Highway), *Pien ch'iang shih ch'ing* (Sept., 1947).

Yin Fu-i. Hsi-tsang chi yao (A Record of the Important Facts concerning Tibet). Published by the Mongolian and Tibetan Affairs Commission, Nanking, 1932.

Yü Tao-ch'üan. "I chu Ming Ch'êng-tsu chien shih chao Tsong-k'a-pa chi chih chi Tsong-k'a-pa fu Chêng-tsu shu" (Ming Chêng-tsu's Invitation and Tsong-k'a-pa's Reply), Academia Sinica's Ts'ai Yüan-p'ei Anniversary Volume, II, pp. 939-62. Peiping, 1935.

Yüan-chao. Wu-k'ung ju chu chi (Wu-k'ung's Pilgrimage to India).

Yüan Shih-k'ai. Yüan tai tsung t'ung shu tu (Correspondence of President Yüan Shih-k'ai).

Yüeh Shih. T'ai-p'ing huan yü chi (Gazetteer of the Sung Realm and Its Dependencies). 976-983.

B. IN WESTERN LANGUAGES

Aitchison, Sir Charles Umpherston. A Collection of Treaties, Engagements, and Sanads relating to India and Neighboring Countries. Calcutta, 1929-31. Vol. XIV.

Allan, J., Sir T. Wolseley Haig, and H. H. Dodwell. The Cambridge Shorter History of India. Cambridge, 1934.

Aspinwall, A. Cornwallis in Bengal. Manchester, 1931.

Bacot, J. "Le Marriage Chinois du roi tibetain Sron bcan Sganpo," *Mel. Chin. et boud.*, III (1935).

Bacot, J., F. W. Thomas, and Ch. Toussaint (trans.). Documents de Touen-houang, relatifs à l'histoire du Tibet. Paris, 1946.

Bagchi, P. C. India and China, a Thousand Years of Cultural Relations. 2d ed. Bombay, 1950.

Barrow, John. Some Account of the Public Life and a Selection from Unpublished Writings of the Earl of Macartney. London, 1807.

Beal, S. The Life of Hiuen Tsang. London, 1911.

Bede (Beda Venerabilis, 673-735). Ecclesiastical History of the English Nation. Newly translated into English with notes and introduction by Michael Maclagan. Oxford, 1949.

Bell, Sir Charles. The People of Tibet. Oxford, 1928.

——— Portrait of the Dalai Lama. London, 1946.

——— The Religion of Tibet. Oxford, 1931.

——— "Tibet and Its Neighbors," *Pacific Affairs,* X, No. 4 (Dec., 1937).

——— Tibet: Past and Present. Oxford, 1924.

——— "Tibet's Position in Asia Today," *Foreign Affairs,* X (Oct., 1931).

——— "While Europe Prepares for War, Pious Tibet Searches for Child Ruler," *China Weekly Review,* LXXXI (July 10, 1937).

Bernard, Theodore. "The Peril of Tibet," *Asia,* XXXIX (Sept., 1939).

Borenius, Tancred. Field-Marshal Mannerheim. London, 1940.

Bretschneider, E., in Medieval Researches from Eastern Asiatic Sources, II (1888), 25.

Bushel, S. W. "The Early History of Tibet from Chinese Sources," *Journal of the Royal Asiatic Society,* New Series (1880), XII, Part IV.

Cammann, Schuyler. "The Panch'en Lama's Visit to China in 1780; an Episode in Anglo-Tibetan Relations," *The Far Eastern Quarterly,* IX (1949).

——— Trade through the Himalayas. Princeton, 1951.

Candler, Edmund. The Unveiling of Lhasa. London, 1905.

Chapman, F. Spencer. Lhasa the Holy City. New York, 1939.

Chavannes, Edouard. Voyage de Song-Yun dans l'Udyana et le Gandhara. 1903.

Chen, Kenneth K. S. "Buddhist-Taoist Mixtures in Pa-shir-i-hua-t'u," *Harvard Journal of Asiatic Studies,* XIX (1955).

——— "The Tibetan Tripitaka," *Harvard Journal of Asiatic Studies,* IX (1945).

"China as It Stands To-day," *China Critic,* VII, No. 24 (1934).

China Year Book, ed. by H. T. M. Bell and H. G. W. Woodhead.

Chinese Year Book. Later editions prepared by the Council of International Affairs.

Clark, Grover. Tibet, China and Great Britain. Peking, 1924.

Creel, H. G. Birth of China. London, 1936.

Crosby, Oscar T. Tibet and Turkestan. London, 1905.

Csoma de Körös. "Enumeration of Historical and Grammatical Works to Be Met With in Tibet," *Journal of the Asiatic Society of Bengal,* 1838, VII, Part 1.

Csoma, Sandor. A Grammar of the Tibetan Language. Calcutta, 1834.

Das, Sarat Chandra. "Contributions on the Religion, History . . . of Tibet," *Journal of the Asiatic Society of Bengal,* L, Nos. 3, 4 (1882).

—— "The Monasteries of Tibet," *Journal of the Asiatic Society of Bengal,* New Series, I (April, 1905).

—— "A Short History of the House of Phagdu, Which Ruled over Tibet on the Decline of Sakya till 1432 A.D.," *Journal of the Asiatic Society of Bengal,* New Series, I (Aug., 1905).

—— "Tibet, a Dependency of Mongolia, 1643-1716," *Journal of the Asiatic Society of Bengal,* New Series, I (May, 1905).

—— "Tibet under Her Last Kings (1434-1642 A.D.)," *Journal of the Asiatic Society of Bengal,* New Series, I (June, 1905).

Das, Taraknath. British Expansion in Tibet. Calcutta, 1927.

Dauvillier, Jean, in Melangés offerts au R. P. Federand Lavallera à l'occasion de la quarantième année de son professorat à l'Institut Catholique. Toulouse, 1948.

David-Neel, A. "Tibetan Border Intrigues,"*Asia,* XLI (May, 1941).

Davis, Sir John F. China during the War and since the Peace. London, 1852.

—— Chinese Miscellanies: A Collection of Essays and Notes. London, 1865.

"Death of Dalai Lama of Tibet Spurs China to Regain Control," *Trans-Pacific,* XXII (Aug. 30, 1934).

Diskalkar, D. H. "Tibeto-Nepalese War 1788-1793," *Journal of Bihar and Orissa Research Society,* XIX. Patna, 1933.

Edgar, J. Huston. "The Tibetan and His Environment: An Interpretation," *Journal of the Royal Asiatic Society,* LVII (1926).

Enders, Gordon B. "A New Role for the Panch'en Lama," *Asia,* XXXIV (Aug., 1934).

Fairbank, J. K. and S. Y. Têng. "On the Ch'ing Tributary System," *Harvard Journal of Asiatic Studies,* VI, No. 2 (June, 1941).

Fay, S. B. The Origins of the World War. New York, 1928.

Fenwick, Charles. International Law. 3rd ed. New York, 1948.

Filippi, Filippo de (ed.). An Account of Tibet: the Travels of Ippolito Desideri. London, 1932.

Fischer, Louis. The Soviets in World Affairs. New York, 1930.

Fitzgerald, Charles P. China, a Short Cultural History. Rev. ed. London, 1950.

Francke, A. H. A History of Western Tibet. London, 1907.

Franke, Otto, and Berthold Laufer. Lamaistische Klosterinschriften aus Peking, Johol und Si-ngan, in Epigraphische denkmäler aus China, mit unterstützung der Hamburgischen wissenschaftlichen stiftung. Berlin, 1914.

Georgi. *Alphabetum Tibetanum.*

Goodrich, L. Carrington. A Short History of the Chinese People. Rev. ed. New York, 1951.

—— "Trade Routes of China from Ancient Times to the Age of

European Expansion," in Labatut and Lane (eds.), *Highways* (1950).

Grenard, F. Le Tibet; le Pays et les Habitants. Paris, 1904.

Griswold, A. Whitney. The Far Eastern Policy of the United States. New York, 1938.

Grousset, René. Histoire d'Extreme-Orient. Paris, 1929.

Hackin, Joseph. Asiatic Mythology. London, 1932.

Hall, William Edward. A Treatise on International Law. 8th ed. Oxford, 1924.

Hertslets, Sir Edward. China Treaties. Vol. I. 3rd ed. London, 1908.

Hoang, Le Rév. Père P. Concordance des Chronologies Néoméniques Chinoise et Européenne. Shanghai, 1910.

Howard, Harry Paxton. "Dalai Lama's Death Brings Crisis to Tibet," *China Weekly Review,* LXVII (Jan. 27, 1934).

Howorth, Sir Henry Hoyle. History of Mongols. 4 vols. London, 1876-1927.

Hu Shih. "The Indianization of China. A Case Study in Cultural Borrowing," in Independence, Convergence and Borrowing. Harvard Tercentenary Publications (1936).

Huc, Evariste Regis. Souvenirs d'une Voyage dans la Tartarie, le Thibet et la Chine pendant les années 1844, 1845, et 1848. 2d ed. Paris, 1853.

Hummel, Arthur W. (ed.). Eminent Chinese of the Ch'ing Period. Washington, 1943-44.

Hung, William. "The Secret History of the Mongols," *Harvard Journal of Asiatic Studies,* XIV (Dec., 1951).

Hyde, Charles Cheney. International Law, Chiefly as Interpreted and Applied by the United States. 2d ed. Boston, 1945.

Kawaguchi, Ekai. "Russia's Policy in Tibet," *Open Court,* XXX (1916).

——— Three Years in Tibet. London, 1909.

Kirkpatrick, William. An Account of the Kingdom of Nepaul. London, 1811.

Klaproth, J. H. Description du Tibet (extrait du nouveau *Journal Asiatique*). Paris, 1831.

Kohn, Hans. History of Nationalism in the East. New York, 1929.

Lai Tze-sheng. Le Problème Thibetain. Paris, 1941.

Landon, Perceval. The Opening of Tibet. New York, 1905.

Laufer, Berthold. "Bird Divination among the Tibetans . . . with a Study of Tibetan Phonology of the Ninth Century," *T'oung pao,* XV (1914).

——— "Loan-Words in Tibetan," *T'oung pao,* XVII (1916).

——— "Origin of Tibetan Writings," *Journal of the American Oriental Society,* XXXVIII (1918).

——— "Was Odoric of Pordonone Ever in Tibet?" *T'oung pao* (1914).

Law of Treaties. The Harvard Research, Part III, supplement to *American Journal of International Law,* Vol. 29. Concord, 1935.

Lee Wei Kuo. Tibet in Modern World Politics. New York, 1931.

Legge, James (trans.). A Record of Buddhistic Kingdoms (1886).

——— (trans.). The Shoo King. Vol. III, Part 1. London, 1876.

Levi, Sylvain. "Les Missions de Wang Hiuen-tze dans l'Inde," *Journal Asiatique* (Paris, 1900).

Levi, Sylvain, and E. Chavannes. "L'itenéraire d'Ou-kong," *Journal Asiatique,* VI (1895).

Lin Tung-hai. "Three Months in Lhasa," *China Critic,* VIII, No. 8 (Feb., 1935).

Ludwig, Earnest. Visit of the Tashoo Lama to Peking. Chien Lung's *Inscription.* Peking, 1904.

Macdonald, David. Tibet. Oxford Pamphlets on Indian Affairs, No. 30. Bombay, 1945.

——— Twenty Years in Tibet. London, 1932.

MacMurray, John V. A. Treaties and Agreements with and concerning China. New York, 1921.

McNair, Sir Arnold D. Law of Treaties. Oxford, 1938.

Majumdar, R. C., H. C. Raychaudhuri, and Kalikinkar Datta. An Advanced History of India. 2d ed. London, 1950.

Mannerheim, C. G. Across Asia from West to East in 1906-1908. Helsinki, 1940.

Markham, Clements R. Narratives of the Mission of George Bogle to Tibet and of the Journey of Thomas Menning to Lhasa. London, 1876.

Martin, H. Desmond. The Rise of Chingis Khan and His Conquest of North China. Baltimore, 1950.

Meng, C. Y. W. "Miss Liu's Mission to Tibet," *China Weekly Review,* LIV (Sept. 6, 1930).

——— "Tibetans Are Praying for China's Victory," *China Weekly Review,* LXXXVIII (April 15, 1939).

Moon, Parker Thomas. Imperialism and World Politics. New York, 1928.

Morse, H. B. The Chronicles of the East India Company Trading to China 1635-1834. Oxford, 1926-29.

——— The International Relations of the Chinese Empire. Vol. II. London–New York, 1910-18.

Morse, H. B., and H. F. MacNair. Far Eastern International Relations. New York, 1931.

Mowat, R. B. A History of European Diplomacy, 1815-1914.

Muir, Ramsay. The Expansion of Europe. 6th ed. London, 1939.

Nicolson, Harold. Portrait of a Diplomatist. Boston, 1930.

Obermiller, Eugene. "Tson-kha-pa le pandit," *Mélanges Chinois et Buddhiques,* July, 1935.

Oppenheim, L. F. L. International Law. 7th ed. by H. Lauterpacht. London, 1952.
Overlach, T. W. Foreign Financial Control in China. New York, 1919.
Parker, E. H. "Manchu Relations with Tibet or Sitsang," *Journal of the Royal Asiatic Society* (China Branch), New Series, XXI (1886).
——— "Mongolia after the Genghizides and before the Manchus," *Journal of the Royal Asiatic Society* (North China Branch), XLIV (1913).
Pelliot, Paul. *Journal Asiatique,* May-June (1913), p. 639; CCX (1927), 372; CCXXXI (1939), 133-34.
——— "Les Mots A H Initiale, Aujourd'hui Amuie dans le Mongol des XIIIe et XIVe Siècles," *Journal Asiatique,* CCVI (1926).
——— "Notes sur quelques artistes des six dynasties et des T'ang," *T'oung pao* (1923).
Pelliot, Paul, and Hambis. Histoire des campagnes de Gengis Khan. 1951.
Petech, Luciano. China and Tibet in the Early 18th Century. Leiden, 1950.
——— A Study on the Chronicles of Ladakh (Indian Tibet). Calcutta, 1939.
Pokotilov. History of the Eastern Mongols during the Ming Dynasty from 1368 to 1634. Translated from the Russian by Rudolf Loewenthal. Chengtu, 1947.
Price, Ernest B. The Russo-Japanese Treaties of 1907-1916 concerning Manchuria and Mongolia. Baltimore, 1933.
Price, Frank W. (trans.). San Min Chu I. Shanghai, 1927.
Pritchard, Earl H. "Anglo-Chinese Relations during the 17th and 18th Centuries," *University of Illinois Studies in the Social Sciences,* XVII, Nos. 1-2 (1929).
——— "The Crucial Years of Early Anglo-Chinese Relations, 1750-1800," *Research Studies of the State College of Washington,* IV, Nos. 3-4 (1936).
Rapson, E. J. (ed.). The Cambridge History of India. Cambridge, 1922.
Rawlinson, H. G. A Concise History of the Indian People. Rev. 2d ed. London, 1950.
——— Indian Historical Studies. London, 1913.
Reincourt, Amaury de. Roof of the World, Tibet, Key to Asia. New York, 1950.
Richardson, Hugh Edward. Ancient Historical Edict at Lhasa and the Mu Tsung/Khri Gtsug Lde Brtsan Treaty of A.D. 821-822 from the Inscription at Lhasa. London, 1952.
Ritscher, Walter Holmes. Criteria of Capacity for Independence. Jerusalem, 1934.
Rockhill, W. W. "The Dalai Lamas . . . ," *T'oung pao,* XL (1910).

—— The Dalai Lamas of Lhasa and Their Relations with the Manchu Emperors of China 1644-1908. Leyden, 1910.

—— The Life of Buddha (derived and translated from the Tibetan works in the Bkah-hgyur and Batan-hgyur). London, 1884.

—— "Tibet"—a Geographical, Ethnographical, and Historical Sketch Derived from Chinese Sources," *Journal of the Royal Asiatic Society,* New Series (1891).

Roerich, George N. Blue Annals (a translation of the Deb-ther snon-po). Published by the Royal Asiatic Society of Bengal, 1949-53.

Sanang Setsen. Geschichte der Ost-Mongolen (trans. into German from the Mongolian by I. J. Schmidt). 1829.

Sandberg, Gratham. The Exploration of Tibet. Calcutta, 1914.

Sarcar, S. C. "Some Notes on the Intercourse of Bengal with the Northern Countries in the Second Half of the 18th Century," Bengal, Past and Present, XLI. Calcutta, 1931.

Satow, Sir Ernest. A Guide to Diplomatic Practice. 3d ed. rev. by H. Richie. London, 1932.

Schlagintweit, Emil. Die Könige von Tibet. 1866.

Schwarzenberger, Georg. A Manual of International Law. London, 1951.

Scott, A. MacCallum. The Truth about Tibet. London, 1905.

Sen, D. K. "China, Tibet and India," *India Quarterly,* VII, No. 2 (April-June, 1951).

Shen, James. "New Dalai Lama Is Found," *Living Age,* No. 357 (Jan., 1940).

Shen Tsung-lien and Liu Shen-chi. Tibet and the Tibetan. Stanford, 1953.

Smith, Vincent A. The Early History of India. 3d ed. Oxford, 1914.

—— The Oxford History of India. 2d ed. Oxford, 1923.

Spykman, Nicholas John. America's Strategy in World Politics. New York, 1942.

Staël-Holstein, Baron A. von. "On the Sexagenary Cycle of the Tibetans," *Monumenta Serica,* Vol. I (1935-36).

Statesman's Year Book; Statistical and Historical Annals of the States of the World. London.

Steele, A. T. "Boy Ruler of Shangri-la," *Saturday Evening Post,* April 13, 1946.

Stein, R. A. "Récentes Études Tibetaines," *Journal Asiatique,* CCXL (1952).

Teichman, Eric. Travels of a Consular Officer in Eastern Tibet. Cambridge, 1922.

Terenzio, Pio-carlo. La Rivalité Anglo-Russe en Perse et en Afghanistan jusqu'aux Accords de 1907. Paris, 1947.

Thomas, Lowell. Out of This World; across the Himalayas to Forbidden Tibet. New York, 1950.

——— "Out of This World: A Journey to Lhasa," *Collier's* Feb. 25, 1950.

"Three Nations Hunt a Lama," *Living Age,* No. 357 (Jan., 1940).

Tibet, Peace Handbooks, No. 70. Published by the Historical Section of the British Foreign Office, 1920.

Tolstoy, I. "Across Tibet from India to China," *National Geographic Magazine,* XC (Aug., 1946).

Tucci, Giuseppe. Tibetan Painted Scrolls. Rome, 1949.

Turner, Captain Samuel. An Account of an Embassy to the Court of the Teshoo Lama in Tibet. London, 1800; 2d ed., 1806.

"Tzarist Russia and Mongolia in 1913-14," *The Chinese Social and Political Science Review,* Vol. XVI, No. 4; Vol. XVII, No. 1.

Vassilief, M. V. Le Bouddhisme. Paris, 1865.

Viscount Grey of Fallodon. Twenty-five Years, 1892-1916. New York, 1925.

Waddell, L. Austine. " Ancient Historical Edicts at Lhasa," *Journal of the Royal Asiatic Society* (1909 and 1911).

——— "Chinese Imperial Edict of 1808 on the Origin and Transmigrations of Grand Lamas of Tibet," *Journal of the Royal Asiatic Society* (1910).

——— Lhasa and Its Mysteries. London, 1905.

Wang, S. T. The Margary Affairs and the Chefoo Agreement. London, 1940.

Watters, Thomas. On Yüan Chwang's Travels in India (629-645 A.D.). 2 vols. London, 1904-5.

Wessels, C. Early Jesuit Travellers in Central Asia 1603-1721. The Hague, 1924.

Westlake, John. International Law. Cambridge, 1910-13.

White, John Claude. Sikkim and Bhutan, Twenty-one Years on the North-East Frontier 1887-1908. London, 1909.

Willoughby, M. E. "Relation of Tibet to China," *Journal of the Central Asian Society,* II (1924).

Wu, Ai-ch'ên. China and the Soviet Union. London, 1950.

Younghusband, Sir Francis E. India and Tibet. London, 1910.

Zabriskie, Edward H. American-Russian Rivalry in the Far East. Philadelphia, 1946.

IV. *Periodicals and Newspapers*

A. PERIODICALS

China Critic

China Weekly Review

Current History

The Far Eastern Review

Hsi-ch'ui hsuan-hua-shih kung-shu yueh-k'an (Panch'en Lama Headquarters Monthly)
K'ang tsang ch'ien feng
The Japan Weekly Chronicle
Mêng tsang chou pao (The Mongolian and Tibetan Weekly)
Mêng tsang hsün k'an
Mêng tsang yüeh pao (The Mongolian and Tibetan Monthly)
North China Herald
Pien shêng pao (Chengtu)

B. NEWSPAPERS

China Daily News (New York)
Chung yang jih pao (Central Daily News)
Hong Kong Standard
Jên min jih pao (Chinese Communist organ, Peking)
The New York Times
North China Daily News (Shanghai)
Shanghai Daily News
South China Morning Post (Hong Kong)
Ta kung pao (Chungking)
The Times (London)
News Dispatches of AEP, AP, Hsin-hua, Pan Asia, Reuter

SUPPLEMENTARY BIBLIOGRAPHY

U. S. Bureau of Foreign and Domestic Commerce, *Special Consular Reports*. No. 72 (1915).

Demieville, Paul. (trans. from the Chinese Tun-huang [in French, Touen-Houang] manuscript) *Le Concile de Lhasa*. Paris, 1952.

Kachru, D. N. "Ladakh," *India Quarterly*, Vol. 6, No. 1 (1950).

Kundra, Jagdish Chandra. *Indian Foreign Policy 1947-1954*. New York, 1955.

Li, Tieh-Tseng. "The Legal Position of Tibet," *American Journal of International Law*, Vol. 50, No. 2 (April 1956).

Rockhill, W. W. *Diary of a Journey Through Mongolia and Tibet in 1891 and 1892*. Washington, 1894.

Survey of China Mainland Press issued by the American Consulate-general in Hong Kong.

Winnington, Alan. *Tibet Record of a Journey*. London, 1957.

Yamagata, Hatsuo. *Hsi-tsang T'ung-Lan* ("Chibetto tsuran") revised by Wu Chi-po, 1910 ed.

APPENDIX 1

THE SEVENTEEN-ARTICLE AGREEMENT OF MAY 23, 1951

Text of "Agreement of the Central People's Government and the Local Government of Tibet on Measures for the Peaceful Liberation of Tibet" as issued by the New China News Agency on May 27, 1951.

... In order that the influences of aggressive imperialist forces in Tibet might be successfully eliminated, the unification of the territory and sovereignty of the People's Republic of China accomplished, and national defence safeguarded: in order that the Tibetan nationality and people might be freed and return to the big family of the People's Republic of China to enjoy the same rigths of national equality as all the other nationalities in the country and develop their political, economic, cultural and educational work; the Central People's Government, when it ordered the People's Liberation Army to march into Tibet, notified the Local Government of Tibet to send delegates to the central authorities to conduct talks for the conclusion of an agreement on measures for the peaceful liberation of Tibet. At the latter part of April 1951, the delegates with full powers of the Local Government of Tibet arrived in Peking. The Central People's Government appointed representatives with full powers to conduct talks on a friendly basis with the delegates with full powers of the Local Government of Tibet. As a result of the talks, both parties agreed to establish this agreement and ensure that it be carried into effect.

1. The Tibetan people shall unite and drive out imperialist aggressive forces from Tibet; the Tibetan people shall return to the big family of the motherland—the People's Republic of China.

2. The Local Government of Tibet shall actively assist the People's Liberation Army to enter Tibet and consolidate the national defences.

3. In accordance with the policy towards nationalities laid down in the Common Programme of the Chinese People's Political Consultative Conference, the Tibetan people have the right of exercising national regional autonomy under the unified leadership of the Central People's Government.

4. The central authorities will not alter the existing political system

in Tibet. The central authorities also will not alter the established status, functions and powers of the Dalai Lama. Officials of various ranks shall hold office as usual.

5. The established status, functions and powers of the Panchen Ngoerhtehni shall be maintained.

6. By the established status, functions and powers of the Dalai Lama and of the Panchen Ngoerhtehni are meant the status, functions and powers of the 13th Dalai Lama and of the 9th Panchen Ngoerhtehni when they were in friendly and amicable relations with each other.

7. The policy of freedom of religious belief laid down in the Common Programme of the Chinese People's Political Consultative Conference shall be carried out. The religious beliefs, customs and habits of the Tibetan people shall be respected, and lama monasteries shall be protected. The central authorities will not effect a change in the income of the monasteries.

8. Tibetan troops shall be re-organised step by step into the People's Liberation Army, and become a part of the national defence forces of the People's Republic of China.

9. The spoken and written language and school education of the Tibetan nationality shall be developed step by step in accordance with the actual conditions in Tibet.

10. Tibetan agriculture, livestock raising, industry and commerce shall be developed step by step, and the people's livelihood shall be improved step by step, in accordance with the actual conditions in Tibet.

11. In matters related to various reforms in Tibet, there will be no compulsion on the part of the central authorities. The Local Government of Tibet should carry out reforms on its own accord, and when the people raise demands for reform, they shall be settled by means of consultation with the leading personnel of Tibet.

12. In so far as former pro-imperialist and pro-Kuomintang officials resolutely sever relations with imperialism and the Kuomintang and do not engage in sabotage or resistance, they may continue to hold office irrespective of their past.

13. The People's Liberation Army entering Tibet shall abide by all the above-mentioned policies and shall also be fair in all buying and selling and shall not arbitrarily take a needle or thread from the people.

14. The Central People's Government shall have centralised handling of all external affairs of the area of Tibet; and there will be peaceful co-existence with neighbouring countries and establishment and development of fair commercial and trading relations with them on the basis of equality, mutual benefit and mutual respect for territory and sovereignty.

15. In order to ensure the implementation of this agreement, the

Central People's Government shall set up a military and administrative committee and a military area headquarters in Tibet, and apart from the personnel sent there by the Central People's Government shall absorb as many local Tibetan personnel as possible to take part in the work.

Local Tibetan personnel taking part in the military and administrative committee may include patriotic elements from the Local Government of Tibet, various districts and various principal monasteries; the name-list shall be set forth after consultation between the representatives designated by the Central People's Government and various quarters concerned, and shall be submitted to the Central People's Government for appointment.

16. Funds needed by the military and administrative committee, the military area headquarters and the People's Liberation Army entering Tibet shall be provided by the Central People's Government. The Local Government of Tibet should assist the People's Liberation Army in the purchase and transport of food, fodder and other daily necessities.

17. This agreement shall come into force immediately after signatures and seals are affixed to it.

Signed and sealed by:

Delegates of the Central People's Government with full powers:

Chief Delegate:
LI WEI-HAN
Delegates:
CHANG CHING-WU
CHANG KUO-HUA
SUN CHIH-YUAN

Delegates with full powers of the Local Government of Tibet:

Chief Delegate:
KALOON NGABOU NGAWANG JIGME
Delegates:
DZASAK KHEMEY SONAM WANGDI
KHENTRUNG THUPTEN TENTHAR
KHENCHUNG THUPTEN LEKMUUN
RIMSHI SAMPOSEY TENZIN THUNDUP

Peking, May 23, 1951.

Appendix II

THE SINO-INDIAN PACT ON TIBET OF APRIL 29, 1954

Text of "Agreement Between the People's Republic of China and the Republic of India on Trade and Intercourse Between Tibet Region of China and India" as issued by the New China News Agency.

The Central People's Government of the People's Republic of China and the Government of the Republic of India, being desirous of promoting trade and cultural intercourse between Tibet Region of China and India and of facilitating pilgrimage and travel by the peoples of China and India, have resolved to enter into the present Agreement based on the following principles:

(1) Mutual respect for each other's territorial integrity and sovereignty,
(2) Mutual non-aggression,
(3) Mutual non-interference in each other's internal affairs,
(4) Equality and mutual benefit, and
(5) Peaceful coexistence,

And for this purpose have appointed as their respective plenipotentiaries:

The Central People's Government of the People's Republic of China, His Excellency Chang Han-fu, Vice-Minister of Foreign Affairs of the Central People's Government; the Government of the Republic of India, His Excellency Nedyam Raghavan, Ambassador Extraordinary and Plenipotentiary of India accredited to the People's Republic of China, who, having examined each other's credentials and finding them in good and due form, have agreed upon the following:

Article One

The high contracting parties mutually agree to establish trade agencies:

1. The Government of India agrees that the Government of China may establish trade agencies at New Delhi, Calcutta and Kalimpong.

2. The Government of China agrees that the Government of India may establish trade agencies at Yatung, Gyantse and Gartok.

The trade agencies of both parties shall be accorded the same status and same treatment. The trade agents of both parties shall enjoy freedom from arrest while exercising their functions, and shall enjoy in respect of themselves, their wives and children who are dependent on them for livelihood freedom from search.

The trade agencies of both parties shall enjoy the privileges and immunities for couriers, mailbags and communications in code.

Article Two

The high contracting parties agree that traders of both countries known to be customarily and specifically engaged in trade between Tibet Region of China and India may trade at the following places:

1. The Government of China agrees to specify (a) Yatung, (b) Gyangtse and (c) Phari as markets for trade.

The Government of India agrees that trade may be carried on in India, including places like (a) Kalimpong, (b) Siliguri and (c) Calcutta, according to customary practice.

2. The Government of China agrees to specify (a) Gartok, (b) Pulanchung (Taklakot), (c) Gyanimakhargo, (d) Gyanimachakra, (e) Ramura, (f) Dongbra, (g) Pulingsumdo, (h) Nabra, (i) Shangtse and (j) Tashigong as markets for trade; the Government of India agrees that in future, when in accordance with the development and need of trade between the Ari District of Tibet Region of China and India, it has become necessary to specify markets for trade in the corresponding district in India adjacent to the Ari District of Tibet Region of China, it will be prepared to consider on the basis of equality and reciprocity to do so.

Article Three

The high contracting parties agree that pilgrimage by religious believers of the two countries shall be carried on in accordance with the following provisions:

1. Pilgrims from India of Lamaist, Hindu and Buddhist faiths may visit Kang Rimpoche (Kailas) and Mavam Tso (Manasarovar) in Tibet Region of China in accordance with custom.

2. Pilgrims from Tibet Region of China of Lamaist and Buddhist faiths may visit Benaras, Sarnath, Gaya and Sanchi in India in accordance with custom.

3. Pilgrims customarily visiting Lhasa may continue to do so in accordance with custom.

Article Four

Traders and pilgrims of both countries may travel by the following passes and route: (1) Shipki La Pass, (2) Mana Pass, (3) Niti

Pass, (4) Kungri Bingri Pass, (5) Darma Pass, and (6) Lipu Lekh Pass.

Also, the customary route leading to Tashigong along the Valley of the Shangatsangpu (Indus) River may continue to be traversed in accordance with custom.

Article Five

For travelling across the border, the high contracting parties agree that diplomatic personnel, officials and nationals of the two countries shall hold passports issued by their own respective countries and visaed by the other party except as provided in Paragraphs One, Two, Three and Four of this Article.

1. Traders of both countries known to be customarily and specifically engaged in trade between Tibet Region of China and India, their wives and children who are dependent on them for livelihood and their attendants will be allowed entry for purposes of trade into India or Tibet Region of China, as the case may be, in accordance with custom on the production of certificates duly issued by the local government of their own country or by its duly authorized agents and examined by the border check-posts of the other party.

2. Inhabitants of the border districts of the two countries who cross the border to carry on petty trade or to visit friends and relatives may proceed to the border districts of the other party as they have customarily done heretofore and need not be restricted to the passes and route specified in Article Four above and shall not be required to hold passports, visas or permits.

3. Porters and mule-team drivers of the two countries who cross the border to perform necessary transportation services need not hold passports issued by their own country, but shall only hold certificates good for a definite period of time (three months, half a year or one year) duly issued by the local government of their own country or by its duly authorized agents and produce them for registration at the border check-posts of the other party.

4. Pilgrims of both countries need not carry documents of certification but shall register at the border check-posts of the other party and receive a permit for pilgrimage.

5. Notwithstanding the Provisions of the foregoing Paragraphs of this Article, either Government may refuse entry to any particular person.

6. Persons who enter the territory of the other party in accordance with the foregoing Paragraphs of this Article may stay within its territory only after complying with the procedures specified by the other party.

Article Six

The present Agreement shall come into effect upon ratification by both Governments and shall remain in force for eight years. Extension of the present Agreement may be negotiated by the two parties if either party requests for it six months prior to the expiry of the Agreement and the request is agreed to by the other party.

Done in duplicate in Peking on the 29th day of April, 1954, in the Chinese, Hindi and English languages, all texts being equally valid.

Chang Han-fu, Plenipotentiary of the Central People's Government, People's Republic of China.

Nedyam Raghavan, Plenipotentiary of the Government of the Republic of India.

* * *

Indian Ambassador Raghavan's Note to Chang Han-fu

Following is the full text of the note of Nedyam Raghavan, Ambassador Extraordinary and Plenipotentiary of the Republic of India to the People's Republic of China, dated April 29, 1954, to Chang Han-fu, Vice-Minister of Foreign Affairs:

Your Excellency Mr. Vice-Foreign Minister:

In the course of our discussions regarding the Agreement on Trade and Intercourse between Tibet Region of China and India, which has been happily concluded today, the Delegation of the Government of the Republic of India and the Delegation of the Government of the People's Republic of China agreed that certain matters be regulated by an exchange of notes. In pursuance of this understanding, it is hereby agreed between the two Governments as follows:

(1) The Government of India will be pleased to withdraw completely within six months from date of exchange of the present notes the military escorts now stationed at Yatung and Gyantse in Tibet Region of China. The Government of China will render facilities and assistance in such withdrawal.

(2) The Government of India will be pleased to hand over to the Government of China at a reasonable price the postal, telegraph and public telephone services together with their equipment operated by the Government of India in Tibet Region of China. The concrete measures in this regard will be decided upon through further negotiations between the Indian Embassy in China and the Foreign Ministry of China, which shall start immediately after the exchange of the present notes.

(3) The Government of India will be pleased to hand over to the Government of China at a reasonable price the twelve rest houses of the Government of India in Tibet Region of China. The concrete measures in this regard will be decided upon through further negotiations between the Indian Embassy in China and the Foreign Ministry

of China, which shall start immediately after the exchange of the present notes. The Government of China agrees that they shall continue as rest houses.

(4) The Government of China agrees that all buildings within the compound walls of the trade agencies of the Government of India at Yatung and Gyantse in Tibet Region of China may be retained by the Government of India. The Government of India may continue to lease the land within its agency compound walls from the Chinese side. And the Government of India agrees that the trade agencies of the Government of China at Kalimpong and Calcutta may lease lands from the Indian side for the use of the agencies and construct buildings thereon. The Government of China will render every possible assistance for housing the Indian trade agency at Gartok. The Government of India will also render every possible assistance for housing the Chinese trade agency at New Delhi.

(5) The Government of India will be pleased to return to the Government of China all lands used or occupied by the Government of India other than the lands within its trade agency compound walls at Yatung.

If there are godowns and buildings of the Government of India on the above-mentioned lands used or occupied and to be returned by the Government of India and if Indian traders have stores, godowns or buildings on the above-mentioned lands so that there is a need to continue leasing lands, the Government of China agrees to sign contracts with the Government of India or Indian traders, as the case may be, for leasing to them those parts of the land occupied by the said godowns, buildings or stores and pertaining thereto.

(6) The trade agents of both parties may, in accordance with the laws and regulations of the local governments, have access to their nationals involved in civil or criminal cases.

(7) The trade agents and traders of both countries may hire employees in the locality.

(8) The hospitals of the Indian trade agencies at Gyantse and Yatung will continue to serve personnel of the Indian trade agencies.

(9) Each Government shall protect the person and property of the traders and pilgrims of the other country.

(10) The Government of China agrees, so far as possible, to construct rest houses for the use of pilgrims along the route from Pulanchung (Taklakot) to Kang Rimpoche (Kailas) and Mavam Tso (Manasarovar); and the Government of India agrees to place all possible facilities in India at the disposal of pilgrims.

(11) Traders and pilgrims of both countries shall have the facility of hiring means of transportation at normal and reasonable rates.

(12) The three trade agencies of each party may function throughout the year.

(13) Traders of each country may rent buildings and godowns in accordance with local regulations in places under the jurisdiction of the other party.

(14) Traders of both countries may carry on normal trade in accordance with local regulations at places as provided in Article Two of the Agreement.

(15) Disputes between traders of both countries over debts and claims shall be handled in accordance with local laws and regulations.

On behalf of the Government of the Republic of India I hereby agree that the present note along with Your Excellency's reply shall become an agreement between our two Governments which shall come into force upon the exchange of the present notes.

I avail myself of this opportunity to express to Your Excellency Mr. Vice-Foreign Minister, the assurances of my highest consideration.

His Excellency N. Raghavan
Ambassador Extraordinary and Plenipotentiary
of the Republic of India

To His Excellency Mr. Chang Han-fu, Vice-Minister of Foreign Affairs, Central People's Government, People's Republic of China.

* * *

Chang Han-fu's Note to Indian Ambassador

Following is the full text of the note of Chang Han-fu, Vice-Minister of Foreign Affairs of the Central People's Government of the People's Republic of China in reply to Nedyam Raghavan, Ambassador Extraordinary and Plenipotentiary of the Republic of India to the People's Republic of China:

Your Excellency Mr. Ambassador:

I have the honor to receive your note dated April 29, 1954, which reads:

"In the course of our discussions regarding the Agreement on Trade and Intercourse between Tibet Region of China and India, which has been happily concluded today, the Delegation of the Government of the Republic of India and the Delegation of the Government of the People's Republic of China agreed that certain matters be regulated by an exchange of notes. In pursuance of this understanding, it is hereby agreed between the two Governments as follows:

"(1) The Government of India will be pleased to withdraw completely within six months from date of exchange of the present notes the military escorts now stationed at Yatung and Gyantse in Tibet Region of China. The Government of China will render facilities and assistance in such withdrawal.

"(2) The Government of India will be pleased to hand over to the Government of China at a reasonable price the postal, telegraph and public telephone services together with their equipment operated by the Government of India in Tibet Region of China. The concrete measures in this regard will be decided upon through further negotiations between the Indian Embassy in China and the Foreign Ministry of China, which shall start immediately after the exchange of the present notes.

"(3) The Government of India will be pleased to hand over to the Government of China at a reasonable price the twelve rest houses of the Government of India in Tibet Region of China. The concrete measures in this regard will be decided upon through further negotiations between the Indian Embassy in China and the Foreign Ministry of China, which shall start immediately after the exchange of the present notes. The Government of China agrees that they shall continue as rest houses.

"(4) The Government of China agrees that all buildings within the compound walls of the trade agencies of the Government of India at Yatung and Gyantse in Tibet region of China may be retained by the Government of India. The Government of India may continue to lease the land within its agency compound walls from the Chinese side. And the Government of India agrees that the trade agencies of the Government of China at Kalimpong and Calcutta may lease lands from the Indian side for the use of the agencies and construct buildings thereon. The Government of China will render every possible assistance for housing the Indian trade agency at Gartok. The Government of India will also render every possible assistance for housing the Chinese trade agency at New Delhi.

"(5) The Government of India will be pleased to return to the Government of China all lands used or occupied by the Government of India other than the lands within its trade agency compound walls at Yatung.

"If there are godowns and buildings of the Government of India on the above-mentioned lands used or occupied and to be returned by the Government of India and if Indian traders have stores, godowns or buildings on the above-mentioned lands so that there is a need to continue leasing lands, the Government of China agrees to sign contracts with the Government of India or Indian traders, as the case may be, for leasing to them those parts of the land occupied by the said godowns, buildings or stores and pertaining thereto.

"(6) The trade agents of both parties may, in accordance with the laws and regulations of the local governments, have access to their nationals involved in civil or criminal cases.

"(7) The trade agents and traders of both countries may hire employees in the locality.

"(8) The hospitals of the Indian trade agencies at Gyantse and Yatung will contniue to serve personnel of the Indian trade agencies.

"(9) Each Government shall protect the person and property of the traders and pilgrims of the other country.

"(10) The Government of China agrees, so far as possible, to construct rest houses for the use of pilgrims along the route from Pulanchung (Taklakot) to Kang Rimpoche (Kailas) and Mavam Tso (Manasarovar); and the Government of India agrees to place all possible facilities in India at the disposal of pilgrims.

"(11) Traders and pilgrims of both countries shall have the facility of hiring means of transportation at normal and reasonable rates.

"(12) The three trade agencies of each party may function throughout the year.

"(13) Traders of each country may rent buildings and godowns in accordance with local regulations in places under the jurisdiction of the other party.

"(14) Traders of both countries may carry on normal trade in accordance with local regulations at places as provided in Article Two of the Agreement.

"(15) Disputes between traders of both countries over debts and claims shall be handled in accordance with local laws and regulations."

On behalf of the Central People's Government of the People's Republic of China, I hereby agree to Your Excellency's note, and your note along with the present note in reply shall become an agreement between our two Governments, which shall come into force upon the exchange of the present notes.

I avail myself of this opportunity to express to Your Excellency, Mr. Ambassador, the assurances of my highest consideration.

Chang Han-fu, Vice-Minister, Ministry of Foreign Affairs, People's Republic of China

To His Excellency Nedyam Raghavan, Ambassador Extraordinary and Plenipotentiary, Republic of India.

INDEX